People, Taxation, and Trade in Mughal India

'Shireen Moosvi commands an enviable combination of statistical skills with a close study of the primary sources that has enabled her to explore a number of fields of the economic history of Mughal India, some of them little touched by previous research. The present collection of her papers should be of much interest to all who wish to know how our people lived and worked three to four hundred years ago.'

—Irfan Habib
Professor Emeritus of History, Aligarh Muslim University

'This comprehensive volume is characterized by a striking richness of source material, wealth of statistical data, and astute inquiries into a range of issues connected with Mughal economic and social history. It indeed reflects the author's prolonged and committed engagement with the subject.'

—Sabyasachi Bhattacharya
Chairman, Indian Council of Historical Research

Aligarh Historians Society Series

General Editor: Irfan Habib

People, Taxation, and Trade in Mughal India

Shireen Moosvi

OXFORD
UNIVERSITY PRESS

OXFORD
UNIVERSITY PRESS

Oxford University Press is a department of the University of Oxford. It furthers the University's objective of excellence in research, scholarship, and education by publishing worldwide. Oxford is a registered trademark of Oxford University Press in the UK and in certain other countries

Published in India by
Oxford University Press
22 workspace, 2nd Floor, 1/22 Asaf Ali Road, New Delhi 110002

First Edition published in 2008
Oxford India Paperbacks 2010

ISBN-13: 978-0-19-806631-6
ISBN-10: 0-19-806631-7

Typeset in Times Roman 10/12

Printed in India by Repro India Limited

To the memory of my mother
Dr Zahra Musavi

Contents

MAPS

FIGURES

Preface

The present volume that I offer to (I hope) an indulgent readership contains papers that in their original form appeared in different journals or collaborative volumes. They have this in common that they deal with various aspects of the economic life and institutions of Mughal India. Since they appeared at various times, I found it necessary, before their inclusion in this volume, to revise them carefully and update the references; I have also taken the liberty of making changes and additions to take into account new questions and fresh evidence. The result is that in many cases the chapters in this volume are practically new versions of the original papers; even the titles of some have been modified. In the Introduction I have endeavoured to focus attention on some larger issues of debate.

The opportunity has been taken to make spellings of names and terms as uniform as possible. For diacritical marks the system followed in Steingass's *Persian-English Dictionary* has been adopted with a few changes introduced for reasons of simplification.

Professor Irfan Habib has been liberal with guidance, advice and encouragement (including the encouragement to differ!). I have, throughout the preparation of the original papers and in the course of their revision for this volume, obtained unstinted help from the members of the staff of the library of the Department of History (AMU) at all odd times. I am especially grateful to Mr Arshad Ali, Mr. Bansi Dhar Sharma and Mr Salman Ahmad.

The processing of the text has been carried out under the aegis of the Aligarh Historians Society, mainly by Mr Muneer Uddin Khan. Mr Sajid Islam has also borne part of the burden.

It was good to work with Oxford University Press again. It has been a special pleasure to have worked with the editorial team at the Oxford University Press.

Shireen Moosvi

Aligarh, 2008

ORIGINAL SITES OF PUBLICATION

The Indian Economic Experience 1600-1900: A Quantitative Study, *The Making of History: Essays Presented to Irfan Habib,* ed. K.N. Panikkar, T.J. Byres, U. Patnaik, Delhi, 2000. The first version appeared in *Economic Growth and Structural Change: Comparative Approaches over the Long Run (B13 Proceedings Eleventh International Economic History Congress*, Milan, 1994) edited by A. Maddison and H. Van der Wee, Italy, 1994.

The Silver Influx, Money Supply, Prices and Revenue- Extraction in Mughal India, *Journal of the Economic and Social History of the Orient,* Vol.XXX, Part 1, The Netherlands, 1987.

A Note on Movement of Interest Rates in India: Sixteenth-Eighteenth Centuries, *History of Money and Banking in India,* edited by A.K. Bagchi, Delhi, 2002.

Ecology, Population Distribution and Settlement Pattern in Mughal India, *Man and Environment*, XIV(I), 1989.

Data on Mughal-Period Vital Statistics – A Preliminary Survey of Usable Information, *PIHC, 58th Session*, Bangalore, 1997.

Urban Population in Pre-Colonial India, *Society and Ideology in India*, edited by D.N. Jha, 1995. Presented at Second International Congress of Historical Demography, Paris, 1987.

Work and Gender in Mughal India, *Socio-Economic Consequences of Sex-Ratio in Historical Perspective*, (*B5: Proceedings of the Eleventh International History Congress*, Milan, 1994), edited by A. Fauve-Chamoux & S. Songer. Italy, 1994.

Todarmal's Original Memorandum on the Revenue Administration, March 1582, *PIHC, 49th session*, Dharwad, 1988.

Aurangzeb's *Farmān* to Rasikdās, 1665, *Medieval India*, edited by Irfan Habib, Vol.I, OUP, Delhi, 1992.

Administering Kashmir: An Imperial Edict of Shahjahan, *Aligarh Journal of Oriental Studies*, Vol.III, No.2, 1986.

Expenditure on Buildings under Shahjahan — A Chapter of Imperial Financial History, *PIHC*, *46th Session,* Amritsar, 1985.

The Mughal Empire and the Deccan — Economic Factors and Consequences, *PIHC*, *42nd Session,* Kurukshetra, 1982.

Scarcities, Prices and Exploitation: 'The Agrarian Crisis', 1658-70, *Studies in History*, New Series, Vol.I, No.1, New Delhi, 1985.

Shipping and Navigation under Akbar, *PIHC, Diamond Jubilee (60th) Session*, Calicut, 1999.

Mughal Shipping at Surat in the First Half of Seventeenth Century, *PIHC*, Calcutta, 1991.

Travails of a Mercantile Community – Aspects of Social Life at the Port of Surat (Earlier Half of the Seventeenth Century), *PIHC*, Delhi, 1992.

Gujarat Ports and their Hinterland *Ports and Hinterland in India*, 1700-1900, edited by J.S. Grewal, 1991.

Abbreviations

Āʾīn	Abūl Faẓl, *Āʾīn-i Akbarī*, ed. H. Blochman, 2 vols., Bib. Ind., Calcutta, 1867-77
A.N.	Abūl Faẓl, *Akbarnāma*, ed. Ahmad Ali and Abdur Rahim, 3 vols., Bib. Ind., Calcutta, 1873-87
ASMI	Irfan Habib, *Agrarian System of Mughal India,* second revised ed. Delhi, 1999
Atlas	Irfan Habib, *Atlas of the Mughal Empire*, Delhi, 1982
CEHI	*Cambridge Economic History of India* Vol.I edited by Tapan Raychaudhuri and Irfan Habib, Cambridge, 1982 Vol. II edited by Dharma Kumar and Meghnad Desai
EME	Shireen Moosvi, *Economy of the Mughal Empire — A Statistical Study*, Delhi, 1987
EFI	*The English Factories in India*, ed. W. Foster, 13 vols., Oxford, 1906-27. The volumes are not numbered and are cited by the years given under the title in each volume.
IESHR	*Indian Economic and Social History Review*, Delhi
IHR	*Indian Historical Review*, Delhi
JESHO	*Journal of the Economic and Social History of the Orient,* The Netherlands
PIHC	*Proceedings of the Indian History Congress* (the number, place and year of the annual session follow the abbreviation)

Introduction

The papers assembled in this volume were written over a period of years, upon divergent impulses, but all concerned with various aspects of the economy (and the connected social and political framework) of India during Mughal times. As I have indicated in the Preface, I have done my best not only to revise them and update the references, but also to introduce, wherever the specific themes so allowed, new questions that have been raised in the meantime or struck me while going over the ground again. But it has seemed to me that there still remain a number of points that these essays touch upon, or, indeed, themselves suggest, but do not develop in any fullness. Since these appear to me to be of some significance for understanding the nature of Mughal-Indian economy and the processes of change affecting it, I propose to address some of them in this Introduction, admitting in advance that many of my own positions remain tentative, and in some cases, alas, even indefinite.

Population

Let us, first, take up a few issues relating to demography. Behind most historical processes, especially behind economic trends, historians have often discerned the decisive role of changes in population size, which is itself determined by rates of mortality and fertility. M. Dobb in his influential study of the history of capitalism stressed the cruciality of the ratio between labour and land in a society where peasant production predominates. Applying, tacitly, the Malthusian model to the pre-industrial society of Western Europe, Dobb argues that the increase in population between 1000 and 1300 outpaced the extension of the area of cultivable land resulting in a decline of labour productivity, inasmuch as the land newly brought under the plough could only be claimed from the less fertile waste, which had been hitherto left untouched for that very reason. At the same time the shortage of land was bound to raise the level of real rents. These conditions, in turn, in the classic Malthusian manner, brought about a fall in the level of subsistence of the poor, causing higher mortality and thereby a decline of population (and so of rents) even before the outbreak of the Black Death in Europe in the middle of the fourteenth century.[1]

A more explicit Neo-Malthusian approach is followed in Emmanual Le Roy Ladurie's formidable work, *The Peasants of Languedoc*. In his chapter 2, 'Malthusian Renaissance', he sets out to show how a population, expanding beyond the available resources, caused famines, pestilence and violent conflicts, and how these in turn brought down the population back to a level that was manageable in relation to resources.[2] M.M. Postan, a votary of demographic determinism, identified the rise in West European population, rather than the increasing money supply, as the main factor behind the Price Revolution.[3] A discordant note seemingly comes only from Robert Brenner, who has questioned this approach *in toto*, and raised afresh the question of the internal structure of the economy concerned, the pattern of distribution of wealth or control of resources within it, and the mode of class-exploitation.[4]

It is, indeed, a fair argument that population size, whether in the process of enlargement or constriction, cannot be separated from the nature of the economic structure. Let us suppose that the state levies a claim on the surplus produce of the land generally and not on that of particular plots of land. Such a situation exists where the system of individual rents is either not prevalent or very limited in extent, while the dominant position is occupied by a system of land-tax levied on behalf of the state — the characteristic basis of the Mughal agrarian system.[5] In such circumstances, the extension of cultivation may have

[1] Maurice Dobb, *Studies in the Development of Capitalism* (revised ed.), London, 1963, pp.47-9.

[2] Emmanual Le Roy Ladurie, *Peasants of Languedoc*, translated by John Day, Urbana, 1976.

[3] M.M. Postan, *Essays on Medieval Agriculture and General Problems of the Medieval Economy*, Cambridge, 1973.

[4] Robert Brenner, 'Agrarian Class Structure and Economic Development in Pre-Industrial Europe', *Past and Present*, No.70, February, 1976. See also *The Brenner Debate*, edited by T.H. Aston and C.H.E. Philpin, Cambridge, 1985.

[5] This is the position of both W.H. Moreland (*Agrarian System of Moslem India*, Cambridge, 1929) and Irfan Habib (*Agrarian System of Mughal India*, 2nd ed., 1999, New Delhi).

results different from those of economies where private rents are the mode. In the former case, if productivity per acre declined, the land-tax collection per capita would also decline, whereas in individual-rent economies, rents are presumed to rise. If the decline in land-tax per capita led to any change, it would, perhaps, reflect in a relative decline of the urban population, maintained on rural revenue, rather than in a demographic crisis for the whole society. Secondly, where we are speaking of a large empire, and, of a fairly high degree of peasant mobility,[6] the fact of newly cultivated land being necessarily less fertile cannot be assumed. If there are virgin forest areas where clearings can be made, which are potentially as fertile as the lands previously cultivated, an increase in population might not result in a decline of labour productivity.[7] The rise in population might therefore be sustained for a long time, and any declines might simply stem from environmental accidents, such as failures of the monsoons, or the spread of epidemics which can strike even a prosperous population. On the other hand, it is possible that the high revenue-demand in the Mughal Empire, forming the bulk of the surplus and leaving the peasant only with bare subsistence, might constantly obstruct population growth. The lack of resource-reserve with the peasant would easily turn even a seasonal shortfall in rains, or a rampage by a moving army, into a fatal famine visitation. In Gujarat a complete failure of the rains in 1630, followed by attacks of mice and locusts and then excessive rains in subsequent years, resulted in such a devastating famine that the decline of cultivation caused by it was not made up till *c*.1665 and the extent of cultivation still remained much below the level it had reached in 1595.[8]

It is thus possible that in an economy like that of the Mughal Empire, an increase or decline in population need not have had its roots in a previous demographic process in the opposite direction, as is suggested by neo-Malthusian historians for feudal and post-feudal Western Europe. Indeed, since even in Europe, prior to the eighteenth century, the death rate among the aristocracy was practically the same as that among the common people,[9] it may be difficult to assume, as an

[6] *ASMI*, pp.130-35.

[7] Chapter 4 in this book suggests such a situation.

[8] See Chapter 1 in this volume. For a detailed account of the famine see *ASMI*, pp.114-5.

[9] As in the case of England: see T.R. Edmons, 'On Duration of Life in the English Peerage' in *Population Studies*, Vol.IX, London, 1957. For trends in mortality

established fact, a direct relationship between falling productivity and higher mortality rate.

Nothing that has been said above should, however, be construed as a denial of the impact of demography on the extent of cultivation, the revenue system and the levels of subsistence. The essential data must, in the first instance, come from demography itself. One realizes that no census for any large territory comes to us from Mughal times. But the enormously rich data in Abū'l Faẓl's *A'īn-i Akbarī* enable us to attempt estimates of the population of the Mughal Empire, and, on this basis that of India, valid for *c*.1601.[10] Such statistical wealth, however, is not available to us for any large area of India until the nineteenth century. One result of this is that we are unluckily in no position to offer an estimate of Indian population at any point within the two centuries between 1601 and 1801.

What is possible within this period is an estimation of population for some localities and towns. There is, for example, exceptionally detailed information furnished for Marwar (Western Rajasthan) in Nainsi's *Vigat* (c.1665).[11] This provides us data on villages, the number of ploughs, wells, etc., and gives for some *qasbas* (townships) and towns the numbers of houses. For Khandesh, too, detailed village-level records of Aurangzeb's time are available in the Inayat Jang Collection of the National Archives, New Delhi.

It is possible that if further explorations are made, e.g. in the Rajasthan Archives, Bikaner, and the Andhra Pradesh Archives, Hyderabad, statistical reconstructions would be possible for other localities as well. When such further work has been carried out, it may be possible to derive larger conclusions for, say, the size of mid-seventeenth century population and its composition than can be attempted at the moment from a very small sample (as in Chapter 6, where Nainsi's data have been used for estimating the population of some towns in Marwar).

Until these data are quarried and analysed, one is left only with the choice of speculative theorizing. It has been suggested that Neo-Malthusian assumptions of the type made for pre-modern Western Europe are not necessarily valid for societies where not private rents,

---

and fertility rates in Mughal imperial family see Chapter 5.

[10] *EME*, pp.395-406.

[11] Munhta Nainsi, *Mārwār rā Pargana rī Vigat* (*c*.1666), ed. N.S. Bhati, 2 vol.s., Jodhpur, 1968-9.

but the state's land-tax shaped the most dominant economic relationships. It would be of some interest to economic historians when this hypothesis can be actually tested from hard data. That time, however, still seems far-off.

Gross Domestic Product

The gross domestic product (GDP) or national income is today considered a critical indicator for the performance of an economy. The present estimates of GDP are controlled by internationally set standards for national accounts, where totals of income received by producers and service-providers are compiled on one side, and values of goods consumed and services paid for, are put on the other. Allowing for balance of trade/ payments, the total on one side should match the other.

Such compilation of national accounts has so far not been attempted for even nineteenth-century India. Atkinson had to combine estimates for production in some sectors and consumption in others to construct his estimates of the National Income of British India in 1875 and 1895.[12] Sivasubramonian has adopted basically the same method, though in a much more refined manner, for calculating the GDP of India from 1901 onwards.[13]

It is again the rich statistics provided by Abu'l Fazl in his *Ā'īn-i Akbarī*, the marvellous gazetteer of Akbar's India, that makes it possible to attempt the an estimation of GDP for *c.*1600 by a method similar to the one used by Atkinson and Sivasubramonian. The value of agricultural product has to be worked out here either on the basis of the size of the cultivated area and estimates of yields or by making use of figures for land-revenue that represented a known fixed share of the value of gross crops. Since the cropping pattern (the area under different crops) is not known the use of land-revenue statistics to estimate the total value of produce seems to offer a more serviceable procedure. Adding the estimates of values of pastoral, mineral and forest product the share of the primary sector can then be estimated.

The value of manufactures must be worked out from estimates of income distribution and consumption pattern in the absence of any

[12] Fred J. Atkinson, 'A Statistical Review of the Income and Wealth of British India', *Journal of the Royal Statistical Society,* Vol.LXV (part ii), June, 1902.

[13] S. Sivasubramonian, *The National Income of India in the Twentieth Century*, New Delhi, 2000.

direct statistics. The share of the tertiary sector can be estimated with help of stated salaries of the *manṣabdārs*, wage-rates, transport-costs and trade statistics.

The margin of error in estimating the GDP by such means must indeed be fairly large and it could at best be a guesstimate, but the attempt has nevertheless to be made. I tried to calculate the GDP for India, *c*.1600, in an earlier paper,[14] and now present in this volume a revision of the estimates.[15] A comparison with modern GDP cannot be made in terms of units of silver or gold, since these are money metals whose intrinsic values have greatly changed. A better comparison can perhaps be made by converting the money figures into units of weight of wheat at the prices prevailing at the times in question. This has its own pitfalls, since wheat loses its prime position in an industrial society, though this would be of no relevance when we compare the GDP of *c*.1600 with that of *c*.1900, when modern industry was hardly of much importance in India.

I do not wish here to anticipate the inferences I draw from the GDP estimate for *c*.1600, but venture to offer one particular defence of such an ambitious computation on the basis of admittedly limited data. In 1920 W.H. Moreland wrote his path-breaking book, *India at the Death of Akbar*, where he aimed at a comparison of per-capita productivity, *c*.1600, with that estimated for around 1900. Except for a few hard estimates it was a largely impressionistic effort. One should surely aim now to replace such a 'qualitative' exercise with a more quantitative one, and then judge how far the results of both the efforts match each other.

The Supply of Capital

The nature of capital before capitalism approximates to those text-book definitions of 'capital', which link it merely to money or titles or goods that are used to produce an income for the owner. Under such a definition even a rent-receiving landlord's rights would constitute capital, just as would be a modern company's brand-name. What is overlooked here is not only the Marxist stipulation about the hiring of labour as the means of income ('surplus value'), but also any necessary link of capital to production or value-addition (e.g. by transport). One

[14] 'The Gross National Product of the Mughal Empire', *IHR*, Vol.XIII, Nos.1-2, pp.75-87.

[15] Summary statement in Chapter 1 in this book.

is reminded of the remark of a fourteenth-century *sufi* of Delhi that every person pursuing an occupation needs capital (*māya*): "for example a merchant (*baqqāl*) needs capital for trade, viz., money (*māl*), shop and commodities (*qumāsh*); a peasant needs capital to undertake cultivation, viz. seed, cattle, goods and tools; and so too a cloth-seller, a cook [i.e. cooking food for sale], etc. — whoever is [in some business] needs capital."[16]

Since commodity production had developed in Mughal India and all goods could be bought and sold, capital existing in the form of goods could be theoretically converted into money and *vice versa*. Such convertibility of capital could also enhance its degree of mobility. But, in fact, the convertibility in various sectors of production came at a cost, and this cost was generally much higher for the rural poor. This may be illustrated by the large difference in interest rates set for the well-to-do debtors and for the poor.

In the famous official enquiries into the conditions of the poor in the present Uttar Pradesh in 1887-88, we find the description of a *zamindar* (a Thakur) in a village of District Etah, who was able to borrow from a Bohra (professional moneylender) the sum of Rs 2000, at 0.75 per cent. per month, and lend it out to poor borrowers at 3.125 per cent. per month, making an annual net profit of Rs 750 (*rect.* Rs570) for himself.[17] In other words, the intermediary charged interest at a rate four times he himself, presumably as a reliable debtor, paid to the primary creditor. This difference indicated where the roots of rural usury lay.

While this piece of information comes to us from the late nineteenth century, it can hardly be doubted that conditions of rural usury in Mughal times, where our information about it is so limited, could not have been much different. We know, at least, that indebtedness was widespread: 'small peasants' (*reza ri'āya*), who "engage in cultivation, but are wholly in debt for their subsistence and seed and cattle", were numerous enough to require a special *farmān* from Aurangzeb declaring them exempt from the *jizya* or poll tax. *Mahājans* (professional money-lenders) lent money to the village as a body to pay the land-tax, and to

[16] Hamid Qalandar, *Khairu'l Majālis* [Conversations of Shaikh Nasiru'ddīn, 1354], ed. K.A. Nizami, Aligarh, 1959, p.140.

[17] *Collection of Papers connected with an Inquiry into the Conditions of the Lower Classes ... in the North Western Provinces and Oudh, instituted in 1887-88*, Naini Tal (?), 1890, pp.91-93.

zamīndārs apparently on the security of their lands.[18] The high rates of interest for ordinary peasants made it imperative for the government to provide *taqāvī* (modern 'taccavi') loans to them, to sustain existing cultivation and encourage its improvement and extension.[19] Such intervention by the state was in fact a form of capital supplied to agriculture out of the state's own revenue resources. Its total size has not been estimated, but it was certainly considerable.

Turning to commercial credit, there is luckily little need here to say much on the institutions of deposit banking, bills of exchange and insurance by which capital was channelled into commercial credit, since much has been written on it.[20] It could be supposed that some capital became available for commercial operations through deposits by wealthy nobles and officials (the latter including treasurers who lent out treasury money illegally) with *ṣarrāfs* or bankers, and this would, again amounted to a conversion into capital of part of the agrarian surplus, extracted through land-revenue by the state. If the *ṣarrāfs* had to offer attractive rates to obtain such deposits, these must have determined the minimum levels below which the commercial interest rates would not fall. From Agra it was reported in 1645 that the *ṣarrāfs* accepted deposits from "greate monied men" at 0.625 per cent. per month to lend at 1 to 2.25 per cent. The higher rates were charged on loans to "persons of qualletie", where much risk was incurred.[21] In the latter case no enhancement of merchant capital was involved. But the *ṣarrāfs'* main business, for which they could use these deposits, was the discounting of bills, which in India, as in Europe, were the main instruments by which commercial credit was extended.

Another possible source of supply of capital for commerce in India needs to be investigated. In Chapter 3 in this volume I raise the question whether the higher rates of commercial interest prevailing in India during the seventeenth century did not generate a transfer of money-capital to India. In other words, if all the silver imported was not used

[18] Cf. *ASMI*, pp.137-8, 154, 202, for the facts cited above. It is a pity that while describing agrarian conditions, Irfan Habib does not enter into a discussion of rural usury and its impact on the agrarian structure in Mughal times.

[19] Ibid., pp.295-96.

[20] See, e.g., Irfan Habib, 'Banking in Mughal India' in: T. Raychaudhuri (ed.), *Contributions to Indian Economic History*, Vol.I, Calcutta, 1960, pp.1-20.

[21] *EFI, 1642-45*, p.303.

up for purchases of goods, but a part remained to be lent out at interest, then this would in effect amount to a transfer of money-capital. The curious coincidence of a fall in interests rate in the late 1640s in both Europe and India may be taken to suggest that speculation about such capital transfer may not be entirely out of place.

'The Price Revolution'

The Price Revolution of the sixteenth and seventeenth centuries has for the last hundred years become a theme of debate among Europe's historians almost at par with that on the nature of the Reformation. The critical initial contribution came from Earl J. Hamilton who in 1929 not only assembled evidence for the transfer for American silver to Spain during the period, but also raised the question of its effects on the internal economy of Western Europe, in that the inflation it created led to extra profits leading to the rise of capitalism.[22] The Price Revolution has been seen by most supporters as well as critics of the Hamilton thesis, as a monetary phenomenon, and, on that score, there have been disavowals of the effect of American silver on prices in Europe, as by Postan,[23] and a rejection also of the connection between inflation and the rise of capitalism.[24] In this debate a major context appears to be overlooked, viz., the very root of silver exports, the forcibly enforced hegemony of Spain over Amerindian peoples, constituting the initial phase of colonialism on the world scale. In 1869 in a famous passage, Karl Marx had put "the discovery of gold and silver in America, the extirpation, enslavement and entombment in mines of the aboriginal population" as the first among "the chief momenta of primitive accumulation [of capital]."[25] The monetary phenomenon was thus created by acts of force and brutality seldom seen in human history.[26] If one, for the moment, overlooks what the

[22] Earl J. Hamilton, 'American Treasure and the Rise of Capitalism, 1500–1700', *Economica*, November 1929; and idem, *American Treasure and the Price Revolution in Spain, 1501-1652,* Cambridge (US), 1934.

[23] M.M. Postan, 'The Rise of a Money Economy', *Economic History Review*, XIV (1944), Part 2.

[24] Cf. P. Vilar, 'Problems of the Formation of Capitalism', *Past and Present*, No.10 (November 1956), pp.15-38.

[25] Karl Marx, *Capital*, I, transl. by Samuel Moore and Edward Aveling, ed. Frederick Engels, London, 1887, p.775.

[26] It is in the context of this and other "idyllic proceedings" of colonialism that Marx made his famous pronouncement: "Force is the midwife of every old society pregnant with a new one. It is itself an economic power". (ibid., p.776).

influx of American silver did to the internal economy of Western Europe, and simply take Western Europe as a single economic unit, the silver influx placed in its hands a huge mass of precious metal, by which it could buy immense quantities of goods from the rest of the Old World, without, in effect, paying for them out of its own products. Though what may appear as a mere monetary mechanism, it could now levy a tribute on the whole world, gathering for its own use Chinese silk, Indian cotton textiles and spices, and African slaves, in exchange of silver, that had been secured at the expense merely of Amerindian lives.[27]

It was inevitable, therefore, that while retaining much of the imported silver within Western Europe, a large part of it should be exported eastwards in search of physical products. Estimates of such exports vary, but according to one accepted by W. Barrett, during 1601-1700 a total of 12,750 metric tons of silver out of a total of 30,875 tons, i.e. over 41 per cent. of the total silver received in Europe, was exported, in bulk, of course, to Asia.[28] In Chapter 2 of this volume where I attempt a quantification of the growth of coined silver stock in India, I reach the conclusion that the growth in Indian stock between 1500 and 1650 amounted to about a third of the quantity of silver that legally reached Spain (the owner of the American silver mines) during that period, according to Hamilton's calculations. This matches Barrett's estimates fairly well.

One, then, needs to look at how the silver influx affected the Indian economy James Grant deserves credit for raising this question in 1789 and stipulating a 50 per cent rise in the silver price of gold in the course of the seventeenth century.[29] The entire matter was practically

[27] This particular implication of silver influx has not at all been perceived by many Marxist historians (despite the remarks of Marx himself that we have quoted) partly because there has been a curious distrust among them of treating monetary circumstances as elements of fundamental economic processes. As Prabhat Patnaik points out ("The Other Marx's in: *Karl Marx on India*, ed. Iqbal Husian, New Delhi, 2006, pp.lxi-lxiii), Marx was very well aware of the function of money as "a store of value", which was precisely the primary function of the silver brought over from America to Europe.

[28] Ward Barrett, 'World Bullion Flows', in: James D. Tracy, ed., *The Rise of Merchant Empires*, Cambridge, 1990, pp.242-43.

[29] James Grant, 'Analysis of the Finances of Bengal', in: *The Fifth Report* from the Select Committee on the Affairs of the East India Company, London, 1812-13, pp.649-50.

left untouched until Irfan Habib raised the question afresh as to whether India could have been affected by the Price Revolution; but his evidence consisted mainly of the shifting trimetallic ratios in India.[30] As more evidence from coin-hoards and European commercial and customs statistics has been gathered, it is possible to get more precise data. It would appear that the per-capital coined silver stock in Northern India during 1600–1700 grew only by about 62 per cent. The silver price of copper seems to have first fallen and then recovered, while the silver price of gold rose by over 31 per cent.[31] This means that despite the heavy influx of silver, the annual rate of inflation (if gold represented the general price-level) was barely 0.3 per cent., a rate so low as to hardly affect even the rate of interest and so hardly one to provide the kind of extra profits that Hamilton postulated for the proto-capitalists of Europe. It is also a reminder for us of the sheer relative size of the Indian economy in the seventeenth century, that enabled it to absorb such a large influx of silver without any perceptible effects on its economic stability.

Processes of Labour

The term 'labour process' in Marxist discourse essentially encompasses the conditions in which production of goods is undertaken. It embraces the quality of labour (skilled, unskilled; intensity, duration); its recompense (wages, contract rates, 'profits' as owner-labourer, balance in hand left for tax- or rent-paying peasant, etc.); the legal status of the labourer (slave, partly servile, free); and the conditions of wage determination (custom *versus* market). In a pre-industrial society, forms of labour process are expected to vary in the extreme, since the uniformities imposed by capitalism and machine-industry are absent. Still two major categories can be identified in Mughal India: self-employed labour (peasant, artisan) and wage-labour. In peasant-agriculture with abundance of arable land, even ordinary peasants would need the help of hands from outside the family at sowing and harvesting times. This would be the case still more with the higher strata of peasants, who, with a larger number of draught cattle and cultivating a larger number of crops, would need many extra hands. Without advancing such an argument, W.H. Moreland still assumed

[30] I. Habib, *Agrarian System of Mughal India*, first ed., Bombay, 1963, pp.392-94.

[31] The figures are based on Tables 2.9 and 2.10 in Chapter 2.

the presence of large number of landless labourers in Mughal-Indian countryside.[32] For this Irfan Habib has adduced documentary evidence; and he has also argued that the caste system, by denying the lowest castes the entitlement to hold land, helped create a rural proletariat to meet the needs of peasants and *zamindars*.[33]

The caste system may not only be seen as determining the property system, but also as modifying the role of the labour market. Wages did not need to be determined wholly by the supply of and demand for labour, but could be manipulated by constraints on particular castes and communities. Such constraints prevented 'menial' castes not only from aspiring to landed property but also from benefiting from occupational mobility. They were compelled to keep to professions, which met only part of their subsistence needs. For the rest they had to depend on the low-paid labour in peasants' fields. It must be realized that customs were often different for middling castes. While hereditary profession or duty was duly prescribed, the impediments to occupational mobility were often much lighter for them. Morris D. Morris in a notable article and Fukazawa in his study of conditions in eighteenth-century Maharashtra have shown how readjustments in occupations could take place for whole, or sections of, particular artisanal castes.[34] One has also to take into account the flexibility obtained through the capacity of some castes to claim higher status by shifting to higher-caste ritual and customs. This is, of course, the burden of Srinivas's theory of 'Sanskritisation'.[35] Finally, the presence of legally non-caste communities, notably Muslims, among artisans, also introduced occupational flexibility. It may be marked here that unlike the case with the so-called 'menial' castes, the possibility of inter-occupational mobility favoured the interests of the ruling and mercantile classes, because as market demand shifted there could be an influx of new labour into the craft sector, faced with increasing demand, and such influx could keep the wages under control there.

In one respect, namely, gender, India shared with the 'civilized'

[32] W.H. Moreland, *India at the Death of Akbar*, p.112.

[33] *ASMI*, pp.142-5.

[34] Morris D. Morris, 'Values as an Obstacle to Economic Growth in South Asia', *Journal of Economic History*, Vol.XXVII, pp.588-62; H. Fukazawa, 'Rural Servants in the Eighteenth Century Maharasthrian Village-Demiurgic or Jajmani System', *Hitotsubashi Journal of Economics*, Vol.XII, No.2, 1972, pp.14-40.

[35] Cf. M.N. Srinivas, *Caste in Modern India and Other Essays*, Bombay, 1962.

world generally in assigning particular branches of labour to women: This form of division of labour is the concern of Chapter 7 in this volume.

Why certain professions, such as spinning, rice-transplanting and weeding have been assigned to women in most societies remains a theme of ongoing discussions. Some of the reasons lie in physiological attributes, such as women's higher gracility, small size, greater control over fingers, etc. Other specializations may have originated in male oppression, one example of this being hand-spinning which (before the arrival of the spinning wheel) put an almost unbearable strain on the spinner's fingers. Similarly, work with pestle and mortar and grain-milling also required long periods of strenuous labour. Indeed, jobs requiring very hard labour could also be assigned to women. In India women were employed in the building industry as pounders of rubble, and they had to carry bricks, lime-mortar and bitumen to masons, by going up the planks. These occupations assigned to women are described in Chapter 7, but there is need to examine the gender division in labour in further detail and to reflect on how it came to be established and enforced. Far too little, one confesses, is known of the recompense women received for their labour — a point Chapter 7 does address. But nothing can still be said about who really ultimately got the money that the women did receive!

The State and the Economy

My suggestion earlier that an economy with private rent must be considered very differently placed in demographic situations from one where the land-tax substituted for rent, necessarily raises questions about the nature of the state that could impose such a land-tax, and how it was constituted. One can certainly detect many shifts in the theorctical cxpositions of the pre-colonial Indian state. Francois Bernier (1620-85), who was in India during the years 1659-66, considered that there being no private property in India, the despotic tax-receiving state was a great drag on the economy. Presuming that the king claimed to be the owner of the soil and the transfer of *jagirs* caused an unrelenting degree of oppression of the peasantry, he held that the miserable conditions of the people did not stem from any intrinsic weakness of theirs, but from the authoritarian institutions of the state.[36]

[36] François Bernier, *Travels in Mughal Empire, 1656-68*, translated by I. Brocke and A. Constable, revised by V.A. Smith, London, 1916.

Among India's earliest economic historians, Moreland maintained the same assumptions about the nature of the Mughal empire, and practically drew the same conclusions.[37]

Karl Marx saw the rent-tax equivalence as the major foundation of the Despotic State, but also saw it as co-existing with the village community, which though self-sufficient, could yet produce a surplus on which the state subsisted. In return, the state carried out irrigation works, which, we may infer, aided agriculture and so enlarged its own revenues. He also held that in this system, a large craft sector could thrive, and the conversion of the surplus into commodities (marketable goods) could sustain a large market and an urban economy.[38] Though Irfan Habib has rejected irrigation as a major concern of the Mughal state, his interpretation of the Mughal Empire[39] could be accommodated well within the framework of Marx's Asiatic Mode of Production.

On the other hand, Ashin Das Gupta[40] and M.N. Pearson,[41] mainly concerned with the world of merchants, view the state as one for which commerce and other aspects of economy were of little concern, so long as its taxation was not affected: an atmosphere of indifference, almost amounting to *laissez-faire*, therefore, prevailed.

Burton Stein, applying the notion of 'segmentary state' developed by Aidan Southan, an anthropolist working on African tribal societies, eventually asserted that all pre-colonial Indian polities (including the Mughal Empire) were essentially segementary in nature,[42] and since such a state co-existed with divergent institutions and, local authorities, each customarily sovereign in its own sphere, no consistent picture of the state's role in the economy could really be drawn. The net result is that Stein sees the state as rather irrelevant to the economic processes that went on unaffected by its interference. It almost seems — though this is seldom asserted in precise terms — that in the view

[37] W.H. Moreland, *Agrarian System of Moslem India*.

[38] Irfan Habib, 'Marx's perception of India', in his *Essays in Indian History: Towards a Marxist Perception*, New Delhi, 1995, pp.22-29.

[39] *ASMI*

[40] *Indian Merchants and the Decline of Surat c.1700-1750*, Wiesbaden, 1979.

[41] *Merchants and Rulers in Gujarat: The Response to the Portuguese in the Sixteenth Century*, California, 1976.

[42] B. Stein, 'Eighteenth Century in India: Another View', in P.J. Marshall ed., *The Eighteenth Century in Indian History: Evolution or Revolution,* New Delhi, 2003.

of Stein and his fellow-thinkers the detailed documentation for land-tax collection notwithstanding, the heavy land tax was an ideal, seldom realized, and much of the documentation itself is to be treated as mere paper-work or normative. At this level it becomes difficult for more conventional historians even to enter into an argument with some of the "revisionists."[43]

As for the amount of the land-tax levied, one can do no better than to go back to the Grant–Shore controversy of the 1780s, when Grant argued that the land-revenue taken by the Mughl state allowed much leakage, and Shore refuted this.[44] It is surely unhelpful to go on challenging the evidence for both centralization and systematization without any detailed criticism of the evidence itself. This is very much the case with Andre Fink's use of the *fitna* in the sense of compromise (a sense for it unknown to lexicographers) as the basis of Indian polities.[45] Similarly, Frank Perlin roots for *watan* (eighteenth-century term for service-grant in Maharashtra) as the core unit of the Indian political structure.[46]

It is quite a relief, then, to read J.F. Richards' assertion of his firm conclusion that "the Mughal centralized power was a reality and that its effect on Indian society was considerable". One should not, of course, forget his further comment, that "whether this was good or bad is a different question."[47] I am, however, a little wary of a simple docketing of the Mughal Empire with the larger category of Despotic States, even with the important qualifications that Marx was apparently inclined to introduce into the concept. The land-tax was heavy in both the Mughal Empire and Safavid Iran; and yet both the states had markedly different features. Safavid Iran lacked anything akin to the *manṣab* system for public office and military organization that gave to the Mughal Empire such a powerful bureaucratic and command framework. One result was that Iran could not also develop the kind

[43] For a stimulating critique, however, see M. Athar Ali, *Mughal India*, New Delhi, 2006, pp.82-93.

[44] James Grant's 'Analysis of the Finances of Bengal' and Sir John Shore's long minute are both contained in *The Fifth Report* from the Select Committee on the Affairs of the East India Company, London, 1812-13.

[45] Andre Wink, *Land and Sovereignty in India: Agrarian Society and Politics Under the Eighteenth Century Maratha Swarajya*, Cambridge, 1986.

[46] Frank Perlin, 'State Formation Reconsidered, Part Two', *Modern Asian Studies*, Vol.XIX, No.3, 1985, pp.415-80.

[47] John F. Richards, *The Mughal Empire*, Cambridge, 1993, p.xv.

of *jāgīr* system, with regular transfers of assignments, that the Mughal Empire possessed.[48] M. Athar Ali also stressed the force of conventions (almost in the nature of an unwritten 'constitution') that, from the reign of Akbar to Bahadur Shah I (d.1712), governed the relations between the Emperor, and the nobility and bureaucracy.[49] These conventions necessarily modified the range of despotic decisions available to the monarchs as persons, and enabled the Empire to pursue well-established long-term policies in such economic spheres as currency, taxation, protection to merchants, 'free trade', etc. As an economy the Mughal Empire was more open than was possibly the case with many European states.[50]

Crisis of the Empire

When Irfan Habib's *Agrarian System of Mughal India* was published in 1963, it elucidated fairly definitively a large number of problems of the history of Mughal administration, through a critical and extensive scrutiny of an impressive mass of evidence. These strengths have been enhanced in the revised edition of 1999, which takes account of a still larger store of published and unpublished material. There have been surprisingly few dissents to the bulk of the details of his work: what has attracted reservations, notably from M. Athar Ali and J.F. Richards, is his theory of the agrarian crisis of the Mughal Empire, which occupies a whole chapter of his book and apparently sums up his own view of the direction in which the Mughal system was moving, and the outbreaks of violent revolts from the agrarian classes it thereby called forth.[51] Both Athar Ali and J.F. Richards have urged that Irfan Habib's argument about a high degree of exploitation of the peasantry is overstated.[52] However, neither provide any direct refutation of the

[48] The best study (available to me) of the agrarian administration of Safavid Iran is still A.K.S. Lambton, *Landlord and Peasant in Persia*, London, 1953, chapter V (pp.105-28).

[49] M. Athar Ali, *Mughal India*, p.67.

[50] In the words of Edward Terry, "a free trade, a peaceable residence and a very good esteem with that king and people", found by the English in India under Jahangir (quoted by W. Foster (ed.), *The English Factories in India, 1618-1621*, Oxford, 1906, p.ix). A grateful tribute must be paid here to Foster's outstanding service to Indian economic history through his monumental series, *The English Factories in India*, 13 vols.

[51] *ASMI*, New Delhi, 1999, pp.364-405.

[52] M. Athar Ali, *The Mughal Nobility under Aurangzeb*, Bombay, 1966, pp.89-92; J.F. Richards, *The Mughal Empire*, Cambridge, 1993, pp.291-92.

evidence adduced by Irfan Habib; and, indeed, M. Athar Ali himself objected to J.F. Richards' criticism of the concept of the crisis of *jāgīrs* as the mismatch between revenue and expenditure within the Empire increased.[53] It may be admitted that the fact of oppressive exploitation is as well established as any facts can be on the basis of available data. But this is not the sole issue to be settled in Habib's thesis of an Agrarian Crisis.

If the reader were to refer to Chapter 13 in this volume he or she may well feel that while examining a period of rural depression (late 1650's and the whole decade of the 1660's), I have managed to skirt the larger question of the maturing of internal class contradictions and the agrarian revolts that are thereby thought to have ensued.[54] The criticism would be just; and I append below my own tentative submissions on the matter.

It is obvious that Irfan Habib's theory is set in a Marxist framework, with a clear sympathy with the view that class struggle intensifies as exploitation increases, and that in a mainly agrarian society, this must be reflected in the outbreak of peasant revolts.[55] Those who do not necessarily view this connexion as universally applicable may find Habib's evidence for the oppression of the peasants more persuasive than that for the underlying roots of the agrarian revolts. He has himself noted that demands on the part of the rebels for the relief of peasants do not at all figure in any of the extant documents or accounts of these revolts.[56] It may be argued that revolts, without a consciousness of peasant grievances, can hardly be called "peasant revolts." Further, so long as peasants were able to desert land in one *jāgīr* and accept better terms in another,[57] such mobility could counteract the destructive

[53] M. Athar Ali, *The Mughal Nobility under Aurangzeb*, second ed., Delhi, 1997, Introd. to the new ed., pp.xx-xxii.

[54] Irfan Habib retained in his second ed. (p.405) the footnote admiringly quoting Mao Zedong's statements about the peasant revolts in China and the reasons for their failure. See also his essay 'Forms of Class Struggle in Mughal India', in: his *Essays in Indian History: Towards a Marxist Perception*, New Delhi, 1995, pp.232-58, especially p.257.

[55] Cf. however, M. Athar Ali, who held in the Introduction to the new ed. of his *Mughal Nobility under Aurangzeb*, Delhi, 1997, p.xxiv, that my essay supported his "doubts" about Irfan Habib's thesis.

[56] Cf. *Essays in Indian History*, op.cit., pp.257-58.

[57] *ASMI*, pp.133-34. He himself quotes Buchanan (1800) to the effect that such migrations were an important check on "arbitrary oppression" under "native governments".

effects of *jāgīr* transfers, as well as provide to the peasant an escape from oppression without the need of revolt. Were, then, the agrarian revolts as extensive and as dangerous for the Mughal Empire, as their enumeration by Habib makes them out to be?

In fact, except for the Marathas (which Habib counts among his agrarian revolts on the basis of a single though important passage in Bhimsen's *Dilkusha*),[58] none of the revolts posed any serious danger to the Mughal Empire, including those of the Jats, Satnamis, or Sikhs. Moreover, they were not by any means simultaneous, so that the combined effect of these revolts, at a particular moment, could not have been life-threatening for the Mughal Empire. The single raid of Nadir Shah (1739-40) undermined the authority of the Empire much more than all the revolts put together, the Maratha uprising alone excepted.

All this is said by way of qualification, not refutation. It is not my case that peasant unrest was not an important factor in the situation: the evidence to this effect, brought together by Habib, cannot be brushed away, as is often done by 'revisionist' historians, like C.A. Bayly or Muzaffar Alam. The real point at issue should be about the net weight that can be assigned to what may be called the purely agrarian factor in the collapse of the Mughal Empire. In other words, there are other causes too that merit attention.[59]

Satish Chandra, for example, has emphasized the decay of the *mansab* and *jāgīr* system as an important source of the Mughal breakdown.[60] But one asks, then, what beyond mere inertia, was the cause, in turn, of the failure of a system that had worked fairly well in enlarging and maintaining the Mughal Empire until the middle of Aurangzeb's reign. M. Athar Ali made an important point here, with Iqtidar Alam Khan's researches in mind, that the *mansab* system, based essentially on cavalry enumeration, could not work or continue as an efficient mechanism of military organization once the musketeer began to replace the mounted archer as the key element in the army.[61] The Mughal

[58] *ASMI*, pp.400-01.

[59] In terms of Marxist historiography, I would support Althuser against Plekhanov in urging the importance of multi-causal factors as against mono-causal.

[60] Satish Chandra, *Parties and Politics at the Mughal Court*, Aligarh, 1959, pp.xliii-xlix, where he outlines the features of the 'Crisis of the Jagirdari System'.

[61] M. Athar Ali, Introd. to the new ed. of *Mughal Nobility under Aurangzeb*, pp.xix-xx. For Iqtidar Alam Khan's work, see his *Gunpowder and Firearms: Warfare in Medieval India*, New Delhi, 2004, esp. pp.142-163. He has also argued (pp.164-90) that musket diffusion made peasant resistance more effective.

failure to shift from matchlock to flintlock also weakened the strength of imperial fire power. This is, on another plane, a further reflection of the increasingly technological stagnation of the Empire relative to Europe — a part of what M. Athar Ali aptly called a "cultural failure" of eastern societies.[62]

In the end, there is one thing more to be said about a study of the economy of Mughal India. Since India was not only the largest colony of the first industrial nation, but one most fully subjugated, a comparison of the economy of the Mughal Empire with that of India under British rule can offer us valuable insights about the economic processes underway in pre-colonial times and after the colonial subjugation. Chapter 1 makes a tentative attempt at this by essaying the economic history from *c.*1600 to *c.*1900. One hopes that as our knowledge grows of both periods, we will be able to understand our own pre-modern conditions better, as also what happened to us under colonialism.

[62] M. Athar Ali, *Mughal India*, New Delhi, 2006, p.342.

THE ECONOMIC EXPERIENCE

1

The Indian Economic Experience 1600–1900*

A Quantitative Study

I

The statistical cornerstones for any efforts at arriving at India's Gross Domestic Product and determining its structure were provided only in the latter half of the nineteenth century: the *Prices and Wages of India* from 1861, the all-India censuses from 1872, and the all-India *Agricultural Statistics* from 1884. Any attempt to build national income figures for a period before 1861 is a hazardous enterprise unless backed by a massive collection of statistics from archival repositories, many of which have so far not been explored extensively even for general historical purposes. The one exception is offered by the rich statistical material in Abū'l Faẓl's *Ā'īn-i Akbarī*, c. 1595–8, which has been aptly credited with providing the 'base-line' for the economic history of India.[1] Moreland himself carried out a detailed comparison of production per-capita between c. 1600 and c. 1911.[2] Since then there have been a number of studies[3] leading finally to a speculative estimate

* This is a revised version of a paper presented at the Eleventh International Economic History Congress, Milan, 1994. In revising it I have greatly benefited from the discussion there and at the Leuven (Belgium) Pre-conference and from the comments very kindly made by Professor Angus Maddison.

[1] W.H. Moreland, 'The *Ain-i Akbari*: A Possible Baseline for the Economic History of Modern India', *Indian Journal of Economics*, Vol. I, Allahabad, 1916, pp. 44–53.

[2] W.H. Moreland, *India at the Death of Akbar*, London, 1920, pp. 286–300.

[3] Brij Narain, *Bengal: Economic Life Past and Present*, Lahore, 1929; Irfan Habib, *Agrarian System of Mughal India*, Ist edn., Bombay, 1963; M. Mukherjee, *National Income of India: Trends and Structure*, Calcutta, 1969; A.O. Maddison, *Class Structure and Economic Growth: India and Pakistan since the Mughals*, New York, 1971; Shireen Moosvi, *Economy of the Mughal Empire: A Statistical Study c. 1595*, Delhi, 1987.

by me of the GDP for 1601.[4] One has to acknowledge, however, that there is no possibility yet for an all-India estimate of this kind for 1701 or even 1801. What one can do is to consider such other quantitative data as can help us in pursuing the course of economic change. (India here and throughout this paper means India of the pre-1847 frontiers, but excludes Burma, which was separated in 1935).

Coming to the possibility of estimating GDP for 1601, one must always remember that merely to reconstruct GDP on the basis of annual values assigned to goods and services in economic sectors (primary, secondary, and tertiary) would be misleading, unless there is a description of the pattern of distribution as well. The GDP for the Mughal empire c. 1601 was in fact built up by me on the basis of an understanding of the taxation system (based on the well-known tax-rent equation) and after working out the distribution of tax-resources among the ruling class, the bureaucracy, soldiery, and other dependants of the ruling class, and the rural hereditary right-holder (*zamīndārs*). The details of my estimate in a revised form are reproduced in Table 1.1.

Table 1.1: GDP 1600

	'000 *dāms*	% of Total
PRIMARY SECTOR		
Agriculture and orchards	1,13,66,256	50.771
Animal husbandry	27,06,251	12.088
Forests	2,70,625	1.209
Fisheries	54,125	0.242
Total of Primary Sector	1,43,97,257	64.310
SECONDARY SECTOR		
Value added to Primary Products by		
Urban manufactures consumed by		
imperial establishment, etc.	5,98,248	2.672
imperial land grantees	27,064	0.121
zamīndārs, headmen, etc.	73,372	0.328

[4] I had first attempted an estimate of the GDP in c.1600 in *IHR*, Vol.XIII, Nos.1–2, pp.75–87. But I have now revised it and the new estimates are due to appear in an additional chapter to the second edition (forthcoming) of my book, *The Economy of the Mughal Empire, c.1595*.

local revenue staff	8,486	0.038
ordinary townspeople	5,50,000	2.447
mercantile classes	55,000	0.245
peasants	49,033	0.219
Total	13,61,203	6.080
Rural manufactures consumed by		
peasants and *zamīndārs'* retainers	5,73,023	2.560
zamīndārs and headmen	90,617	0.405
rural artisans	36,336	0.162
Total	6,99,976	3.127
Manufactures exported	2,80,000	1.251
Minting	5,382	0.024
Mining, quarrying, construction, etc.	1,36,120	0.608
Total of Secondary Sector	24,82,681	11.090
TERTIARY SECTOR		
Salaries and Individual Incomes		
Manṣabdārs	8,27,455	3.696
Aḥadis (imperial soldiery)	82,857	0.370
Tābīnān (manṣabdārs' retainers)	6,90,141	3.083
Other imperial staff	1,04,581	0.467
Revenue staff	4,06,518	1.816
Zamīndārs' retainers	8,12,294	3.628
Domestic servants	6,50,000	2.903
Unattached professionals	65,000	0.290
Village servants	1,22,531	0.547
Total	37,61,377	16.801
Transport and communications	8,95,903	4.002
Merchants' profits, house rents	8,50,000	3.797
Total of Tertiary Sector	55,07,380	24.600
Grand Total	2,24,87,320	100.000

Note: Allowance for seed set at 6.8 per cent of crop value as against Sivasubramonian's allowance of 6 per cent and making an allowance of 10 per cent for mining, quarrying, and other uncovered items.
Source: See text.

The primary sector with share of over 64 per cent is thus held to contribute the major part to the GDP while the secondary sector accounted for a little over 11 per cent and the share of the tertiary sector was nearly 25 per cent. These figures are rather different from those suggested by Maddison.[5] According to my estimates the village and tribal economy (product of primary sector + value-added by rural manufactures) accounted for 67.447 per cent of GDP as against the 48 per cent suggested by him. The respective figures for the urban economy are 31.702 per cent and 52 per cent.[6] I saw no way in which the working force could be estimated. By assigning a labour force of 82 per cent to the village and tribal economy, but allowing it a share of only 48 per cent of GDP (after tax), Maddison perhaps wishes to emphasize the highly urban-based exploitative nature of Mughal rule, which one would not of course dispute as a general proposition.[7] At the end of British rule, however, Maddison argues for a relative improvement in the share of the village and tribal sector; with the same share of labour force (82 per cent), it now produced 56 per cent of the GDP (after tax).

While it is difficult to agree or disagree with Maddison's basic assumption of the gain of the rural sector in the colonial era, there is little doubt that the Mughal social structure displayed an enormous concentration of resources gained from a land tax that was practically identical with rent. The concentration in terms of total receipts of nobles (*manṣabdārs*) against both *ẕāt* (numerical rank determining personal salary) and *sawār* (numerical rank indicating size of military contingent and payment allowed for it) claims as a percentage of total revenue has been worked out for 1595 and 1647 (Table 1.2).

Table 1.2 shows a tendency towards intensified concentration; even though the number of *manṣabdārs* tended to increase in the higher ranks, there was simultaneously a general reduction of salaries.

The GDP estimate offered above does not make use of any assumptions about size of population. The population for 1601 has been estimated, on the basis of the extent of cultivation as well as percapita revenue, at 145 millions for India (pre-1947 frontiers).[8]

[5] Maddison, *Class Structure and Economic Growth*, pp. 33, 69.

[6] Ibid., pp. 33, 69.

[7] On this see also *EME*, pp. 347–8, where I suggest that the conditions of urban labour in c. 1595, were better than those in c. 1900, but the conditions of rural labour were possibly worse.

[8] *EME*, pp. 395–406. Moreland had estimated the population of India at 100

Table 1.2: Salary Income of Nobles as Percentage of Total Revenue

	1595		1647	
Rank	No. of *manṣabdārs*	Salary income as % of total revenue	No. of *manṣabdārs*	Salary income as % of total revenue
5,000-10,000	12	18.590	25	24.22
500-4,500	13	11.714	48	13.10
500-2,000	97	21.579	372	23.50
100-400	365	13.812	N.A.	N.A.
10-80	1,184	16.464	N.A.	N.A.

Source: EME, pp.221-29 (for 1595); A.J. Qaisar, 'Distribution of Revenue Resources of Mughal Empire among the Nobility, *PIHC, 27th session*, Allahabad, 1965, pp.237-43.

Unfortunately, the data from the seventeenth and eighteenth centuries do not warrant even a guestimate for the total population. However, if we take the population counted in the first all-India census of 1872 as modified by Davis for fuller territorial coverage, namely, 225 million,[9] the compound rate of growth over the period during 1601–1871 works out at 0.21 per cent per annum. The population estimates for 1801 range from 198 million[10] to 207 million.[11] If the compound rate of 0.21 per cent per annum had been maintained unchanged throughout the period 1601–1871, we should have had an Indian population of 210 million in 1801. This would also give us a population increase of 45 per cent in two hundred years, which, though not spectacular, suggests that the economy was not entirely stagnant in the intervening period.

From the seventeenth century we do not have measured-area statistics for the whole Empire, similar to the detailed *pargana*-wise

million in c. 1600 (*India at the Death of Akbar*, p. 22), which Kingsley Davis raised, to allow for uncovered regions, to 125 million (*Population of India and Pakistan*, Princeton, 1951, p. 24). See also Irfan Habib, in *CEHI*, Vol. I, pp. 163-71.

[9] Kingsley Davis, *Population of India and Pakistan*, p. 27.

[10] M.D. Morris, 'The Population of All India, 1800–1951', *IESHR*, Vol. XI, Nos 2–3, pp. 303–13.

[11] D. Bhattacharya, *Report on Population of Eastern India*, Vol. III, New Delhi, 1985, pp.1811–20.

figures of the *Ā'īn-i Akbarī*, c. 1595. Nevertheless, the *ṣūba*-and *sarkār*-level figures of measured area along with the breakdown of measured and unmeasured villages preserved in the late work *Chahār Gulshan* of Rai Chaturman (c. 1720) corroborated by *ṣūba*-level statistics from other documents, assignable from internal evidence to c. 1665, can be used to give some indication of changes in the extent of cultivation.

A comparison of gross-cropped area in four large blocks of the Mughal empire, comprising present-day Uttar Pradesh, Haryana, Delhi, Punjab (pre-1947), and Gujarat is offered here. The estimate for gross cultivation (i.e., area under the two seasonal crops separately totalled), c. 1595, based on the statistics in the *Ā'īn-i Akbarī* as worked out by me earlier,[12] is compared here in Table 1.3 with that for gross cultivation, c. 1665, established by applying the same method to the area statistics of this year. The figures for 1909–10 are taken from the official *Agricultural Statistics.*

Table 1.3: Growth of Gross-Cropped Area, 1595, 1665, and 1909-10

	c. 1665 as % of 1595	1909-10 as % of c. 1665
Uttar Pradesh	132.185	138.856
West Punjab	90.338	282.439
East Punjab (including Delhi)	130.401	171.539
Gujarat (excluding Saurashtra)	88.604	194.767
Total	117.554	170.983
Compound Rate of Annual Growth	0.23%	0.37%

Source: See text.

In considering the individual regions, the contraction in Gujarat during 1595–1665 makes sense in view of the devastating famine of 1630–2, which left a deep scar on the region's agriculture, and caused a long-lasting setback to its total revenues.[13] The contraction in West Punjab is less explicable, though the drying up of the long lower channel of the Beas[14] could have had a serious effect on cultivation in the area.

[12] *EME*, pp. 139–72

[13] 'Abdu'l Ḥamīd Lāhorī, *Bādshāhnāma*, K. Ahmad and A. Rahim, eds., Vol. II, Calcutta, 1872, pp.711–12.

[14] *Atlas*, Delhi, 1982, p. 11.

Overall, the cultivated expanse seems to have expanded by a little less that 18 per cent in all the four regions together, giving a compound rate of expansion of 0.23 per cent for 1595–1665. It is possible that the survey of c. 1665 was undertaken in response to the Mughal administration's anxiety to establish the area actually cultivated so as to monitor the place of agricultural development in a situation of acute agrarian distress.[15] But the actual rate of expansion of cultivation at 0.23 per cent is nonetheless above the annual population growth of 0.21 per cent found for the entire period 1601–1871.

Statistical studies of the more limited area of eastern Rajasthan broadly corroborate these findings for the large zones. In six parganas the measured (mainly cultivated) area recorded at various dates, 1649–1767, was 121.36 per cent of the measured area recorded in the *Ā'īn-i Akbarī*, taken as true for 1595.[16]

There has been considerable debate on the contribution of the Mughal empire to economic growth. Irfan Habib suggested that the revenue pressure tended to increase progressively and that this had a depressing effect on agriculture: he took this to be the explanation of the modest increase in estimated revenues (*jama*') of the Empire.[17] My figures do not seem to bear out this judgement, but the uncertain factors are many and one cannot be wholly certain.

One major economic factor for change in the seventeenth century was the silver influx from Europe, raising the question of the existence (and extent) of a price revolution in India. For estimating the silver influx in India the major device has been the counting of Mughal coins (whose legends give years and mints of issue), found in museums[18] and hoards.[19] The latter study, based on a correlation of surviving hoard-coins with coin-output, suggests scales of net coin-

[15] Shireen Moosvi, 'Aurangzeb's *farmān* to Rasikdas', in Irfan Habib, ed., *Medieval India*, Vol. I, Delhi, 1992, pp. 198–208, (revised version in this volume, Chapter 9).

[16] S.P. Gupta, *The Agrarian System of Eastern Rajasthan*, Delhi, 1986, p.43.

[17] *ASMI*, pp. 366-78.

[18] A. Hasan, 'The Silver Currency Output of the Mughal Empire and Prices in India During the 16th and 17th Centuries', *IESHR*, Vol. VI, 1969, pp. 85–116.

[19] Shireen Moosvi, 'The Silver Influx, Money Supply, Prices and Revenue-Extraction in Mughal India', *JESHO*, Vol. XXX, No. 1, 1987, Netherlands, pp. 47–94 (revised version in this volume, Chapter 2). See also Najaf Haider, 'Precious Metal Flows and Currency Circulation in the Mughal Empire', in *JESHO*, Vol. XXXIX, No. I, 1996, Table 11, p. 340. Haider's figures are slightly different from mine.

output (excluding recoinage) from North Indian mints, given in Table 1.4.

These data are important for showing that the seventeenth-century Indian economy could have gone through a constant, though perhaps moderate, inflationary process. But prices in proper series for major agricultural products are very difficult to come by and only tentative conclusions are possible.

Table 1.4: Net Coin Output

Years	Metric tons Per year	Years	Metric tons per year
1556–65	110.12	1636–45	140.30
1566–75	67.48	1646–55	111.90
1576–85	131.02	1656–65	102.62
1586–95	246.29	1666–75	71.98
1596–1605	290.70	1676–85	82.80
1606–15	145.22	1686–95	127.36
1616–25	121.46	1696–1705	188.39
1626–35	213.12		

Source: See text.

Accepting the prices in the *Ā'īn-i Akbarī* as those of Agra, Irfan Habib has compared them with the average monthly prices at Agra in 1637 and 1638 quoted by a Dutch source and with those for 1670 recorded in the *Ma'aṣir-i 'Alamgīrī.*[20] The prices of 1638 are clearly high and of 1670, clearly low. Table 1.5 sets out the relative prices (with 1595 prices as base =100):

Table 1.5: Agriculture Prices

	1595	1637	1638	1670
Wheat flour	100	218	338	250
Gram	100	338	629	190
Ghi (Clarified butter)	100	244	278	286
Moth (a millet)	100	260	367	N.A.

Source: CEHI, Vol.1, p.373.

[20] Sāqī Musta'idd Khān, *Ma'āṣir-i 'Ālamgīrī*, Bib. Ind., Calcutta, 1870-3, p.98.

The prices of Bayana indigo quoted in the records of the Dutch East India Company[21] and the English East India Company[22] offer a better means of studying price trends in the same (Agra) region. Table 1.6 gives the decennial average of these prices.

Table 1.6: Bayana Indigo Prices (Prices of 1595=100)

Years	Price Indices
1595	100
1609	154
1611–20 (7 years)	238
1621–30 (9 years)	245
1631–40 (9 years)	333
1641–50 (8 years)	292
1651–60 (4 years)	293
1663–64 (2 years)	773

Note: A monopoly imposed in the 1630s caused an abnormal rise in indigo prices in that decade.

Source: See text.

For the last four decades of the seventeenth century foodgrain prices have been collected from another area adjoining Agra, namely, eastern Rajasthan. Converted into ten-yearly unweighted averages, the aggregate prices of wheat, barley, grain, and millets (*bajra*, *juar*, and *moth*) are presented in Table 1.7.

Table 1.7: Grain Prices

Years	Rs/maund
1665–70 (5 years)	0.66
1671–80	0.76
1681–90	1.50
1691–1700	1.03

There is only one quotation from the 1660s.

Source: S. Nurul Hasan and S.P. Gupta, 'Prices of Food-grains in the Territories of Amber, c. 1650', *PIHC, 29th session*, Patiala, 1967, pp. 350–71.

[21] H.W. van Santen, *De Verenigde Ost-Indische Compagnie in Gujarat en Hindustan, Proefschrift,* State University, Leiden, 1982, p. 143.

[22] *ASMI*, pp. 94–5.

Arasaratnam suggests a rise in prices in the Coromandel (including Golconda) in the first half of the seventeenth century, which was becoming steeper towards its close.[23] Prices of rice, wheat, moth, *ghi*, and *gur* (jaggery) in Gujarat (mainly Surat) during the first half of the seventeenth century have also been published in Dutch records (Table 1.8).

Table 1.8: Rice and Wheat Prices (in rupees per maund)

Year	Rice	Wheat
1609 1.75	N.A.	
1611–20 (Average 4 years)	1.11	N.A.
1618 N.A.	0.77	
1620–9 (Average 3 years)	1.20	N.A.
1627 N.A.	0.99	
1630–40 (Average 5 years)*	7.54*	6.24*
1641–5 (Average 5 years)	1.65	1.39
1693–4 (Average 2 years)	1.99	1.49
1700 2.19	N.A.	

* Decade contained famine years

N.A. = not available.

Note: 1 maund = 37.523 kg.

Source: van Santen, *De Verenigde Oost Indische Compagnie*, pp. 92–5.

Remembering that the prices of the 1630s could not have been normal since these contain years of acute famine (1630–2), a steady rise is clear enough. Prices for other foodgrains and products are unluckily not numerous enough for any reasonable analysis.

It is only for Bengal that price-trends remain debatable. Those for rice and wheat do not either support or negate the possibility of a secular ascent.[24]

The increase in prices of gold and copper in terms of silver between 1615 and 1705 works out at 33 per cent for gold and 110.4 per cent

[23] S. Arasaratnam, *Merchants, Companies and Commerce on the Coromandel Coast 1650–1740,* Delhi, 1986, p. 337.

[24] Om Prakash, *The Dutch East India Company and the Economy of Bengal, 1630–1720*, Princeton, 1985, p. 285.

for copper.[25] This means that the price of gold in terms of silver rose at a compound rate of 0.28 per cent per annum and of copper at 0.83 per cent per annum. It is unlikely, then, that the overall rate of the general price-increase exceeded 0.83 per cent over the century: in the journalistic parlance of today, it was a less than one-digit inflation, but inflation all the same.

If the Indian Price Revolution occurred in the seventeenth century, in the moderate form that we are arguing for it here, it would be pertinent to set statistics of land-revenue against changes in prices. The officially estimated revenue (*jama*‘) figures have been culled together in a tolerably regular series. Table 1.9 gives the *jama*‘ indices, 1595–1707, for the Mughal empire (excluding the Deccan, so as to maintain uniformity of territorial coverage) as given by Irfan Habib. These are set against the silver prices of gold and copper.

Table 1.9: Revenue (Jama‘) Figures in Relation to Prices of Gold and Copper

Year	*Jama*‘ index	Silver price of gold	Silver Price of copper
1595	100	100	100
1605	115.54	-	105
1625	134.54	140	66.5
1635	130.00	125	80
1665	183.75	150	123.6
1690	178.23	132.5	102.6

Source:*ASMI*, Table 8, p. 375, Chapter 2, Table 2.9.

Irfan Habib assumed that the silver price of copper represented the maximum for price movements; and he, therefore, found that adjusted to prices, the total revenues did not show any real increase.[26] He deduced from this that cultivation did not really expand—a deduction which, as we have seen, is not tenable in view of fairly firm evidence now obtained of an expansion in the cultivated area.

The reason for the failure of Mughal fiscal resources to increase in real terms, despite an increase in the taxable resources, could be better attributed to a failure of the cash revenue-rates to adjust to price

[25] Moosvi, ‘The Silver Influx’, p. 85.

[26] *ASMI*, p.375.

fluctuations. This is borne out by a comparison of prices and cash-revenue rates (*ẓabtī*) from eastern Rajasthan indexed with 1715 as the base year = 100 restated in annual averages by decades (Table 1.10).

Table 1.10: Comparison of Price and Cash-Revenue Rates, Eastern Rajasthan (Reference Year 1715, Base = 100)

Years	Agricultural Prices	*Ẓabtī* rates
1661–70	36.52	106.34
1671–80	60.57	112.16
1681–90	44.30	105.99
1691–1700	60.24	171.81
1701–10	54.06	99.81
1711–20	122.34	117.05

Source: S.P. Gupta and Shireen Moosvi, 'Weighted Price and Revenue-Rate Indices of Eastern Rajasthan', *IESHR*, Vol. XII, No. 2, 1975, pp. 183–92.

Owing to the inelasticity of the cash-rates, there was a shift from the cash-nexus to tax-demand in kind (often commuted into money at current prices);[27] but such a process too could not entirely overcome the lag if we remember that a fundamental principle of Mughal administration was to hold on to demand fixed in money.

While the low rate of inflation (about 0.83 per cent per annum) over the century could hardly have much upward effect on the interest rates, the silver-influx, if it enlarged the liquid resources in the hands of merchants, might be expected to press the rates down. This appears indeed to have happened in at least three of the four zones into which seventeenth-century India could be divided on the basis of interest-rate levels, namely, Gujarat; northern India (mainly Agra); Bengal and Orissa; and the Deccan and South India. The interest rates per month for these regions are set out in Table 1.11.

It can be seen that in Gujarat the rates of interest on un-secured commercial loans ranged from 1.00 to 1.25 per cent a month until about 1650, and thereafter ranged between 0.50 and 0.75 per cent. A fall in interest rates in the 1640s occurred also in the Agra markets. For Bengal the data are available only for the second half of the

[27] *Ibid.*, p.277.

Table 1.11: Interest Rates per Month

Year	Rate per month%	Place
Gujarat		
1622	1	Ahmadabad
1622	1	Surat
1626	1.25	Surat
1628	1	Ahmadabad
1628	0.5	Ahmadabad
1630	1.2	Surat
1634	1 or 1.25	Surat
1635	1	Surat
1639	1.25–1.5	Surat
1640	above 1.2	Ahmadabad
1642	1 or 1.25	Surat
1647	above 0.7	Ahmadabad
1647	above 0.81	Ahmadabad
1650	1	Surat
1651	0.5	Surat
1652	0.75	Surat
1652	0.5	Surat
1652	0.625	Surat
1654	0.5–0.625	Surat
1657	0.625	Surat
1658	0.75	Ahmadabad
1658	0.625	Ahmadabad
1659	0.5 and 0.625	Surat
1659	0.75	Surat
1659	0.625	Surat
1665	0.75	Surat
1666	0.50	Surat
1669	0.33–0.50	Gujarat
1702	over 0.75	Surat
1702	0.80	Surat
1703	0.75	Surat
Northern India		
1626	0.83–1	Agra
1628	2	Agra

1645	0.625	Agra
1645	1–2.5	Agra
1645	0.75	Agra
1647	0.75	Agra
1657	0.75	Agra
Eastern India		
1650	3	Balasore
1660	1.5	Hugli
1670–2	1.37	Hugli
1676	25	Hugli
1679	1.25–2	Bengal
1679	1.5	Hugli
1679	1.5	Balasore
1679	1.5	Balasore
1703	1	Calcutta
1704	1	Calcutta
1706	1	Calcutta
1711	1	Calcutta
1711	1	Calcutta
1720	0.9	Bengal
The Deccan		
1635	2 and 2.5	Masulipatam
1636	2.5 and 3	Masulipatam
1639	3	Masulipatam
1642	1.5	Golkunda
1642	1.125	Rajapur
1645	1.5	Golkunda
1647	1.25	Raybag
1647	1.063	Golkunda
1648	1.5	Madras
1650	2.5	Karwar
1654	1.5	Coromandel
1658	1.50	Coromandel
1660	1	Rajapur
1661	0.75	Madras
1663	0.83	Madras
1665	1.5	Madras

1640–67	1.5	Bijapur
1666–8	1	Calicut
1667–76	2-3	Masulipatam
1665	1.25	Madras
1674	1.25	Karwar
1676	2	Masulipatam
1675	1.25	Karwar
1683	0.5	Madras
1711	0.83	Madras

Source: Irfan Habib, 'Usury in Medieval India', *Comparative Studies in Society and History*, VI-4, 1964, pp. 393–419, *EME*, p. 373. Certain quotations are added mainly from English records.

seventeenth century; here the rates continued to fluctuate around 1.5 per cent until 1679. Quotations are not available for the last two closing decades of the century, but at the turn of the century these were about 1 per cent per month and remained stable for the next two decades.

In the Deccan the rates were higher than in the other three regions prior to 1640. A great fall occurred between 1639 and 1642 and the rates thereafter fluctuated generally between 1.25 and 1.5 per cent.

The mid-seventeenth-century fall in rates[28] opens another speculative line of enquiry. Since interest rates were higher in India than in Western Europe, did the incentive of a larger usurious profit induce any money-capital movement to India? Such a movement remains concealed from us (except where the European companies are involved), largely perhaps, because the international eastward movement proceeded in stages (Italy-Levant-Red Sea/Gulf-Gujarat/Coromandel), and not directly.

II

The eighteenth-century post-imperial, pre-colonial regimes were seen, until recently, in a rather dim light as far as their economic performance is concerned. Contemporary indigenous historians had been generally of one voice in comparing them unfavourably with the past empire; and British officials and observers of a later time saw in them a hollow

[28] *Contra* K.N. Chaudhuri, *Trading World of Asia and the English East India Company*, Cambridge, 1978, p. 129.

shell concealing lawlessness and disorder, to be contrasted with the Pax Britannica of the next century. The view was so strong that K. Davis let it shape all his estimates of population at various points of time before 1871–2.[29] With Bayly leading the revisionist onslaught,[30] there has now been a swing of the pendulum in the opposite direction. The regimes are seen as creative responses to new circumstances, their alleged vices like revenue-farming now appear as products of creative ingenuity. But the interpretations have rested largely on qualitative evidence. Statistics have played little role in the arguments on either side, partly because they are exceptionally hard to get.

For one thing, the eighteenth century is bereft of any population estimates. But if there is any substance in our finding that the area under cultivation increased by no more than 0.23 per cent per annum, between c. 1595 and c. 1665, it would seem unlikely that the seventeenth century saw a population-growth rate of more than 0.23 per cent per annum. The all-India population would have been around 181 million in 1701. If so, for it to reach the vicinity of 207 millions by 1801, the eighteenth century must have seen an overall rate of growth of around 0.14 per cent per annum. The absolute stagnation assumed by Davis for both the seventeenth and eighteenth centuries[31] is, therefore, hardly credible, though it is possible that the eighteenth century saw a lower rate of population growth than the seventeenth.

Unfortunately, our inferences about population growth are unmatched by any dependable statistics for gross cultivation. Not that they do not exist; the sad fact is that the Nizam's Deccan, Maharashtra and Rajasthan still await explorers and interpreters of their rich eighteenth-century agrarian archives: there have as yet only been pioneers.

There are indications, however, that even if the eighteenth-century indigenous regimes were not as progressive in their economic performance as Bayly and like-minded historians[32] tend to portray them, they were not as destructive of internal commerce and good order as the apologists of British rule so often thought. Interesting

[29] Kingsley Davis, *Population of India and Pakistan*, Table 6, p. 25.

[30] C.A. Bayly, *Rulers, Townsmen and Bazaars: North Indian Society in the Age of British Expansion, 1770–1870*, Cambridge, 1983.

[31] Davis, *Population of India and Pakistan*, p. 26.

[32] F. Perlin, 'Proto-Industrialization and Pre-Colonial South Asia', *Past and Present*, No. 98, Oxford, 1983, pp. 30–95; Muzaffar Alam, *The Crisis of Empire in Mughal North India: Awadh and the Punjab, 1707–48*, Delhi, 1986.

evidence comes to us in the detailed tabulation of insurance rates on short and long distance transport within the Maratha dominions in 1795 and under the British hegemony in 1820 (Table 1.12).

Table 1.12: Insurance Rates, Short and Medium Distance (% of insured value)

From	To	Merchandise	1795	1820	1795 as % of 1820
Indore	Rutlam	Cloths	0.38	0.38	100
Ditto	Ditto	Kuranah	0.25	0.25	100
Ditto	Katchrode	Cloths	0.38	0.25	150
Ditto	Ditto	Kuranah	0.25	0.19	150
Kotah	Indore	Cloths	1.50	0.88	171
Indore	Kotah	Opium	1.25	0.88	143
Jeypoor	Indore	Cloths	2.00	1.50 to 1.75	114 to 133
Ditto	Ditto	Gold	1.00	0.38 to 0.50	200 to 267
Ditto	Ditto	Jewels, pearls & c.	0.75	1.00	75
Shujahalpoor	Indore	Cloth	1.00	0.38	267
Ashta	Ditto	Ditto	1.50	0.50	300
Mhysir	Ditto	Ditto	0.38	0.25	150
Ditto	Ditto	Silver	0.19	0.19	100
Oojein	Ditto	Cloth	0.19	0.19	100
Ditto	Ditto	Silver	0.75 to 1.00	0.75 to 0.88	100 to 133
Long Distance					
Indore	Ahmadabad Baroda, Broach	Opium & cloth	2.00	1.00 to 1.50	200 to 233
Ditto	Guzerat	Coins & bullion	1.25	1.00	125
Ditto	Ditto	Gold *mohurs*	1.50	0.80	150 to 171
Surat	Indore	Pearls & precious stones	0.75	2.00 to 2.50	30 to 38
Poonah	Malwa	Money & silver bullion	2.00 to 2.50	2.50	80 to 100
Naniapoor	Ditto	Cloths	0.50 to 0.63	1.00 to 1.50	33 to 63
Oomraw-Touttee	Malwa	Cloths, kuranah	0.63	3.00 to 1.50	20 to 42

Hyderabad	Ditto	Silver and gold coin & bullion			
Jaulnah	Indore	Cloths	2.00	1.25 to 1.50	133
Berhanpore	Ditto	Cloths	0.75	0.75	100
Mirzapoor, Mhow, and Jhansi	Ditto	Cloths	1.50 to	1.75 2.00	86 to 114
Ditto	Ditto	Kuranah	1.25 to 1.50	1.25 to 1.50	88 to 100
Chanderee & Bundelcund	Ditto	Cloths	2.00 2.25	2.00 to	100 to 88
Indore	Bhopal	Kuranah	1.25	1.50 to 2.00	83 to 100
Seronge	Indore	Cloths	1.75	1.50 to 2.00	88 to 117

Source: John Malcolm, *A Memoir of Central India Including Malwa and Adjoining Provinces*, London, 1833, pp. 366–8.

These tables show that insurance rates in 1795 were by no means such as to be prohibitive or render commerce difficult. They certainly testify to fairly orderly conditions. When one turns to the last column, one finds a rather surprising result. For local and short-distance trade, insurance rates under the Marathas were generally higher than under the British; but for long-distance trade they were at the same level or even lower. Should one then conclude that the major routes were as well protected under the Maratha Confederacy as under the Company?

The movement of interest rates for the century has still to be worked out in sufficient depth. At least in the Coromandel, they did not rise very greatly. Arasaratnam, whose statements as to the rates themselves are not very clear, suggests a slight rise by the 1730s over the seventeenth century (8–10 per cent as against 6–8 per cent on secured loans earlier).[33] He considers it remarkable that the interest rates moved up so sluggishly, 'as everything else had risen in price.' This would suggest an increase in the supply of liquid capital so as to press down interest rates till at least well into the first half of the century.

[33] Arasaratnam, *Merchants, Companies and Commerce*, pp. 279–82.

Of prices (foodgrains) over the century I have been able to locate three important series which give us some indication of secular changes (Table 1.13).

Table 1.13: Prices of Food Grains in Rs/maund

Year	Rice Bengal	Foodgrains Eastern Rajasthan	Wheat Delhi
1701–10	0.58	1.70	-
1711–20	0.71	2.64*	-
1721–30	0.97	1.85	-
1731–40	1.05	1.95	-
1741–50	1.48	1.55	-
1751–60	1.47	1.84	-
1761–70	2.91*	1.11	1.16**
1771–80	1.55	0.99	1.55
1781–90	1.55	-	1.98
1791–1800	1.14	-	1.16

* Decade includes famine years.

** For 1763–70.

Source: Brij Narain, *Bengal, Economic Life*, pp. 95–7, 100–102; N. Hasan and Gupta, 'Prices of Foodgrains', pp. 238–71; D. Singh, *The State, Landlords and Peasants – Rajasthan in the 18th Century*, Delhi, 1990, pp. 95, 98–9, 101; Jevons, *Investigations in Currency and Finance*, London, 1909, quoted from A. Siddiqi, 'Money and Prices in the Earlier Stages of Empire: India and Britain 1760–1840', *IESHR*, XVIII, 3–4, 1981, pp. 259–62.

We can see here an important break around the 1750s. Until then, there was by and large long-term stability in foodgrain prices in eastern Rajasthan, though a rise in rice prices occurred in Bengal. But in the next half century, the price rise in Bengal tapers off, and both in Bengal and at Delhi there is a great fall in the 1790s. The turn-around in price-behaviour cannot be unconnected with Plassey.

Until 1757, India went on receiving silver supplies on an increasing scale (the English East India Company's treasure exports in 1750 amounted to £1.10 million); but now these stopped altogether, as the English Company financed its purchases from revenues raised here; and other foreign companies began to do so from private remittances of the new, white *nobobs*. Moreover, the Company began to make its purchases in China from silver rupees collected in taxes in Bengal and exported to China.[34] The cessation of treasure imports and then its net outflow could not but have generated strong deflationary pressures, with consequent constriction of merchant capital.

With Plassey began also the 'Tribute' or 'Drain of Wealth' from India to England. Furber offers an estimate of £1.78 million annually for the years 1783–4 to 1792–3;[35] but this is much on the lower side. A detailed contemporary estimate covering trade of all kinds between India and Europe, puts India's annual export surplus during 1780–90 at £4.94 million.[36] Allowing an increase of 25 per cent for undervaluation and smuggling, India's export surplus, by English custom house records, should have been £3.59 million per annum in 1795–9 and £3.62 million in 1800–4.[37]

Even as estimated by Furber, the drain has been estimated by Irfan Habib at 9 per cent of GDP of the Company's territories. This calculation must probably be remade, because both the drain and the GDP of the Company's territories have here been underestimated.

An argument arose between James Grant and John Shore in the 1780s as to what was the actual gross product of land in Bengal (including Bihar and Orissa) in 1765, when the Company assumed its fiscal authority over the area. Grant in 1786 estimated the agricultural product at Rs 210 million and the value added by manufacture at Rs 30 million.[38] Shore scaled the former down to Rs 60 million, but did not contest the latter figure.[39] Moreover, he argued that the population, though increasing currently, had not yet returned to the level before the 1770 famine, which had caused the deaths of a fifth of the population. It may be recalled that in my estimate of the GDP in 1601, the value added by urban and rural manufactures was set at 22.93 per cent of the value of the product of agriculture (excluding orchards).

[34] A. Siddiqi, 'Money and Prices in the Earlier Stages of Empire: India and Britain 1760–1840', *IESHR*, Vol. XVIII, 1981, p. 253.

[35] Holden Furber, *John Company at Work*, Cambridge, 1951, pp. 112–16.

[36] K.N. Chaudhuri, 'Foreign Trade and Balance of Payments (1757–1947)', in *CEHI*, Vol. II, pp. 804–77.

[37] Calculated from B.R. Mitchell and P. Dean, *Abstract of British Historical Statistics*, Cambridge, 1962, p. 247. Cf. the recent estimates of 'inflows from India' to Britain in J. Cuenca-Esteban, in *Explorations in Economic History*, Vol.44, 2007, p.162.

[38] J. Grant, 'Analysis of the Finance of Bengal', in *Fifth Report from the Select Committee on the Affairs of the East India Company, 1812*, pp. 245–50.

[39] J. Shore, 'Minute dated 18 June 1789', *Fifth Report*, pp. 169–238.

Grant's estimate of the value of manufacture was 50 per cent of Shore's estimate of agriculture. Since they calculated only on the basis of area of cultivated land to arrive at the value of 'normal' produce, neither Grant nor Shore seem to have allowed for animal husbandry, fishery, and forestry, which, in my estimate for c. 1601, together with orchards, was 33 per cent as large as agricultural production. Nor did they estimate the value of the product of the tertiary sector. Clearly, the GDP (even if one ignores income from services) of the British territories was much larger than has been estimated by Irfan Habib, on the basis of Grant and Shore.[40] However, since Furber's estimate of the Tribute was also on the lower side, the ratio of Tribute of GDP of British India in the 1780s might not ultimately turn out to be very different from where Habib puts it.

III

In the nineteenth century, the major issues of debate among historians, namely, the Tribute, de-industrialization, de-urbanization, and population growth, have all led to extensive quantitative explorations. Dadabhai Naoroji was the first to see that, if the central question was India's pauperization, estimations of total value of production must be attempted: and he was the first to provide one.[41] His estimate then provoked a controversy which has continued to this day.

The assumption of Davis, that the beneficent impact of colonial rule led to an unprecedented increase in population in the period 1801–71,[42] no longer commands wide assent. Morris set the population in 1801 at 198 million by merely applying backwards the compound annual rate of population growth (0.3619 per cent) disclosed from the early official censuses 1871–1921.[43] Bhattacharya, using substantive 'pre-census' data gave an estimate of 207 millions for 1801,[44] and this gives a compound rate of growth of 0.21 per cent per annum for the period 1801–71, and 0.30 per cent for the entire century (1801–1901). Going by these rates of population growth, then, India's British

[40] Irfan Habib, 'Studying a Colonial Economy without Perceiving Colonialism', *Modern Asian Studies*, Vol. 19, No. 2, Cambridge, 1985, pp. 355–81.

[41] Dadabhai Naoroji, *Poverty and Un-British Rule in India*, rpt, Delhi, 1988, pp. 495–8.

[42] Davis, *Population of India and Pakistan*, pp. 25–6.

[43] 'The Population of All India, 1800–1951', *IESHR*, Vol. XI, Nos 2–3, p. 313.

[44] Bhattacharya, *Report on Population*, Vol. XLVI.

century could hardly boast of much of an improvement, if at all, over the earlier regimes, particularly when we remember that the 'improvement' which came was at least in part due to improvement in counting, marked especially between the 1881 and 1891 censuses, yielding a growth of nearly 1 per cent per annum. The extent of undercounting in censuses before 1891 has not yet been properly investigated.

Owning to the fact that official agricultural statistics begin from the 1880s, it is difficult to estimate the expansion in cultivation resulting from population growth. Table 1.3, comparing Gross Cultivation in 1901–10 as percentage of Gross Cultivation c. 1665 in four regions shows a higher overall compound rate of expansion in cultivation than that attained between 1595 and 1665. This is not surprising since the regions include western Punjab where the British-laid canal system undoubtedly contributed much to the expansion of cultivation in the area, duly reflected in its having the highest rate of expansion of all the four regions. A steady though modest growth of population, with little or no change in agricultural technology, was bound to lead to a point where further extension of cultivation must lead to diminishing returns and, therefore, must lag behind the growth of population. In UP, in 1880, with a population of 45 million, 36.5 million acres were cropped (double-cropped area being double counted); in 1947 with 63 million people the cultivated expanse (again double-counting the double-cropped area) was only 46 million acres,[45] a decline from 0.81 acre per head to 0.73 acre. Over the whole of India crop acreage grew only by 8 per cent between 1913 and 1946,[46] whereas population increased by 28 per cent between 1911 and 1946. The first official outcry over India's excessive population was raised by Lord Dufferin in 1888, clearly with the Irish population controversy green in the memory of this great English landlord of Ireland. There grew thereafter a British official dogma of India's growing 'overpopulation'. But essentially what had happened in at least the nineteenth century was simply that despite its rather modest population growth, colonial India was confronted with barriers raised by technological stagnation, urban decay and de-industrialization or obstructed industrialization.

[45] E. Stokes, 'Agrarian Relations: Northern and Central India', in *CEHI*, Vol. II, pp. 36–85.

[46] G. Blyn, *Agricultural Trends in India, 1891–1947*, Philadelphia, 1986, p.316; R.W. Goldsmith, *The Financial Development of India, 1860–1977*, Delhi, 1983, p. 128.

Singularly representative of the stagnation of Indian agriculture was the growing importance of opium, which upon the failure of cotton and indigo as major export goods in the 1820s, became India's major export item, accounting for 30.1 per cent of total export value in 1850–1 and 30.9 per cent in 1860–1.[47] Britain's infamous Opium War against China (1840–2) was clearly forced by India's inability to pay the Tribute to Britain in any other commodity.

The construction of the railways in the latter half of the nineteenth century initiated an economic change of undoubtedly important dimensions. Agricultural prices over different regions began to converge,[48] and inland India became linked to the world market. The latter process led to an improvement in agriculture's terms of trade. With 1870=100 as base, they moved up from 101.0 in 1861–5 to 135.9 in 1891–5, reaching 152.6 in the famine period of 1896–1900.[49]

But the impact of this improvement in agriculture's terms of trade was in part wiped out by increased taxation, where indirect taxes tended to rise as the proportion of land-revenue declined (Table 1.14).

Table 1.14: Total Revenue in Proportion to Size of Land Revenue 1858–1902

Year	Total revenues (Rs million)	Increase (%)	Share of land revenue
1858–9	360.6	42.57	50
1870–1	514.1	20.53	40
1877–8	619.7	20.53	32
1901–2	1145.2	84.80	24

Source: *CEHI*, Vol. II, p. 916; R.C. Dutt, *Economic History of India*: *Victorian Age*, London, 1905, p. 595.

Adjusted to price changes, the total tax revenues increased by no less than 75 per cent between 1870–1 and 1901–2.[50] The significance

[47] Chaudhuri, *CEHI*, Vol.II, p. 844.

[48] Z.A. Khan, 'Railways and the Creation of National Market in Foodgrains', *IHR*, Vol. IV, No. 2, Delhi, 1978, pp. 336–53; J. Hurd, *IHR*, Vol. II, p. 746.

[49] M. McAlpin, 'Price Movements and Fluctuations in Economic Activity (1860–1947)', in Kumar and Desai, eds., *Cambridge Economic History of India*, Vol. II, pp. 878–904.

[50] Irfan Habib, 'The Processes of Accumulation in Pre-Colonial and Colonial

of such an increase was far more in the Indian economy where the land-tax in theory (and at the beginning of the nineteenth century largely in practice), comprised the bulk of rent or economic surplus. In the scheme of Permanent Settlement (1790) it had been assumed to amount to 91 per cent of the rent, and in the Ryotwari system of the Madras Presidency (1822) at 33.33 per cent of the produce. As late as 1855, it was deemed a concession to the landholders in the Mahalwari areas of northern India, when under the so-called Saharanpur Rule, the land-tax was to be set at half the rental. The figures already tabulated show that after the 1850s the land revenue increased at a lower rate than prices, but the lag was more than compensated by an enormous absolute and relative increase in indirect taxation. This undercuts much of the argument advanced by Michelle McAlpin in favour of an actual lightening of the tax burden in the latter half of the nineteenth century.[51]

The gains from the favourable turn in terms of trade for agriculture were not, however, wholly appropriated by the colonial state. There were considerable enhancements in rents owing to commercialization of agriculture; and, therefore, land-values in areas which were drawn into international trade by the railways increased massively. In the Punjab the average land price rose from 31 times the annual revenues in 1875 to 127 times in 1910;[52] in UP it was estimated as equal to five years' revenue in 1861, but at twenty-eight years' revenue in 1899–1900.[53] On the other hand, in Bengal and Bihar, where railways did not help establish any new export crop, and protected sub-leases restricted zamindars' power to increase rents, land-values tended to decline after an initial spurt (Table 1.15)

One may here have an 'economic' explanation for the moderate nationalism of the zamindars of Bengal as against the strident loyalism of their counterparts in the Upper Provinces during the closing decades of the century.

The effects of railway-induced commercialization in the Ryotwari Presidencies (Bombay and Madras) are less clearly demarcated. Upper peasants were sometimes able to improve their circumstances, explaining much of the evidence McAlpin offers.[54] But moneylenders

---

India', *IHR*, Vol. XI, Nos 1–2, 1988, pp. 65–9.

[51] M. McAlpin, *Subject to Famine*, Princeton, 1983, pp. 198–205.

[52] Goldsmith, *The Financial Development of India*, Table 1.24, col.5, p. 5.

[53] Stokes, in *Cambridge Economic History of India*, Vol. II, p. 59.

[54] McAlpin, *Subject to Famine*.

Table 1.15: Land Values in Bengal 1853 to 1908

Years	Land Values in Bengal and Bihar as multiples of land revenue		
	Bengal & Bihar	Bengal	Bihar
1853–4 to 1857–8	8.77	—	—
1858–9 to 1863–4	10.25	—	—
1865–6 to 1868–9	10.16	—	—
1869–70 to 1873–4	7.72	—	—
1874–5 to 1878–9	8.79	7.43	14.63
1879–81 to 1883–4	6.91	4.92	18.24
1884–5 to 1888–9	6.10	4.45	11.68
1889–90 to 1893–4	6.64	4.19	11.59
1898–90 to 1902–3	6.36	—	—
1903–4 to 1905–8	4.90	—	—

Source: B. Chaudhury, 'Eastern India', in *CEHI*, Vol. II, pp. 104–332.

benefited still more.[55] Agricultural indebtedness increased from Rs 1.25 billion in 1860 to Rs 5.00 billion in 1913—an increase of 300 per cent,[56] while prices increased by only 106 per cent.[57] (These should not be compared with Goldsmith's figures for values of agricultural land, which are vitiated by his taking Punjab land values as valid for the whole of India).

A class that did not benefit, and probably increased steadily in size, was the agricultural labourers. The agricultural wages drawn from the official district-wise *Prices and Wages*, converted into real wages at 1873 prices by Moni Mukherji[58] is given below in five-yearly averages in Table 1.16.

This is the only firm real-wage index for agricultural labour available; a very low (unsourced) wage rate for 1857 in another of Mukherji's tables[59] has given rise to a misleading representation of his agricultural

[55] Habib, 'Processes of Accumulation', p. 86.

[56] Goldsmith, *Financial Development of India*, Table 1.28, p. 61,.

[57] M. Mukherji, 'National Income', in V.B. Singh, ed., *Economic History of India, 1857–1965*, Bombay, 1965, p. 685.

[58] M. Mukherji, *National Income of India: Trends and Structure*, p. 89.

[59] Ibid., p. 91.

Table 1.16: Real Wages

Years	Rs/Year
1873–5 (for 3 years)	35.33
1876–80	33.60
1881–5	41.60
1886–90	39.00
1891–5	34.40
1896–1900	36.20

Source: M. Mukherjee, *National Income of India: Trends and Structure*, p. 89.

real-wage index.[60] It is clear from the official *Prices and Wages* that over the last three decades agricultural wages remained stable or stagnated, an ascent in the early 1880s being soon cancelled thereafter.

Together with the land crisis and the accompanying attenuation of agricultural wages went the two processes of 'de-industrialization' and 'Tribute', on which much has been written. Here we are essentially concerned with the statistical data.

On the process of de-industrialization, the two major areas of controversy that have emerged are the changes in urban composition of population and the fortunes of the Indian textile handloom industry. On urban population the estimated pre-census populations of individual towns suggest a considerable overall decline until 1871 in Bengal, Bihar, and Awadh; but a notable increase (of 77 per cent) in the small province of Sind between 1831 and 1881.[61] Much, of course, depends on the weight that is to be assigned to the available pre-census counts or estimates. After the censuses began in 1872, urban population largely stagnated as percentage of total population (Table 1.17).

The premise of decline in the textile craft industry was challenged by Morris on two counts: the import of British machine-made yarn strengthened the Indian weaver, and there was a 'shift to the right

[60] A. Heston, 'National Income', in *CEHI*, Vol. II, Table 4A II, col. 5, p. 445 (how Heston manages to find an increase during the period 1857 to 1900–1, in ibid., col. 6, on the basis of the same data remains a mystery).

[61] Shireen Moosvi, 'De-industrialisation, Population Change and Migration in 19th Century India', *IHR*, Vol. XVI, Nos 1–2, 1993, pp. 149–62.

Table 1.17: Urban Population

Year	% of total population
1872	8.7
1881	9.3
1891	9.4
1901	10.0
1911	9.4

Source: L. Visaria and P. Visaria in *CEHI*, Vol. II, p. 519.

of the demand curve' for cloth in India.[62] To put the first argument in proper perspective one needs to consider the value of imported yarn as a percentage of the value of imported piece goods: see Table 1.18.

Table 1.18: Imported Yarn as % of Indian Imports

Year	Value of imported Yarn as % of value of imported piece-goods	Value of piece-goods as % of total value of Indian imports
1828–9	35.6	22.0
1839–40	45.0	32.3
1850–1	28.6	31.5
1860–1	18.7	39.6
1870–1	21.5	47.0
1880–1	16.3	45.5
1890–1	13.7	37.9
1900–1	9.2	33.8

Source: Calculated from K.N. Chaudhuri, *CEHI*, Vol. II, Tables 10.17 and 10.18, pp. 857–8.

Table 1.18 establishes clearly that the import of yarn, in value, relative to imported cloth declined heavily as competition from British textiles intensified in the Indian market from 1850 onwards.

[62] M.D. Morris, 'Towards a Reinterpretation of 19th Century Indian Economic History', *IEHSR*, Vol.V, No. 1, 1968, pp. 1–15.

As for the 'shift to the right of demand curve', this is hard to prove or disprove statistically (much depending too on one's view of what happened to India's per capita income). But two statistical endeavours have raised questions as to Morris's basic assumption that Indian handicraft production smoothly weathered English competition. Towmey estimated Indian handicraft textile employment in terms of million FTJEs (full-time job-equivalents) (see Table 1.19).

Table 1.19: Full-Time Job-Equivalents (Millions)

Year	Total textile workers	Weavers
1800	3.9–6.3	1.1–1.8
1850	6.0	1.8
1880	2.5	1.0
1913	2.4	1.5

Source: M.J. Towmey, 'Employment in Nineteenth Century Indian Textiles', *Explorations in Indian Economic History*, Vol.20, No.1, 1983, p. 522.

Amalendu Guha carried out an extensive survey of cotton acreage;[63] in an unpublished paper he calculated from these the total production of cotton. Deducting from the production figures, the total cotton exported and consumed in Indian factories, and adding imports of machine-made yarn, he formed the following estimates of availability of cotton for the Indian handloom industry in million avdp (Table 1.20).

Table 1.20: Cotton Consumed in Indian Handloom Industry

Years	Million avdp.
1850	419
1870	240
1900	184 or 221

Source: A. Guha, 'Growth of Acreage under Raw Cotton in India, 1851–1901: Quantitative Account', *Artha Vijnana*, Vol. XV, No. 1, Calcutta, pp. 1–56.

[63] A. Guha, 'Growth of Acreage under Raw Cotton in India, 1851–1901: Quantitative Account', *Artha Vijnana*, Vol. XV, No. 1, Calcutta, pp. 1–56.

Until further quantitative effort challenges these findings, the 'received' view of de-industrialization is likely to prevail.

The size of the Tribute to Britain has similarly called for much statistical and theoretical effort since the last century, especially since Dadabhai Naoroji began making his calculations in the papers he laid before the East India Association in London in 1876.[64] The latest and most careful calculation gives a picture of India's adverse balance of payments on the current account in current rupees (millions) and is reproduced in Table 1.21.

Table 1.21: Indian Adverse Balance of Payments

Year	Rupees (Millions)
1858–9	224.8
1868–9	171.7
1878–9	122.8
1888–9	276.3
1897–8	395.3

Source: A.K. Banerji, *Aspects of Indo-British Economic Relations 1858–1898*, Bombay, 1982, pp. 168–9.

There is, therefore, no justification for the extremely low figure for the Drain adopted by S. Sivasubramonian, of a mere Rs 191 million for 1900–1 in current rupees, adopting A.K. Banerji's earlier calculations for the later period of 1921–2 to 1938–9 and totally rejecting Y.S. Pandit's estimates for 1898–1913. When Heston accepts Sivasubramonian's figure for 1900 (converting 1938–9 into 1946–7 prices) and works back all the figures to 1868–9 by assuming a growth at 1.5 per cent in foreigners' earnings each year,[65] he unnecessarily extends guesswork into an area for which much precise data are, in fact, available. In so doing he reduces the Tribute, which should have been 3.4 per cent of his own 'Net Produce' for India in 1899–1900, to just 1.6 per cent.

A subsistence economy like that of eighteenth-century India can hardly be expected to have attained a rate of saving higher than 3 or 4 per cent of its national income; yet if this is the share of its national

[64] Dadabhai Naoroji, *Poverty and Un-British Rule in India*, rpt, Delhi, 1988.
[65] Heston, in *CEHI*, Vol. II, , pp. 376–462.

income that it lost year after year throughout the eighteenth century, there would be little room left in it for capital formation. It is, therefore, not surprising that there was a continuous capital scarcity in India throughout the eighteenth century which is marked by persistently high rates of interest in India.

Buchanan reported 2 per cent a month as interest at which manufacturers borrowed from merchants at Bangalore in 1800; and cultivators borrowed at 23.5 per cent per annum.[66] In Calcutta in 1801, 12 per cent treasury-bills were selling at a discount of 3 or 4 per cent, suggesting a rate of interest of 15 per cent per annum on strongest credit.[67] In Patna in 1807–16 interest on loans secured by bullion deposits was 12 per cent a year; commercial loans had previously carried 15 per cent interest but were now carrying 18 or 20 per cent.[68] In the 1830s the commercial rate of interest at which Indians borrowed was 12 per cent in Calcutta, where this was the legal limit; in the provinces it was 24 per cent or 30 per cent. In 1837 the agency houses paid depositors at 10 per cent and advanced loans at 12 per cent per annum.[69] Even on loans secured against goods the rates of interest remained fairly high in the 1840s and 1850s, as Table 1.22 shows.

These rates on heavily secured loans might have attained a slightly lower level (5.5 and 6 per cent) in the period after 1860, but they were still 2 per cent above the rates in London. 'The bazar or commercial rates were in the neighbourhood of 9 per cent from 1867–79; somewhat lower around 7.5 per cent in the 1880s; again at about 9 per cent in the 1890s.'[70] Such high rates after the full establishment of Free Trade and practically perfect ease for capital movement into India can only be explained by the constant outward pressure exerted by the Tribute, which prevented any net capital inflow into India, and so kept Indian rates so much higher than those in the London money market. It should not surprise us that in 1900 there were just 363 joint-stock companies with a total capital of Rs 648 million, of which

[66] F. Buchanan, *A Journey from Madras through the Countries of Mysore, Canara and Malabar*, p. 212.

[67] A.K. Bagchi, *Evolution of the State Bank of India*, Vol. I, Bombay, 1987, p. 62.

[68] F. Buchanan, *An Account of the Districts of Bihar and Patna in 1811–12* (*Patna-Gaya Report*), Patna, 1934, p. 699.

[69] Bagchi, *Evolution of the State Bank of India*, Vol. I, pp. 127–8.

[70] Goldsmith, *Financial Development*, p. 16.

Table 1.22: Interest on Loans Secured against Goods (mean for each year)

	Rate per annum(%)		
	Calcutta	Bombay	Madras
1840	–	7	–
1841	8	7	–
1842	8.5	8.2	–
1843	8.6	6.7	5.5
1844	–	6.5	5.0
1845	8.5	8.1	6.25
1846	10.5	9.6	7.75
1847	10.5	9.2	8.25
1848	8.5	9.6	5.5
1849	7.0	7.0	6.0
1850	8.5	8.6	8.0
1851	10.3	8.5	9.5
1852	7.2	6.0	8.5
1853	5.6	6.5	5.0
1854	6.25	7.9	4.75
1855	10.7	8.5	8.0
1856	8.1	9.4	8.5

Source: Bagchi, *Evolution of the State Bank*, Vol. I, pp.188–205, 327–30, 425–6.

only Rs 184 million was invested in factories;[71] and in 1911, in a population of 303 million, those engaged in 'Manufacturing employment' numbered just 11.7 million.[72] There is thus a considerable case for a Drain-induced capital famine which greatly retarded Indian industrial growth in the nineteenth century, crippled as it already was by an utter lack of protection against British competition.

Dadabhai Naoroji in 1876 attempted an estimate of India's per capita physical product (with no account taken of services).[73] The data on which such an estimation could be attempted were only then becoming available. The official response to Naoroji's pioneer effort was slow

[71] Ibid., p. 52.

[72] J. Krishnamurty, in Kumar and Desai, eds., *Cambridge Economic History of India*, Vol. II, Table 6.2, p.535.

[73] Naoroji, *Poverty and Un-British Rule*, p. 22.

in coming. At last, Fred J. Atkinson, a high official of the government's accounts department came up with two national-income and per-capita income estimates, for 1875 and 1895.[74] The increase of nearly 30 per cent in per-capita income that he showed was actually wiped out by the increase in prices that took place in the intervening period, that was noted by Atkinson himself. V.K.R.V. Rao in 1939 found that Atkinson's figures for per-capita income for 1895 had to be scaled down by over 20 per cent, showing that in fact there had been no per-capita income growth over these twenty years.[75] Moni Mukherjee's restoration[76] of the growth by scaling down Atkinson's 1875 figure by 20 per cent as well, on the rather irrelevant plea that Atkinson was 'an independent observer', hardly carries much conviction. Heston's more recent endeavour to reconstruct national-income figures, which show it rising in constant prices by 70 per cent between 1860 and 1920,[77] pulling up the per capita income by 35 per cent, has been heavily criticized for both his assumptions and calculations.[78] These criticisms have weight. Prima facie, too, Heston's optimistic estimation of a steady growth of per-capita income from 1868–9 onwards stands in direct contradiction to some other crucial indices, contained in Table 1.23.

A secular fall or stagnation in real wages, and a fall in the expectation of life by one-fifth, in a period of little industrial growth can hardly be consistent with a growth in per-capita income of over a third. A lily can be gilded only if it exists.

As our 'quantitative' survey of the Indian economy comes to a close, it is tempting to draw a balance-sheet of India's economic performance over the three centuries, 1601–1901. After a detailed sector-by-sector study of Indian production about the time of Akbar's death, comparing it with Indian production in his own time, c. 1911, W.H. Moreland concluded with some degree of satisfaction, that by and large, per-capita production and also real wages were about the same at either end of the three-hundred-year period.[79] Even this was

[74] 'A Statistical Review of the Income and Wealth of British India', in *Journal of the Royal Statistical Society*, London, 1902, pp. 210–59. See also Irfan Habib, *Indian Economy, 1858-1914*, New Delhi, 2006, pp.7–8.

[75] Bipan Chandra, *Rise and Growth of Economic Nationalism in India*, Delhi, 1966, pp. 16–17.

[76] M. Mukherjee, *National Income*, pp. 69–82.

[77] Heston, *CEHI*, Vol. II, p. 402.

[78] Habib, 'Studying a Colonial Economy', pp. 368–74.

[79] Moreland, *India at the Death of Akbar*, p. 202.

Table 1.23: Per-Capita Income, 1861–1920 (1900=100)

Decade	Estimate of per-capita income at end of decade (a)	Real Wages—annual average per decade (b)	(c)	Life-expectation years (mean of men and women) (d)
1861–70	83.33	108.25	–	–
1871–80	89.58	106.84	–	–
1881–90	92.36	108.41	127.5	25.07
1891–1900	100.00	100.50	110.5	23.80
1901–10	106.94	99.18	112.6	22.95
1911–20	113.89	91.58	94.2	20.14

Source: (a) Heston, *CEHI*, Vol. II, p. 402. Table 4.5, col. (3), recalculated (with slight adjustments of years in the first two decades); (b) K. Mukherji, 'National Income', V.B. Singh, (ed.) *Economic History of India, 1857–1965*, Bombay, 1965, cols. 5 and 7, pp. 657–9; (c) J. Kuczynski, 'Conditions of Workers (1880–1950)', in *Economic History of India*, Table IV, p. 656; (d) K. Davis, *Population of India and Pakistan*, p.62.

strongly contested by R. Mukerjee who saw a substantial decline in real wages between Akbar's time and the end of the nineteenth century.[80]

I have tried a rather crude comparison of the per-capita income in 1595 and 1901–10, by converting the two estimates (mine for 1595 and that of Sivasubramonian for 1901–10) into maunds of wheat at the prices in the imperial camp c. 1595 and the average prices for 1901–10 from Agra. The per-capita income in terms of wheat in 1595 turns out to be about 4.5 per cent higher than that in 1901–10.[81] Of course, a different picture could emerge if we were to take cloth as the medium for stating per-capita income. But in a subsistence economy foodgrain consumption has better claims to be considered as the key index of the quality of material life.

Not only did per-capita income stagnate over the three centuries, but even the structure of GDP remained very similar. A comparison of the share of the sectors in c. 1595 and 1901–10 presents the following picture (Table 1.24).

[80] R. Mukerjee, *Economic History of India, 1600–1800*, Allahabad, 1967, p.58.

[81] Moosvi, 'Gross National Product of the Mughal Empire', p. 86.

Table1.24: Distribution of GDP

	c. 1595 (%)	1901–10 (%)
Primary sector	64.310	63.027
Agriculture	50.770	50.994
Secondary sector	11.090	11.562
Tertiary sector	24.600	25.412

Sources: For 1595, Moosvi, *IHR,* XII (1–2), pp. 75–87 (revised for this paper); for 1901–10, Sivasubramonian, '*National Income of India*'.

The share of agriculture was lower by 0.44 per cent in c. 1595 than in 1901–10. Since it is not clear whether Sivasubramonian includes horticulture in his figure for agriculture, the relative share of agriculture for 1595 would be smaller if we exclude orchards from it. At 48.138 per cent of GDP it would be 5.60 per cent lower than in 1901–10. The secondary or manufacturing sector was also lower by about 4.08 per cent. The shares of all these sectors, including the tertiary sector, in GDP were lower in 1595 than in 1901–10, the reason being the larger share of non-agricultural primary sector (livestock, forestry, etc.) in 1595 by some 12.5 per cent.

These figures, then, do not suggest any great alteration in the structure of the Indian economy by the end of the nineteenth century in spite of the introduction of railways and 'commercialization' of agriculture. The reason is not far to seek: the process of colonial exploitation of India, marked by the Tribute and de-industrialization, was obviously the crucial factor in this picture of stagnation, and not merely, if at all, the pre-colonial low per-capita income, which Morris would identify as the main culprit.[82]

[82] *IESHR*, Vol. V, No. 1, 1968, pp. 5–6.

2

The Silver Influx, Money Supply, Prices and Revenue-extraction in Mughal India

The sixteenth and seventeenth centuries are recognized on all hands as constituting a period of worldwide monetary disturbance. The period was marked by the global commercial expansion of Western Europe, the influx of bullion from the New World, and the phenomenon (now disputed) called the Price Revolution. The questions as to how far the influx of silver from the Spanish American mines was a causative factor in inflation in Europe and how far the latter, in turn, was a factor in capital formation for the subsequent Industrial Revolution, have engaged the attention of economic historians for a long time.[1] Individual opinions on the cause-and-effect sequence may vary; but there is hardly any disagreement that the actual configuration of European economic history of the two centuries bore a notable imprint of these processes upon it.

Students of Mughal Indian economic history, too, have inevitably to face the question whether the influx of bullion from the New World was extended to the Mughal empire, and, if so, with what larger economic consequences. This must primarily involve a study of the size of the bullion influx during the two centuries, as well as of the impact that the influx had on money supply, prices, and taxation within India.

[1] See, e.g., Earl J. Hamilton, *American Treasure and Price Revolution in Spain, 1501–1652*, Harvard University Press, 1934; P. Vilar, 'Problems of the Formation of Capitalism', *Past and Present*, No. 10, November, 1956, pp. 15–38; Braudel and Spooner, 'Prices in Europe from 1450 to 1750', in F.E. Rich and Wilson, eds., *Cambridge Economic History of Europe*, (*CEHE*), Vol. IV, Cambridge, 1967, pp. 378–486. The debate is summed up by Immanuel Wallerstein, *The Modern World System: Capitalist Agriculture and the Origins of the European World Economy in the Sixteenth Century*, New York, 1974, pp. 68–80.

The problem has already attracted some attention.[2] Irfan Habib studied the movements of prices in India with special attention to changes in the ratios of silver to gold and copper during the seventeenth century.[3] He was followed by Aziza Hasan who offered estimates of the relative changes in the size of silver money in circulation and sought to relate the changes to movement of prices.[4] But, as we shall see, there are certain problems relating to the evidence used by both Irfan Habib and Aziza Hasan; and there is much fresh information that needs to be considered.

Constructing a Silver-Currency Output Histogram

India did not produce any noticeable amount of silver herself,[5] and so practically the entire stock of silver in India in, say, 1595, over and above the stock accumulated by 1500, must have been built up through imports during the sixteenth century. The imports during this century as well as the next are likely to have originated almost entirely in Spanish America, and to have been channelled mainly through Europe and partly across the Pacific. This is the burden of the statements by a number of contemporary observers.[6] Since the Mughal empire had

[2] As early as 1784 James Grant raised the question of the effects of import of the bullion on prices in India (and of the size of bullion influx) during the period of the Mughal Empire, in his 'Political Survey of the Northern Circars', in *Fifth Report from the Select Committee on the Affairs of the East India Company*, the Irish University Press Series of *British Parliamentary Papers; Colonies, India*, Vol. III, Shannon (Ireland), pp. 649–50.

[3] Irfan Habib, *Agrarian System of Mughal India*, Bombay, 1963, pp.392–4. For his revised exposition see *ASMI*, pp.445–9.

[4] Aziza Hasan, 'Silver Currency Output of the Mughal Empire and Prices in India During the 16th and 17th Centuries', *IESHR*, Vol. VI, No. 1, March, 1969, pp. 85–116. The paper appeared in a French version in *Annales E.S.C.*, Vol. XXIV, 1969.

[5] It transpires from Abū'l Faẕl, *Akbarnāma*, edited by Beveridge, Bib. Ind., Vol. I, p. 283, that the once famous silver mines of Panjshir in Afghanistan were no longer worked by the mid-sixteenth century. (For early medieval descriptions of these mines, see G. Le Strange, *Lands of the Eastern Caliphate*, Cambridge, 1930, p. 350.)

[6] Hawkins, *Early Travels in India (1583–1619)*, edited by W. Foster, London, 1927, p. 112; Francois Bernier, *Travels in the Mughal Empire 1656–68*, translated by A . Constable, London, 1916, pp. 202–4; Mīr G͟hulām 'Alī Āzād Ḥusainī Bilgrāmī, *K͟hizāna-i 'Āmira*, Nawal Kishore, Kanpur, 1871, p. 111.

an open system of coinage,[7] it is to be assumed that the imported silver bullion or coins were rapidly melted down and minted into rupees (the silver coinage established in 1540). Variations in the silver currency output are, therefore, likely to provide us with a fairly accurate index of the variations in imports of silver during the corresponding period, subject, of course, to allowance for remintage of rupees previously coined.

Aziza Hasan devised an ingenious means of measuring the silver currency output of the Mughal empire by counting the surviving silver coins by help of all published museum catalogues.[8] Mughal coins of the period in question are of uniformly pure metal, and, with the exception of some special rupee issues of Jahāngīr, of a uniform weight (Aurangzeb's increase of the weight of the silver rupee from 178 to 180 grains is too trifling to affect calculation). Thus they are easily comparable. Since each rupee coin bore the name of the mint as well as the year of issue, Aziza Hasan made a count of the catalogued Mughal coins on the basis of mints and years. She then argued that the variations in the number of surviving coins of different years must represent fluctuations in the total currency output. The curve showing the number of preserved coins relating to various years, could thus be taken as the curve of the currency output of the Mughal empire, though on an 'unknown scale'. In order to establish geographical comparability over time, Hasan confined her count to North Indian mints only.

Hasan's effort must be recognized as a pioneering one; but there was a possible bias in her evidence, which has led to criticisms by John S. Deyell. [9] He urges that since there is always an element of selectivity in the coins retained or acquired by museums, which do not aim at possessing more than a pair of coins of the same type (i.e.,

[7] Irfan Habib, 'The Currency System of the Mughal Empire (1556–1707)', *Medieval India Quarterly*, Vol.IV, Nos. 1–2; see also Irfan Habib, 'Monetary System and Prices', *CEHI*, Vol. I, Cambridge, 1982.

[8] Aziza Hasan, *IESHR*, Vol. VI, No. I, pp. 85–116.

[9] John S. Deyell, 'Numismatic Methodology in the Estimation of Mughal Currency Output', *IESHR*, Vol. XIII, No. 3, July–September, 1976, pp 392–401. Aziza Hasan's effort was earlier commented upon by Om Prakash and J. Krishnamurthy, but they made no fundamental criticism of her method, and their objections were largely met in a reply by Hasan herself in the same issue of *IESHR*, VII No. I, pp. 139–60.

the same mint/date/legend/design), the years in which coins of the more varied styles were minted tend to be more heavily represented in museum collections. Changes in style, rather than changes in quantities of silver minted, might therefore provide an alternative explanation for the great fluctuations displayed by Aziza Hasan's currency output histogram.

On the plane of theoretical arguments, Deyell's critique is partly unobjectionable; it is also partly overstated since he tends to ignore the fact that most individual museum collections often lack coins of particular mints in some years (though such coins *are* represented in other collections and, therefore, were certainly minted), while in other cases particular mints in certain years are practically fully represented in all collections.[10] Clearly, fluctuations in output must be heavily responsible for such variations in representation in museum collections.

In any case, Deyell's principal objection can be met by an elementary empirical check: Let us set aside the catalogued collections and go to the records of the coin-finds where no element of selectivity is possibly involved. It is well known that the Lucknow Museum has one of the richest collections of Mughal coins in the world, and this mostly derives from the large number of coins found in the treasure-troves in UP or Uttar Pradesh (previously, 'United Provinces').[11] The region is very large and also occupies a central position in northern India; it contained a large part of the core-area of the Mughal empire including its capital city, Agra. Coin-finds within it are therefore likely to represent fairly well not only the issues of the entire period we are concerned with, but also the issues of the various parts of northern India, without any particular geographical bias. I, accordingly abstracted information for all treasure-troves found in Uttar Pradesh during the period 1880–1968; from unpublished official reports.[12] The number of such

[10] In Deyell's own Table 2, *IESHR*, Vol.XIII, No.3, July–September, 1976, p.399, which he regards as a conclusive demonstration of the weakness of A. Hasan's thesis, the range of number of coins of each type is as wide as 1.60 to 3.00.

[11] Deyell himself refers to the UP treasure-troves as providing the material from which the Lucknow Museum made its collections on a selective basis; he cites a personal letter from Dr A.K. Srivastava, numismatic officer of the Museum, to this effect (*IESHR*, Vol. XIII, No. 3, pp. 395–6).

[12] For particulars of these reports, see A.K. Srivastava, *Coin Hoards of Uttar Pradesh*, Vol. I, (the author kindly let me read his pre-publication copy). I have worked from the original reports in the State Museum, Lucknow, since Srivastava does not, unfortunately, record the number of duplicates in each find.

recorded Mughal coins (North Indian mints only) comes to 7,382; this total represents coins belonging to the reigns of emperors Akbar to Aurangzeb only (See Table 2.1). The record constitutes as random a sample as one is perhaps likely to get.[13]

Table 2.1

		Total	Dates with mint	Datable by decade	Mintless with date	Dateless with mint	Mintless and dateless
Akbar	1556–1605	2,653	1,719	421	373	86	54
Jahāngīr	1606–27	1,109	790	0	30	281	8
Shāhjahān	1628–59	1,678	1,283.5	9	57.5	80	248
Aurangzeb	1660–1707	1,942	1,696	0	0	246	0

Source: *EME*, p.355.

I have excluded (like A. Hasan) the coins uttered by the Deccan mints in order to have the same area to consider during the entire period in question. A noticeable feature of this sample is that the rupee coins from Akbar's reign considerably outnumber those from each of the other reigns. In spite of the fact that the number of mints (and hence the coin-types) largely increased during Aurangzeb's reign,[14] Aurangzeb's rupee coins in the sample are substantially less than those of Akbar. In Hasan's count the reign-wise breakdown is quite different, namely,

Akbar	1,739
Jahāngīr	1,346
Shāhjahān	1,556
Aurangzeb	2,426

Source: *IESHR*, Vol. IV, No.2, 1969, pp. 85-16.

[13] Like A. Hasan, I count 8-anna or 4-anna pieces as 0.5 and 0.25 rupee respectively in arriving at my coin-totals. I have also converted Jahāngīr's heavier rupees into ordinary rupees by taking into account their actual weight: A *sawāī* rupee is thus treated as equal to 1.25 rupees.

[14] I take it that most museums have been concerned with the mint-name and year (*ilāhī*, regnal, *ḥijrī*) as determinates of type rather than the *ilāhī* month (when used). If this had not been the case the possible coin-types of Akbar's reign would have been far more numerous than the catalogued types counted by Deyell for his Table 2, *IESHR*, Vol. XII, No. 3, July–September, 1976, p. 399.

The smaller number of Akbar's coins in the museum collections is probably owing to the smaller number of mints and early types of Akbar's rupees, while, conversely, the larger number of mints of Aurangzeb explain the larger contribution of his reign in Aziza Hasan's count. There is, therefore, the probability of some bias in her sample, whose precise degree is, of course, difficult to determine.

I have constructed a five-yearly histogram from my own sample based on coin-find reports, on the same lines as those adopted by Hasan (Fig. 2.1). The only departure from her method has been that I have also included coins which are datable in terms of decades only (through loss of the last digit), by dividing them into two equal halves for assignment to the five-year periods. I have also not neglected the dateless coins which are at least assignable to reigns. For example, it would give a distorted picture of the currency output of Jahāngīr's reign if as many as 281 dateless coins of his reign are disregarded. I have, therefore, distributed the dateless coins among the various five-year periods in the same proportions as the dated coins.

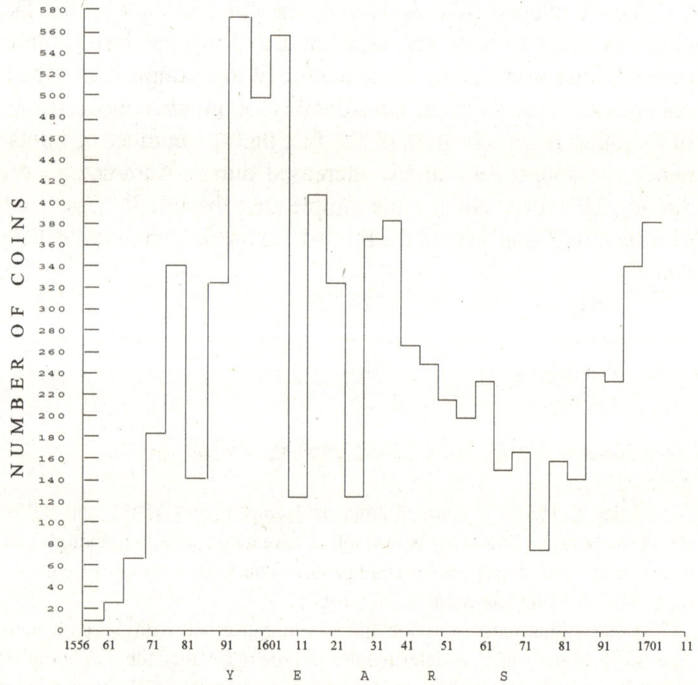

Fig.2.1: Mughal Rupees (North Indian Mints) Quinquennial Histogram Based on U.P. Coin Finds

A comparison of this histogram, with Aziza Hasan's histogram (redrawn in Fig. 2.2) does partially vindicate her attempt, if not the whole of her method, since the correspondence between the two is too close to be merely accidental. The trend (towards increase or decline) is the same in the two figures in respect of as many as twenty-five out of the total of thirty quinquennial periods. This is close correspondence indeed. The substantial ascents during 1586–90 and 1611–15 and the declines during 1606–10, 1671–75 and 1636–40, which have been attributed by Deyell merely to fluctuations in coin-types, are equally reflected in the treasure-troves where 'survival-by-type' would have had no part to play.[15]

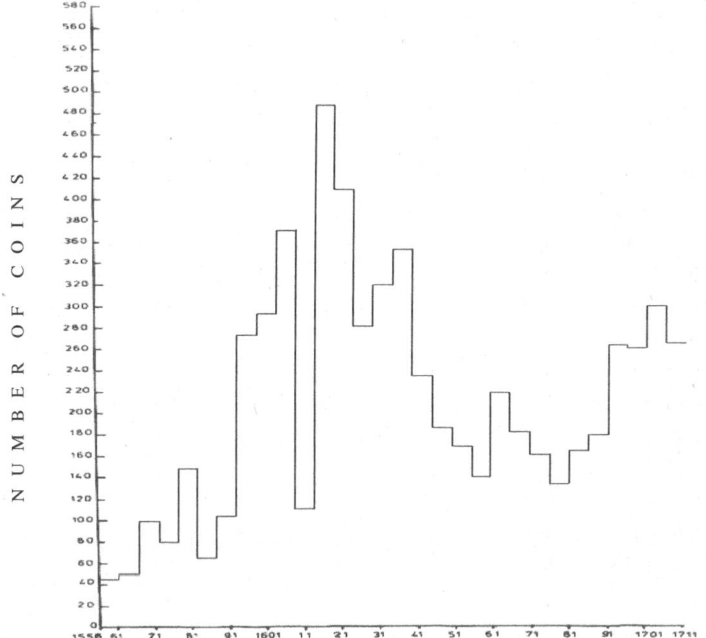

Fig. 2.2: Mughal Rupees (North Indian Mints) Quinquennial Histograph Based on Cataloguged coins

[15] Thus while Hasan's sample is not perhaps useful for establishing secular trends on a firm basis, it is still of value for showing changes in short periods within which coin-types are not known to have changed substantially. In other instances, it would appear that coin-types multiplied as the silver mintage increased; and this perhaps explains the correspondence here between the ascents in Hasan's sample and my own.

SILVER CURRENCY OUTPUT AND THE INFLUX OF TREASURE

Our histogram should theoretically enable us to follow movements in the silver money supply. In Table 2.2 where the information is converted into terms of decades, an analysis of the regional composition of the total number of coins is also offered. Column 'G', standing for Gujarat, represents the output of the Ahmedabad, Surat and Cambay mints; the North-Western ('NW') mints include Lahore,

Table 2.2: Coins from treasure-troves in UP
(Those of Deccan and South Indian Mints excluded)

Decades	Total	G	NW	B	C	Mintless
1556–65	36	0	2	0	25	9
1566–75	240.5	30	13	0	151.5	46
1576–85	466.5	97.5	15	0	228	126
1586–95	876.5	294.5	47	0	320	215
1596–1605	1,034	592	202	43.5	165.5	31
1606–15	516.5	91	139	28	241	17.5
1616–25	432.5	37	177	43	155	20.5
1626–35	758	118.5	221.5	291.5	92	34.5
1636–45*	499.5	105	199.5	48.5	44.5	101.5
1646–55*	395.1	127	83.6	33.5	55.5	95.5
1656–65	365	103.5	98.5	41.5	121.5	-
1666–75	256	139	32	63	22	-
1676–85	294.5	153	35.5	39.5	66.5	-
1686–95*	453	104.5	31.5	51.5	266	
1696–1705	670	92.5	26.5	52	499	-
1706–07*	86	7.5	5.7	6.5	66	-

* Small differences in totals are due to rounding.

Note: In this table the *alf* (1,000 = *Alf*) coins are all attributed to the decade 1586–95, though, as Najaf Haider has shown, ('Disappearance of Coin Minting in the 1580s? — A Note on the *Alf* Coins', in Irfan Habib, ed. *Akbar and His India*, New Delhi, 1997, pp.55–65.) the *alf* coins had begun to be minted from 1582–83 onwards. We cannot, however, determine how many *alf* coins belonged to the years 1582–85; and, in any case, the general picture at the decade-level is not likely to be much affected, even if we were to place some *alf* coins in the decade 1576–85. In any case, the number of *alf* coins in the hoards is small, being just 24.

Multan, Thatta, Kabul, and Qandahar. Column 'B' represents the Bengal mints ('Bengala', Akbarnagar or Rajmahal, Makhsusabad, Jahangir Nagar or Dacca, and Patna). The remaining mints are grouped together as inland or central mints under column 'C'.

For reasons already stated, it should be valid to treat Table 2.2 as indicative of the relative size of the average annual output (decade-figures in Table 2.2 divided by 10) of rupee coinage from the north Indian mints.[16] It, of course, does not define the scale and we must seek other sources for data of mint output that would help us to convert our figures based on hoards into absolute figures of coin output. This can be done if we can know, for example, what the average output of a particular mint in a particular period was, and count its issues in our sample. Luckily, this can be done for the Surat mint during the 1630s.

Statements made by English factors indicate that the Surat mint ordinarily turned out Rs 6,000 a day for the English in 1636, when 'we have the mint alone'. Earlier in 1634, the mint output was said to have ordinarily exceeded Rs 8,000 daily (coining Rs 5,000 for the English and 3,000 for the Dutch); in the absence of the Dutch, the English had been able to obtain as many as Rs 9,000 daily.[17] Apparently, by the time the English and Dutch delivered their bullion, the silver brought through the Red Sea and the Gulf had already been coined. These figures then suggest a daily output of more than Rs 8,000 for the Surat mint during the years 1634–6. Now in our sample there are 46 coins of the Surat mint assignable to the four Regnal Years 7–10, corresponding to 1634–7.[18] Given an annual output of Rs 8,000 x 365 for the Surat mint, we may then take it that each surviving coin in the UP treasure-troves represents 2,53,913 rupee coins actually minted.[19]

[16] There may be a geographical bias in my sample since it consists of coin-finds in UP only — a large region, certainly, but still rather distant from the Deccan, which may possibly be under-represented in it. But there is likely to be no under-representation of any north Indian region; silver coinage must always have had a high degree of mobility.

[17] W. Foster, ed., *EFI, 1634–6*, Oxford, 1906–7, pp. 68 and 218. Malcolm gives the *maximum* capacity (not average output) of the central Indian mints during the early years of the nineteenth century as 10,000 rupees a day (*Memoirs of Central India*, London, 1824, p. 85).

[18] The number of Surat coins bearing regnal years seven to ten, of Shāhjahān in the UP treasure-troves is actually forty. But this number has been increased by six to allow for the dateless Surat coins of the reign of Shāhjahān.

[19] The Surat mint could not have been kept open all the 365 days. Supposing

Assuming this ratio to apply to coins of different years, we can go on to estimate the total coin output of the Mughal empire. It is true that in view of the survival rate being presumably higher for the period subsequent to the years 1634–7 and lower for the preceding period, the result would understate the earlier coin production, and overstate the latter. Moreover, it would have been better if there had been similar data for mints other than Surat to enable a cross-check to be made. Nevertheless, a minimum output of 8,000 rupees a day for Surat does not seem unreasonable since in 1676, when the production at the Rajmahal mint was at an especially low ebb, the English expected to get 10,000 rupees minted there in three or four days.[20]

Converting, then, the numbers of coins reported from the UP treasure-troves as set out in Table 2.2 into absolute figures of coins actually uttered, at the rate indicated above, we can reconstruct the following figures of average annual output for each decade. We can further convert the coin-output into metric tons, by allowing 170.88 grains of pure silver in each coin[21] and so supposing that one metric ton of silver was made up of Rs 90,324.90 in coin.

The fluctuating quantities of tonnage of silver minted as shown by Table 2.3 will be considered presently, after being arranged in certain identifiable phases. But before such detailed consideration is offered, a comment on the general scale of output of silver coinage that the table brings out may not be out of place. The French mints between

---

it was closed once a week, our estimated output should be reduced by 1/7. But our estimate of the daily average output is itself very conservative: We have not fixed it at Rs 9,000, but Rs 8,000. Moreover, the English seem to have overlooked petty claimants on the mint other than the Dutch, so that the actual output might well have been in the region of Rs 9,500. Thus the output ascribed to the closed days can be adjusted against the larger output on the working days.

The mint output of Surat may seem to be rather small in view of a later report (14 October 1672) in Surat Factory Outward Letter Book, Vol.II, 1663–71/72, p. 187 (Maharashtra State Archives, Bombay), which gives its daily output as Rs 30,000 (according to Irfan Habib's reading of it in *Essays in Indian History*, p.222 & n.) But the document, as transcribed by Aziza Hasan shows that minting at this scale was an exceptional measure undertaken by special arrangement with the Mint-master; it cannot be construed as indicating the *average* daily output of the mint.

[20] Streynsham Master, *The Diaries of Streynsham Master, 1675–80, & other Contemporary Papers Relating Thereto*, in R.C. Temple, ed., Indian Record Series, Vol. I, London, 1911, pp. 401–2.

[21] Irfan Habib in *Medieval India Quarterly*, Vol. IV, Nos.1–2, p. 9.

1631 and 1660 issued 2,259 tons of silver money (including silver equivalent of the gold minted), giving an average annual output of 75.3 metric tons.[22] Given the size of the Mughal empire relative to France, a silver currency output, averaging 151.69 metric tons a year from 1576 to 1705, is by no means unreasonable.

Table 2.3

	Total Annual Output*		Annual Output by Regions in Metric Tons				
Decades	Rupees	Metric Tons	G	NW	B	C	Mintless
1556–65	9,14,087	10.12	0.00	0.56	0.00	7.03	2.53
1566–75	61,06,608	67.48	8.43	3.66	0.00	42.60	12.93
1576–85	1,18,32,346	131.02	27.41	4.22	0.00	64.10	35.43
1586–95	2,22,55,474	246.29	82.80	13.21	0.00	89.97	60.45
1596–1605	2,62,54,604	290.72	166.44	56.79	12.23	46.53	8.72
1606–15	1,31,14,606	145.22	25.59	39.08	7.87	67.87	4.92
1616–25	1,09,81,737	121.46	10.40	49.76	12.09	43.58	5.76
1626–35	1,92,46,605	212.85	33.32	62.14	81.82	25.87	9.70
1636–45	1,26,70,259	140.30	29.52	56.08	13.64	12.51	28.53
1646–55	1,01,05,737	111.90	35.71	24.32	9.42	15.60	26.85
1656–65	92,67,824	102.62	29.10	27.69	11.67	34.16	0.00
1666–75	65,00,173	71.98	39.18	9.00	17.71	6.19	0.00
1676–85	74,77,738	82.80	43.02	9.98	11.11	18.70	0.00
1686–95	1,15,02,259	127.36	29.38	8.86	14.48	74.51	0.00
1696–1705	1,70,12,171	188.34	26.01	7.45	14.62	140.02	0.00

Source: See text.

Abbreviations: G = Gujarat; NW = North-Western; B = Bengal; C = Central

Note: The figures for metric tons are directly calculated from the totals of rupees; slight differences would therefore be noticed if the regional figures are totalled.

We now propose to correlate our data of mint-output with the information we have of imports of silver during successive periods marked by specific recognizable trends.

The Latter Half of the Sixteenth Century

Tables 2.2 and 2.3 indicate a steady increase in the output till 1605, which is exactly what one would expect. Akbar's empire from its

[22] Braudel and Spooner in *Cambridge Economic History of Europe*, Vol. IV, p. 444.

relatively small core area in the period 1556–65 expanded to embrace the whole of northern India by the 1590s; and so, naturally, the number of mints and the coins uttered grew from year to year to serve the expanding area of the Empire. There was, in addition, the process of replacement of copper money by silver; this must naturally have meant that the increase of silver coinage had to be on a far greater scale than what corresponded simply to the territorial expansion of the Empire. To an extent, this must have involved the minting of internal silver stock, which because of the previous prevalence of copper coinage had remained uncoined or had been minted in the form of coarse silver money in Malwa, Gujarat, and Khandesh.[23] This perhaps explains the domination of the 'Central' or inland mints until the decade ending 1585; these mints provided in that decade as many as 64.10 tons out of a total of 131.02 tons annually coined within the Empire.

But in the twenty years following 1585 it is Gujarat which assumes a dominating position. Gujarat (i.e., the Ahmedabad mint) contributed 82.80 tons per annum during 1586–95 out of an estimated total of 246.29 tons of silver minted and then a phenomenal 166.44 tons out of 290.72 tons during 1596–1605.[24] Gujarat was one of the principal areas of entry of silver; and the Gulf and the Red Seas as well as the Cape of Good Hope routes converged here. The province, therefore, had been receiving enormous quantities of bullion by these channels during the whole of the latter part of the sixteenth century. Some of it must have previously been coined in the coarse-silver money (*maḥmūdīs*) minted in Gujarat before the Mughal conquest (1573). After the Mughal conquest the Ahmedabad mint must have had to coin into rupees the large previously accumulated quantities of silver (whether bullion or *maḥmūdīs*) as well as the silver that entered in the current stream. But even if a major portion of the rupees minted in these two decades was out of the silver coin and bullion accumulated previously,[25] the mint output of these decades is high enough to suggest a very large size of silver imports into Gujarat.

[23] This domestic stock must itself have accumulated out of previous imports, much of it coming into the country during the sixteenth century.

[24] If this estimate is correct, the Ahmedabad mint must on average have coined about Rs 40,000 a day during this decade.

[25] Najaf Haider (*Medieval History Journal*, Vol. II, No. 2, 1999, pp.328–9), emphasizes this, but insists that it was only in 1592 that 'an imperial order was issued to demonetize all precious metal coins of previous emperors', based on a statement in Badāūnī, *Muntakhabu't Tawārīkh*, II (not III as in Haider), p.380.

The reader of Hamilton's work on the transfer of American silver to Europe would of course, not be surprised at the large influx of silver into India at this time, because, as his celebrated histogram of the Spanish imports of American silver show, this is the period during which the volume of bullion transported from America to Spain achieved its highest scale (undergoing a dramatic rise in 1576–80). The peak was, indeed, reached in the years 1591–5, and there was only a marginal descent in the next half-decade.[26] That a large part of the American silver was spilling into Asia is recognized by most scholars. Geoffrey Parker estimates the loss of silver by Europe to the East around 1600 at 80 metric tons a year;[27] P. Vilar puts it at 64 tons.[28] But both these estimates probably understate the size of silver that was actually entering Asia at the close of the sixteenth century.

Parker suggests, for example, that the annual flow of silver from Europe to the Levant amounted to 1.5 million ducats, or 39.7 metric tons.[29] But the silver that annually left the port of Ormuz on the Persian

---

Actually, Badāūnī himself says, prefacing this passage, that the orders now issued merely repeated earlier ones. Todar Mal's memorandum, approved by Akbar, in 1582, laid down that only coins bearing Akbar's name were to be accepted, so that the coins of earlier regimes had naturally to be melted down. Moreover, like Todar Mal's memorandum, the *farmān* quoted by Badāūnī also insisted that no discount should be levied on coins issued in past years of the reign (the so-called *sanwāt* discount) (on which see Irfan Habib, 'The Currency System of the Mughal Empire', in *Medieval India Quarterly*, Vol. IV, Nos.1–2, p.5, *n.3*). This part of the imperial orders was obviously designed to discourage remintage of Akbar's own coins. Thus there is no reason at all to suppose either that the large coin output of the Ahmedabad mint, 1592–1605, represented mainly 'recoinage' or that it followed a brand 'new monetary policy' formulated in 1592 (*Medieval History Journal*, Vol. II, No. 2, p.331). Even, otherwise, it is most unlikely that the melting of the previous stock of coarse silver coins like *maḥmūdīs*, could have sustained such enormous mint output year after year.

[26] See Hamilton, *American Treasure and Price Revolution in Spain*, Harvard, 1934.

[27] Geoffrey Parker, 'The Emergence of Modern Finance in Europe 1500–1730', in Carlo M. Cipola, ed., *Fontana Economic History of Europe*, Glasgow, 1974, p. 529.

[28] P. Vilar, *A History of Gold and Money, 1450–1920*, London, 1976, p. 101.

[29] Certain interesting figures for the Venetian exports of silver to Syria during 1593–6 (6.7 tons per annum) and 1610–14 (8 tons per annum) are given in Parker, 'The Emergence of Modern Finance in Europe 1500–1730', p. 529, and Braudel and Spooner in *Cambridge Economic History of Europe*, Vol. IV, p. 448 & *n*. The latter authors apparently consider 37,529 ducats to be equal to one metric ton of

Gulf alone is said to have amounted to 2 million cruzadoes or the equivalent of some 41.7 metric tons.[30] Precise information of this kind is unfortunately lacking for the Red Sea route. But Indian trade with the Red Sea was normally brisker than with the Gulf: whereas the Ormuz trade was connected with Aleppo (Syria), the Red Sea trade was linked to Cairo and Alexandria.[31] For the Cape of Good Hope route, Chaunu has estimated that during the sixteenth century Portugal paid for its imports from India by 150 tons of gold, seized from Africa, and an amount of silver far less than the 6,000 tons nominally equivalent to the remaining value of the imported spice.[32] It may then be thought that since Chaunu is speaking of the entire century, imports of silver to the East through the Portuguese by the end of the sixteenth century must have considerably exceeded 60 tons per annum.

It should be observed here that Portugal brought in silver not only by the Cape-of-Good-Hope route, but also from the Far East. The American silver brought to the Philippines reached enormous proportions during the 1590s, when at one time almost as much silver was transported across the Pacific as across the Atlantic. The tonnage

---

silver; but Parker puts a slightly higher silver-value on the ducat.

It may be noted that Venetian silver exports to Alexandria are not included in these figures; nor the Genoese exports to the Levant. Parker recognizes that Marseilles exported more silver to the Levant than Venice did; but its figures too are not available.

[30] Neils Steensgaard, *The Asian Trade Revolution of the Seventeenth Century: The East India Companies and the Decline of the Caravan Trade*, Chicago, 1974, p. 199. I have calculated the tonnage by using values given in ibid., pp. 417–19. I have used the lower value of the reis of Goa, one mark silver (229.5 grammes)=4398 reis. One cruzado was worth 400 reis. The values given by Steensgaard are broadly corroborated by the Jesuits at Agra, who in 1607 equated one cruzado with 2 or 2 ½ rupees (*Jahangir and the Jesuits*, translated by C.H. Payne, London, 1930, pp. 37–8).

[31] For the connection of the Gulf with Aleppo see a 1640 report from Basra in the *EFI, 1637–41*, pp. 247–8; and for the linkage between Mokha (Red Sea) and 'Grand Cairo', see report of a visit to Mokha in 1625–6 in *EFI, (1624–9)*, pp. 349–51.

[32] Cited in I. Wallerstein, *The Modern World System*, p. 329 *n*. J.F. Richards, on the basis of P. Vilar's data, estimates the annual imports of gold by the Portuguese at the close of the sixteenth century at 1.5 tons, a figure which is in accord with the estimate offered by Chaunu.

exceeded 500 tons in single years.[33] If the Portuguese had imported only 2 tons of silver from Japan (which itself received American silver) in the 1580s,[34] their silver imports from the Far East must have been considerably more in the 1590s. Moreover, there were direct mercantile connections between the Gujarat ports and Acheh; and some bullion must have travelled through them. Even if a fifth of the trans-Pacific silver reached India, it would have meant something like 30 to 100 tons coming to India annually during the 1590s.

In view of these large quantities of silver entering the Indian Ocean area during the 1590s (probably approaching 150 tons per annum), the estimated annual output of the Gujarat and North-Western mints amounting to 159.62 tons during the two decades 1586 to 1605 should not seem unreasonable, especially if we make an allowance for the minting of coins of older currencies and of bullion previously hoarded.

1605–30

Immediately after 1605, a decline in the total Mughal currency output becomes noticeable (see Table 2.3). The average estimated output fell from 290.72 tons per year during 1596–1605 to 145.22 during 1606–15 and 121.46 during 1616–25. One can see that this decline is almost totally due to a dramatic fall in the output of the Gujarat mints, sliding from 166.44 tons during 1596–1605, to 25.59 during 1606–15 and only 10.40 tons during 1616–25. However, the North-Western mints, that were receiving bullion by overland routes (or the coastal routes from the Gulf to Thatta) continued to maintain their high level, displaying a steady increase from the decade 1596–1605, until an output of 62.14 tons per annum was reached during 1626–35. Clearly, this was owing to the brisk overland trade via Qandahar that had developed at this time.[35] This is corroborated by the fact that Venetian exports of silver to Syria did not undergo any decline between the 1590s and 1610s; on the contrary they tended to increase.[36]

[33] J.H. Parry, 'Transport and Trade Routes' in *Cambridge Economic History of Europe*, Vol. IV, pp. 209–10. The quantities sent from Mexico to the Philippines reached 12 million *pesos* (or the equivalent of 485.765 tons of silver) in 1595. In other years it ranged from 3 to 5 million pesos.

[34] J.F. Richards in *Comparative Studies in Society and History*, Vol. 23, Part 2, April 1981, p. 302.

[35] For this development, see Steensgaard, *The Asian Trade Revolution of the Seventeenth Century*, pp. 206–7.

[36] Ibid., see f.n. 31 on these exports.

As for the decline in silver mintage in Gujarat, it is possible that the coining of previously accumulated bullion and coined silver had been completed by 1605. But this alone cannot explain the radical contraction in mintage. The total flow of silver to India seems to have received a setback during the two decades after 1605. This fits in with what we know of the position of silver supply and conditions of the Indian Ocean trade during this period.

There was a contraction in the amount of silver entering Spain from America during the period 1601–05 and again during 1611–15; and this could not but have adversely affected the total silver outflow from Europe.[37]

As for the Cape of Good Hope route, the English and Dutch exports of silver to India were small, while the Portuguese trade was forcibly blocked by the two new intruders. According to the figures given by Bal Krishna[38] and reproduced by K.N. Chaudhuri,[39] the English East India Company during the first twenty-three years of the century exported to the East a total of treasure worth £753,336, or the equivalent of 76.84 metric tons of silver. The volume of the Dutch trade judging by its value was about twice that of the English East India Company during the first quarter of the seventeenth century.[40] If the relative shares of bullion and goods in the Dutch exports were of the same order as those of the English East India Company, the companies together should have exported over 230 metric tons of silver, that is, just about ten metric tons per annum. During the same period the Portuguese trade declined substantially, so that it is difficult to imagine the Portuguese adding even as much as this tonnage to the silver

[37] In 1621 Sir John Woltenholme estimated the annual outflow of silver from Christendom to Asia at 150 English tons (K.N. Chaudhuri, *English East India Company, 1600–1640*, London, 1965, p. 120). Of these 150 tons, considerable quantities must have been absorbed by the Ottoman Empire and Iran; and, therefore, even if one accepts the estimate, it is difficult to conjecture how much of the tonnage reached India. At its face value, when compared to our other indicators (equally nebulous, perhaps) for the 1590s, Woltenholme's estimate would suggest a decline in the annual silver imports into India by the 1620s.

[38] Bal Krishna, *Commercial Relations between India and England*, London, 1924, p. 283.

[39] K.N. Chaudhuri, *The English East India Company, 1600–1640*, p. 117.

[40] Bal Krishna, *Commercial Relations between India and England.* The ratio has been worked out by the help of the figures for Dutch trade stated in florins on p. 289 and for the English on p. 282.

imports of India. The Gujarat mints, to the extent that they depended upon silver imports around the Cape, therefore, must have had their supplies reduced considerably.

These could have been made up by silver coming through the Levant, by the Red Sea and the Gulf; but the conflicts between the English and the Portuguese, and the English seizures of Mughal ships sailing to the Red Sea greatly obstructed this commerce as well, as Pelsaert noted in 1626.[41] There was therefore a natural drying up of the flow of bullion over the sea routes;[42] and, in partial compensation,

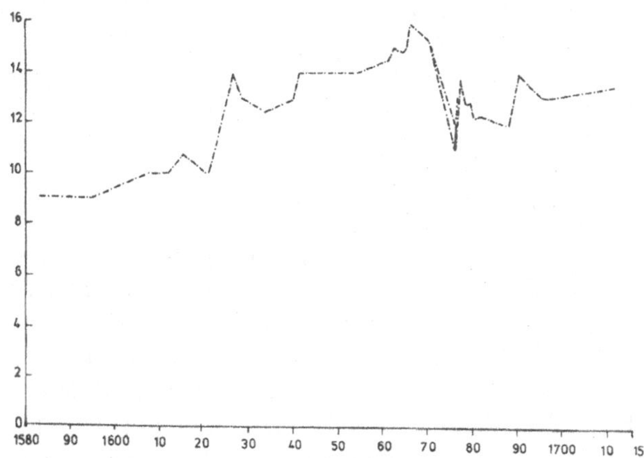

Fig.2.3: The Silver Value of Gold (Rupees per *Muhr*)

[41] See F. Pelsaert's description of the enforced stagnation of this trade (*Jahangir's India*, translated by W.H. Moreland and P. Geyl, pp. 39–41). In 1623 the English seized Indian junks returning from the Red Sea (*EFI, 1622–3*, pp.282, 327, 341). In 1624 the Surat factors of the English Company recommended a seizure of all Red Sea junks for the attractive reason that 'they will be rich enough to countervail the English goods ashore ("being per estimate about 26 or 27 thousand pounds sterling"), for often one ship from Jidda is worth more in treasure' (*EFI, 1624–9*, p.29). But among the Red Sea junks seized in 1623, the *Shāhī* from Surat was found to have carried only 20,000 rials of eight (less than half metric tons of silver) (*EFI, 1622–3*, p.327). Another ship (unnamed) carried 40,000 or 60,000 rials, but this was bound for Chaul, not Surat (ibid. pp.282, 341).

[42] One must remember that the major immediate source of European silver entering Gujarat must still have been the Levant. In 1618 the Surat ship *Rahimi* returning from Mocha was carrying 29 'tunnes of silver' (John Hatch 'Relations & c.' in Mac Lehose, ed., *Purchas His Pilgrims*, Vol. IV, Glasgow, 1905, p. 537. The shipping 'tunnes' of that time cannot unfortunately be converted into 'metric tons' (weight).

an increased flow overland. This could have been the main factor behind the high output of the North-Western mints during the period that we have noted above.

This net decline in the annual silver currency output, as well as the inflow of silver imports, was bound to check the decline in the price of silver in relation to gold, if one could assume that the supply of gold during this period also remained small. In Fig. 2.3, I offer a curve constructed on the basis of the available quotations of the rupee prices of the gold *muhr*.[43] The silver price beginning with Rs 9 in 1595–6, had risen to Rs 14 in 1628; but it fell to Rs 12.5 in 1633, whereafter it showed a gradual recovery. Thus there was a fall in the silver-value of gold between the years 1628 and 1633, precisely as our data, showing a restricted flow of silver, would lead us to expect.

1631–1655

The recovery in the value of gold (in terms of silver) subsequent to 1633, in turn, matches the good evidence we have for a spurt in the influx of silver chiefly through the Levant, and the large increase in currency output, that our Table 2.3 shows for the two decades subsequent to 1625. In 1641 before the arrival of the English ships, the junks from Mokha (the principal Red Sea port) had already landed at Surat upwards of 1.7 million ryalls/rials,[44] which at the moderate value of Rs 2.20 per rial should have represented a little over 40 metric tons of silver. Similarly in 1646, 'noe lesse then 1,167,853 rayalls of eight' had been brought in apparently from the Red Sea and the Gulf before the arrival of the English ships;[45] this implied the importation of about 27.9 tons of silver by sea from the Levant to Surat alone within a part of the year 1646. To this one must add imports through the agency of the English and the Dutch, for which satisfactory figures are unfortunately not available for this period. But the figures for sea-borne imports from the Levant alone are a sufficient corroboration of the high average annual output of the Gujarat mints, set in our Table 2.3 at 33.32 tons during 1626–35 (contrasting with only 10.40 tons in 1616–25), 29.52 tons during 1636–45 and 35.71 tons during 1646–

[43] Irfan Habib has collected and organized much of the available data in his 'System of Trimetallism during the Price Revolution' in J.F. Richards, ed., *The Imperial Monetary System of Mughal India*, Delhi, 1987, p.148.

[44] *EFI, 1642–45*, p. 17.

[45] Ibid., *1646–50*, p. 249.

55.[46]

The heavy imports of silver by the overland routes from the Levant must also have continued during these years, since the North-Western mints were more active than the Gujarat mints, annually coining 62.14 tons during 1626–35 and 55.25 tons during 1636–45. The sharp decline in the North-Western mints during 1646–55 to an annual output of 24.32 tons only is clearly attributable to the repeated wars over Qandahar which took place between the Persians and the Mughals during the years 1648–53. Trade over that route must have been practically blocked for most of these years.[47] Indeed, one can see that the decrease in the total mint output of the Mughal empire between the decades 1636–45 and 1646–55 was almost entirely made up by the decline in the output of the North-Western mints.

1656–75

The decline in the total output of the Mughal mints continued during the decades 1656–65 and 1666–75. Our estimated annual total is 102.62 tons for 1656–65, and only 71.98 tons for 1666–75. This can be convincingly ascribed to a substantial contraction of silver imports. The figures of treasure exported by the English East India Company (see Table 2.4 below) cited by Chaudhuri indicate that gold exceeded silver in the Company's exports during 1666–75.

The same compulsions led to gold entering India through the Levant. In 1665 the English factors at Surat reported the imports of 'many hundred thousand pounds (of gold) from Bussora, Persia and Red Sea yearly'.[48]

[46] A further corroboration of this may be found in the reported increase of Indian shipping at Surat from fifteen to twenty ships to eighty during the ten years preceding 1660 (*EFI, 1655–60*, p. 301).

[47] The trade with Persia was already affected in the late 1630s because the war between the Persians and Turks retarded passage of goods between the Gulf and Syria (*EFI, 1637–41*, p. 202). Shāhjahān's seizure of Qandahar in 1638 first brought about a stoppage of overland trade (ibid., pp. 125–6), and then a positive Mughal prohibition of all traffic with Persia in 1639–40 (ibid., p. 242).

With the Persian attempt to retake Qandahar in 1648–9, overland trade was again obstructed (*EFI, 1646–50*, p. 261); and an embargo was laid on all Indian exports to Persia even by sea (ibid., pp. 300, 308, 310, 324). The land route was not yet opened in 1651 (*EFI, 1651–54*, p. 64). Some decline was noticeable in the sea trade with the Gulf as well. In 1656, Surat exported £332,000 worth of goods to Gombroon; in 1657 only £112,500 (*EFI, 1655–60*, p. 172).

[48] *EFI, 1661–64*, p. 95.

Table 2.4

Years	Silver (kg)	Gold (kg)	Average silver Price of gold (weight for weight)	Silver Equi-valent of gold (kg)	% of gold in Total Treasure
1660–65	40,145	1,074.47	15.01	16,129.6	28.66
1666–70	22,910	1,673.66	15.46	25,874.8	53.04
1671–75	49,828	3,669.50	15.00	55,042.5	52.49
1676–80	179,252	5,156.62	11.33	58,431.0	24.58
1681–85	240,952	6,931.61	12.53	86,870.4	26.50
1686–90	30,567	879.18	12.00	10,550.2	25.66
1691–95	7,687	221.14	13.25	2,930.1	27.60
1696–1700	131,511	491.22	13.13	6,449.7	4.67
1701–05	166,885	-	-	-	-

Source: K.N. Chaudhuri, p.177; *CEHI*, Vol.I, p.366-69.

The relative increase in gold imports at Surat appears from the following data of treasure brought by the English ships (Table 2.5):

Table 2.5

	Ships	Gold (Kg)	Silver (Kg)	Reference
1662	4	1,385	27,349	*EFI, 1661–64*, p. 95
1664	2	8,384	26,717	*EFI, 1661–64*, p. 326
1668	3	8,993	22,171	*EFI, 1668–69*, p. 13

Note: *EFI* stands for the *English Factories in India* series

It is, therefore, not surprising that there had to be ultimately a fall in the price of gold, or an appreciation of silver in terms of gold in India. This fall occurred rather sensationally in 1676: Gold had appreciated steadily since 1633, when the gold muhr fetched Rs 12.50; the price touched Rs 15.25 by 1676. But in that year, it suddenly crashed to as low a rate as Rs 11.[49] This must have put an end to the substitution of gold for silver in treasure exports to India, as Table 2.4 so clearly brings out.

1676–1705

After declining to a level of 72 tons of coined silver per annum during 1666–75, the Mughal currency output began to increase again. Table 2.3 shows it rising to 82 and 127 tons annually in the two subsequent decades, and, finally, to 188 tons during 1696–1705. The curious feature in this increase is that it is not accompanied by any sustained increase in the output of mints of the regions directly receiving imports of silver. The output of the North-Western mints did not undergo any particular increase; the Gujarat mints show a continuous decline after 1676–85; and the annual output of the Bengal mints remained below 15 tons. The increase in the total output is accounted for practically entirely by the inland or central mints whose annual output climbed up dramatically from 96.19 tons during 1666–75 to 140 tons during 1696–1705. On the face of it the evidence suggests that the Mughal empire went on receiving large quantities of silver from abroad, but that much of the silver influx evaded the coastal mints and streamed directly to the inland mints for conversion into coin of the realm.

The first inference, namely, the importation of large quantities of silver during the last quarter of the seventeenth century fits in with our actual evidence of the import of treasure around the Cape of Good Hope and through the Levant. K.N. Chaudhuri's figures for export of treasure by the English East India Company, already set out in Table 2.4 above, show the scale of increase in silver exports by the English Company. The figures are for exports to the East as a whole, but we should be able to determine from these figures the size of the bullion influx into northern India if we can establish what proportion of the English East India Company's silver exports to Asia was directed to northern India. This is luckily made possible by Chaudhuri's own data of the total values of the Company's imports from Surat/Bombay and Bengal, from which we have simply to deduct the values of imports of pepper which, though exported through Surat/Bombay, came from Kanara and Malabar.

49 For the specific evidence of the 1676 'crash' in gold, see W. Foster's communication, *Journal of the Royal Asiatic Society*, 1925, pp. 314–16; see also Fig. 3 in this paper.

A part of the English East India Company's treasure exports was in gold.[50] From the fact that the gold pagoda (*hun*) was the basic currency in Southern India we may assume that the imports from Madras were paid for in gold, and no silver was normally retained at Madras except during such years as when the proportion of gold exports was less than the proportion of value of imports from Madras to the total value of the company's imports. In such cases it had been assumed that the excess of value of imports from Madras over that of gold brought by the Company was met out of silver. The ratio of the total costs of the English East India Company's purchases in the Mughal empire to its total purchases in the East based on Chaudhuri's data[51] can then be worked out as follows (see Table 2.6).

Table 2.6

	(A) Value of Total Imports (£)	(B) Net Value of Imports from Bombay (£)	(C) Value of Imports from Bengal (£)	B as % of A	C as % of A	Value of Imports from the Mughal Empire as % of total
1664–65	195,437	93,143	48,749	47.66	24.94	72.60
1666–70	310,722	153,421	49,416	49.37	15.90	65.27
1671–75	779,002	329,997	203,664	42.36	26.14	69.51
1676–80	1,555,565	382,507	326,106	24.59	20.96	45.55
1681–85	2,470,596	842,323	681,094	34.09	27.56	61.65
1686–90	603,947	208,382	224,010	34.50	37.09	71.59
1691–95	247,503	40,920	146,310	16.53	59.11	75.64
1696–1700	1,322,528	341,104	659,385	25.79	49.86	75.65
1701–05	1,342,485	177,598	638,503	13.23	47.56	60.79

Source: See text.

Taking the figures of the English East India Company's total exports of silver to the East (Table 2.4), we can now attempt a rough estimate

[50] *Trading World of Asia*, p. 177.

[51] Ibid., p.510. Table C. 2. The Mokha coffee is *not* covered in K.N. Chaudhuri's figures for Bombay; it should have been assigned a column in Table C. 2, where without it the percentages under the various columns do not add to 100.

of the amount of silver brought into northern India during the successive five-year-periods by the English Company. All the figures in the table are in metric tons. The estimates of silver coin output, made on the same basis as for Table 2.3, are set out in the right-hand columns for comparison.

Table 2.7
Silver Imported through the English East India Company
(All quantities in metric tons)

				Estimated Mint-output		
	Gujarat	Bengal	Total	Gujarat	Bengal	Total
1660–65	10.04	19.13	29.17	223.32	105.43	328.75
1666–70	3.64	11.31	14.95	268.50	47.80	316.30
1671–75	13.18	21.36	34.54	122.30	42.17	164.47
1676–80	37.57	44.09	81.66	196.81	36.55	233.36
1681–85	66.41	82.14	148.55	233.36	66.08	299.44
1686–90	11.34	10.55	21.89	163.07	53.42	216.49
1691–95	4.54	1.27	5.81	130.74	36.55	167.29
1696–1700	65.57	33.92	99.49	122.30	33.74	156.04
1701–05	79.39	22.08	101.47	129.33	42.17	171.50

Source: See text.

The Dutch East India Company also exported considerable quantities of bullion to the East.[52] Its total volume of trade exceeded that of the English, though, as far as commerce with northern India was concerned, the difference in size of the trade of the two companies was probably marginal during the last quarter of the seventeenth century. Moreover, the Dutch partly paid for their imports in Japanese copper. From a comparison of Glamann's data of the Dutch exports of Japanese copper to India[53] with the figures of the total value of the Dutch imports from the East, offered by Bal Krishna,[54] it appears that copper exported to Surat accounted for 6.7 per cent of the total costs of Dutch imports from the East during 1666–70. Thereafter, the Dutch

[52] Chaudhuri, *The English East India Company, 1600–1640*, pp. 455–6.

[53] K. Glamann, 'The Dutch East India Company's Trade in Japanese Copper, 1645–1736', *Scandinavian Economic History Review*, Vol. I, pp. 63–5.

[54] Bal Krishna, *Commercial Relations between India and England*, p. 289.

export of Japanese copper to Surat increased substantially. From 1671 onwards until 1684, when Glamann's series ends, copper exports to Surat paid for 12 per cent of the total value of the Dutch imports from the East. The copper brought to Bengal between 1679 and 1684 was a little less than half the quantity sent to Surat.[55] In view of such large payments in copper, it would perhaps not be wrong to assume that the amount of silver brought into the Mughal empire by the Dutch East India Company was less than the silver brought in by the English. The intrusion of the French Company and, still less, of the Danes, was not of much account but cannot entirely be ignored. On the whole, therefore, we can assume that the total silver influx into northern India by the Cape of Good Hope route was probably about, but not much more than, double the quantities brought by the English by that route.

As the three left-hand columns of Table 2.6 show, the English imports of silver into Gujarat became substantial only during 1676–80, but were still dwarfed by the silver coined at the mints. In 1680–5, however, the imports through the English reached a respectable 28.5 per cent of the silver minted in Gujarat.

The next decade saw a great decline in silver imports by the English;[56] there was a decline too in the total mint output of Gujarat, almost corresponding proportionately to the decrease in English imports. During 1696–1705 the English imports of silver rose phenomenally, while the mint-output of Gujarat remained largely stationary: The silver imports through the English at over 13 tons per annum now exceeded a half of the total silver minted in Gujarat. If the Dutch imported as much silver, the imports of the two Companies would have accounted for the entire mint-production of Gujarat.

But the English and the Dutch imports were not the only, or even the principal, source of silver imported into Gujarat. During the fourth quarter of the seventeenth century the Red Sea and the Gulf trade still brought in large quantities of silver;[57] and the commerce was still

[55] The copper sold in Surat was 4,972,2041 lbs (Dutch) during this period (1679–84) while in the same years the factories in Bengal sold 2,483,472 lbs. (*Scandinavian Economic History Review*, Vol. I, p. 57.)

[56] For this decline owing to the rise of prices of silver in the London market, see K.N. Chaudhuri, *Trading World of Asia*, p. 171.

[57] See Bernier, *Travels*, pp. 202–3; J. Fryer, *New Account of Persia and India being Nine Years Travels, 1672–81*, edited by W. Crooke, Vol. I, London, 1902, pp. 282–3; J. Ovington, *A Voyage to Surat, in the Year 1689*, edited by Rawlinson,

important in the 1690s. In 1695 when the ship *Ganj-i Sawai* returning from Jeddah to Surat, was plundered by the English, it reputedly carried treasure estimated at 5 million rupees (=55.37 metric tons of silver), said probably erroneously to be in gold.[58] The knowledgeable English Captain Hamilton sets the value of the booty at 2.6 million rupees,[59] which, though lower, is high enough. Ashin Das Gupta tells us that the Gujarat ships every year took 4 million rupees' worth of textiles to Mokha and Jeddah in the Red Sea at the beginning of the eighteenth century.[60] If this figure is made up of sale prices and the entire value was received in bullion, the annual inflow of silver from the Red Sea to the Gujarat ports should have amounted to 44.5 metric tons, by far in excess of the Cape-route imports. This would surely mean that the larger part of the silver entering Gujarat during the 1690s and later, was not simply taken to the Gujarat mints; the alternative, which seems in fact to have been adopted, was to carry it to the inland regions.

The issues of the Bengal mints are so few as to render implausible any suggestion, that these could at any time have absorbed a large part of the bullion imported into Bengal. Table 2.6 shows that during 1676–85 and again during 1696–1700, the total estimated output of the Bengal mints (including Patna) was less than the estimated imports of silver by the English alone. We must remember that we have to make allowance for the silver brought in by the Dutch as well; direct imports from the Levant into Bengal, on the other hand, were probably on so small a scale as to be not worth notice.

It seems that the Bengal mints were not very popular with bullion importers. The English East India Company had serious misgivings about the exchange rates for the Spanish rials prevailing at these mints, the rates being much lower here than those allowed at the Gujarat mints. From 1685, the Company started exploring possibilities of

London, 1929, pp. 270–1. Ovington, however, blamed the English for harming this trade, saying that in 1691 they seized £120,000 worth of goods from merchants trading between Surat and Mokha.

[58] Abū'l Faẓl Ma'mūrī, 'History of Aurangzeb's Reign', MS. Or 1671, f. 187b. The *zar-i surkh* may possibly be a mistake for *zar-o-sim* (gold and silver).

[59] *A New Account of the East-Indies—Being the Observations and Remarks of Capt. Alexander Hamilton from the Year 1688-1723,* Edited by W. Foster, 2nd ed., Vol. I, London, 1930, p.43.

[60] Ashin Das Gupta, 'Gujarati Merchants and the Red Sea Trade, 1700–25', Blair B. Kling and M.N. Pearson, eds., *The Age of Partnership*, Honolulu, 1979, p. 124.

getting its silver coined at its Madras mint; and from 1692 the English began to mint rupees at Madras for export to Bengal.[61] Since the Madras rupees were not generally accepted in Bengal, except at a disadvantageous discount, the Company used to sell the treasure imported to local merchants, without taking it to the mint.[62] It is possible that these merchants instead of getting the silver coined in the Bengal mints took them to the inland mints. When the 'exchange' rose owing to large payments made from Bengal to Agra and the Court,[63] it would have been immaterial to the merchants whether they took bullion or minted rupees; and they would have preferred the former course if the Bengal mints were not efficient or not offering sufficiently attractive terms in comparison with the inland mints. This seems the only persuasive explanation of the low level of output of the Bengal mints compared to the large quantities of silver imported into the region.

We can see, therefore, that the expanded output of the inland mints in the later years of the seventeenth century must in large part have been due to the overflow of silver from Gujarat and a bypassing of the Bengal mints. The ebb and flow of the mint output of the Mughal empire as a whole continued to reflect fairly faithfully the fluctuations in the volume of silver imports into India.

COINED SILVER STOCK

It is hoped that in the previous section, we have largely established that our estimates of changes in the size of silver-coin output based on UP treasure-troves (Table 2.3) are consistent with such information as we have on bullion imports and the movements of gold and copper prices. The question arises whether we can go further and venture an estimate of coined silver-stock from our coin-find data, so as to have some impression of the size of the total silver-money supply.

Aziza Hasan drew a curve which she assumed to be that of 'currency-in-circulation'. She took the cumulative totals of catalogued

[61] Susil Chaudhuri, *Trade and Commercial Organisation in Bengal*, Calcutta, 1975, pp. 103–10.

[62] *Early Annals of the English in Bengal*, Vol. II, No. 1, p. 106. Consultation at Fort William, 23 February 1713: Only 'a chest of silver ... remaining which we cannot sell' at a high enough price was sent to the Makhsusabad mint. The rest of the silver was sold to local merchants. See also Susil Chaudhuri, *Trade and Commercial Organisation in Bengal*, pp. 103–7.

[63] Susil Chaudhuri, *Trade and Commercial Organisation in Bengal*, pp.118–19.

coins for each year, after making a deduction of 2.5 per cent from the previous total at each stage treating it as allowance for reminting.[64] But the curve she constructs cannot be one of 'currency-in-circulation', since it represents the coins minted, and thus must include those which were in circulation as well as those which went into hoard. For it was be coined money which was mainly hoarded, and not bullion or 'silver plate'. Akbar's treasure, for example, contained a vast quantity of coined silver (in rupees) with only an insignificant amount in bullion.[65]

Furthermore, Hasan's curve is naturally based on her own count of catalogued coins, which as we have seen has a built-in bias. Can we, then, build a similar curve on the basis of the UP treasure-troves?

Before we do so, the deduction of 2.5 per cent per annum that Aziza Hasan allows for reminting has to be considered. The evidence on this score is admittedly scanty. Hawkins seems to suggest that a coin remained in circulation for twenty years only,[66] while from Tavernier's statement that payments were normally made in coins that were fifteen or twenty or more years old,[67] one would infer a much longer period of life for the average coin. Hasan made her allowance of 2.5 per cent by fixing the life of an average coin at forty years on the ground that if a coin lost 0.5 per cent of its value every three or four years (as stated by Tavernier),[68] it should have needed a period of thirty-three to forty-four years during which the entire premium of 5.6 per cent, equal to minting charges and seigniorage,[69] would have been lost. But it must be remembered that a coin which wore off through use and so lost in weight, could still remain in

[64] Aziza Hasan, *IESHR*, Vol. VI, No. 1, p. 100.

[65] Pelsaert (*A Contemporary Dutch Chronicle of Mughal India*, translated by Brij Narain and S.R. Sharma, Calcutta, 1957, p. 33) gives the amount left by Akbar in his hoarded treasure as ten crores of rupees. Qazwīnī (*Bādshāhnāma*, Br. Mus. Add. 20734, pp. 444–5, Or. 173, ff. 221a–b) gives the figures as seven crores of rupees. The latter is an official work. The uncoined silver was only 70 *mans* (Nawal Kishore, ed., *Tārīkh-Firishta*, Lucknow, 1869, p. 272), that is, the equivalent of 1,52,285 rupees, taking the weight of a rupee as 178 grains troy and seigniorage and minting costs as 5.6 per cent (cf. Irfan Habib, *Medieval India Quarterly*, Vol. IV, Nos.1–2), pp. 2–3, for seigniorage and minting costs).

[66] Foster, ed., *Early Travels*, London, 1921, p. 112.

[67] Jean Baptiste Tavernier, *Travels in India*, translated by V. Ball, edited by W. Crooke, Vol. I, London, 1925, p. 29.

[68] Ibid.

[69] Irfan Habib, *Medieval India Quarterly*, Vol. IV, Nos.1–2, pp.1–2.

circulation for as long as it was exchangeable for its value as bullion. In fact, it should have lingered on further since in the process of the reminting of coins, 1.5 per cent of the silver was wasted.[70] Moreover, since a large number of coins was kept out of circulation for a long duration by being hoarded, the wearing-off of silver coins would have been quite a slow process on the average.

It is, therefore, difficult to accept Aziza Hasan's deduction of 2.5 per cent per annum merely to cover re-coinage.[71] It is also rendered dubious by the shape of the curve that results, since it shows large and sharp declines, taking her total down to even three-fourths of the level previously reached. This might have been possible if her curve was that of currency in circulation, though even in that case one would have to imagine that at a particular point something like one-fourth of the total currency went additionally into hoard. But, as we have seen, her curve is really that of coined stock; and while a marginal contraction of coined stock over a short period (to allow for silver going into ornaments), is not inconceivable, a substantial decline in total coined stock seems very difficult to accept.

The allowance of remintage must accordingly be much lower than what Hasan assumed it to be in order to cover coins that wore off or were wasted besides those that were actually brought for reminting. It must be reduced further in view of the necessity of adjusting our figures to take account of the difference in the 'survival rates' of the coins, which must be lower for the earlier coins and higher for the later. The difference in the ratio of surviving to actual coins from various periods cannot, of course, be determined with any pretence at even good guesswork; but for that reason alone it cannot also be ignored.

With all these considerations in mind, I have fixed the remintage rate at 1 per cent per annum, on the assumption that (a) the life of the average coin was considerably more than fifty years, and the remintage

[70] Abū'l Faẓl (*Ā'īn-i Akbarī*, Vol. I, edited by Blochmann, Bib. Ind., Calcutta, 1867, p. 32) records that in the coining of pure silver, 5 *tolcha* 4.75 *surkh* were wasted out of each 969 *tolcha*, 9 *māsha*, and 4 *surkh*, i.e., 0.5 per cent. But in the case of baser silver and coins, 14 *talcha*, 10 *masha*, and 1 *surkh* silver were wasted out of each 989 *tolcha*, 7 *māsha*; i.e., the wastage was 1.462 per cent (Abū'l Faẓl seems to have rounded off the waste to 1.5 per cent since he puts it at 1.5 *tolcha* in every hundred *tolcha*). Malcolm, in *Memoirs of Central India*, Vol. II, London, 1824, p. 844, gives the loss as 0.72 per cent.

[71] Aziza Hasan, *IESHR*, Vol. VI, No. 1, 1969, p. 101.

rate must accordingly have been well below 2 per cent per annum; and (b) the deduction has to be reduced further to allow for the lower surviving rates of earlier coins.

In applying the deduction rate of 1 per cent, I have differed again from Aziza Hasan in not calculating it on the inverse compound principle. If that were used, the actual remintage rate would be much lower than 1 per cent as time passed, amounting to only 0.61 per cent of the original stock after fifty years, and 0.38 per cent after ninety-nine years. Indeed, even after 100 years instead of (theoretically, at least) all the original coins being reminted, over 37 per cent of the coins would escape remintage.[72] I have, therefore, calculated 1 per cent as a simple rate on the original stock taking five-year periods for convenience of calculation.

Under our mode of counting, the deductions for remintage on account of each addition of stock during a five-year period cease after the expiry of 100 years. Thus if x coins were added during the years 1571–5, we would subtract 5x/100 from the stock at the end of every subsequent five-year period until the quinquennium ending with 1675 is reached.

In making my calculations on this basis, I have found little purpose in offering a coined stock curve for the period before 1596, since it would simply reflect the territorial expansion of the Empire and not be true for northern India as a whole. Moreover, it must have taken some time before the rupee coinage replaced the bullion and copper coinage in the core-area of the Empire and other (mainly silver or coarse silver) coinages in the outlying regions. I have, therefore, totalled up all rupee coins of the years 1556–95 to get the base-figure for the initial stock. For this period I have ignored deductions for remintage. Such remintage as might have been taken place can be set off against the rupee coins issued during the period 1540–56 (the Sur interregnum) and the underestimation resulting from lower rate of survival of coins from the sixteenth century (when compared with the seventeenth).

The estimated coined silver stock of the Mughal empire (northern India) as calculated on these lines for quinquennial periods is tabulated below. The conversions from treasure-trove coins into metric tons have been made on the basis of the equivalence already hypothesized, namely, one rupee coin from the UP treasure-troves equals 2.811 tons.

[72] This would also have the result of proportionately reducing the relative significance of additions to coined stock after the passage of years.

According to these estimates the silver stock in the form of coin must have risen from about 4,550 metric tons in 1595 to over 9,235 tons in 1645 (average annual increase: nearly 94 tons). Thereafter, there was a slow decline, the coined stock losing on average 17.5 tons annually until 1675. An increase in stock again took place now, with an annual average addition of some 67 tons, so that the quantity of coined silver exceeded 10,700 tons by 1705.

Table 2.8

	Coins in UP Treasure-troves (total after allowance for remintage)	Estimated coined silver stock in metric tons	Index
1595	1,619.0	4,551.90	100.0
1600	2,028.0	5,701.85	125.3
1605	2,466.5	6,934.72	152.0
1610	2,456.5	6,905.20	151.7
1615	2,730.1	7,675.85	168.0
1620	2,890.3	8,126.26	178.5
1625	2,838.3	7,980.06	175.3
1630	3,032.9	9,927.19	187.3
1635	3,226.0	9,070.10	199.3
1640	3,272.2	9,199.99	202.1
1645	3,284.9	9,235.70	202.9
1650	3,257.2	9,157.82	201.9
1655	3,195.9	8,982.66	197.3
1660	3,165.2	8,899.16	195.5
1665	3,151.0	8,859.24	194.6
1670	3,160.0	8,884.54	195.2
1675	3,098.6	8,711.92	191.4
1680	3,114.5	8,856.61	194.2
1685	3,125.7	8,890.92	193.1
1690	3,237.0	9,109.03	199.9
1695	3,351.0	9,421.55	207.0
1700	3,579.0	10,062.59	221.1
1705	3,861.0	10,728.93	238.5

Source: See text.

These figures of estimated coined stock match fairly well with Hamilton's data of silver flow from the New World.[73] It is almost certain that the entire addition of 4,684 tons between 1595 and 1645 came from the influx of New World silver; it is also likely that about 1,500 tons of the 1595 stock originated in the New World. We may thus suppose that northern India absorbed some 6,000 tons of silver between 1500 and 1650.[74] Hamilton estimated that Spain legally imported 16,886.8 metric tons of silver from the Americas between 1500 and 1650; this undoubtedly constituted the bulk of the total quantity of silver that entered Europe from across the Atlantic.[75] This figure excludes, however, the fairly large quantities of silver that for some time reached the Philippines, China, and Japan,[76] through which India too received quantities of American silver. But since India drew her silver mainly from the west, it would seem that over one-third of silver flowing into Europe between 1500 and 1650 was ultimately carried to India through the Levant and by the Cape route. This, in view of contemporary European alarm at the drain of bullion eastwards, does not seem to be an implausibly high proportion.

For this very reason, the decline in India's Mughal coined silver stock between 1645 and 1675, that Table 2.8 indicates, seems to deserve remark. Although our evidence for bullion imports for these thirty years is very patchy, it does seem as if the Cape route carried comparatively smaller quantities of silver during the period and there was a spurt in gold flow in partial substitution of silver both on the Cape route and in the Levant trade (see the second section above). The shift seems to have ended with the great crash in gold prices in India in 1676. But even if the silver flow drained off considerably during the third quarter of the seventeenth century, why should it

[73] They also tie up well-enough with James Grant's estimate of an annual influx of silver equal to one crore of rupees or 109 metric tons from 1583 to his own time (1784) (*Fifth Report*, Irish University Press facsimile reprint, p. 650).

[74] It may be remembered that the estimated coined stock for 1650 is slightly less than that for 1645.

[75] Hamilton believed that the unrecorded imports might have ranged from 10 per cent to 50 per cent of the recorded; but he felt the true figure would have been closer to 10 per cent.

[76] See above. Also Aziza Hasan, *IESHR*, Vol. VII, No. 1, p. 152, where she cites Takakoshi, *The Economic Aspects of the History of the Civilization of Japan*, London, 1930, Vol. II, pp. 395–6, for the observation that much of silver exported by Japan during the seventeenth century had originated in the Americas.

have had the effect of diminishing the coined silver money in India in absolute terms?

The answer seems to lie partly at least in what Bernier says (1667) about Indian demand of precious metals for non-monetary use.[77] There had to be a minimum annual supply of silver to make up for the precious metal lost in melting and refashioning of ornaments and for the additional demand for new ornaments. If the silver imports fell below this minimum, there would have to be a transfer from coined stock; and this would naturally take the form of a fall in the number of coins re-minted.

There is also the possibility that there was some silver outflow from India, notably to Central Asia from which, according to Bernier, some 25,000 good horses were imported every year.[78] This probably explains the use of seventeenth-century Mughal rupees in the Uzbek dominions till as late as the earlier part of the nineteenth century.[79] Moreover, Shāhjahān's expensive war in Balkh and Badakhshan (1646–7) might well have resulted in a substantial drain of silver from India to Central Asia.[80]

Silver coins that went out of India would not turn up in Indian hoards, and, therefore, would be excluded from any calculation of mint output (and thence of coined stock) that we may attempt on the basis of treasure-troves. In other words, any export of Indian rupees to Central Asia would mean a reduction in coined stock as estimated from treasure-trove finds within India.

[77] Bernier, *Travels,* pp. 223–4: 'In the first place a large quantity is melted, re-melted and wasted, in fabricating women's bracelets, both for the hands and feet, chains, ear-rings, nose and finger rings and a still larger quantity is consumed in manufacturing embroideries; alaches, or striped silken stuffs; touras, or fringes of gold lace, worn on turbans; gold and silver cloth; scarf turbans and brocades. The quantity of these articles made in India is incredible. All the troops, from the Omrah to the man in the ranks will wear gilt ornaments; nor will a private soldier refuse them to his wife and children, though the whole family should die of hunger; which indeed is a common occurrence'.

[78] Bernier, *Travels*, p. 203. Manucci raises the number to one hundred thousand. (*Storia do Mogor* , 1656–1712, translated by W. Irvine, Vol. II, London, 1907–8, pp. 390–1).

[79] A. Burnes, *Travels to Bokhara*, Vol. I, 1973, pp. 241–2.

[80] 'Abdūl Ḥamīd Lāhōrī, *Bādshāhnāma*, edited by Kabiruddin, Vol. II, p. 2, Asiatic Society, Calcutta, 1868, pp. 562–3, describes how Shāhjahān ordered silver *K͟hānīs* to be minted at Balkh in his own name; these were designed to replace the billon *k͟hānī* of the Uzbeks.

The second period of expansion of coined silver stock beginning after 1675 corresponds with the rapid expansion in bullion exports to India by the English and Dutch Companies and the restoration of a substantial influx of silver through the Red Sea. On this we have here nothing to add to the information that we have already set out at some length above.

SILVER–MONEY SUPPLY AND PRICES

The index of the coined silver stock in Table 2.7 may logically stand even if there are some reservations about the conversions into absolute size. At the same time, the corroboration from our other evidence of the estimates of absolute tonnage not only show them to be plausible but by so doing reinforces our stock index as well.

According to the index, the coined silver stock practically doubled between 1595 and 1635; after a long plateau, the index rose to 238.5 in 1705 (with the stock in 1595 as 100).

If we follow the conventional quantity theory of money, this expansion in money supply should have had the result of proportionately raising prices in terms of silver-money, had T (the total volume of transactions, or trade) and V (velocity of circulation) remained constant.[81]

It is difficult, however, to treat T (transactions) as constant over a long period. In the first place, this is because the number of transactions could not have remained the same owing to variations in the GDP. In so far as GDP equals average productivity per capita multiplied by population, possible changes in these two factors must be given consideration. It may be reasonable to assume that the average

[81] Here it may be admitted that coined silver stock is not the same thing as money supply. At least, the imperial hoard should be deducted from it. In 1605, this amounted according to a conservative official account of some thirty years later, to Rs 7 crore (Amīn Qazwīnī, *Bādshāhnāma*, Br. Mus. Add. 20734, pp.444-5, Or. 173, f 221a–b) and, according to earlier contemporary non-official statements, to 10 crore of rupees (F. Pelsaert, 'Chronicle' in *A Contemporary Dutch Chronicle of Mughal India*, translated by Brij Narain and S.R. Sharma, Calcutta, 1957, p. 33). According to our estimates (converting coins in the hoard into actual coins at the ratio of 2,53,913:1), the coined silver hoard at the time should have been 62.63 tons. The imperial hoard thus amounted to between one-ninth and one-seventh of the coined stock. Complete dishoarding at that time could not have, therefore, raised the prices, on its own, by more than 13 per cent or 17 per cent. For all long-term purposes, therefore, one may take the index of coined silver stock as an index of silver-money supply.

per-head productivity remained constant in the Mughal empire since no noticeable change in production technology is known to have occurred during the period in question,[82] and there was as yet no 'scarcity' of land.[83] But the population could hardly have remained absolutely constant. For 1601, I have offered an estimate of Indian population (14.5 crore)[84] that, when compared with the corrected census figure for 1871,[85] suggests an average annual increase of 0.211 per cent per annum during the intervening period (at the compound rate). For purposes of judging its effect on prices, we should convert the index of total coined silver stock into a per-capita index through scaling it down according to the assumed rate of population growth. Obviously, since population growth in the short-run (five-year period or decades) could hardly have progressed uniformly, the index could be misleading for the shorter intervals but is likely to be more relevant for longer periods.

In qualification of what is said in the preceding paragraph, T is not only determined by GDP; T may increase if the portion of GDP entering the market sector expanded, without a proportionate increase in GDP. Such an expansion of the market sector in the latter half of the sixteenth and seventeenth centuries is not unlikely in view of what we know about the extension of the cash nexus and the growth of commerce during this period.[86] But in terms of Fisher's equation, such increase in T could have been counter-balanced by an increase in V, or velocity of money, due to the greater use of bills of credit/exchange, and the system of deposit banking which is heard of for the first time in the seventeenth century.[87] It is also possible that velocity was increased

[82] For a survey of production technology in Mughal India, see Irfan Habib, 'Technology and Economy of Mughal India', *IESHR*, Vol. XVII, No. 1, pp. 1–33; 'Technology and Barriers to Technological Change in Mughal India', in *Indian Historical Review*, Vol. V, Nos. 1–2, 1978–9, pp. 152–74; 'Changes in Technology in Medieval India', in *Studies in History*, Vol. II, No. 1, 1980, pp. 15–38.

[83] W.H. Moreland, *India at the Death of Akbar*, pp. 110–11; Irfan Habib, *Agrarian System of Mughal India*, 2nd ed., pp.133–4.

[84] *EMI*, p.405. See also Moosvi, *Population*, No. 2, Paris, March, 1984, pp, 10–25.

[85] Kingsley Davis, *Population of India and Pakistan*, Princeton, 1951, Table VI, p. 25.

[86] Irfan Habib, 'The System of Bills of Exchange (Hundis) in the Mughal Empire', *Proc. Indian History Congress*, Muzaffarpur Session, 1972, pp. 298–9.

[87] Irfan Habib, 'Banking in Mughal India', in Tapan Ray Chaudhuri, ed., *Contributions to Indian Economic History*, Calcutta, 1960, p. 17.

by the replacement of copper by silver coinage. A silver coin being lighter has much greater geographical mobility; on the other hand, the individual copper coins may go on being employed in petty transactions while the silver coin awaited a transaction large enough for it to be used. As in every matter involving 'V' one can hardly say anything with any degree of confidence. What may at present be said is that both T and V are likely to have increased, but the former proportionately more than the latter. Given this broad picture, the coined stock per capita (absolute coined stock adjusted to population growth) would still appear to be the best index of the size of the effective silver-money supply per head.

There do not exist any indices of prices of goods of mass consumption with which we can compare our index of coined stock. This is because any series of whatever reliability does not simply exist for seventeenth-century prices, even for eastern Rajasthan from which we have data in relative abundance during the next century.[88] The only series, though broken and inadequate, are those of gold and copper prices in terms of silver.[89] We know something about the state of the supply of both gold and copper; and we can, therefore, consider their price movements as reflective of the general purchasing power of the rupee, subject to such deviations as must have taken place by changes in the demand-and-supply position of the other two metals (gold/copper).

Table 2.8 sets out the indices of silver prices of gold and copper along with the index of silver coined stock per capita. Wherever the quotations for gold and silver prices of the last year of a quinquennium are not available, the prices quoted within ± two years of that year are used.

In Table 2.9 the copper price index has been revised to take into account the corrections that need to be made after Najaf Haider's persuasive rejection of the supposition by all previous writers on Mughal monetary history, including the present writer, that *paisa* (the 'pice') of English accounts had come to mean half-*dām* in the seventeenth century, and that *ṭaka* now meant the dām rather than the double-*dām* as in the time of Akbar.[90] The new reading of the evidence has implications, which Haider has not considered, but must now be

[88] *IESHR*, S.P. Gupta and S. Moosvi's Weighted Price and Revenue, Rate Indices of Eastern Rajasthan, Vol. XII, No. 2, pp. 183–93.

[89] See Irfan Habib, 'The Monetary System and Prices', in *CEHI*, Vol. I., pp.360-81

[90] Najaf Haider, in *Medieval History Journal*, Vol. II, No. 2, pp.342–4.

addressed. It implies, first of all, a heavy decline in copper price in 1608–15, when the value of the rupee rose from 40 to about 80 *dāms*/ 'pice';[91] the second implication is that thereafter, there was a slow and steady recovery in the price of copper for the rest of the century.

Table 2.9

1595 = 100			
Year	Per capita silver coined stock: Total coined stock index of Table 7 adjusted to population growth	Silver Price of Gold	Silver Price of Copper
1595	100.0	100	100
1600	124.3	-	-
1605	149.6	-	105
1610	148.1	100	100
1615	162.8	107.00	47.5–50
1620	171.6	-	-
1625	167.3	140	66.5
1630	177.4	127.5–130	80.5
1635	187.1	125	80
1640	188.3	130–140	71.5
1645	187.7	-	-
1650	184.8	-	-
1655	179.8	-	89.5
1660	176.8	146	133.5
1665	174.5	150	123.6
1670	173.7	151–152	-
1675	169.1	150	-
1680	170.2	122.5–130	111.1
1685	167.9	123.8–125	106.5
1690	172.5	132.5	108.7
1695	177.4	131.3	102.6
1700	188.01	-	-
1705	201.3	145(1711)	105.2

Source: See text.

[91] The period during which the crash in copper prices occurred can be further

Whereas the per capita silver stock index rose from 100 to 162.8 between 1595 and 1615, gold prices in terms of silver remained stable during that period, gold rising only by 7 per cent.[92] The dramatic decline in copper value during this phase can only be explained by the hypothesis that Irfan Habib first put forward, namely, the large-scale replacement of copper money by the silver rupee.[93] Since the large

---

narrowed down on the basis of the information culled from various sources tabulated below:

Year	Price per rupee	Reference
1605–6	50 or 66 *dāms*	*Tuzuk,* 34
1606	38 *dāms*	(*'tankas' at Kabul*) Dastūr Kaiqubād, *Petition and Laudatory Poem* [1617], ed.& transl. Jivanji Jamshedji Modi, Bombay, 1930
1607	40 *dāms*	*Tuzuk,* 46-47
1609	80 pice (1 '*man*'=32 or 31 pice)	*Letters Received,* I, 54
1611	80 pice (1 'man' = 32 pice)	Ibid., 141
1614	85 pice (1 'man' = 34 pice)	*Supl. Cal.,* 46-47
1614	79.5 pice	*Letters Received,* II, 214
1614	84 pice	Ibid., 249-50
1615	80 to 86 pice	Ibid., III, 87
1626	57.6 to 72 pice (28.8 to 36 *takas* = 1 rupee)	Pelsaert, 42, 60

If 'pice' are the same as *dām* then, one would have to conclude that the copper price began fluctuating as early as 1605–6, and a fall to as low a rate for copper as 64 *takas* or 128 *dāms* at the Court in the Punjab in 1606 was recalled by Kaiqubād. But as we see in the Table, Kaiqubād found the *taka* back at 19 to a rupee at Kabul, and in 1607 Jahāngīr gives the equivalence of 40 *dāms* to the rupee. But from 1609 the English records began putting the *dām/pice* value as at low as 80 to the rupee. So the main fall in copper values must belong to 1609—11.

Kaiqubād's poem is also interesting in that it implies that while his money stock held on royal account was in the form of *dāms*, he required rupees to make payments while accompanying the royal camp. It thus is one of the rare pieces of evidence of replacement of copper money by silver.

[92] In view of Najaf Haider's note no.86 in *Medieval History Journal,* Vol. II, No. 2, p.340, about the value of Rs 8 given to the *ashrafi* in a document of 1608 (NAI-2671/2), it needs to be stated that the rupee in the quotation is designated *muhrī,* and so was apparently the one minted by Jahāngīr, was 120 per cent of the ordinary rupee in weight and value. The *ashrafi* in terms of ordinary rupees would then have had the value of Rs 9.6.

[93] Irfan Habib, 'A System of Trimetallism during the Price Revolution' in John

increase in coined silver stock took place at the expense of copper, the gold:silver ratios would be largely unaffected. On the other hand, copper by being expelled from monetary circulation would fall heavily in price until the bottom was reached in or about 1615. Indeed, even in 1619 copper was cheap enough at Surat to be exported to Persia.

The increase in price-level in terms of silver money, therefore, ought to have occurred only after c. 1615, by which year the replacement of copper money by silver had been completed. Any further influx of silver now was bound to increase prices of both gold and copper.

If we then compare the increase in coined silver stock between 1615 and 1705 and the increase in gold and copper prices in terms of silver in the same period, the percentage of the increase turns out to be as follows:

Total silver stock	42%
Per capita silver stock	24%
Gold price	33%
Copper price	110.4%

One must remember that the two percentages representing the increase in absolute stock of silver and in silver stock per capita are at best rough approximations. Yet the above set of figures conforms very closely to what we know otherwise about the state of supply of gold and copper.

The scale of increase in the price of gold falls between the scale of increase in the absolute stock of silver and that in silver stock per capita. In other words, it implies that there were some additions to gold supply between 1615 and 1705, since otherwise the increase in the price of gold over the whole period would have fallen well short of 15 per cent, by which (actually 14.5 per cent) we have assumed the population to have increased between 1615 and 1705. Since there was little gold production in India (beyond the gold dust from river-sand), all substantial additions came from imports. Except for the spurt in the 1660s, gold imports were at best modest; and there was, in any case, no spectacular increase in gold production on the world

---

F. Richards, ed., *The Imperial Monetary System of Mughal India*, Delhi, 1987, pp.146–7. John S. Deyell supplemented this paper by a note on Mughal copper coinage which shows that after 1605 the coining of copper declined remarkably (ibid., pp.160–4).

scale to compare even remotely with silver. Indeed, Braudel and Spooner allow only an increase of 5 per cent in European gold stock between 1500 and 1650, though this may be an underestimate.[94]

In contrast to gold, the rise in the price of copper was remarkably high leaving far behind the increase in the total stock of silver, let alone the silver stock per capita.

That this should have happened may be expected from what we know about copper. Though there was a certain amount of internal copper production, there is some evidence that this declined in the seventeenth century.[95] The copper import data are more satisfactory, since we have an almost comprehensive record of quantities for certain definite periods. This is because the Dutch East India Company was practically the sole importer of copper into the Mughal empire, bringing its supplies from Japan. The data have been collected by Glamann, who shows that imports reached their peak in 1679–84. Given the prices which the Dutch obtained at Surat, the Dutch annually imported through Surat and Bengal (the two inlets into the Mughal empire) quantities of copper that were equal in value to 13.76 metric tons of silver.[96] If this was the peak figure, the copper imports compared quite poorly with those of silver estimated by us at an average of 67 metric tons per annum during 1675–1705. It should further be borne in mind that copper is subject to corrosion and waste much more than silver, and that there had to be a large addition to copper supply every year simply to maintain the total existing level of stock.

It was, therefore, to be expected that the net supply of copper should increase by a lower percentage than gold; it follows that the price of copper ought to have increased by a higher proportion than the price of the yellow metal. But the percentage of actual increase in price would seem to suggest a relative contraction of copper supply since at 110.4 per cent the percentage of increase in copper price is so substantially larger than the estimated percentage of increase in silver stock (42 per cent).

[94] Braudel and Spooner, in *CEHE*, Vol. IV, pp. 445–6.

[95] Shāhjahān's historian Wāriṣ tells us that the fall in the production of copper mines at Bairat and Singhana induced the Emperor to change their management in 1655 (Muḥammad Wāriṣ, *Bādshāhnāma*, Br. Mus. Add. 6556, f 448a). Moreland (*From Akbar to Aurangzeb*, London, 1920, p. 184) cites a Dutch letter from Surat in 1661 referring to the scarcity of copper owing to disorganization of Indian copper mines as well as the inadequacies of foreign supply.

[96] K. Glamann, *Scandinavian Economic History Review*, Vol. I, p. 51.

The answer seems to lie in the simple fact that whereas, all said and done, gold was essentially only a substitute (though a better or preferred one) of silver, copper was not only such a substitute (though inferior and imperfect) of silver, but was a substitute of iron as well. In the seventeenth century there was much demand for bronze (copper alloyed with tin) and brass (copper alloyed with zinc), the basic alloys, from which artillery pieces and muskets were made. There was, further, a market for copper and brass utensils (which should have expanded at least by as much as the population increased). The need of artillery for larger quantities of copper must have drained away copper from circulation as money. By the 1660s a scarcity of copper seems to have been strongly felt (this was significantly after the internecine war in the Empire during 1658–9). Copper coinage disappeared, and Aurangzeb had to replace the older copper *dām* with a coin one-third lighter.[97]

We can say, then, that if we forget for the moment our estimates of silver stock, our information about copper alone should have suggested that the general price-level could not have doubled between 1615 and 1705, since, as we have seen, there were special reasons for the rise in the value of copper on this scale. On the other hand, gold (33 per cent) is more likely to give a true reflection of the rise in the general price-level since the conditions of its demand remained about the same and its supply increased modestly. This reinforces our confidence in the two other indices we offer, based on our estimates of silver stock: a 45 per cent rise in the total stock, and 27 per cent rise per capita rise. If we go by these indices, the price-level did not probably rise as much as 42 per cent, since GNP must have increased in the meantime; in other words the price-level probably increased only by 27 per cent or thereabouts over the whole period, though large fluctuations in a mainly agricultural country must have created a complex picture in shorter periods.

THE SILVER INFLUX, REVENUE EXTRACTION, AND THE ECONOMY

The picture of price movements in terms of silver that we can now reconstruct is one of general stability from about the early 1580s till after 1615, and of an increase of no more than a third over the entire period, 1615–1705. This moderate actual impact of the bullion influx

[97] 'Alī Muḥammad Khān, *Mir'āt-i Aḥmadī*, edited by Nawab Ali, Baroda, 1927–8, pp. 265, 267, 385.

on prices casts some doubt on the applicability of the theory of Price Revolution to Mughal India,[98] insofar as a term of that kind suggests a steep long-term inflation. If the stability of the Mughal Indian economy was subverted, its source, then, could not lie, as far as we can see, in any monetary factors.

Table 2.10

Year	(A) *Jama'-dāmī* per-capita 1615=100	(B) Coined Silver Stock per-capita, 1615=100
1595	84.5	61.4
1600	–	76.4
1605	93.2	91.9
1610		91.0
1615	100.0	100.0
1620	–	105.4
1625	106.7	102.8
1630	102.1	108.9
1635	115.1	114.9
1640	–	115.7
1645	130.9	115.3
1650	–	113.5
1655	–	110.4
1660	–	108.6
1665	134.8	107.2
1670	–	106.7
1675	–	103.1
1680	–	104.5
1685	–	103.9
1690	125.0	105.9
1695	–	108.9
1700	–	115.5
1705	120.4	123.6

Source: See text below.

[98] First stated directly in Irfan Habib, *Agrarian System of Mughal India*, 1st ed., Bombay, 1963, pp. 392–4.

The data we have presented help us to offer a solution to a particular inconsistency in the comparison of *jama'-dāmī* (estimated revenue) of the Mughal empire with the previous estimates of secular price movements. If it is held that the prices greatly increased over the course of the seventeenth century,[99] the *jama'-dāmī* should have gone up considerably, for the *jama'-dāmī* figures tended to be artificially inflated as time passed, so as to be more and more in excess of actual collections,[100] which themselves would have grown as tax collection expanded to keep pace with the rising prices.[101]

Since the *jama'-dāmī* figures are believed to have reflected (with some exaggeration) the extension of cultivation or the increase in population (if the two processes broadly synchronized), Table 2.10 in its column A scales down Irfan Habib's index of *jama'-dāmī* of north Indian provinces by our assumed rate of population increase with the assumed per-capita *jama' dāmī* for 1615 (medial between the 1605 and 1625 figures) taken as base =100.[102] It is set alongside column B which indexes growth in silver stock per-capita with 1615 as base. The latter (column 'B') should better represent the movement of prices after 1615 since we know that the earlier increase in silver stock through the absorption of silver in money supply did not have any effect on the general price-level (in terms of silver).

Reading column B as above, suggests that the *jama'-dāmī* per capita (column A) increased at a greater pace than the rise in price-level in terms of silver (as indicated by changes in silver stock per-capita) until 1690, whereafter, the per capita silver stock began to increase. Since the *jama'* was perhaps always artificially inflated, the actual collections following at a lower level might have broadly kept pace with the increase in prices. There is little room left for any conjecture about the lightening of the fiscal burden in real terms in the latter half of the seventeenth century on this score at any rate.

A study of the *jama' dāmī* statistics, in its turn, suggests a solution of the apparent contradiction between our estimates of the scale of

[99] Irfan Habib in *CEHI*, Vol. I; Aziza Hasan, in *IESHR*, Vol. VI, pp. 104–9. See also Irfan Habib's survey of agricultural prices in *ASMI*, pp.90–102.

[100] *ASMI*, pp.305–7, and M. Athar Ali, *The Mughal Nobility under Aurangzeb*, Bombay, 1966, p. 46.

[101] *ASMI*, pp.367–8.

[102] Ibid., p.375.

the rise of the general price-level in the whole of the Mughal empire and the evidence of the price data from the Agra region. It is the latter data that have mainly given support to the hypothesis of a seventeenth-century price revolution in India. The conclusion that Irfan Habib has drawn from a critical study of agricultural prices of the Agra–Delhi region and eastern Rajasthan is that a great increase in prices occurred between 1610 and the mid-1630s, the price level rising to 1.5 times or double that of 1595. It rose again in the 1660s, but declined in the 1670s, though only to a level that was still above that of the 1630s (and only about 230 per cent of that of 1595).[103] Subsequent price data from eastern Rajasthan suggest secular stability until about 1710 when a great leap upwards in prices took place;[104] but that is outside our period. Here, then, the price-level rose much above the point it should have reached under the sole impetus of the injection of silver into the Indian economy.

Now the *jama‘ dāmī* statistics appear to suggest that this was a more or less regional phenomenon. The *jama‘ dāmī* index of the Agra and Delhi *ṣūbas* and of the Ajmer *ṣūba* also show an increase far above the average for the Empire. Indeed, the increase in the *jama‘ dāmī* of these three *ṣūbas* is by and large consistent with a doubling of prices in the region over the century.

Table 2.11 compared with the previous one shows that the price movements and the increase in the *jama‘ dāmī* in the central or core region of the Empire during the seventeenth century were not representative of the average or general changes for the Empire as a whole. This is not the place to go into the reasons for such regional exceptions or variations, though, given the high costs of transport of bulky goods and other limitations of the technology of the period, these are what one should expect; the draining of tribute from outer regions to the core area should also have had the result of unduly increasing silver-money supply in the Agra–Delhi region, and so raising prices there much more than in other areas. What is directly relevant to my argument is simply the existence of such variations, which means that we would have to assemble price information for individual regions before we can hope to have an accurate depiction of the general movement of prices in the Empire as a whole. Until then the estimates

[103] Irfan Habib in *CEHI*, Vol. I., pp.375-6.

[104] S.P. Gupta, and Shireen Moosvi, 'Weighted Price and Rate Indices in Eastern Rajasthan', *IESHR*, Vol. XII, No. 2, p. 191.

of bullion influx or additions to coined-silver stock together with the gold and copper prices must remain the best sources for determining the approximate scale of that movement.

Table 2.11

Year	*Jama' dāmī*		*Jama'-dāmī* Adjusted to Population-Increase	
	Agra & Delhi	Ajmer	Agra & Delhi	Ajmer
1595–6	100	100	100	100
1605	122	107	120	103
1627	129	146	123	138
1628–36	122	107	120	100
1633–8	146	186	136	173
1646–7	169	208	153	191
1656	254	224	231	204
1667	193	221	173	197
1687–1709	205	225	174	191
1690	206	226	175	191
1709	206	227	175	192

Source: The *jama'-dāmī* indices drawn from *ASMI*, pp.375 and 454–61. The *jama'-dāmī* figures of Agra and Delhi have to be combined because of substantial boundary changes between the two provinces.

The evidence we have adduced so far may help to put the size and influence of the bullion received through the East India companies (English and Dutch) in a proper perspective. The transfer of treasure to India through the activities of the Dutch and English companies before 1660 was by no means substantial when set by the side of treasure imported through other channels; even the additions to Indian silver stock made through the companies' trade after 1660 were not on such a scale as to enhance phenomenally the silver stock already accumulated in India. The silver influx through the companies certainly increased after 1675, but it is, in any case, difficult to find reason for K.N. Chaudhuri's enthusiastic applause at that phenomenon:

The economies of the two great empires of Asia (The Mughal empire and China) greatly benefited from the expansion of economic relations with the West. The

> huge influx of bullion which resulted from the new demand was only one indication of the growth in income and employment. The export of textiles turned the coastal provinces of India into major industrial regions, and the bullion imported by the Companies passed into circulation as payments of export goods.[105]

It is surprising that Chaudhuri should be able to speak of the conversion of certain areas into 'major industrial regions' without any information as to the relative volumes of agricultural and non-agricultural production in these area; and to speak of immense benefits of bullion influx without any proof of how a mere infusion of metal could expand employment in India (unless India re-exported it to obtain capital or wage-goods). Indeed, since silver steadily depreciated in value, India stood to lose a great deal in the long run by receiving and retaining that metal. Finally, even if a simple mercantile approach is adopted, and the import of bullion considered virtuous in itself, it is yet to be established not only that the English and Dutch companies were the main agents in the transfer of American silver to India, but even (in view of the trade through the Levant) that the companies were the irreplaceable media by which Indian exports could reach Europe to meet the expanding demand for them.

Om Prakash follows K.N. Chaudhuri in assuming the same virtues in treasure imports, but he actually goes into quantities. He estimates the 'export surplus' of Bengal 'generated' by the companies' commerce at Rs 3.32 million annually for the period 1709–10 to 1717–18, and then speaks on its basis of an increase in income of the order of 33.54 million rupees per annum.[106] This is not the place to consider in detail the nebulous theoretical basis for this estimate of increase in 'national income' generated by the export surplus channelled through the companies' trade; but surely the assumption that the figures of the influx of bullion for just one decade could apply to the previous century has to be treated with much reserve.[107] For the rest, his arguments are open to the same objections as those of K.N. Chaudhuri.

The influx of treasure by itself could not, then, have caused an absolute increase in total income and internal consumption. But could

[105] K.N. Chaudhuri, *The Trading World of Asia*, p. 462.

[106] Om Prakash, 'Bullion for Goods: International Trade and the Economy of Early Eighteenth Century Bengal', *IESHR*, Vol. XIII, No. 2, pp. 169–78.

[107] Susil Chaudhuri is far more cautious with regard to the impact of the silver brought by the companies in his *Trade and Commercial Organisation in Bengal, 1650–1720*, Calcutta, 1975, pp. 207–10.

it have led to significant internal redistribution of wealth within the economy, notably by adding to merchant capital at the expense of the resources of other classes? Our study raises serious doubts over such a possibility. If the total rise in the price-level owing to monetary phenomena over the seventeenth century was as moderate as we have suggested, namely, about 0.3 per cent per annum at the simple rate, there is little room for the supposition that the distance between prime costs and sale-prices was being constantly enlarged so as to yield abnormally high profits to merchants. In other words, it is not likely that merchant-capital was able to expand at the cost of raw-material producers and artisans, through drawing benefits from inflation. Indeed the rate of monetary inflation (if the term can at all be used) was so low that it would have been largely submerged in the fluctuations in prices caused by variable harvests. Adjustments in prices and wages made for those variations would have easily absorbed the dislocations caused by monetary inflation. It would seem then that it is unlikely to have a significant 'Hamilton factor' working to generate extra profits for merchant capital (and so to provide a source for capital accumulation) in Mughal India.

3

A Note on Interest Rates in the Seventeenth and Early Eighteenth Centuries

A rudimentary history of interest rates in the Mughal period can be constructed almost solely from European accounts. Mughal sources that offer us considerable information on the system of coinage, bills of exchange (*hundī*), and the institution of *ṣarrāf* have unfortunately yielded little on rates of interest.[1]

The data on interest rates from the English records were first collected by Irfan Habib.[2] This collection was subsequently augmented by more data, notably relating to Gujarat (1622–33 and 1701–3) and other regions.[3] Drawing on Dutch records, van Santen has given us considerable information on Gujarat and Agra.[4]

The interest rates in the seventeenth and early eighteenth century can be conveniently assigned to four rather distinct zones, namely, Gujarat, northern India (mainly Agra), Bengal and Orissa, and the Deccan and South India. The interest rates so distinguished can be put on a graph (Fig. 3.1), which shows both the common trends in movement and the disparities between their levels.

[1] Data on the principal and interest to be repaid on loans (*musa'ādāt*) given by Akbar to nobles is given in Abū'l Faẓl, *Ā'īn*, Vol.1, p. 196, but there is no reference to interest rates on commercial loans.

[2] Irfan Habib, 'Usury in Medieval India', *Comparative Studies in Society and History*, Vol. VI, No. 4, The Hague, 1964, pp. 402–4.

[3] The data up till the end of Shāhjahān's reign (1658–9) with full references are set out in Shireen Moosvi, 'The Silver Influx, Money Supply, Prices and Revenue-Extraction in Mughal India', *JESHO*, Vol. XXX, 1987, pp. 373–4.

[4] H.W. van Santen, *De Verenigde Oost-Indische Compagnie in Gujarat en Hindustan*, 1620–1660, Leiden, 1983, Table 13, p. 120. Om Prakash also mentions the borrowings by the Dutch East India Company at Surat on interest and the differences in interest rates in his *European Commercial Enterprise in Pre-Colonial India*, The New Cambridge History of India Series, Cambridge, 1998, pp. 61–4.

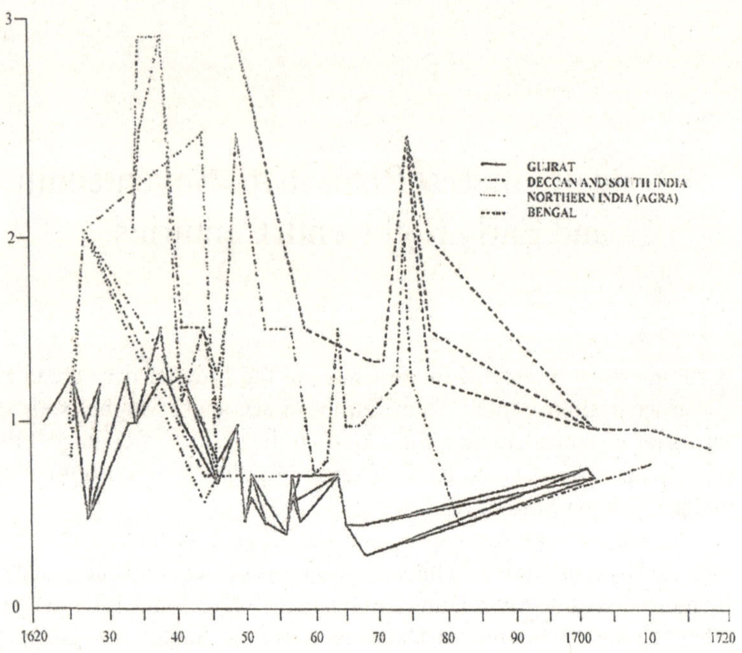

Fig. 3.1: Interest Rates

All the four graph lines depict an unmistakable fall in the interest rates around the middle of the seventeenth century in all the zones, though the scale of decline varies.[5] In Gujarat the monthly rate fluctuated between 1 and 1.25 per cent from 1622 to 1650, barring the rate quoted for 1628 at Ahmadabad where the loan was procured against gold pledged with the lender at 0.5 per cent interest per month.[6] Around 1650 there was a considerable fall: from 1651 to 1703 the rates ranged between 0.33 to 0.8 per cent. At Agra, for which our information is rather meager, a fall seems to have occurred during the course of 1647 when the cost of credit declined from 1–2.5 per cent to 0.625 per cent and did not rise above 0.75 per cent thereafter.

In the Deccan, on the other hand, the interest rates were higher than in Gujarat and Agra. But as in the other two zones, a great fall in

[5] K.N. Chaudhuri rather cursorily remarks that 'there was no long-term downward movement in interest rates in India', *The Trading World of Asia and the English East India Company, 1660–1760*, Cambridge, 1978, p. 159.

[6] W. Foster, ed., *English Factories in India 1624–9*, Oxford, 1906, p. 23.

commercial interest rates seems to have occurred between 1639 and 1642. Before 1642 the rates seem to have always remained higher than 2 per cent, whereas after 1642 the interest per month appears to have varied between 1 and 1.5 per cent, though in some years at Madras it fell below this level, while in the 1670s at Masulipatnam it even touched 2 per cent.

The rates in Bengal for the first half of the seventeenth century are unfortunately not available and there is only one quotation from Bengal (or rather Balasore) for 1650. The subsequent quotations are much lower and a fall in the rates may be inferred for the 1650s. But the monthly rates in Bengal still remained around 1.5 per cent. No information about them is available from the last two decades of the seventeenth century, but during the opening two decades of the eighteenth century the rates apparently remained stable at 1 per cent per month. Thus, even after the decline of rates in Bengal, the interest rates there remained substantially higher than those at Agra and Gujarat. On the basis of information in the records of the Dutch East India Company, Om Prakash also infers that 'the average rate of interest in a money market such as Surat was lower—at times substantially lower—than in a somewhat less developed market such as Hugli in Bengal'.[7]

What do these trends in the movement of interest rates suggest? Not only does the noticeable fall in the rates in all the four zones around the middle of the seventeenth century call for some explanation, but the regional variations in interest rates also demand attention.

The seventeenth-century decline in interest rates was not confined to India; it seems to have been a phenomenon that occurred in Europe as well. It appears from the data collected by Sidney Homer that in England there was a fall from about 10 per cent per annum in the first quarter to less than 6 per cent in the last quarter of the seventeenth century. In Holland too, where the rates were in any case lower than in England, a steady decline took place in the first half of the seventeenth century, the rate falling from 8.5 per cent to 4 per cent per annum, even taking it to below 4 per cent in the next half of the century: the only exceptions were the few years of war. A similar decline in rates also occurred in France and other parts of Europe about the middle of the seventeenth century.[8] Rates of interest appear to have registered a

[7] Om Prakash, *European Commercial Enterprise in Pre-Colonial India*, p. 161.

[8] Sidney Homer, *A History of Interest Rates*, New Brunswick, 1963, pp. 125–9, 139.

steady decline in Italy (Genoa) from the last decade of the sixteenth century onwards, the dip becoming more pronounced in the second decade of the seventeenth century during which these even dipped to below 2 per cent per annum.[9]

It has been suggested that the 'increase in liquidity' which in itself was a result of 'greater supply of precious metal brought down the interest rates in some major financial centres of Europe'.[10] The question arises whether the fall in the interest rates in India at about the same time was a consequence of similar developments. In a perfect market the interest rates should be determined simply by the supply and demand of money. In pre-modern times, prior to the introduction of paper currency, money supply would seem largely to have depended on the availability of precious metals. Here, however, one point must be clarified, since this seems to be missing in many texts where it is simply held that an influx of bullion should normally lower interest rates, in the belief that a rise in prices of commodities must result in a fall of the value of money. In fact, interest rates represent not prices of money but hire-prices of capital. Now if there is an influx of a precious metal, say, silver, and its supply is doubled, leading to a halving of its own price (the prices of commodities being doubled), capital would not really increase in real terms at all, since what was purchased by one kilogram of silver is now purchased by two kilograms. The rate of interest should then not fall at all, because in real terms no more capital has come into the market than before.

Seen in this light it is less easy theoretically to relate the fall of interest rates to the influx of silver during the sixteenth and seventeenth centuries from the Americas.

The silver influx by itself thus would not increase effective money supply and force a reduction in interest rates. If interest rates fall, this could mean either a fall in money demand, for example, through a fall in production, or market orientation. Alternatively, it could follow expansion in money-capital in real terms, that is, an accumulation of silver in lenders' hands which was greater, say, in gold value than before (if gold values remained steady).

The transfer of money capital in large quantities from the Atlantic area to India, through various conduits, during the late sixteenth and seventeenth centuries, is well established and much has been written

[9] Carlo M. Cipolla, *Before the Industrial Revolution, European Society and Economy, 1000–1700*, London, 1976, pp. 227, 229.

[10] Ibid., p. 229.

on it.[11] The imports of silver in the sixteenth and early seventeenth century, according to Irfan Habib, went mainly to replace the copper currency and was absorbed by increasing monetization of the economy through a cash nexus. The value of silver thus did not fall in proportion to the influx of silver.[12] Even after the replacement of copper by silver currency had been mainly completed, that is, during 1615–1705, the increase in prices of gold and copper in terms of silver works out at 33 per cent for gold and 110.4 per cent for copper.[13] Now, if silver largely, served as the medium of payment, it would by the same token not add to capital at all, by merely replacing copper, as it did until 1610, by which time the value of silver had not fallen. In this case, then, there ought to have been no effect on the rate of interest until after 1610. Since, unfortunately, we have practically no information on the movements of interest rates before 1610, this hypothesis cannot be checked with the available data.

The ideal situation would have been if we had with us at least approximate figures of gold, silver, and copper stock in India, say c. 1610, and their annual variations. We would then have been able to determine whether or not the variations in the relative values of the three metals were in proportion to the changes in their stock. Despite an attempt to establish the amount of stock of silver coins that I once undertook,[14] the exercise would be meaningless for our present purpose since there are no similar reconstructions of gold and copper stocks.

We thus deal with the quantitative factor by considering possibilities. Let us begin with the supposition that though the price of silver fell after 1610 it did not fall in proportion to the increase in its supply. This could happen if there was a more-than-proportional increase in the consumption of silver for purposes of hoarding and of making ornaments. It must, however, be pointed out that the English factory records always relate the demand for silver in India to minting rather

[11] Aziza Hasan, 'The Silver Currency Output of the Mughal Empire and Prices in India during the 16th and 17th Centuries', *IESHR*, Vol. VI, No. 196, pp. 85–116; Shireen Moosvi, 'The Silver Influx, Money Supply, Prices and Revenue-Extraction in Mughal India', *JESHO*, Vol. XXX, Part 1, 1987, pp. 373–4; Najaf Haider, 'Precious Metal Flows and Currency Circulation in the Mughal Empire', *JESHO*, Vol. XXXIX, Part 3, 1996, pp. 298–336.

[12] Irfan Habib, 'The System of Trimetallism', in J.F. Richards ed., *The Imperial Monetary System of Mughal India*, Delhi, 1987, pp.139–60.

[13] Shireen Moosvi, *JESHO,* Vol.XXXIX, Part 1, p.35. (revised version in this volume Chapter 2).

[14] Ibid., pp.47–94.

than to hoarding or demand for ornaments. It is unlikely, therefore, that there was any large increase in silver hoarding.

A much more important consideration is the difference in the interest rates between western Europe and India. The large margin of difference would be obvious from the rates in Europe we have already mentioned. The rate of interest in England was reported to be only 4 per cent per annum in 1650, when at Surat (even after the fall in the interest rates) it was 7.5 to 9 per cent per annum according to the factors of the English East India Company, so that, the factors argued, the Company would gain by sending capital to India.[15] If this was so, then there would be a built-in pull for drawing silver to India from the Atlantic to South Asia merely for usurious purposes. Such transfers could exercise a downward pressure on the rates of interest in India. Indeed, in 1682 the Court of Directors of the East India Company claimed that by sending 'great stocks of money' to Surat they had forced down the interest rates prevailing there to as low as 6 per cent per annum (0.5 per cent per month).[16]

The matter requires greater attention to be devoted to it than has hitherto been the case. It is to be borne in mind that it would not be necessary for money-capital to move directly from England, Holland or France to India; it could also move from the Mediterranean through the Levant to India, once the pull was there. Such transfers need to be studied in connection with the Ottoman empire (controlling the Red Sea) and Safavid empire (controlling the Persian Gulf). What we are arguing is that the exports of specie to India did not cover imports of Indian goods to Europe; these also represented, in part, a continuous export of money-capital. If this happened, then the supply of credit in India was bound to expand and force a fall in the interest rates.[17]

A second factor that could explain the fall in interest rates is one that has not so far been considered at all: an increase in the elements of liquidity, or, in other words, territorial and inter-sectoral mobility of money, which for Europe has been held to be a major causal factor in the process. In an early article, Irfan Habib pointed out that in the seventeenth century there were certain striking practices in Indian indigenous banking, in which the *ṣarrāfs* played a key role; there was

[15] Susil Chaudhuri, *Trade and Commercial Organization in Bengal, 1650-1720*, Calcutta, 1975, p.117.

[16] K.N. Chaudhuri, *Trading World of Asia*, p.159.

[17] This paragraph develops a suggestion made by me in *Economy of the Mughal Empire, c. 1595*, Delhi, 1987, p. 374.

extensive deposit banking and insurance provided by the *ṣarrāfs*,[18] along with their issuance and discounting of *hundīs* (bills of exchange). Hundis, being transferable,[19] were crucial to the increase in the liquidity of money-capital.

The problem here, however, is that we do not know if the practices were of recent growth. The fact that these were not evidenced earlier is not decisive when we remember that before Irfan Habib's paper of 1960s, no one had noted the existence of deposit banking and insurance in India in the seventeenth century either.

We may close here with the problem of the regional differences in rates. The difference between North India (Agra and Gujarat) and the Deccan may at first sight be ascribed to the fact that the chief currency metal in the Deccan and South India was gold (since the basic coin for all price quotations was the *hūn*), so that money supply in the Deccan was not likely to be affected as much by the silver influx as in northern India; not, that is, until after the Mughal annexations of Bijapur and Golkonda in 1686 and 1687. Gold supply would have become abundant (relatively) only in so far as silver replaced gold as currency metal in the peripheral areas of the Deccan (bordering the Mughal empire) or in some of the ports. Attractive as this argument may be, it encounters a serious objection in that we are concerned not with money supply, but with supply of capital in real, not nominal, magnitudes; and this would not be affected by the South Indian coinage being in gold. Indeed, one may argue that, with Gresham's law operating, gold would be driven out of the Mughal empire as more silver flowed in to be minted into rupees; and there then might have been an actual gold influx into the southern states.

I should rather see the higher level of the rates in South India to lie in the lack of development of those financial practices of which we have spoken above. Arasaratnam, in his detailed study of seventeenth-century mercantile organization in South India, fails to record any institution of brokerage in South India.[20] If deposit banking in India is seen essentially as an extension of brokerage practices, the absence of brokerage could suggest a relative lack of liquidity, and this in turn

[18] Irfan Habib, 'Banking in Mughal India', T. Raychaudhuri, ed., *Contributions to Indian Economic History*, Calcutta, 1960, pp. 1–20.

[19] Irfan Habib, 'The System of Bills of Exchange (Hundis) in the Mughal Empire', *PIHC*, 33rd Session, Muzaffarpur, 1973, pp. 290–303.

[20] S. Arasaratnam, *Merchants, Companies and Commerce on the Coromandel Coast 1650-1740*, Delhi, 1986.

could be a better explanation of higher interest rates in South India.

The prevalence of high rates of interest in Bengal is rather more difficult to explain. One possibility is that there was a steady drain of revenues from Bengal from the imperial *khālişa* lands and *jāgīrs* of nobles to the capital seats of the Mughal empire. But whether this required a continuous loss of specie is questionable. If there was commerce of a sufficiently large volume by which the monetary circuit was completed by a corresponding amount of purchases, of 'exports' to the other parts of the Mughal empire, no large amount of specie (in the net) need have actually been transported out of Bengal. The loss of specie that Grant and Shore supposed to have occurred during the first half of the eighteenth century when, during some years, about a crore of rupees were annually remitted by the Niẓāms of Bengal to the Mughal Court,[21] need not really have taken place. We would then have to look for factors other than specie movements. One possibility not to be ignored is that the fall in interest rates to the levels of Agra and Gujarat was obstructed by the need for extra capital owing to the great expansion of silk trade, which made Bengal, in the latter half of the seventeenth century, into one of the great silk-exporting regions of the world.[22]

I should like to end by admitting that by the very nature of our evidence there is a great deal of speculation involved in all the points I have made; but, while our search for relevant data proceeds, there is also the need to seek clarity on the causative factors behind the economic processes of the seventeenth century. My purpose would be served if this note brings into focus the problems involved when one seeks to go behind observable facts, like the movements of interest rates.

[21] Fifth Report from the Select Committee on the Affairs of the East India Company with an Appendix and Glossary to the Report, 1812–13; Irish University Press, Series of *British Parliamentary Papers, Colonies: East India 3*, Shannon, Ireland, 1969, p. 321, lines 6–10, (Grant). Shore, in his Minute, agrees that the money must have come back by channels of trade; yet, he cites Grant for the figure of Rs 8.12 crore as being sent out to Delhi within a period of ten and a half years during Shujauddin Khan's viceroyalty; some more might have been sent, he says, to meet bills at Delhi (ibid., p. 183, paragraphs 133 and 134). Apparently, he supposes the specie to have been transported back physically to pay for Bengal exports.

[22] Susil Chaudhuri, *Trade and Commercial Organization in Bengal, 1650–1720*, Calcutta, 1975, pp.114–25.

ECOLOGY, DEMOGRAPHY AND GENDER

4

Ecology, Population Distribution, and Settlement Pattern in Mughal India

A basic shift in ecology occurs in all agricultural societies whenever the plough makes inroads into the forest or grassland. There are other man-made factors too which reduce and otherwise affect the domain of nature, such as timber-cutting and overgrazing; but it is the limits of the agricultural zone which constitute the main frontier between the territories of nature and of man. The ecological change since AD 1600 can therefore be grasped, in general terms at least, by tracing the extent of cultivation at that time, with a view to comparing it with what it has come to be in more recent times.

An important statistical record exists for computing the extent of cultivated land around c. 1600. The *Ā'īn-i-Akbarī*, the gazetteer of Akbar's Empire compiled by his minister Abū'l Faẓl, gives us measured area (*ārāẓī*) statistics for the whole of northern India (except some parts of Bihar, Bengal, Sind, and Kashmir). Moreland and Habib made use of these figures to work out the extent of cultivation in Akbar's time,[1] and I have tried to go over the same ground again.[2]

The estimates worked out by me have been for the cultivated area in only three regions of Akbar's Empire:[3] *(a)* UP, comprising the Mughal *ṣūbas* of Awadh, Allahabad, most of Agra, and parts of Delhi; *(b)* Gujarat, excluding Kutch and Saurashtra (the Mughal *ṣūba* and the present state of Gujarat had practically identical boundaries); and *(c)* the British province of the Panjab, consisting of the Mughal *ṣūba* of Delhi west of the Yamuna, provinces of Lahore and Multan, excluding the sarkār of Bhakkar [See Maps. 4.1 (a), (b), and (c)].

[1] W.H. Moreland, *India at the Death of Akbar*, London, 1930, pp.20–2; *ASMI*, pp.12–15.

[2] *EME*, 1987, pp.39–71.

[3] The *Ā'īn-i Akbarī* also gives measured area figures for parts of Rajasthan and Madhya Pradesh but as these are incomplete, a reliable estimate is not possible.

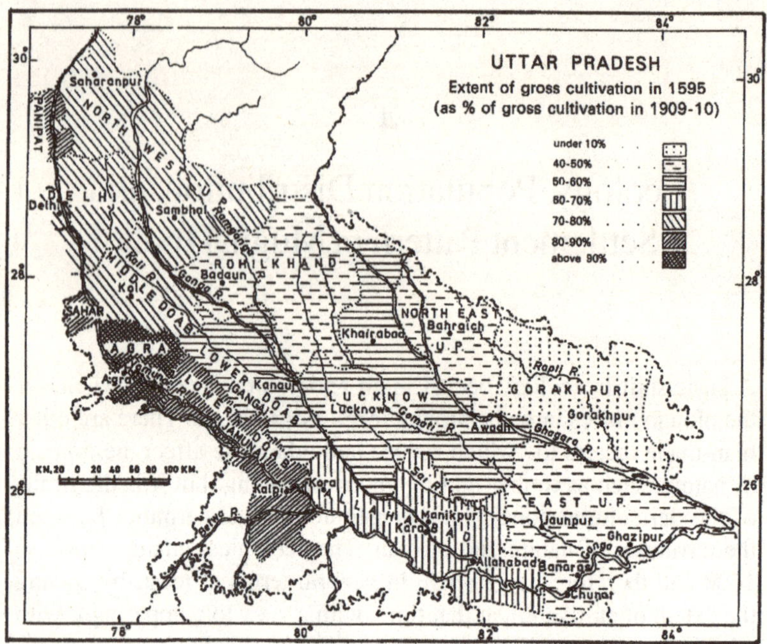

Map 4.1(a): Uttar Pradesh: Extent of Gross Cultivation in 1595 (As % of Gross Cultivation in 1909-10)

(a) Within the large tract corresponding to UP the proportion of the total area under cultivation in c. 1600 varied greatly from one part to another. In the revenue-circle of Agra, cultivation was almost as high as in 1909–10; in the lower Yamuna Doab and North-West U.P., it was above 80 per cent of what it was in 1909–10. Of the other hand, the area between the Ghaghara and the Ganga was much less densely cultivated, the area under cultivation amounting, in 1600, to 40 to 60 per cent of that in 1909–10. In the extreme northeastern block of Gorakhpur, on the other hand, cultivation in c.1600 was so sparse as to cover less than 10 per cent of the sown area in 1909–10.

(b) In Gujarat some parts were already highly cultivated. In Baroda, Surat and Nadaut the extent of cultivated land reached almost 90 per cent of what it was in 1903–4. In Ahmadabad it was 68 per cent, but in Patan, only around 43 per cent. The cultivated area was the lowest in the sarkārs of Champaner and Godhra (28 per cent and 37 per cent respectively of the 1903–4 level).

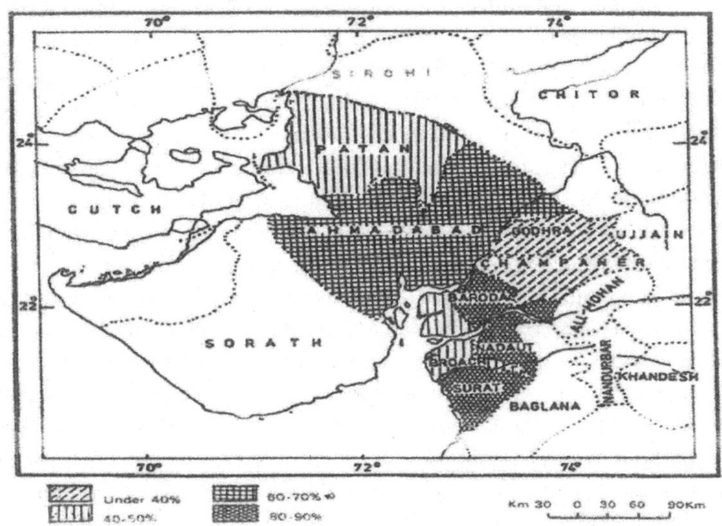

Map.4.1(b): Gujarat: Extent of Gross Cultivation in 1595 (As % of Gross Cultivation in 1903-4)

(c) The extent of cultivation in East Panjab, that is, the Mughal sarkārs of Rewari, Hissar Firuza, Sirhind, and Delhi west of the Yamuna, was about 45 per cent and in Multan a little over a quarter of the cultivated area in 1909–10. In West Panjab, comprising all the territory west of the Sutlej, cultivation in c. 1600 was nearly 40 per cent of what it was in 1909–10.

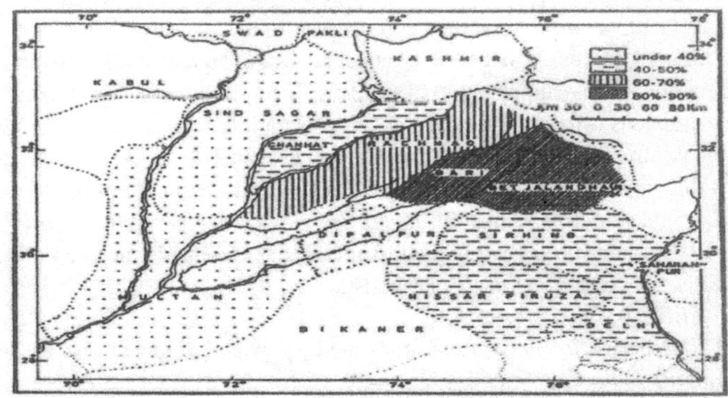

Map 4.1(c): Panjab: Extent of Gross Cultivation in 1595 (As % of Gross Cultivation in 1909-10)

If one can generalize from these samples covering around a third of the total area of Akbar's Empire, the extent of cultivation in Mughal India might be put at 50 to 55 per cent of what it was in the opening decade of the twentieth century.[4] A doubling of the extent of cultivation during the three centuries since 1600 must have meant an immense retreat of forest and wasteland. The retreat, however, has been on varying scales in particular zones or localities. The middle Doab (in Western UP) was already practically fully cultivated by c. 1600. The extensive stretches of forest, which were once found here—in the thirteenth century, a traveller faced the danger of encountering tigers in the area—had by now been cleared.[5] Pelsaert particularly notices a lack of trees in the countryside, the surest sign of forest clearance.[6]

The very large sarkārs of Gorakhpur (East UP) were 'full of forest' in the middle of the seventeenth century.[7] Here forests large enough to harbour wild elephants are recorded down to the beginning of the nineteenth century.[8] The increase of cultivation by over tenfold in this region, as indicated by our area statistics, has been almost entirely at

[4] These estimates are criticized by Neeladri Bhattacharya, in *Studies in History*, Vol. 14, No.2, 1998, pp.168–70, on the basis of an elementary misunderstanding. After correctly repeating that my estimates of the cultivated area for c.1600 put it at a little over half of what it was in c.1900, he goes on to treat it thereafter as half of the total map area! He then goes on to point out that since in the 1880s actual cultivation, according to 'the Duke University project', occupied only 32 per cent of the total area, my estimate of cultivation must be wrong! If the situation in the 1880s represented, for argument's sake, the one in c.1900, then according to my estimate the actual cultivation would have occupied only 16 per cent. of the total area in c.1600. K.K. Trivedi's estimate, putting it at 28 per cent, would then set the extent of cultivation at a much higher proportion of the total area, than my estimates. It is besides the point that both Bhattacharya and Trivedi totally disregard the large amount of documentary evidence that I had presented in *EME*, Chapter 2 . An example is offered by Bhattacharya's declaration (with no data given) that in colonial times the area under the category of cultivable waste did not at all expand with the expansion of cultivation (p.169n.) despite the data offered by me in *EME*, Table 2.3 (p.45) that this is precisely what happened between 1909–10 and 1946–7 in districts where the cultivable area represented a small proportion of the total area, according to official statistics.

[5] *CEHI*, p.48.

[6] F. Pelsaert, *Remonstrantie*, translated by W.H. Moreland and P. Geyl as *Jahangir's India,* Cambridge, 1925, p.48.

[7] Jean-Baptiste Tavernier, *Travels in India*, translated by V. Ball, edited by W. Crooke, Vol.II, London, 1925, p.20.

[8] Ghulām Ḥaẓrat, *Kawā'if-i Ẓila' Gorakhpur*, 1810, MS. I.O. 4540, f.9b.

the expense of these forests.

If in the Gangetic basin too the advance of the plough has been at the expense of forest, towards the west it has been largely at the expense of desert, grassland and scrub.

In the Haryana block of British Panjab the extent of cultivation was two-fifths of what it was in 1901–10. But there are no forests here beyond the thin sub-montane tract. In the sixteenth–seventeenth centuries, imperial hunting grounds, where cheetahs were caught, were located in the *sarkārs* of Hissar Firuza and Sirhind. The *Ā'īn* notes the existence of desert in the southwestern part of *sarkār* Hissar Firuza,[9] as is indeed the case today as well. In this region the introduction of canal irrigation in the last quarter of the nineteenth century helped to extend cultivation over dry grassland. But the impact of the introduction of canal irrigation has been more spectacular in Western Panjab. In the *sarkārs* of Multan and Dipalpur, cultivation in c. 1600 comprised only a quarter of the cultivated area at the beginning of the present century. A large part of the area was covered by extensive dryland. But there was also jungle like the Lakhi jungle in *sarkār* Dipalpur, created by flood-channels of the Beas and Sutlej rivers.[10] The Lakhi jungle has now disappeared, and much dry wasteland (previously serving for pastures) brought under cultivation with water from the canals. Some areas, e.g., in Sind, have been cultivated by directly reclaiming tracts from the Thar Desert.

The retreat of the forest in the face of the peasant's plough can also be established for different areas from direct contemporary evidence about forests where they no longer exist. Abū'l Faẓl in his description of the geography of the provinces of Akbar's Empire, gives an account of the forests as well. Other Mughal historians often mention forests in their accounts of the topography of the regions where Mughal arms penetrated. European travellers too have left records of forests they had to pass through on their journeys. Much of this information has been collected and represented in the notes and maps of Irfan Habib's *Atlas of the Mughal Empire*. Sheets 8B, 10B and 11B of the *Atlas* show these forests in greater detail, presumably because for this region (UP, Bihar, and Bengal), James Rennel's mapping of forests is available as a kind of floor-line. By

[9] *Ā'īn*, p.257.

[10] Sujān Rai Bhandārī, *Khulāṣatu-t Tawārīkh*, edited by Zafar Hasan, Delhi, 1918, p.63.

about 1780, Rennel had prepared maps of the Gangetic Basin on the basis of what later official mappers would have called 'reconnaissance survey'; and these showed forests as they then existed.[11]

On the basis of Sheets 8B and 10B of the *Atlas*, I have prepared a map of forests, c. 1600, in the upper and middle Gangetic Basins (Map 4.2).

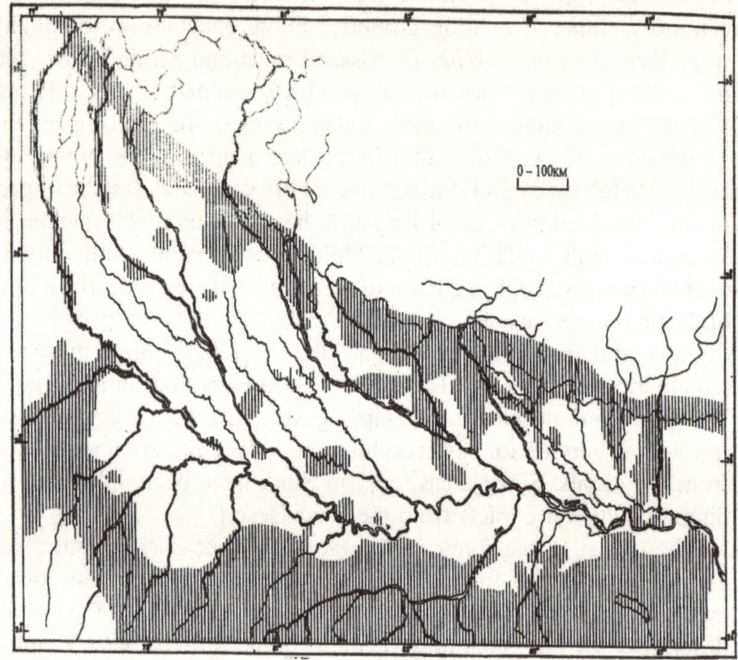

Map 4.2: Upper & Middle Gangetic Basin: Forests & Scrub (Excluding Himalayan Forests) 17th Century

Map 4.2.incorporates some additions for southern Awadh based on Butter's report on the topography of the area.[12] He reports 'an immense forest' in Pratapgarh and another of three miles diameter in Salon (UP). Butter distinguishes two types of forests in the region: one occupying lowlands annually overflowed by the Ganga and Deoha, which could not be reclaimed for cultivation; such forests lay mainly

[11] James Rennel, *Bengal Atlas*, London, 1781,

[12] Donald Butter, *Outlines of the Topography and Statistics of Southern Districts of Oudh and the Cantonment of Sultanpur Oudh*, Calcutta, 1839, pp.116–25.

in Bainswara. The other type of forests were more numerous but more vulnerable to encroachments. The land being very fertile these forests, usually interspersed with stretches of cultivation, were already fast disappearing. A large forest (20 by 8 miles), in the vicinity of Manikpur, had by then been almost entirely cleared within the short span of four years between 1833 and 1837. However, there were still some 'silvan' stretches near Niwardipur, Faizabad, Pali, and Rudauli that were deliberately preserved either for pasturage or as possible places for refuge by the zamindars. These forests were mostly dry and therefore free of wild elephants.

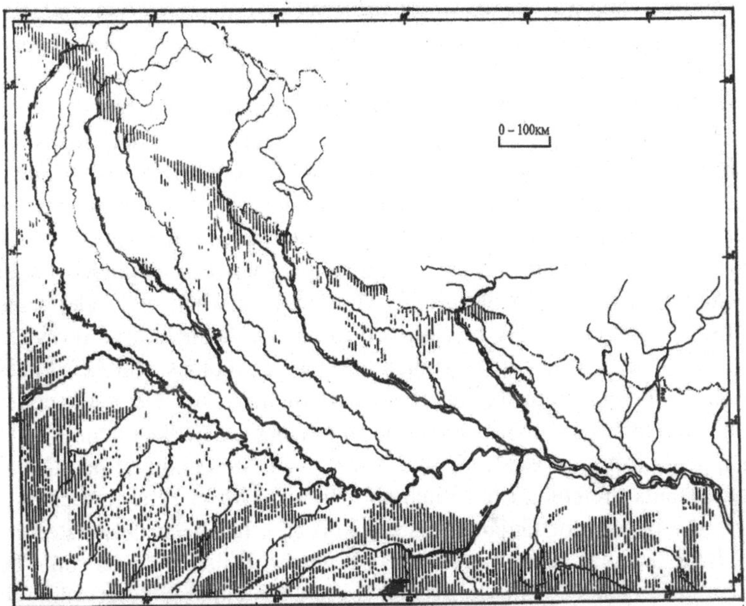

Map 4.3: Upper & Middle Gangetic Basin: Forests & Scrub (Excluding Himalayan Forests) 1951

The Map 4.3. is based on the *National Atlas of India* (sheets 102–5) and shows the area covered by forest and scrub in the same region till 1951. Both Maps 4.2 and 4.3 omit depiction of forests in the Himalayas and north of the India–Nepal frontier. A comparison of Maps 4.2 and 4.3 shows that the *Tarai* forests, which was very broad and continuous in the seventeenth century right from Purnea in Bihar to Bahraich in Awadh (UP) have disappeared in the east (south of the India–Nepal frontier), while the remaining stretch of *Tarai* now survives in broken fragments and strips. In the seventeenth century, the forest line curved sharply southwards to enclose much of Rohilkhand. Further east, the forest pierced the Ghaghara. But now only a little of it survives north of the Ghaghara, and none to its south. All stretches of forest and scrub scattered in South Awadh as late as 1837 have been completely cleared. The forests of Central India showed a less dramatic change by c.1900, though the withdrawal and fragmentation here too was very considerable.

Evidence regarding the presence of animals such as wild elephants, cheetahs, and wild buffalo is also of help in identifying certain areas as forests and wastelands where these species flourish. Such evidence enables us to extend our study of forest and grassland zones beyond the Gangetic Basin as well.

The presence of wild elephants offers, perhaps, the firmest evidence about forests. There would, of course, be forests without elephants, but there could be no wild elephants without dense stretches of forest, undulating or hilly ground and fresh water streams. Since on an average an elephant consumes about 200 kg of green fodder a day, and wastes an equal amount in the process, a small, sparse, or degraded forest cannot sustain elephant herds.[13] Thus regions where wild elephants were found can safely be assumed to have contained large forests.

Elephants were much sought after in Mughal times, and Abū'l Faẓl offers in detail information about tracts where wild elephants could be caught.[14] This evidence can be supplemented by later sources.[15] It appears from our evidence that a wide belt containing herds of wild elephants stretching from Bihar and Orissa to Malwa and further west to the borders of Gujarat existed. This belt has been designated by Habib as the 'Great Central Indian Forest'.[16] Wild elephants could be caught in the areas of Dohad and Rajpipla in Gujarat.[17] According to the author of the *Mi'rāt-i Aḥmadī,* sometime before 1761 wild elephants no longer came to Rajpipla because their 'forest route' linking Rajpipla with Malwa had been cut off by human settlements.[18] Now the forests

[13] S. Israel and T. Sinclair, eds, *Indian Wildlife, Srilanka, Nepal,* Singapore, n.d., p.83.

[14] *Ā'īn*, Vol.I, p.132.

[15] *Atlas*, Sheet 4B, 8B–11B, 13B–16B and notes on these sheets.

[16] Ibid., p.38.

[17] 'Abdu'l Ḥamīd Lāhorī, *Bādshāhnāma*, edited by K. Ahmad, A. Rahim and W.N. Lees, Vol. I, Calcutta, 1866–72, p.331.

[18] 'Alī Muḥammad K͟hān, *Mi'rāt-i Aḥmadī*, edited by Nawab Ali, Vol. I, Baroda, 1927, p.214.

in Malwa and much of Madhya Pradesh have become so fragmented and sparse that the area where wild elephants can roam have been reduced to the border districts of Madhya Pradesh and Orissa. In the Deccan, wild elephants roamed near Tirupati: none are found here today. Another Map 4.4 brings out the extent of the retreat of elephant-forests all over India since c. 1600.[19]

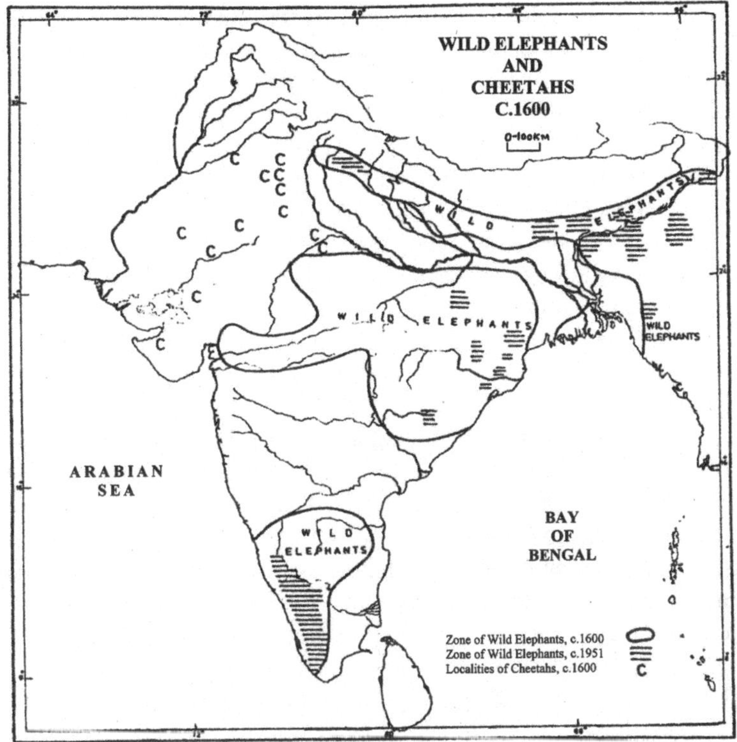

Map 4.4: Wild Elephants and Cheetahs c.1600

Mughal Emperors were very fond of hunting. Akbar had cheetahs caught to be tamed and used in hunting deer. The localities where these animals were caught are therefore well documented in Mughal accounts. The cheetah's habitat lies not in thick tree forests, but in rocky tracts or low rugged hills bordering on wastelands and land with tall grass where he could find his prey. Cheetahs were found in

[19] The depiction of the limits of the zone of wild elephants and localities of Cheetah c.1600 on this map (Fig.4.4).

West Panjab in the Lakhi jungle on the northern bank of the Sutlej, and in the territories of Pattan, Bhatnair, Bhatinda and Sunam, where imperial hunting grounds were located. The other localities of cheetahs in Rajasthan were the scrub in close proximity of rocky regions or desert at Jodhpur, Merta, Nagaur, Jhunjhunu and Amarsar. Cheetahs were also found in Gujarat, near Patan and Navanagar, and within Madhya Pradesh, in or near the Chambal ravines, close to Gwalior. While it is possible that human preying on deer has been responsible for the cheetah's extinction in India, a great reduction in grassland owing to the expansion of cultivation might be a more probable cause.

Another animal to consider is the wild buffalo whose presence attests the existence of swamps and large expanses of wastelands with tall grass or drier grounds drained by nullahs and scattered trees. In the sixteenth–seventeenth centuries wild buffaloes were found in Awadh.[20] As late as the 1830s their presence is attested in southern Awadh.[21] An Uzbek traveller noticed large herds of them, near Burdwan in Jahangir's reign.[22] Manucci found them in the Sundarbans in Bengal.[23] At present, wild buffaloes are found in none of these areas, being confined to Assam, North Bihar and parts of southern Madhya Pradesh.

Some evidence is forthcoming about the presence of rhinoceros in regions where it is now absolutely unknown. For example, Abū'l Faẓl reports its presence in sarkār Sambhal.[24] However, there are two distinct species of this animal in India with totally different habitats, namely, the great one-horned rhinoceros, which being a grazer lives in tall grass jungles in swampy and marshy ground, and the lesser one-horned species that is found in swampy forests since it is not a grazer but a browser.[25] The evidence about rhinoceros is not of much help to us in establishing the presence of dense forests.

The impact of this immense change in the extent of forest and grassland has naturally had far-reaching consequences for the

[20] *Āīn*, Vol. I, p.433.

[21] Butter, p.5.

[22] Maḥmūd b. Amīr Walī Balkhī, *Baḥr-ul-Aṣrar*, (c.1640) edited by Riazul Islam, Karachi, 1980, pp.30—1.

[23] Manucci, *Storia*, Vol.II, p.87.

[24] *Āīn*, Vol.I, p.514.

[25] B.K. Tekadar, *Threatened Animals of India*, Calcutta, 1983, pp.89—91.

economy. The much larger extent of forest in Mughal times must have provided certain important products. First, there was a larger supply of timber for construction and ship building, fire-wood, charcoal, gum lac, and tasar silk. Second, animals such as wild elephants were economically important when caught not only as war animals but also as beasts of burden. Cheetahs were caught and trained to hunt deer, and were much in demand from the Imperial Court and the aristocracy.

The forests in the proximity of Agra and Lahore provided 150,000 *mans* of fire-wood annually to the imperial household alone. For bringing this quantity 600 carts were reserved.[26] In the 1680s timber worth Rs 5000 was brought from Khelaghar in Dehradun to Delhi for use in construction of a noble's house.[27] It was the abundant supply of good quality teak wood from the forest in southern Gujarat in the seventeenth century[28] that made a revolutionary change in the ship-building industry possible in Surat and neighbouring ports at that time.[29]

Certain forest products have now lost their importance. In the 1860s Cunningham complained that as a result of the gradual disappearance of the 'great forest of Narwar' (Madhya Pradesh) there was a steep increase in prices of charcoal and thereby in prices of iron and some other local manufactures.[30] (Coke produced from coal mines in eastern India was to become amply available to provide a substitute for charcoal only later).

The large area under scrub and forest in c.1600 implied the meant availability of larger tracts of pasture. The fact that four oxen, two cows and one buffalo were allowed free of tax per plough in Akbar's time[31] suggests that the livestock available to the peasant in Mughal India was considerably larger than what his successor had in the opening years of this century. The presence of scrub in close proximity of cultivated zone was ideal for cattle grazing. The ground underneath trees remained thickly covered with grass from the end of June to the

[26] *Ā'īn*, Vol.I, pp.151—2.

[27] Malikzāda *Nigārnāma-i Munshī*, Lucknow, 1882, p.146.

[28] *English Factories, 1668,* pp.65 and 69.

[29] Irfan Habib, 'Change in Technology in Medieval India', *Studies in History*, Vol. II, No. 1, 1980, pp.37—8.

[30] A. Cunningham, *Archaeological Survey of India*, Annual Report, Vol. II, Calcutta, 1864, p.325.

[31] *Ā'īn*, Vol. I, p.287.

middle of January while in the remaining part of the year fodder was provided by fallen leaves. Areas of scrub were also used as breeding grounds for cattle.[32] The larger numbers of cattle relative to ploughed area naturally implied more manure for agriculture even if cattle droppings were not accumulated and part of them was used as fuel.

The smaller size of land under the plough not only implied a favourable land–man ratio but also made possible a shifting of fields to avoid decline in fertility on account of continuous cultivation. In other words, there could be a larger extent of fallows and an easing of pressure on the soil.

From the uninhabited we may now pass on to examine the inhabited zone which, as we have seen, was far more constricted in c. 1600 than in c. 1900.

About the geographical distribution of population one can perhaps only speculate broadly on the basis of the varying degrees of extent of cultivation in different regions that we have already discussed. The level of agricultural technology remaining largely constant between 1600 and 1900, one may legitimately assume a higher concentration of population in areas where a larger proportion of land had been brought under the plough relative to the beginning of the twentieth century. Based on this criterion, the middle Doab seems to have been most thickly populated while the population density in Rohilkhand and eastern UP seems to have been much lower. Another densely populated area of the Mughal empire was Gujarat (excluding Saurashtra). Even on this general level, we can only make an assumption for a limited area of the Empire for which the measured area figures are available. We can, however, form a better idea by comparing the number of villages in various regions in Aurangzeb's time and in 1881.[33]

Interestingly enough the number of villages in Aurangzeb's time in most areas was either appreciably higher than or equal to what it was in 1881. In Bengal, Bihar, Sind, Kashmir and Khandesh, villages in the seventeenth century were as many as in 1881. But in the *ṣūbas* of Awadh, Allahabad and Malwa the number of villages was much higher than in 1881. The villages in Agra, as counted in 1881 were only two-thirds of the numbers reported for the later part of the seventeenth century. In *ṣūba* Delhi this tendency is more pronounced, the number

[32] W.H. Moreland, *Notes on the Agricultural Conditions of the United Provinces and Its Districts*, Allahabad, 1913, pp.1—27.

[33] *ASMI*, pp.11—7.

of villages in 1881 being only one-half of what they were under Aurangzeb. For Ajmer the figures are incomplete but the village lists in Nainsī's *Vigat* indicate that the number of villages in western Rajasthan remained almost constant between the seventeenth and the close of the nineteenth century.[34]

Taking into account the extent of cultivation in these regions one may legitimately infer that the size of villages in Mughal times was on the average much smaller. The population grew from about 145 million in c. 1601[35] to 285 million in 1881.[36] Assuming that there was no big change in the relative distribution of population, one should have expected a corresponding increase in the number of villages if the size of the average village remained the same. Therefore, even if the number of villages remained constant between c. 1700 and 1881, one can safely assume that the average size of villages in Mughal times was about a half of what it was in 1881; and if there were more villages in c. 1600, the average size must have been smaller still. Presumably, where the number of villages had decreased, smaller settlements have been absorbed by the expansion of the larger ones, or have been abandoned altogether. Given these changes, the fields in the Mughal times must ordinarily have tended to be closer to the village sites (and so implied a smaller loss of time in going to the field) than in recent times.

The Mughal empire could well boast of a number of towns that compared with, if they did not exceed, the larger cities of the world in size. Besides these big towns and cities there were a number of smaller towns that were mainly administrative headquarters where the houses were built largely of mud with thatched roofs. Roe reported that between Burhanpur and Surat the 'towns and villages are all built of mudd'.[37] Even in the major towns of the Empire such as Delhi, besides the imperial buildings the use of burnt brick was confined to only a few houses belonging to grandees. As to the other houses belonging to 'petty omrahs, officers of justice, rich merchants and others very few are built entirely of brick or stone, and several are made of clay and straw'. The lower classes, of course, had thatch-roofed mud

[34] Ibid., pp.17—8.

[35] *EME*, p.405.

[36] Kingsley Davis, *Population of India and Pakistan*, Princeton, 1951, p.24.

[37] Thomas Roe, *The Embassy of Sir Thomas Roe, 1615-1619,* edited by W. Foster, London, 1926, p.137.

houses which were liable to be destroyed by the thousand by fire during summer.[38]

Thus while the towns would not have been impressive looking and probably appeared more 'a collection of many villages',[39] the smaller use of burnt bricks would have avoided the adverse impact of brick kilns which today so badly scar the soil and adversely affect horticulture.

On balance, if the changes in ecology have affected the 'human capital' adversely, the situation four centuries ago too was by no means ideal. In spite of all the advantages of favourable land–man ratio and larger number of cattle, the vagaries of nature and the cruelties of man could precipitate famines carrying away hundreds of thousands, if not millions. The 'law of the jungle' prevailed in much of human society.

Quite obviously, if one must look back with a certain sadness at how much of Nature we have lost since 1600, one must at the same time realize that there can be little joy in a peace with Nature, not accompanied by a humane treatment of man by man.

[38] F. Bernier, *Travels in the Mughal Empire 1656-68*, edited by A. Constable, London, 1916, pp.214—6.

[39] Ibid.

5

Data on Mughal-Period Vital Statistics
A Preliminary Survey of Usable Information

The circumstances in which the Mughal empire declined and was destroyed has meant that its major central and provincial archives have perished with only a few survivals. That these archives both of the Mughals at the centre and provinces and of their subordinate principalities were rich, with much material from detailed surveys is known to us from material derived from them by Abū'l Faẓl in his *Ā'īn-i Akbarī* (c. 1595), by Nainsī in his *Vigat* for Marwar (c. 1664) and by 'Alī Muḥammad Khān, the author of *Mir'āt-i Aḥmadī*, for Gujarat (c. 1761), and incidentally or fragmentarily by other contemporary historians and travellers. Even greater evidence of its richness is provided by the few survivals we have just referred to, especially seventeenth century archives from the Mughal provinces of the Deccan (preserved in the AP Record Office, Hyderabad and the Inayat Jang Collection, National Archives, New Delhi) and the records of the Amber principality in the Rajasthan State Archives, Bikaner. But these materials, while a delight for a historian concerned with agrarian economy and administration, give us little information of relevance for determining mortality and life expectation rates. Women and children, were not counted for even the poll-tax (*jizya*), after the imposition of the tax in 1679. The 'absolutely poor' were also excluded, being exempt from the *jizya*. The tax, of course, did not apply to Muslims. Thus even aggregate population change in any particular area cannot be easily calculated. The major short-run index of population growth can only be the change in the recorded cultivated/cultivable area and the size of real tax-collection. This is of course based on the assumption of a constant man:sown-land ratio or a constant man:tax ratio, both of which in the long-terms would be questionable.

I, therefore, thought that one might explore other kinds of information, with which European historical demography is very familiar, namely, the history of births and deaths in families for whose individual members, detailed history is available. By its very nature this is bound to confine us to the Mughal imperial family, and a very limited number of other families; but, after all, in the case of medieval western Europe too it is the ducal, not peasant families, with which beginning has been made in this field.[1]

On the Mughal imperial family the official histories often record births and deaths of princes and princesses and their marriages quite punctiliously, at least, until the reign of Shāhjahān. On emperor Bābur's children, his daughter Gulbadan's memoirs[2] besides his own,[3] provide more or less full information. Abū'l Faẓl's merit is that he not only supplements these data but offers the most reliable account for the offspring of Humāyūn, Akbar, Jahāngīr and his brothers (Murād and Dāniyāl) in Akbar's reign.[4] The comprehensiveness of his evidence can be realized simply from the fact that while Jahāngīr himself mentions only two of his daughters and contents himself by stating that 'several other children had been born to me and had been received into God's mercy',[5] Abū'l Faẓl reports seven more daughters, that is nine in all. The births of Shāhjahān's children are recorded in the *Bādshāhnāmas* of Qazwīnī[6] and Lāhorī[7] as well as in the history of Shāhjahān's reign by Ṣāliḥ.[8] These works are also our source of information though perhaps not complete for the offspring of Shāhjahān's brothers, namely, K͟husrau, Parwēz and Shahryār as well as his sons, Aurangzeb, Dārā Shukōh and Shāh Shujā'. The *Ma'āṣir-i 'Ālamgīrī* has supplementary information on births of Aurangzeb's

[1] S. Peller, 'Studies on Mortality since the Renaissance'; T.R. Edmonds, 'On Duration of Life in the English Peerage'; T.H. Hollingsworth, 'A Demographic Study of the British Ducal Families' in *Population Studies*, Vol. IX, London, 1957.

[2] Gulbadan Begum, *Humāyūn Nāma*, edited and translated by A.S. Beveridge, London, 1902.

[3] *Bāburnāma*, translated by A.S. Beveridge, 2 vols., London, 1921.

[4] *AN*, 3 vols.

[5] *Tuzuk-i Jahāngīrī*, edited by S. Ahmad, Ghazipur and Aligarh, 1863–4, p. 6.

[6] Amīn Qazwīnī, *Badshāhnāma*, transcript of MS Raza Library, Rampur, in Department of History, Aligarh.

[7] 'Abdul Ḥamīd Lāhorī, *Badshāhnāma*, Bib. Ind. Calcutta, 1866–72.

[8] M. Ṣāliḥ Kamboh, *'Amal-i Ṣāliḥ*, edited by G. Yazdani, 4 vols. Bib. Ind. Calcutta, 1912–46.

children. The *Akhbārāt-i Darbār-i Mu'allā* in the India Office Library, London, and the Rajasthan State Archives at Bikaner, contain information of the most dependable nature on births, deaths and marriages in the imperial family from Aurangzeb's reign onward. Unfortunately, I have not yet been able to sift this last mass of evidence.

One realizes that much more spadework needs to be undertaken before one can confidently step into a field on which practically no work has been done so far. Moreover, these statistics suffer from certain lacuna, as for example, in the case of princesses, where, possibly, there is no comprehensive reporting of births of children to them. This is besides the fact that in the seventeenth century many princesses did not marry, as part of imperial policy. We have, therefore, to confine ourselves to the 'male-tree' only.

The data, as far as available, on births, deaths, and marriages of the Mughal imperial family from Bābur to Aurangzeb and their sons other than the succeeding monarchs are set out in the Appendix 5.1 (with full reference). A summary statement is given in Table 5.1.

Table 5.1

	Son	Died in Infancy	Daughters	Died in Infancy	Total Born	Total died in Infancy
Bābur	10	5	7	3	17	8
Humāyūn	5	3	9	3	14	6
Akbar	5	2	4	0	9	2
Jahāngīr	6	2	9	8	15	10
Murād	2	2	1	0	3	2
Dāniyāl	4	1	4	0	8	1
Shāhjahān	9	5	6	3	15	8
Khusrau	3	1	?	?	3	1
Parvez	2	2	1	0	3	2
Shahryār	0	0	1	0	1	0
Aurangzeb	5	0	5	1	10	1
Dārā Shukoh	3	?	2	?	5	?
Shāh Shujā'	2	?	2	?	4	?

Let us begin with Table 5.1 for infant mortality. We learn specifically that Bābur (b. 1483; d. 1530) had from his five wives seventeen children of whom ten were sons and seven daughters. Out of the ten sons, five died in infancy and of seven daughters, three did not survive to adulthood. Thus the infant mortality rate in the case of his children was 47.1 per cent (50 per cent for males and 42.9 per cent for females). Of Humāyūn (b. 1506; d. 1556), as many as three out of five sons did not survive, while three out of nine daughters died in infancy. Thus out of fourteen children from four wives six could not reach adulthood, giving an infant mortality of 42.9 per cent. Akbar (b. 1542; d. 1605) had from his several wives only three sons and four daughters who reached adulthood. Two sons died within a month of birth, but all daughters survived. Thus infant mortality carried off a 22.2 per cent of his children, though they must doubtless have received the greatest care that contemporary medicine and nursing could provide.

The case with his eldest son, Jahāngīr (b. 1569; d. 1627) is even more startling. With numerous wives, like his father (at least nine wives and two concubines bore him children), he had six sons and nine daughters of whom two sons died within a month of birth. Of his daughters six died more or less immediately after birth, one at seven months and another at three years of age. Only two of his daughters attained adulthood. Infant mortality thus claimed two-third of his offspring.

Of Akbar's two other sons, Murād (b. 1570, d. 1599) had two sons, both of whom died in infancy, and only one daughter survived to reach her teens; Dāniyāl (b. 1571, d. 1603) had four sons and four daughters, of whom at least one son died in infancy. In the fourth generation of the imperial house, the infant mortality rate was thus 50 per cent, being 41.6 per cent for males and as high as 57 per cent for females.

Jahāngīr's son Shāhjahān (b. 1592; d. 1666) married his famous wife, Mumtāz Maḥal (born 19 April 1593) in 1612. She died in 1631 after about nineteen years of marriage and bore him fourteen children (six sons and eight daughters). Of these only four sons and two daughters survived their father. One daughter died immediately after birth, one was stillborn. One died at the age of three and another at seven, both of small-pox. One son was stillborn, one died when still less than a year old and another died one and half year old. The only other son Gauhar Sulṭān, born of a different mother also died in infancy. Thus for his children the infant mortality rate was about 53 per cent with the sons being affected slightly more than the daughters.

Our knowledge is incomplete about the families of Shāhjahān's brothers. His eldest brother Khusrau (b. 1587; d. 1607) had three sons, one of whom died in infancy. Both the sons of Parwēz (b. 589; d. 1628) died without reaching adulthood, while Shahryār (b. 1604–d.1626) had no son, and only one daughter survived him.

On the whole in the fifth generation, of the twenty-two children eleven died in infancy giving a rate of 50 per cent for overall infant mortality; 37.5 per cent for females and 57.1 per cent for males.

The offspring of Aurangzeb (b. 1618; d. 1707) were more fortunate. He had five sons and five daughters. Of these only one daughter Zīnnatun Nisā' (b. 1643) seems to have died early, since no further information is available about her, beyond her birth and name. All other five sons and four daughters attained adulthood (for details see Appendix 5.1).

For Aurangzeb's three brothers our information is incomplete. The births of three sons and two daughters of Dārā Shukoh (b. 1615; d.1627) and two sons and two daughters of Shāh Shujā' (b. 1616; d.1659) are reported by Lāhorī.

Though admittedly small our sample helps to provide some data, even if tentative, about the sex-ratio and infant mortality: out of 107 recorded births fifty-six were of males and fifty-one of females, the male–female ratio being 100:91. There is a possibility that the higher number of male births is due to the bias in reporting rather than in actual fact. Still, it can be argued that the fact that reported female births are not much behind male births, gives us some confidence that our information is fairly comprehensive.

A very striking feature of these statistics is that infant mortality rate is extraordinarily high. At least forty-one out of the 107 children born during the period 1504–1667 died in infancy, giving a rate of 38.32 per cent (41.07 per cent for males; 35.29 per cent for females). This is exceptionally high when compared with British ducal families, where for the period 1480–1679, infant mortality has been estimated at 31.5 per cent (for males 34 per cent; females 29 per cent).[9] Interestingly enough the ratios between male and female infant mortality rates were strikingly similar being 100:85.8 for India and 100:85.3 in England; the female infant mortality rate being substantially lower than male infant mortality in both the cases.

Had the Mughals followed a normal marriage policy, the data for marriage age would have been quite interesting, since the princes' and princesses' age at their marriages would be known. But from

[9] Hollingsworth, 'A Demographic Study of the British Ducal Families', p. 8.

Akbar's time onwards the belief that imperial status would be demeaned if princesses were married to persons outside the family kept an exceptionally large number of the princesses unmarried; and, while marriages with cousins did still take place, there could be doubt as to the representative character of such marriages. However, it should be desirable to collect information on such marriages for marriage-age data for males and females. From an earlier period (before 1566), when the taboo on princesses' marriages had not developed, I have traced a few examples.[10] Gulchihra, daughter of Bābur, founder of the Mughal line, was born between 1515–17, and married-off in 1530, at the age of 14±1 years only. She was widowed in 1533, and re-married in 1549, at the age of 33±1 years. Another daughter of Bābur, Dildār, born between 1511–15, was older, 17±2 years, at her first marriage, which took place in 1530. Bābur's son, Humāyūn, had a daughter, Bakhshī Bānu, 1540. She was married to Ibrāhīm in 1550, when she must have been ten years only; the groom was six years older. She was widowed in 1560, to be re-married the same year, at the age of about thirty years. These three instances give an average age of barely fourteen years, for the female entering first marriage. If this, as well as the widow-marriage, has any more general significance, it would be for Muslims only, since among Hindus the marriage customs were different, there being no widow remarriage among Hindu upper castes and child marriages being more common. It may, however, be interesting to investigate at what age Rajput brides were received for Mughal princes in marriage.

As for average lifespan, the data for the Mughal imperial family would be worth exploring though the family, owing to rivalry for succession, had a much larger share of unnatural deaths among males in the seventeenth century (not the sixteenth century, when in this respect better conditions prevailed). The three sons of Akbar, who survived infancy, and none of whom died unnatural deaths attained the ages of fifty-eight, twenty-nine and thirty-three; the average age at death was then forty years. If one takes into account, the sons who died in infancy, this would represent a life expectation (at birth) of twenty-four years only. Of the three daughters, who survived infancy, I have not been able to trace the age at death of the eldest (though doubtless this may be traced), the other two were sixty-five and forty

[10] All these references are from Gulbadan Bānu, *Humāyūn Nāma*, edited and translated by A.S. Beveridge, London, 1902, pp. 231, 225, 214.

years at the time of their deaths. The greater longevity for daughters here indicated may be due to their abstinence from drink which destroyed the health and constitutions of their brothers. The data may, therefore, not again be representative of general conditions.

More data from the sources is to be sifted to present a less fragmentary picture of the Mughal imperial family and, hopefully, draw upon data for some aristocratic families as well.

For the common people, the data are very scarce. However, a merchant, Banārsīdās has obligingly provided us complete information of his own children as well as those of his father in his versified autobiography, the *Aradh Kathanak* (see Appendix 5.2).[11] Banārsīdās was born in 1586 and wrote his autobiography in 1641. This shows that he lived for over fifty-five years. He first married at the age of eleven but brought his bride home when he was fifteen in 1601. She died in 1614 in childbirth and Banārsīdās took in marriage her younger sister immediately after. She too died, along with her son, who was two and a half years old, in 1622. Banārsīdās remarried again a year after, in 1623. He had in all ten children from his three wives, eight sons and two daughters. All of them died in infancy; only one lived for nearly two years. Banārsīdās' case seems an extreme one since his father who himself died at the age of sixty-four had married when he was twenty-two years old. He had five children from his one wife, three of whom were sons and two daughters. Two of the three sons died in infancy while both the daughters survived and were married off at the age of ten. The data about Banārsīdās himself and his brothers and sisters give an infant mortality rate of 40 per cent which may appear to be more typical of the rate prevailing at the time, rather than the 100 per cent infant mortality rate for Banārsīdās's own children.

There may be other ways too by which the problem of lack of data for common people can bc overcome. For example, *zamīndārīs* (superior rights) were, in both Hindu and Muslim custom, divided equally among sons. In a village of Bahraich, which was under the *zamīndārī* of one family, the shares in the village *zamīndārī* were sold to an outsider by separate transactions in Aurangzeb's reign (1556–1707). In each transaction the seller gives his line of descent and his share of *zamīndārī*.[12] This information when collected does not only

[11] *Ardhakathanaka*, edited and translated by Mukund Lath (*Half a Tale*), Jaipur, 1981, text on pp.223–75; translation on pp.1–98.

[12] *ASMI*, p.193.

enable us to reconstruct the family tree but also to establish as to how many sons in each generation reached marriageable age to have children of their own. The following picture (see Table 5.2) emerges:

Table 5.2

First generation	X	had	3 sons
Second generation	Parsu	had	1 son
	Durga	,,	3 sons
	Y	,,	not known
Third generation	Satba	had	2 sons
	Kalyan	,,	2 sons
	Ratan	,,	not known
	Z	,,	1 son
Fourth generation	Dasi	had	not known
	Lachhman	,,	not known
	Kan'i	,,	not known
	Lauki	,,	not known
	Kasi	,,	2 sons
Fifth generation	Patri	had	2 sons

Clearly, the 'not knowns' are far too many here. The known part gives us the figure of 2.1 sons who in each case had at least reached adulthood to inherit and possibly have children.

Of a peasant family near Mathura similar data can be reconstructed from a series of documents from 1595 to 1723(see Table 5.3).[13]

Table 5.3

First generation	Sundar Gaurwa had 1 son
Second generation	Jadu (1599–1600) had 4 sons
Third generation	Lalchand (1640–59) had one son
	Rai Karan (1653)
	Mathura (1653)
	Har Ram (1691) had one son
Fourth generation	Manika (1695-1706)
	Sandal (pre-1701) had three sons

[13] Ibid., p.150.

Fifth generation	Ramchand (1701)
	Sukha (1701)
	Shyam Singh (1701–12)

Note: Years within bracket represent years when the person was alive according to available documentation. The number of sons refers to sons known to us from record.

Thus five persons over five generations had a minimum of ten sons (two on average for each father) who reached adulthood. The result is very similar to that for the *zamīndārī* family from Bahraich. Unluckily, nothing at all can be said about mothers for there is no knowing whether the sons of the same father were born of one or more wives. There is thus no seeming possibility of working out any kind of reproduction rates from such information at the present stage.

There is another kind of material, which may be of use here. Official documents where parties to a sale or contract made an attestation before the *qāẓī*, had their description (*chihra*) inscribed on its margin, in case they were illiterate and could not sign for themselves. These invariably give the ages of the persons and it may be possible to trace the ages to which persons are known to have lived if a sufficient number of such documents are scrutinized.

Irfan Habib has indicated that information may be gathered from such documents for the prevalence of a killer disease like small pox. He notes that out of twenty-five villagers whose descriptions were recorded before *qāẓīs* in the Vrindaban documents, 1653–1717, as many as ten bore the marks of small pox.[14] We may recall here that two daughters of Jahāngīr were carried away by small-pox, and small pox might have been the unmentioned cause of other infant deaths in the imperial family as well.

As I have already said this study is in the nature of a note, written more to draw attention to materials containing demographic information than draw any firm conclusions about expectation of life or reproduction pattern. However, the high infant mortality rates in even the imperial family must force us to adopt a sombre view of the conditions of health and medicine even in households which had access to the best that power and wealth could provide.

[14] Ibid., p.111n.

Appendix 5.1

BĀBUR'S CHILDREN
(b. 1483–1530)

		Reference
by 'Āiysha Ṣulṭāna Begum, (married in 1500)		*BN*, p. 35, Gulbadan, f.6b
1. Fakhrunnisā' Begum	b. 1502 d. within a month	*BN*, p.136
by Māhm Begum (married in 1506)		
2. Humāyūn	b. 1506, d.1556	*BN*, p.344, *AN*, 1, p.92.
3. Bārbol Mirza	b.? d. in infancy	Gulbadan, f.6b
4. Mihrjahān	b.? d.in infancy	Ibid.
5. Īshān Daulat	b.? d. in infancy	Ibid.
6. Fārūq	b. 1526, d.1527	*AN*, 1, p.257.
by Ma'ṣūma Ṣulṭāna Begum (died in Child birth)		
7. Ma'ṣūma (named after mother)	lived long to be married	Gulbadan, f.6b.
by Gulrukh Begum		
8. Kāmrān	d. 1556	*AN*, 1, p.331
9. 'Askarī	b. 1516, d. 1556–7	*AN*, 1, 308
10. Shāhrukh	d. in infancy	Gulbadan, p.146
11. Aḥmad	lived to have a son, d. before 1530	Ibid.
12. Gulezār Begum	lived to be married	Ibid., p.232.
by Dildār Begum		
13. Gulrang	b.1511–15, alive in 1534	Ibid.
14. Gulchehra	b. 1515–17 married 1530 widowed 1533, re-married 1549, alive till 1553	Ibid.
15. Hindāl	b. 1519 killed 1551	*AN*, I, pp.93, 314
16. Gulbadan	b. 1523, d.1603	Gulbadan, pp.1–3
17. Alwār	b. 1529, died in infancy	Ibid.

HUMĀYŪN'S CHILDREN

by Ḥājī Begum		
1. Almān	b. 1528 d. in infancy	*AN*, I, 113.
2. 'Afīfa/ 'Aqīqa	b. 1531 lost at Chausa 1539	Gulbadan, p.208.

by Ḥamīda Bānu Begum

3.	Akbar	b. 1542, d.1605	*AN*, 1, p. 17.
4.	A daughter	b. 1544, d. in infancy	*AN*, I, 220.
5.	A daughter	b.? d.1557	*AN*, II, p.55.
6.	A daughter	b.? d.1557	Ibid.

by Māhchuchak Begum

7.	Bak͟htnisā' Begum	b.1550, lived to have a son	Gulbadan, 214
8.	Sakīna Bānu	lived to be married d.1605	*AN*, III, 839
9.	Amīna Bānu	—	Gulbadan, p.206
10.	Fak͟hrunnisā'	married Shāh Abul Ma'ālī (d.1555), re-married K͟hwāja Ḥasan Naqshbandī	Ibid., 227
11.	Mirza Ḥakīm	b. 1554, d.1585	*AN*, I, p.332, III, p.466
12.	Farruk͟h Fāl	b. 1555, d. in infancy	Ibid., I, p.352

by K͟hānish Āg͟hā daughter of Jujāq Mirza of K͟hwarzim

13.	Ibrāhīm Sulaimān	b. 1555, d. in infancy	Gulbadan, 186; *AN*, I, 337
14.	Bak͟hshī Bānu	b.1540 married 1550 to Ibrāhīm (b. 1534, killed 1560) Widowed at 20 re-married	Gulbadan, 214; *AN*, II, 128.

Akbar's Children

by concubine

1.	Ḥasan] twins	b. 1564, d. within a month	*AN*, II, p.235–6
2.	Ḥusain		

by Maryamu-z-Zamānī

3.	Salīm	b. 1569, d.1627	Ibid., p.343

by concubines

4.	Shāhzāda K͟hānum	b. 1569, alive in 1597	Ibid., pp.349, III, 756
5.	Murād	b. 1570, d.1597	Ibid., II, pp.353, III, 753
6.	Dānīyal	b. 1572, d. 1605	Ibid., pp.34, 837

by grand-daughter of Rawal Harraj, ruler of Jaisalmair

7.	Māhī Begum	b. ? d.1577	Ibid., III, p.200

by Bībī Daulat Shād

8. Shukrun Nisā'	elder to Ārām Bāno lived till Shāhjahān's reign	*Tuzuk*, p.36
9. Ārām Bānu	b. 1584, d.1624	*AN*, III, p.440

JAHĀNGĪR'S CHILDREN

by daughter of Bhagwant Dās

1. Sulṭān Nisā' Begum	b. 1585, d. 1646	*Tuzuk*, p.19 Lahori II, p. 604.
2. Sulṭān Khīrad	b. 1586, d. in infancy	*AN*, III, p. 493.
3. Sulṭān <u>Kh</u>usrau	b. 1587, d. 1607	Ibid., p. 523.

by Jagat Gosain d/Mota Rāja

4. Begum Sulṭān	b. 1590, d. one year old	Ibid., p. 581.
5. <u>Kh</u>urram	b. 1592, d. 1666	Ibid., p. 603.
6. A daughter	b. 1597, d. in infancy	Ibid., p. 733.

by daughter of Sa'īd <u>Kh</u>ān

7. 'Iffat Bānu	b. 1589, d. 3 years old	Ibid., p. 536.

by Ṣāhib Jamāl daughter of <u>Kh</u>awāja Ḥasan

8. Parvez	b. 1589, d. 1627	Ibid., p.568.

by daughter of Daryā Malbhas

9. Daulat Nisā'	b. 1589, d.7 months old.	Ibid., III, p.572, *Tuzuk*, p.20

by Karamasī Kisan Rathor

10. Bahār Bānu Begum	b. 1590, d. in infancy	Ibid., p.581

by Sister of Abiya Chak Kashmīrī

11. A daughter	b. 1592, d. in infancy	Ibid., p. 609.

by daughter of 'Abdullah Balauchī

12. A daughter	b. 1594, d. in infancy	Ibid., p. 662.

by daughter of Ibrāhīm Ḥusain

13. A daughter	b. 1594, d. in infancy	Ibid., p.671

by concubines

14. Jahāndār	b. 1604–5, d. in infancy	*Tuzuk*, p.301
15. Sharyār	b. 1605–6, killed in 1628	Ibid., Lāhorī, I, p.79.

MURĀD'S CHILDREN

by daughter of Khān-i 'Aẓam 'Azīz Koka

1. Rustam	b. 1588, d. in infancy	*AN*, III, p. 529.
2. 'Ālam Sulṭān	b. 1589, d. in infancy	Ibid., p. 581.
3. A daughter	Lived to marry Parwaiz's son	*Tuzuk*, p.38

DĀNIYĀL'S CHILDREN
(Left three sons four daughters, *AN*, III, p. 837)

by daughter of Sulṭān Khāwaja

1. a daughter	b. 1589	*AN*, III, p. 578.
2. Sa'ādat Bānu	b. 1591	Ibid., p.613.
by daughter of Qulīch Khān		
3. A son	b.1597 d. in infancy	Ibid., p.729
4. Bulāqī Begum		Ibid., p.837
5. Hushang	b.? killed in 1627	Lāhorī, I, p.7.
by concubine		
6. Ṭahmūraṣ	b.? killed in 1627	Ibid.
7. Burhānī Begum	—	Ibid.
8. Bayasnghar	b. 1604 killed in 1636–7	Ibid., p. 831, Lāhorī, I, p.207

SHĀHJAHĀN'S CHILDREN

by Mumtāz Maḥal, b. 1593, married 1612, d. 1633, had eight sons and six daughters

1.	Ḥūrliqa	b. 1613, died at 3 of small pox	Ṣāliḥ, I, p.61.
2.	Jahān Arā	b. 1614, d.1681–2	Ibid., *Mā'asir*, p.213.
3.	Dārā Shikoh	b. 1615, killed 1658	Ibid., p. 70
4.	Shāh Shuja	b. 1616, died 1658	Ibid., p. 73
5.	Rohsan Rai	b. 1617, died 1671–2	Qazwīnī, 72, *Mā'asir*, p.110.
6.	Aurangzeb	b. 1618, 1707	Ṣāliḥ, I, p. 96.
7.	Ummid Bakhsh	b. 1619, d. infant	Ibid., p.99.
8.	Ṣurriya Bānu	b. 1620, d. 7 years (of small pox)	Lāhorī, I, p. 197.
9.	Murād Bakhsh	b. 1624, killed 1658	Ṣāliḥ, I, p. 142.
10.	Luṭfullah	b. 1625, d. 1½ yrs	Lāhorī, I, p. 198.
11.	Daulat Afrōz	b. 1628, d. 1629	Lāhorī, I, pp. 198 and 259.
12.	Gauhar Ārā	d. infant	Qazwīnī, p. 198.

13. A daughter	still born	Ibid., p. 271.
14. A son	still born	Ibid.

by daughter of Shāhnawāz Khān, son of 'Abdul Raḥīm Khān Khāna

15. Gauhar Sulṭān	b. 1619 d. infant	Ibid., p. 304.

KHUSRAU'S CHILDREN

by daughter of Khān 'Azam Koka

1. Buland Akhtar	b. 1609, d. in infancy	*Iqbālnāma*, p.38.
2. Dawar Bakhsh	b. ? killed 1628 (had a daughter Hoshmand Bānu married to Hoshang son of Dāniyāl)	Lāhorī, I, p.79.
3. Gurshāps	b. ? killed 1628	Ibid.

PARWEZ'S CHILDREN

by Murād's daughter

1. Dūr Andēsh	b. 1615 d. infant	*Iqbālnāma*, p.73.
2. A son	b. ? d. infant	Ibid.
3. A daughter	b. ? married to Dārā Shukoh	Ibid.

SHAHARYĀR'S CHILD

1. One daughter	b. ?	Ibid.

AURANGZEB'S CHILDREN

by Nawāb Bāī

1. Muḥammad Sulṭān	b. 1639 d. 1676	Lāhorī, 2(I), p. 170, *M.A.*, p.534.
2. Mu'aẓẓam/ Shāh 'Ālam	b. 1643 d. 1712	Ibid.
3. Badrun Nisā'	b. 1647 d. 1670	Ibid.

by Dilras Bānu

4. Ā'zam	b. 1653 killed 1707	*M.A.*, p.536.
5. Akbar	b. 1657 d. 1704	*M.A.*, p.547.
6. Zebunnisā'	b. 1638 d. 1702	*M.A.*, pp.462, 538
7. Zinnatun Nisā'	b. 1643 d.1721.	*Mā'asir-i 'Alamgīrī*, p.539.

8.	Zubdatun Nisā'	b. 1651, d. 1707 married Scpechar Shukoh, 1673	*Mā'asir-i 'Alamgīrī*, pp. 533–9.

by Bāī Udaipuri

9.	Kām Bakhsh	b. 1667 killed 1709	*M.A.*, pp.538-40.

by Aurangabādī Maḥal

10.	Mihrunnisā'	b. 1661, d. 1706, married to Izid Bakhsh son of Murād Bakhsh in 1672, d.1706	Ibid.

DĀRĀ SHUKOH'S CHILDREN

by daughter of Sul. Parwez (married 1632), Lāhorī, 1(1), p. 2)

1.	Sipihr Shukōh	b. 1644, alive in 1658	Ibid., 2(1), p. 388, Kāzim, p.433.
2.	A daughter	b. 1634	Ibid., p.3
3.	Mihr Shukōh	b. 1641	Ibid., p. 1953.
4.	Mumtāz Shukōh	b. 1643	Ibid., p. 337.

Shāh Shujā's Children

by daughter of Mirza Rustām (married 1632)

1.	Dilband Bānu	b. 1634, d. in infancy mother died next day	Ibid.
2.	Zain Muḥammad	b. 1639	Lāhorī, 2(1), p. 165
3.	Gulrukh Bānu	b. 1639	Ibid.

by daughter of Raja Gursen Kishtwar

4.	Buland Akhtar	b. 1646	Lāhorī, 2(1), p. 434

Appendix 5.2

BANĀRSĪDĀS' CHILDREN

b. 1586, fl.1641, married 1597 (p.235) *Ardhkathanak*,

by first wife

1.	a daughter	b. 1603, d. in infancy	Ibid., p.239.
2.	a son	b. 1604, d. in infancy	Ibid., p.241

3.	a son	b. 1607, d. in infancy	Ibid., p.242
4.	a son	b. 1614, d. in infancy	Ibid., p.257

by second wife

5.	a son	b. 1619, in infancy	Ibid., p.269
6.	a son	b. 1620, d.1622	Ibid.

by third wife

7.	a son	b. 1627, d. in infancy (a few days old)	Ibid., p.271
8.	a son	b. 1628, d. one or two year old	Ibid.
9.	a son	b. 1630, d. a few months old	Ibid.
10.	a daughter	b. 1632, d. in infancy	Ibid.

Kharagsen's Children
(b. 1551, d. 1615, p.225)

1.	a son	b. 1578, d. 10 days old	Ibid., p.230
2.	Banārsīdās	b. 1586, alive in 1641	Ibid.
3.	a daughter	b. 1593, married in 1603	Ibid., p.231
4.	a daughter	b. 1597, married in 1607	Ibid., p.232
5.	a son	b. 1604, d. in infancy	Ibid., p.241

6

Urban Population in Pre-Colonial India

The question of urban levels attained in pre-colonial India lay behind much of the controversy over de-urbanization in the nineteenth century.[1] Gadgil has suggested that there was a slight relative decline in the urban population, though there might have been an absolute increase in its size.[2] L. Visaria and P. Visaria have expressed some doubt regarding this,[3] but so far no strong reasons have been advanced (least of all, through any production of statistical data) to show that the decline of a large number of towns was matched by a corresponding increase in the population of other towns. Indeed, if anything, the figures collected by Durgaprasad Bhattacharya suggest not only a relative but an absolute decline in urban population during the first half of the nineteenth century in eastern India.[4] Even if we suppose that the absolute size of urban population remained stable over the nineteenth century at 28.5 millions (its actual size in 1901), that the

[1] The controversy once kindled has continued. A critique of the views propounded in *CEHI*, Vol. II, Cambridge, 1983, is offered by Irfan Habib, 'Studying a Colonial Economy without Perceiving Colonialism', *Modern Asian Studies*, Vol. XIX, No. 3, 1985, pp. 364–8.

[2] D.R. Gadgil, *The Industrial Evolution of India in Recent Times, 1860–1939*, 5th edn, Delhi, 1973, pp. 144ff.

[3] *CEHI*, Vol. II, pp. 519–28.

[4] D. Bhattacharya, *Report on the Population Estimates of India*, Vol. III, Part A, 1811–20, Eastern Region, (Census of India, 1961), pp. xvii–xviii.

I am afraid one can hardly accept C.A. Bayly's judgement that there was 'a clear but not startling growth of the total population living in towns of over 5000' (*Rulers, Townsmen and Bazars*, Cambridge, 1983, p.304 & *n*). This he discovers by comparing house-counts for *chaukīdārī* cess in NWP (North West Provinces) with later urban population estimates, in spite of the very incomplete nature of the house-counts. He also forgets that the under-remuneration of the total population of NWP continued in official reports well after 1850 and was not confined to the earlier decades of the century alone.

population in 1801 was about 200 millions,[5] the relative size of urban population in 1801 have been as high as 14.3 per cent., compared to just 9.9 per cent.

Thus if any de-urbanization occurred in the nineteenth century it must follow that there was a higher proportion of urban population in pre-colonial India than in 1901. Even a percentage as high as 15 per cent cannot therefore be considered implausible given the very simple considerations we have set out above.

The 'de-urbanization' debate alone would require that we have a closer look at the nature of pre-colonial urban economy, so as to enable us to have some kind of estimate of its actual size without being constrained by the low figures of urban population revealed by the censuses from 1872 onwards.

In economic terms the emergence of the town signifies the extraction of a surplus in agriculture, generating a largely uni-directional flow of goods from village to town. At a certain stage of economic development, as at the dawn of the modern period in Europe, this one-way transfer of products from village to town began to be supplemented by a reverse flow, as urban products found an expanding rural market, with the rise of the 'gentry' and rural 'proto-industrialization'. So far as we can judge from our evidence, pre-modern Indian urban economy was likely to be largely in the earlier parasitic phase. Here the urbanization was largely the result of the drain of the surplus from the countryside to the towns without any substantive recompense to the rural economy.

As is widely recognized, the Mughal ruling class was almost entirely town-centred. The Mughal nobles were usually paid through territorial revenue assignments (*jāgīrs*), but seldom directly lived 'off the land' in the sense of directly consuming the agricultural produce. The *jāgīrs* being service assignments were neither hereditary nor permanent, and for political considerations, a system of transfer of posts and *jāgīrs* was deliberately maintained. The relationship between the *jāgīrdār* and the villages in his *jāgīr* revolved usually around his claim to the bulk of the surplus in the form of land revenue. His household

[5] Estimates for 1801, based on different arguments and calculations, range from 198 millions to 208 millions. The first estimate is provided in Morris D. Morris, 'The Population of All India, 1800–1951', in *IESHR*, Vol. XI, Nos. 2–3, p. 311, and the second one in Durgaprasad Bhattacharya, *Report on the Population Estimates of India*, Vol. III, Part A, Table 3.1, p.xxiii.

establishment, as well as most of his retinue, was generally quartered in the towns. The net revenue realized (allowing for costs of collection and concessions to local intermediaries like *zamīndārs*) was thus almost taken away in full from the countryside. A large urban sector could therefore emerge which was almost entirely dependent upon the countryside. The villages were self-sufficient in regard to the bulk of their own requirements, in spite of the fact that grain had to be sold by the peasants to pay the revenue in cash. The main circuit of the rural exploitation can be represented by Fig.6.1.

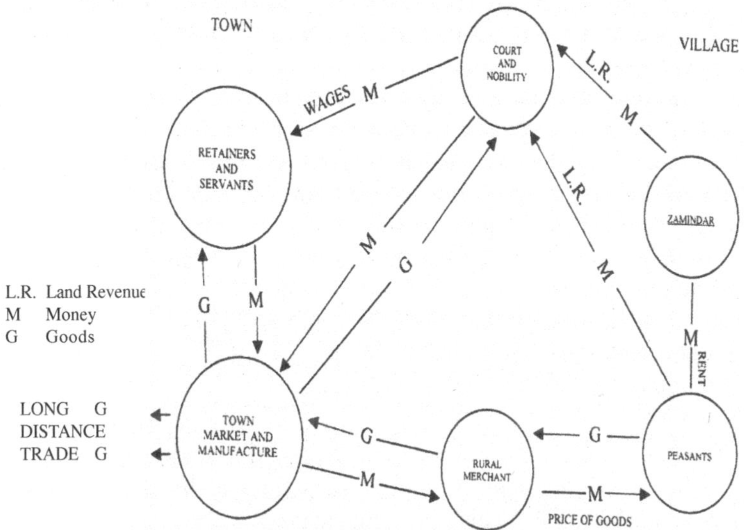

Fig.6.1.:Circulation of the Rural Surplus

Irfan Habib was the first to lay emphasis on this one-sided relationship based on the townward flow of agricultural surplus as the main factor behind Mughal urbanization. He went on to suggest that the size of urban population could be estimated if we could determine the relative size of the 'subsistence' component in the rural produce transferred to the towns in realization of the surplus.[6]

The Mughal administration laid claim to almost one-half of the total agricultural produce,[7] but the net income received after making

[6] Irfan Habib, 'Potentialities of Capitalistic Development in the Economy of Mughal India', in *Essays in Indian History*, New Delhi, 1995, pp.200–13.

[7] *ASMI*, Delhi, 2000, pp. 230–6.

allowances for other subordinate shares and cost of collection was much less.[8] Irfan Habib assumes that the actual drain from the countryside was of the magnitude of one-fourth of the value of the total produce. But since in the drained surplus the proportion of non-food component must have been quite high, he assumes that the urban population in Mughal India was about 15 per cent of the total.[9]

This inference is admittedly hypothetical, though some use has been made of quantitative data. It may still be possible to pursue the device suggested by Irfan Habib in a more specific fashion by using absolute figures of revenue realization, its distribution and the pattern of consumption insofar as it can be reconstructed from our information.

This information comes almost entirely from Abū'l Faẓl's celebrated work, the *Ā'īn-i Akbarī*, a treasure-house of statistical information completed in 1598, with much of its information relating to 1595.[10] These statistics range from tax collection and measured area figures (with detailed geographical break-down) to prices and wages, etc. Moreland and Ashok V. Desai have already used this information for estimating the total population of the Mughal Empire and establishing standards of living.[11] We seek here to throw the net still wider while hoping to use the *Ā'īn*'s information for determining the size of urban population in 1595.

The total effective *jama'* or revenue-income of the Mughal Empire (excluding the Deccan provinces of Berar and Khandesh), on the basis of the detailed *jama'* (revenue) statistics in the *Ā'īn* comes to 3,96,03,27,10 *dām*.[12] This also included taxes other than land revenue, which did not, however, exceed 10 per cent of the total.[13]

[8] *EME*, pp. 129–31.

[9] Irfan Habib, 'Potentialities of Capitalistic Developments', pp. 22–36.

[10] *Ā'īn*. For a discussion of the date of the *Ā'īn's* statistics, see *EME*, pp. 5–8.

[11] W.H. Moreland, *India at the Death of Akbar*, London, 1920, pp. 20–2, 253–7; Ashok V. Desai, 'Population and Standard of Living in Akbar's Time', *IESHR*, Vol. IX, 1972. My own effort at estimating the total population of India in 1595, based chiefly on the *Ā'īn*, was made in 'Estimation de la Population de L'Inde En 1601', in *Population*, No. 2, Paris, 1984. See also *EME*, pp.395–406.

[12] This total is built up from the *pargana*-level figures for the areas that were in actual Mughal control (i.e., excluding those only nominally claimed); it also excludes the amount alienated through revenue grants. The *dām* was a copper coin worth one-fourtieth of a silver-rupee.

[13] Shireen Moosvi, 'Production, Consumption and Population in Akbar's Time', in *IESHR*, Vol. X, No.2, 1973, pp. 193–4.

The statistical information, provided by Abū'l Faẓl, on the imperial household and military establishment and the data on nobles (*manṣabdārs*), according to their ranks and their pay, enable us to work out the distribution of the revenue-income among the court and the nobility (the ruling class) and its further diffusion.

A detailed study of the pattern of consumption of the Emperor and the nobility, that I have made elsewhere,[14] suggests that over 17 per cent of the total effective *jama'* (i.e., 68,43,00,297 *dām*) went directly in wage-payments mostly at subsistence level; and a little above 37 per cent of their revenue-income (1,48,03,40,718 *dām*) was spent by the Emperor and nobility on craft-commodities.[15] A part of this expenditure would, of course, have gone to maintain producers at subsistence level. The ratio between the cost of raw material and value added by labour in various craft-goods cannot obviously be easily worked out. However, we may still attempt a guess on the basis of some rough estimations of the share of labour-costs in product-values. Pelsaert, c. 1626, referring to the articles made of silver and gold (like bedsteads, fan-handles, dishes, cups, betel-boxes, etc.) tells us that 'provided the workmanship is good, half the silver might be paid for manufactures'.[16] This implies that even in the high value manufactures and artifacts the cost of labour could amount to a third of the total value. This might serve us for the lower limit of the value added by labour. For the share of labour-cost in ordinary urban manufacture, we may seek help from the data collected for coarse cloth by Buchanan during early nineteenth century. In coarse cloth the cost of yarn amounted to 72.6 per cent of the total value; and the cost of uncleaned cotton accounted for 44.3 per cent of the value of yarn.[17] This implies that in the case of coarse cloth the value of raw material came to 32.16 per cent and that of labour to 67.84 per cent of thc total value of the final product. This may serve for the upper limit for the proportion of value of labour in craft-goods. Thus taking silverware and coarse-cloth to set the two limits, the share of labour

[14] *EME*, pp. 272–96.

[15] This includes the amount spent on buying imported horses as well as the silver and gold going into hoards: for details and reasons of its inclusion, *EME*, pp.290–4.

[16] Francisco Pelsaert, *Remonstrantie*, translated by Moreland and Geyl, *Jahāngīr's India*, reprint, Delhi, 1972, p. 27.

[17] F. Buchanan, *An Account of the Districts of Bihar and Patna in 1811–12*, Vol. II, Patna, 1928, p. 774.

costs in total craft-values should have ranged between one-third and two-thirds of the total value. We may, therefore, not be far wrong in assuming a parity between the cost of labour and raw material in values of manufactures in general.

However, a slight qualification needs to be introduced here. Both Pelsaert and Buchanan apparently give us the value at which the manufactures were available to the merchant, and not its final full market price; thus their prices seem to exclude the profits of the merchant, middlemen, etc., and also the share of the usurer in the labourer's wages. But we may assume that the merchant's profits out of the last market-ward movement of the craft product must have remained largely within the urban sector, and much of it probably filtered down again to urban workmen in the form of wages. Our assumption of wage costs being half the value of manufactures may thus really not be far from the fact even if part of the merchant's or middlemen's profits have been excluded from the latter.

Proceeding from our assumption of the share of wages in the amount laid out by the ruling class on craft products,[18] the total amount disbursed as wages of craft labour should have been 74,01,70,359 *dām*.[19] To this should be added the direct expenditure on the service sector (68,43,00,297 *dām*). The total sum annually spent by the ruling class upon directly maintaining the urban population should, then, have been 1,42,44,70,656 *dām*.

So much for the maintenance of the urban population out of the net revenue (*jama'*) that reached the court and the nobility. We have now to examine whether an additional segment of the urban population was sustained by expenditure out of the remaining part of the surplus that adhered to the hands of other classes. From the data available to

[18] To meet the possible objection that a significant proportion of expenditure of the ruling class on craft products could have been incurred on buying manufactures imported from outside the Mughal Empire, one may stress the well-recognized fact that the imports in Mughal Empire were almost invariably paid for by exports of goods (mainly cotton textiles). Expenditure on the imported items (including the sums spent on buying imported horses and precious metals) thus in fact induced increased craft production. The expenditure of the ruling class on purchases of imported merchandise and specie can therefore be legitimately included in the amount laid out on craft goods.

[19] *EMI*, p.294. It excludes the part of *jama'* that went to meet the pay-claims of the *jāgīrdārs*' retainers paid through sub-assignments, which imply a largely rural expenditure.

us, we have estimated that about 37 per cent of the gross revenue-claim was realized by subordinate co-sharers or spent on revenue collection.[20]

The class of *zamīndārs* or rural potentates must have spent some amount, however small, upon urban manufactures, such as superior quality cloth woven in towns, jewellery and items of weaponry. The silver and gold hoarded by them as well as any imported horses bought by them should have resulted in an increase in urban craft production insofar as these imports induced exports of craft products to foreign markets.

The retainers of the *jāgīrdār*, who received sub-assignments in the villages, should also have generated some demand for urban products.[21] Moreover, the revenue-collectors, whether imperial or of *jāgīrdārs*, who were more likely to be stationed at administrative headquarters, must have spent part of their allowances,[22] coming out of the amount sanctioned for cost of revenue collections, within the urban sector.

To determine the amount of surplus used to maintain urban population through these conduits, we may seek help from the data available about their shares or the amount appropriated by them and also hazard some guesses about their pattern of expenditure. I have offered a detailed discussion elsewhere of these matters.[23] Table 6.1 below sets out the size of the assumed proportion of their income flowing into the urban craft sector, as estimated by me:

The total amount contributed to the urban sector out of the income of the superior right holders, revenue collectors, and jāgīrdārs' rural retainers thus comes to 27,30,02,662 *dām*. Under our assumption of labour costs being one half of the total value of urban produce, we infer that 13,65,01,331 *dām* went annually to support urban population at subsistence level through sale of craft goods to these classes.

[20] *EME*, p. 131.

[21] Some retainers of the *jāgīrdārs* were paid through sub-assignments; we assume that their number was about a quarter of that of retainers. Their income was, of course, a part of the *jama'* (net income of the court and the imperial ruling class), but it by and large remained within the rural sector and has thus been considered separately here.

[22] The cash allowances to the revenue officials can, on the basis of Todar Mal's recommendations of 1582–3 (*AN*, pp.381–3), be placed at 10 per cent of the total amount sanctioned as cost of revenue collection.

[23] *EME*, pp. 299–304.

Table 6.1

Category	Income		Expenditure on Urban Crafts	
	Relative size	Calculated	% of 2b	Calculated amount (in *dām*)
1	2a	2b	3a	3b
Zamīndār	20.59% of surplus	1,32,01,11,864	10%	3,20,11,186
Headmen	7% of gross revenue	39,60,32,325	5%	1,98,01,616
Revenue collectors	10% of cost of collection	11,31,52,090	75%	8,48,64,067
Sub-assignees of *jāgīrdārs*	12.85% of *jama*'	48,43,43,910	7.5%	3,63,25,793

We assume, despite Tapan Raychaudhuri,[24] that the peasants' purchases of urban goods out of what remained for their subsistence after surplus-realization, were too insignificant to have any influence on the size of urban population.

Combining the total expenditure of the ruling class (1,42,44,70,656 *dām*) and that of the subordinate classes on wages of urban labour, we arrive at the annual total of 1,56,09,71,987 *dām*, as true for the Mughal Empire in 1595. Of this, according to our calculations, the ruling class contributed 91 per cent and the other classes a mere 9 per cent.

To this figure must be added that of the net import of bullion (mainly silver) which was paid for by export of manufactured goods (e.g., cotton textiles), semi-processed agricultural products (e.g., indigo) or agricultural products (e.g., pepper). Our estimate is that c.1595–6, the annual bullion imports amounted to about 30,00,00,000 *dāms*. Assuming that compensatory exports consisted of manufactures to the extent of three-fourths of the value, we may infer that the total value of manufactures exported was 22,50,00,000 *dāms*, and the value added by urban manufactures about 11,25,00,000 *dāms*.[25] This would raise the total value added by urban manufactures to 1,67,34,71,987

[24] Review article 'Agrarian System of Mughal India', *Enquiry*, N.S., Vol. II, No. 1, pp. 92–121.

[25] *EME*, p.304.

dāms.

With our estimates of the amount going to maintain the bulk of the urban population, and the amount left in the countryside for subsistence-level existence, it may now be possible to work out the ratio between urban and rural populations, purely on the basis of the subsistence-level expenditures. For this we make the further reasonable assumption that for the mass of the population in the towns the physical components of subsistence-consumption were the same as for the mass of population in the countryside. The inference would then be that the total amount paid out in wages in the service and craft sectors should have maintained an equal number of people in the towns and the transport sector as would have been maintained in the villages by the same amount of money. The difference in urban and rural price-levels (which must surely have been considerable) would be accounted for at least partly by including wages of transport workers and earnings of middlemen in the urban sector.

The value of the part of the agricultural produce retained in the countryside, according to our estimates, was made up as follows (see Table 6.2).[26]

Table 6.2

	dāms
Amount left with the peasants	4,90,32,57,230
Rural expenditure of the *zamīndārs*, headmen, etc.	1,56,43,31,376
Rural expenditure out of payments to revenue staff	1,01,83,68,809
Rural expenditure by *jāgīrdārs*, retainers	44,80,18,117
Total	7,93,39,75,532

Thc amount for urban wages worked out above being 1,67,34,71,987 *dām*, we get the ratio of 1:5.08 to represent the urban/rural population ratio. In other words, the urban population was 17.42 per cent of the total, and the rural 82.58 per cent.

Our 'urban' population, however, includes, as noticed above, people dependent upon transport of rural goods to the town markets, some of whom, such as grain carriers, cartmen, traders, etc., could well have lived in villages. Unfortunately, there is no means by which one can conceivably estimate the rural portion of the transport workers

[26] The detailed calculations have been offered in *EME*, pp. 299–304.

and tradesmen. In view of the large volume of the country–town trade,[27] their number must have been quite considerable. The best, though rather arbitrary course, seems to be in rounding off the urban population at 15 per cent of the total population, by allowing the rural part of the village-town transport workers a size of 2.4 per cent of the total population. This would include the population of Banjaras, the main long-distance transporters of goods of bulk, whose number Irfan Habib estimates at 400,000 in the seventeenth century,[28] equal to about 0.266 per cent. of the total population of India estimated at 150 millions.

The best way to establish the validity of our estimate of the relative size of the urban population could have been by sample checks with regional estimates. The only one so far offered relates to Marwar. Nainsi in his *Vigat* provides us with the count of houses for certain towns, arranged by caste or profession.[29]

The number of houses in towns given by Nainsi (1659–65) is reproduced in Table 6.3 alongside the number of houses in the same towns in the 1891 census.

Table 6.3

Town		Number of houses	
	(a) 1659–64	(b) 1891	(b) as % of (a)
Sojhat	2,254	3,090	137.09
Jaitaran	1,839	1,189	64.65
Phalodi	657	2,438	371.08
Silwana	188	775	412.23
Sanchor	1,205	448	37.18
Merta	5,860	1,917	32.71
Jalor	3,049	2,341	76.78
Pakran	557	1,633	293.18
Total	15,609	13,831	88.61

[27] *ASMI*, pp. 68–90.

[28] Irfan Habib, 'Merchant Communities in Pre-Colonial India', in James Tracy, ed., *The Rise of Merchant Empires*, Cambridge, 1990, p.376.

[29] Munhata Nainsi, *Marwar ra Pargana ri Vigat* (c. 1666), edited by N.S., Bhati, 2 vols., Jodhpur, 1968–9. These have been discussed by B.L. Bhadani, 'Population of Marwar in the Middle of the Seventeenth Century', *IESHR*, Vol. XVI, No. 4, 1979, pp. 415–27. My own data are, however, directly derived from the published *Vigat*.

If the towns for which house-counts have been given by Nainsi form a fair sample of the towns of Marwar, there must have been an absolute fall in urban population between c. 1660 and 1891 by over 11 per cent.

Had the total population of Marwar remained the same between c. 1660 and 1891, the ratio of the urban population to the total should have been considerably higher in 1660 than in 1891. Bhadani, basing himself on plough-counts in the *Vigat*, offers a surprisingly high estimate for the total population of Marwar in 1660, placing it at above the 1891 level. Yet the size he himself deduces for the urban population still lies within the range of 12.24 to 15 per cent of the total population of Marwar (as compared with 10.60 per cent in 1891). Since his estimate of the total population is indubitably on the high side (the data available for it being far less reliable than those for the urban population), we can almost certainly set his range for the urban population of Marwar as the minimum possible rather than the likely actual. In any case, even this minimum corroborates our estimate of the relative size of the urban population in the Mughal Empire as a whole.

From the size of the urban population in general we may pass on to its distribution: The author of the *Ṭabaqāt-i Akbarī*, c. 1593, reports that Akbar's Empire contained 120 big cities and 3,200 townships (*qaṣba*), each having around it 100 to 1000 villages.[30] Given the total population of Akbar's Empire (not the whole India) as 983 millions,[31] the urban population at 15 per cent works out at 1,47,45,000. Given the *Ṭabaqāt's* number of towns, the population of an average town should have been 4,435.

Such an average is not unreasonable, and Irfan Habib has already argued that this should induce confidence in the estimated size of the urban population (though his estimates are not precisely the same as ours).[32] Thc classification that the *Ṭabaqāt* makes of the towns, setting 120 full-fledged cities besides 3,200 townships, or one city to nearly 27 townships, cannot be tested by any mode of scrutiny. Nonetheless, we can say that some of the towns in the Mughal empire were very

[30] Niẓāmūddīn Aḥmad, *Ṭabāqat-i Akbarī*, edited by B. De, Vol. II, Bib. Ind., Calcutta, 1913–35, pp. 545–6.

[31] Shireen Mossvi, 'Une Estimation de la Population de L'Inde en 1601', in *Population*, No. 2, Paris, 1984, p. 22.

[32] His estimate of the total population of the Mughal Empire is 107 to 115 million, and of its urban population 16 to 17 million; therefore his average population for each town is 5,000, *CEHI*, Vol. 1, p. 170.

large indeed. Monserrate in 1581 considered Lahore, 'second to none either in Asia or in Europe'.[33] Coryat in 1615 compared it to Constantinople.[34] In the seventeenth century Bernier found Delhi as big or bigger than Paris.[35] Ahmadabad was described as comparable to London and its suburbs.[36] European travellers in the seventeenth century also give us numerical estimate of the populations of other major cities of the empire,[37] but since the basis for these estimates is not known it is not possible to use them with much confidence, though generally speaking they support one's impression of the existence of large urban populations in the Mughal empire.

Besides these estimates of the European travellers, the populations of two Mughal cities have been estimated on the basis of contemporary quantitative evidence. Basing himself on the size of the imperial establishment and the workforce required to cater to the needs of the court and the nobility, Irfan Habib has estimated the population of Akbar's capital Fatehpur-Sikri in the 1580s at 220,000.[38] This is corroborated by other evidence. In 1585 when the court was still at Fatehpur-Sikri, Fitch said that 'Agra and Fatepor are two great cities, either of them much greater than London and very populous.'[39] He also thought that Fatehpur-Sikri was 'greater than Agra'.[40] London around 1600 is believed to have contained a population between 150,000 and 200,000.[41]

[33] Fr. A. Monserrate, *The Commentary of Father Monserrate S.J. on His Journey to the Court of Akbar*, translated by J.S. Hoyland and annotated by S.N. Banerjee, London, 1922, pp. 159–60.

[34] *Early Travels in India, 1583–1619*, edited by W. Foster, London, 1927, p. 243.

[35] F. Bernier, *Travels in the Mughal Empire, 1656–68*, translated by Constable, edited by Smith, London, 1916, pp. 281–2.

[36] *Early Travels*, p. 206.

[37] These have been conveniently collected together in tabular form in *CEHI*, Vol.I, p. 171.

[38] Irfan Habib, 'Fatehpur-Sikri—The Economic and Social Setting', in Michael Brand and Glenn D. Lowry, eds., *Fatehpur Sikri,* Bombay, 1987, pp.73–82. He estimates the male workforce employed at Fatehpur-Sikri in the building industry, imperial and aristocratic establishments, market and transport at 45,000. This multiplied by 4.5 gives a population of about 200,000. To this total he adds 20,000 to cover other classes (nobles, officials, scholars, merchants, etc.).

[39] *Early Travels*, pp. 17–18.

[40] Ibid.

[41] R. Mols in *Fontana Economic History of Europe*, Vol. II, ed., Carlo M. Cipolla, Glassgow, 1974, p. 42. Another estimate fixes London's population at

These two sister capital cities of Akbar thus must have contained a population nearly half a million around 1585. This accords with the European travellers' estimate of the population of Agra, when with the abandonment of Fatehpur-Sikri it became the main capital city.[42]

For the population of Delhi, in the 1650s, the same device as used by Irfan Habib has been employed by Fatima A. Imam, who arrives at an estimate of over 600,000.[43] As mentioned above, Bernier thought that the population of Delhi was more or less equal to that of Paris.[44] At that time Paris had a population of 500,000.[45] By this time Delhi had replaced Agra as the major capital of the Empire and some of its growth might have been at the expense of the latter city, though the size of Agra too remained impressive.[46]

It would be interesting to compare the estimates of populations of these Mughal cities with those of the largest cities of Western Europe around 1600:

Paris	200,000 to 300,000
London	200,000
Rome	100,000

Besides Paris and London no other city of Western Europe seems to have reached a population mark of 200,000 during the sixteenth century though a number of them such as Antwerp, Amsterdam, Venice, and Naples crossed the 100,000 mark.[47]

If the size of the largest cities could be an index of urbanization, the Mughal Empire had thus attained a level higher than that of Western

---

that time at 265,000 in H.C. Darby, ed., *Historical Geography of England*, London, 1951, p. 442.

[42] In 1609 its population has been estimated at 5,00,000 by J. Xavier (*JASB*, Vol. XIII, 1947, p. 121); Manrique (1629–43) gives a still higher estimate of 660,000 (F.S. Manrique, *Travels*, translated by C.E. Luard and Hosten, 1927, p. 1562).

[43] Fatima A. Imam, 'Economic History of Delhi—Shahjahanabad to 1739', unpublished M. Phil. Dissertation, M.A. Library, Aligarh Muslim University, Aligarh.

[44] Bernier, *Travels in the Mughal Empire, 1656*–68, pp. 281–2.

[45] *New Cambridge Modern History*, Vol. V, p. 246.

[46] Thevenot describes it in 1666 as 'a great town' and 'as to be able to send out 2000,00 men into the field'. For this see *Indian Travels of Thevenot and Careri*, edited and translated by S.N. Sen, Delhi, 1949, p. 49.

[47] *Cambridge Economic History of Europe*, Vol. IV, E.E. Richard and C.H. Wilson eds., Cambridge, 1967, pp. 82–3.

Europe in 1600.

The final question is, how was urbanization spread within the Mughal Empire, or, in other words, did some regions tend to be more urbanized than others? There seem to exist no data directly bearing on this question. There has, however, appeared to me one device that by establishing the size of urban taxes out of total taxation may give us some indication for regions within a fairly large part of the Mughal Empire.

The *Ā'īn-i Akbarī* gives us *jama'* for individual *pargana* (small territorial units) side by side with those of *ārāẓī* or measured area. Since the *jama'* included urban taxes besides land revenue, we could assume that if the rates of J/A (*jama'* divided by *ārāzī*) vary substantially between contiguous *pargana*, this might be largely due to the varying size of urban taxation (though part of the difference could come from varying patterns of cropping). We can take out the *pargana* containing a known town, and then calculate the J/A (*jama'/ārāzī*) of the remaining ('rural') *pargana*. If we multiply the *ārāzī* of the urban pargana by J/A of the rural, we would get the land revenue component of the *jama'* of the urban *pargana*. The remaining portion of the *jama'* could then represent urban taxation.

This device can, however, be used only for regions where measurement of the taxable land by Mughal administration was by and large complete. In areas where measurement was still in progress when the *Ā'īn* was compiled, this device could be misleading, because of the strong possibility for the *ārāzī* to be more fully measured in the *pargana* containing *sarkār* headquarters or *ṣūba* capitals than in other (purely rural) *pargana*. Here the J/A for rural *parganas* would appear as exceptionally high whereas that of the urban parganas would be much lower. Thus I have had to exclude the Mughal provinces of Ilahabad, Awadh, Malwa, and Multan, from which only incomplete *ārāzī* figures are available.[48]

For the remaining five provinces, containing measured area figures, the levels of urban taxation are given in Table 6.4.

If the urban taxation worked out by us is any index of the degree of urbanization,[49] the *ṣūba* of Gujarat appears at the top. Agra is next

[48] For the lack of completeness of Mughal survey work in these provinces see *ASMI*, pp.11–18.

[49] The size of urban taxation in relation to the *jama'* should have varied according to the rate of taxation and not with the price levels because the price-level would have affected the urban taxes as much as the total *jama'*.

to Gujarat with urban taxation at 15.7 per cent of the *jama'*. Interestingly enough Delhi registers the minimum size of urban taxation relative to *jama'*, namely, 3.37 per cent.

Table 6.4

Ṣūba	(a) Urban Tax (*dām*)	(b) *Jama'* (*dām*)	(a) as % of (b)
Agra	8,56,23,316	54,49,69,546	15.712
Delhi	2,02,53,570	60,06,87,797	3.372
Lahore	2,10,53,617	56,65,60,144	3.716
Gujarat	8,36,34,996	44,83,39,676	18.654
Ajmer	1,36,58,511	28,70,45,025	4.758

At the level of individual towns, Agra records the maximum urban tax-income (namely, 3,18,24,093 *dām*), but the *pargana* of Ahmadabad is a close second with urban taxation amounting to 3,13,02,645 *dām*. Can we then suppose that Ahmadabad was nearly as large a city, c. 1595, as Agra? Curiously, the size of Lahore appears to be rather small: urban taxation here amounted to only 32,64,848 *dām*.

The pre-eminence of Gujarat as the most urbanized region has wider implications for our understanding of the nature of Mughal towns. It has often been asserted that the Mughal towns tended to be 'camp-cities' depending on the court and the potentates' camps. Such towns subsisting directly on the expenditure of the ruling class are thought to be totally dependent on movements of the court or the *jāgīrdārs*' headquarters. But the high level of urbanization in Gujarat could have had almost nothing to do with the military encampments. It can only be explained in terms essentially of the inland long- distance trade generated by the demand for luxuries and other craft products fashioned in Gujarat, from members of the ruling class and their subordinate classes in whatever towns ('camp-cities' or not) in other regions that they might be residing.[50] We must realize that this could not be true just of Gujarat alone. In every region there would be specialized manufacturing centres catering to the demand in distant markets, even if no *jāgīrdār* established his household and stationed

[50] The overseas trade was important for Gujarat, but this alone surely could hardly have sustained more than a small part of its urban economy.

his retainers there. These manufacturing towns were then distinct from the so-called 'camp-cities', though many towns, of course, might well partake of a dual character being both encampments and manufacturing centres.

Though parasitic in nature (being based on consumption of agricultural surplus), the Mughal towns constituted a large demographic and economic sector. The urban populations unevenly spread throughout the empire subsisted on service, manufactures, trade and transport functioning through a complex economic and social network. The urban decline of the late eighteenth and nineteenth centuries, which must be assumed if our estimates of the urban population of the Mughal empire are accepted, was not simply a matter of the disappearance of decadent princes, courts, and their hangers-on; it was part and parcel of the destruction of an entire once-pulsating economy by colonial Tribute and Free Trade.

7

Work and Gender in Mughal India

The study of women as a component of the labour force in pre-colonial India is in infancy as yet. Monographs on women in Mughal India and other pre-modern regimes have tended to concentrate more on their social status, customs, clothing, and fashion, or on individual women.[1] The inadequacy of secondary work is partly explained, perhaps, by difficulties of source material. The kind of profuse documentation which exists for political and fiscal history of the sixteenth–eighteenth centuries is not available for either labour or demographic history. There is no way one can reconstruct sex ratios in the general population or in the non-domestic labour force.

One has, therefore, to cut one's coat according to one's cloth. Where some information is available, though this had not so far been brought together, is in respect of the kinds of work that women did. Incidental references in Indo-Persian and other literature from the fifteenth to eighteenth century provide us with general statements or individual facts from which general conditions may be inferred. Such material has been explored for this paper, notably, Abū'l Faẓl's *Ā'īn-i Akbarī* (c. 1595) and other historical works. Deserving of special mention is Muḥammad Shādiābadī's dictionary, *Miftāḥ-ul Fuẓala*, written in Malwa in 1468–9, with the explicit purpose of explaining words relating to things of everyday life. Its unique manuscript in the British Museum was illustrated probably early in Akbar's reign (1560s and 1570s), and these illustrations often help us when the text itself is silent.[2] In 1825 James Skinner wrote at Hansi (Haryana) his Persian

[1] Rekha Misra, *Women in Mughal India (1526–1748)*, Delhi, 1965; G. Rumer, *Gulbadan, Portrait of a Rose Princess at the Mughal Court*, New York, 1980; C. Pant, *Nur Jahan and Her Family*, Allahabad, 1978; J. Brijbhushan, *Razia Sultan of Hindostan*, New Delhi, 1990; A. Bulenschon, *The Life of a Mughal Princes, Jahan Ara Begum*, London, 1931; J. Brijbhusan, *Muslim Women*, New Delhi, 1980; S. Thomas, *Women of Destiny*, New Delhi, 1979.

[2] British Museum MS Or. 3299.

work on castes, the *Tashrīḥ-ul Aqwām*. The splendid illustrations he provided from hands of Mughal-school artists in the British Museum copy add to the detailed textual information which relates mainly to Haryana and the Delhi region.[3]

These two illustrated works exemplify the importance of pictorial evidence, notably offered by miniatures of the imperial Mughal school of the sixteenth and seventeenth centuries. Its well-known tradition of accuracy and realism invest this school's portrayals of scenes of the court and of everyday life with particular significance for our purpose. The miniatures of the later Mughal-influenced Rajput and Hill schools (eighteenth century) supplement the Mughal school.

The third principal body of evidence comes from British surveys and reports of the early nineteenth century, where conditions and traditions of the pre-colonial society were observed and noted. Most noteworthy among these is Francis Buchanan's set of celebrated *Journey from Madras* (1800–01)[4] and his detailed surveys of districts of the lower and Gangetic basin, prepared between 1806 and 1812.[5] These can be said to form the initial point of all modern economic and anthropological enquiries in India.

What follows is a classified presentation of information of the gender division of labour as one can reconstruct for pre-colonial northern India from this material. At the end I hope to examine the broad inferences one can derive from the description.

Agriculture

Our evidence shows ploughing to be a man's operation: all illustrations from the Mughal and Hill (Pahari) schools, for example, show only men drawing the plough. In line with current practice, a Mughal

[3] Br. Mus. Add. 27,255.

[4] Francis Buchanan, *A Journey from Madras through the Countries of Mysore, Canara, and Malabar, & C.*, London, 1807, 3 vols. I have not used the very rich material contained in this work, because my present paper is confined to northern India only.

[5] Francis Buchanan, *An Account of the District of Purnea in 1809–10*, Patna, 1986 (reprint); *An Account of the Districts of Bihar and Patna in 1811–12* (*Patna–Gaya Report*), Patna, 1986 (reprint); *An Account of the District of Shahabad* (*Shahabad Report*), 1832, *An Account of the District of Bhagalpore, 1831* (*Bhagalpur Report*); see also Motgomery Martin, ed., *The History, Antiquities, Topography, and Statistics of Eastern India*, 3 vols., London, 1838, where these and other district surveys are reproduced in an abridged form.

miniature of c. 1610 depicts a woman sowing seed broadcast, walking directly behind the man driving the plough.[6] In 1811–2 Buchanan reported that in Bihar women earned some wages through sowing seeds, though this was for them a part-time job in addition to spinning.[7]

The work in the field that the women did in the eighteenth century included transplanting, weeding, and helping in harvesting.[8] Though the actual operations carried out by women are not always clear enough in Mughal miniatures, women working in the fields form part of the typical rural scene depicted by the artists. Such illustrations may be seen in the *Anwār-i Suhailī* illustrated in 1575[9] and *Razmnāma*, c.1600.[10] A line drawing of early nineteenth century from Kashmir very clearly depicts a woman transplanting paddy along with a man.[11]

Both men and women were hired for weeding and transplanting work, and, at least in District Purnea (Bihar), c. 1810, their wages were equal, though both were paid generally in kind. Buchanan estimates that a man able to work 270 days in a year could earn about twelve rupees a year. His wife doing the same job could 'make fully as much'.[12]

Besides these direct field operations, there was another task performed by women that too merits classification as field work. They not only cooked food for their men working in the fields, but also carried it to the field. In an illustration in the *Anwār-i Suhailī*, a woman is shown bringing food to her husband standing on the well irrigating the fields.[13]

After the produce was collected from the field, it apparently called for more work from women than men. The beating of rice was exclusively a woman's job, and in the illustration of pestle and mortar (*okhlī*), the *Miftāḥ-ul Fuẓala* shows a woman working with it.[14]

Buchanan writing about Bihar and eastern UP, c. 1810, says that the cleaning of rice was 'performed entirely by the women'. The separation of husk from rice was done by three methods, namely, by

[6] T. Falk and S. Digby, *Paintings from Mughal India*, London, n.d., Plate 18.

[7] *Patna–Gaya Report*, Vol. II, p. 618.

[8] *Purnea Report*, pp. 444 and 446.

[9] *Anwār-i Suhailī* Bharat Kala Bhavan, Varanasi, No.9069, f.18.

[10] Prince of Wales Museum, Bombay, Acc. No.43.35 (dispersed copy).

[11] D.D. Kosambi, *An Introduction to the Study of Indian History*, Bombay, 1956, p. 319, Fig. 41.

[12] *Purnea Report*, p. 446.

[13] *Anwār-i Suhailī*, Bharat Kala Bhavan, Varanasi, MS 9069, f.61.

[14] Or. 3299, f. 89a.

a wooden foot-worked hammer, called *dhengli*; by beating by hand in mortar and pestle (*okhlī*), and by boiling. The first of these methods according to Buchanan was 'very laborious and was generally carried out by two women'. The beating of rice in mortar with a wooden pestle was comparatively lighter work, but the method was less efficient. Only the winter or coarse varieties of rice were cleaned by boiling — that was the easiest method but considered most inferior.[15] The payment for the work was made in kind, the woman being called upon to furnish 9 or 10 measures of husked rice for every 23 or 24 measures of paddy, her wages being simply the husked rice that she had left with her after she had delivered to her employer the fixed measures. Buchanan estimates that the woman was usually left with less than one-fifth of the rice she cleaned (Dinajpur, c. 1810).[16] In Purnea a woman by cleaning rice, around 1810, earned not more than a quarter of a rupee a month and allowing for sickness, etc., she worked about ten months a year, and thus earned not more than Rs 2.50 in a year.[17]

Rice husking was not a full time job as women did it along with their other domestic duties and spinning. In any case beating rice by working the dhengli was so laborious that the women were only able to exert themselves for a limited number of hours.[18]

Not only the cleaning of rice but the milling of all food-grains as well was considered a woman's job. The *Miftāḥ-ul Fuẓala* (1468–9) shows a woman turning a rotary hand-mill, with a single handle.[19] In 1676 Fryer noted about India generally:

> The Indian Wives dress their Husbands, Victuals, fetch Water, and Grind their Corn with Hand-Mill, when they sing, chat, and are merry.[20]

When Buchanan says that two women used to sit on the hand-mill, the labour being very hard, and the work restricted to three hours a day, he must be referring to a larger hand-mill used for grinding of grain for non-domestic use or for the market. He adds that both men

[15] M. Martin, ed., *Eastern India*, Vol. II, pp. 822.

[16] Ibid., p. 823.

[17] *Purnea Report*, p. 444.

[18] *Eastern India*, Vol. II, p. 822.

[19] Or. 3299 f. 119a.

[20] J. Fryer, *A New Account of East India & Persia being Nineteen Year's Travels, 1672–81*, edited by W. Crook, Vol. II, London, 1912, p. 118.

and women were employed at such hand-mills.[21]

Fetching water for domestic needs, as Fryer observed, was another customary chore of Indian women. The way the village women in India carried pitchers, filled with water, balancing them one over the other on their heads, became a popular theme for artists and was a feat remarkable enough to draw the attention of Emperor Akbar who commended Indian women for it.[22] The pictorial representations show women drawing water from wells either by throwing down a rope with pot and pulling it up (c. 1570),[23] or by drawing it over a pulley set up on the well (c. 1700).[24] Some of these and other paintings from the eighteenth century show women carrying filled pitchers.[25]

Fig.7.1: Women at well, women fetching water from well. Line-drawing from *Hamzanama* painting, Victorial and Albert Museum, London

[21] *Patna and Gaya Report*, Vol. II, p. 637.

[22] *Āīn*, Vol. II, p. 228.

[23] Basil Gray, ed., *Rajput Paintings*, Faber Gallery of Oriental Art, n.d., Plate 2.

[24] Laurence Binyon, *The Court Painters of the Grand Moguls*, London, 1921, Plate XVII; T. Falk and S. Digby, *Paintings from Mughal India*, London, n.d., Plate 26; T. Falk and M. Archer, *Indian Miniatures in the India Office Library*, Delhi, 1981, Plate 42d, p.514.

[25] L. Hajek and W. Forman, *Miniatures from the East*, London, n.d., Plates 46 and 47. E. Kuhnel, *Miniatumalerei Im Ishamischen Orient*, Berlin, 1923, p.147.

In 1810s Buchanan found in Bhagalpur 'a great many poor women' who made their living by 'carrying water for wealthy families' and were called '*Panibharin*' (water-fillers). The usual payment for supplying one pitcher daily was 2 paisa (1 rupee=64 paisas) a month and the women were thereby able to earn about half a rupee a month. This income they generally supplemented by some spinning. In Patna the wages for water-carrying were higher.[26]

Looking after cattle and making milk products formed another major sector of women's work. Explaining the term for butter (*maska*), the illustration in the *Miftāḥ-ul Fuẓala*, shows a women sitting and churning butter-milk.[27] In a Kangra painting showing Krishna stealing butter, women are shown making butter.[28] A man is never shown in any illustration similarly preparing butter or butter-milk.

Feeding cattle was also a part of women's domestic chores. A miniature of Kangra school, c. 1750 shows women feeding cows.[29] However, milking cows was a job which men and women both performed; and there seems no strict division of work here for the paintings show men and women both milking cows and goats.[30]

The women did a number of other sundry jobs related to agriculture for which we have traditions but little literary or visual evidence. The jobs included feeding oil seeds or pieces of sugarcanes in the press worked by men, cooking sugarcane juice for making jaggery, etc. Their role could be so important that Akbar's official historian, Abū'l Faẓl writing about Bengal says that the entire agricultural work depended upon women.[31] Bengal being mainly a paddy producing area this statement might not be an exaggeration, since weeding, transplanting, harvesting, and beating rice all essentially fell to the women's share. Women helped in irrigation as well: a nineteenth-century drawing from Kashmir shows a man drawing water from a well while the woman cuts and makes water channels to irrigate the field.[32]

[26] *Patna-Gaya Report*, Vol. I, p. 287.

[27] Or. 3299, f. 89b.

[28] M.S. Randhava, *Kangra Paintings of the Bhagvata Purana*, New Delhi, 1960, Plate III (colour).

[29] Ibid., Fig. 4 (black and white).

[30] D. Barret and B. Gray, *Paintings of India*, British Museum, 1963, pp.74, 88 (c.1595), 156 (c. 1690).

[31] *Āʾīn*, Vol. I, p. 389.

[32] D.D. Kosambi, *An Introduction to the Study of Indian History*, Fig. 43, p. 321.

It appears that the women of common peasants invariably worked along with their men. Only the castes who claimed a higher status tended to keep their women indoors, as in the case of higher ranks among the Jats, according to the *Tashrīḥ-ul Aqwām*.[33]

An interesting evidence of women carrying out actual cultivation comes from the Middle Himalayas, where only hoeing, not ploughing, could be practiced to loosen the soil. Here in 1624 it was reported that 'the women cultivate the soil, while men are weavers'.[34] The conditions in the Kashmir Valley were not identical, but a number of nineteenth-century drawings from Kashmir show women performing almost all agricultural operations along with men, except ploughing.[35]

Textiles

The process of textile manufacture, after cotton was removed from the field, followed fairly well-marked stages. First of all, there was the process of separating the fibre from the seed, a function which seems to have been performed mainly by women. The Ajanta frescoes of the sixth century show a woman using the Indian cotton-gin, now called *charkhī* (two rollers horizontally mounted on a stand, but without worm-gearing).[36] In an eighteenth-century painting a woman is shown carrying the same instrument, now provided with worm-gears as well.[37]

After the seeds were expelled, the fibres had to be separated from each other ('scutched'). The Ajanta frescoes mentioned above show a woman working with a roller and a board, to obtain the separation;[38] but this was a laborious process, which could also damage the fibres. By medieval times, the bow-string device was in wide use for this purpose. This was invariably operated by men so that a semi-itinerant class of men, *dhunyās* or *naddāfs*, went around scutching cotton. In the fourteenth century we are told how, after obtaining cotton, a mother gave it to a *naddāf* (male scutcher) to scutch it.[39] Pictorial

[33] Add. 27,255, f. 157a.

[34] C. Wessels, *Early Jesuit Travellers in Central Asia, 1603–1721*, The Hague, 1924, p. 52.

[35] D.D. Kosambi, *An Introduction to the Study of Indian History*, pp. 318–19, 321.

[36] Reproduced in G. Yazdani, *Ajanta, the Colour and Monochrome Reproductions of the Ajanta Frescoes, based on Photography*, Part I, Plate XII.

[37] L. Hajek, *Miniatures from the East*, London, 1960, Plates 48 and 49.

[38] M.K. Dhavalikar, *Ajanta: A Cultural Study*, Poona, 1973, p.2.

[39] *Khair-ul Majālis*, K.A. Nizami ed., Aligarh, 1956, pp. 190–1.

representations show the cotton-bow was used exclusively by men.[40] But it appears that the bow did not altogether replace hand-beating, and in the 1660s according to an English factor women scutched fibres by this process.[41] Buchanan too reports women beating cotton to separate fibres, c. 1810. He adds, however, that 'for greater part' scutching was done by men using the bow.[42]

Not all *dhunyās* ('carders') went door to door selling their services; a considerable proportion of them (around one-third, according to Buchanan) purchased cotton and scutched it at home.[43] In the case of these 'self-employed' carders the women were entrusted with the job of hawking the cotton scutched at home by their men.[44]

The next process, namely, spinning, was done almost exclusively by women, by hand-spindle or by wheel. Writing at the close of the fourteenth century, Amīr Khusrau likens the needle and spindle to a young woman's spear and arrow.[45] In the dictionary *Miftāḥ-ul Fuẓala*, written in 1468–9 and illustrated about a hundred years later, where the text explains the terms for spindle (*duk* and *praiti*), the illustration depicts it as being worked by women.[46] The same work defines the *charkha*, or spinning wheel, as the device 'by which women spin yarn'.[47] The earliest reference to spinning wheel in India, dates back to 1350, when, while censuring Queen Raẓiyya for claiming to act as sovereign, the historian Isāmī says that a woman is suited only to work on the spinning wheel.[48]

From the succeeding centuries continuous pictorial evidence of women working on the spinning wheel grows in profusion through the miniatures of Mughal painters as well as other Indian schools. A selection is listed below:

[40] Or. 3299, f. 66.

[41] *English Factories in India 1665–7*, Foster ed., Oxford, 1927, p. 174.

[42] *Patna–Gaya Report*, p. 647.

[43] Ibid.

[44] *Purnea Report*, p. 536. A day's sale proceeds are estimated as Re 1 to Rs 2.

[45] *Hasht Bihisht*, M. Sulaiman Ashraf ed., Aligarh, 1918, p. 28.

[46] Or. 3299 f. 151a.

[47] Ibid., f. 94b.

[48] *Futūḥ-us Salāṭīn*, A.S. Usha ed., Madras, 1948, p. 134. Spinning wheel, originally a Chinese device, came to India probably through the Islamic civilization. Interestingly enough in the Persian poetry of twelfth–thirteenth centuries the wheel (*charkhī*) is invariably seen as an instrument worked by women. Cf. Irfan Habib, 'Medieval Technology Exchange between India and the Islamic World' in *Aligarh Journal of Oriental Studies*, Vol. II. Nos. 1–2, 1985, pp. 203–4.

(a) A woman spinning on wheel with no crank handle: illustration in *Miftāḥ-ul Fuẓala*.[49]

(b) Village women carrying spinning wheels, c. 1590.[50]

(c) A woman with a spinning wheel with no handles, dated 1606.[51]

(e) Three women working on spinning wheels, in the foreground, 1617.[52]

(f) A woman and a wheel with a half handle, Shāhjahān's reign (1627–58).[53]

(g) A sturdy village woman sitting in front of a spinning wheel with handle, c. 1670.[54]

Fig.7.2: Woman spinning . Line drawing from painting in F.R. Martin, The *Miniature Painting and Painters of Persia, India and Turkey*, London, 1912, II, Plate 207(a). Current provenance unknown.

[49] Or. 3299 f. 151a.

[50] Cf. p.137 *Razmnāma*, Or. 12076f.

[51] E. Kuhnel and H. Goets, *Indian Book Painting from Jahangir's Album in the State Library, Berlin*, London, 1926, Plate 1.

[52] A.K. Das, *Mughal Paintings During Jahangir's Reign*, Calcutta, 1978, Plate 2.

[53] Ivan Stchoukine, *'La Peinture Indienne a l'Époque des Grands Moghols'*, Paris 1929, Plate XLIV.

[54] F.R. Martin, *The Miniature Paintings and Painters of Persia, India, Turkey, from the Eighth to the Eighteenth Century*, London, 1912, Plate 207a.

(h) Spinning wheel, with handle, being carried by a woman, Kangra painting depicting a scene from the Mahabharata, 1785–90.[55]

As in the case of scutching, the two devices for spinning also remained in use simultaneously. The hand spindle was used by women to spin fine yarn and silk thread even in the nineteenth century.[56]

Buchanan says that spinning was not a taboo for any caste and thus a large number of women from all castes used to spin.[57] We are told in the fourteenth century, that Shaikh Niẓāmuddīn's mother, when making a turban for him, spun half of the yarn herself, while the other half was spun by her slave girl.[58] The *Tashrīḥ-ul Aqwām*, c. 1825, says that the women of the Kayasth caste also spun yarn.[59] Even if women did not spin for wages, they still spun for the use of the family.[60]

Spinning could be adjusted to the working time available to individual women. Thus Buchanan noted that they spun 'when their other occupations permit', spinning often coming after the work of cooking, bringing up children, and beating rice. On the other hand, 'the women of rank' who sat before the wheel for a whole day could do so because they were not obliged to attend to other work.[61] Wages in both cases naturally varied. Women, working part-time, on an average earned Rs 3.25 a year in Bihar,[62] Rs 2.37 in Gorakhpur,[63] and a quarter rupee a month, that is Rs 3 a year, in Purnea.[64] As against this, those who worked full time and spun fine-thread earned fifteen annas a month or Rs 11.25 a year in Purnea.[65]

Women spinners did not usually work for wages, but as self-employed persons, obtaining the raw material themselves. At times they bought even unscutched cotton, had it scutched on payment,[66]

[55] M.S. Randhava, *Kangra Paintings*, Plate V.

[56] *Purnea Report*, pp. 536–7.

[57] Ibid., p. 536.

[58] *Khairul Majālis*, pp. 190–1.

[59] Add. 27,255 f. 105b.

[60] *Patna–Gaya Report*, Vol. II, p. 639.

[61] *Purnea Report*, pp. 536–7.

[62] *Patna–Gaya Report*, p. 647–8.

[63] *Eastern India*, pp. 558–9.

[64] *Purnea Report*, pp. 536–7.

[65] Ibid.

[66] *Eastern India*, pp. 558–9.

and then spun the yarn, and sold it.[67] It was perhaps more convenient and practical for women since this arrangement did not subject them to any strict time-schedule or make them work outdoors. The spinning in case of part-time spinners was done usually in the afternoon, while beating rice occupied them during the mornings.

Cotton was not the only material for women to work in. They also worked at reeling and selling tasar-silk thread. The earnings estimated were 7.5 *annas* a month.[68]

In Kashmir shawl-wool was spun by girls who started work at the age of ten and according to an estimate, a hundred thousand women (out of a supposed total population of 800,000) were engaged in spinning wool in the valley in 1822.[69]

Whereas spinning was strictly women's work, the actual weaving was done mainly by men, though women presumably assisted them in preparing the warp and weft-threads. Mughal and later miniatures show only men with the loom.[70] But Buchanan says that, 'each loom requires one man and woman', the latter to wind, and to assist in wrapping.[71]

In carpet-making, while spinning was again done by women, the weaving was reserved to men. The collective earnings of two men and two women were estimated by Buchanan at Rs 17.89 in a month. Here too the raw material was their own.[72]

In blanket-making, the same division of work prevailed, women spun and men wove. A pair of shepherds (man and woman) in Bihar are reported by Buchanan to have produced a blanket worth one rupee in four days.[73]

In other processes after weaving, it seems the division of work between men and women was not so sharply defined. In dyeing and perhaps bleaching both worked together. Writing in 1675–6 Fryer

[67] *Patna–Gaya Report*, pp. 647–8; *Purnea Report*, pp. 536–7; *Eastern India* (Gorakhpoor), pp.558–9.

[68] *Patna–Gaya Report*, Vol. II, p. 651.

[69] W. Moorcroft and G. Trebeck, *Travels in the Himalayan Provinces of Hindustan and the Punjab in Laddakh and Kashmir from 1819 to 1825*, edited by H.H. Wilson, Vol. II, London, 1937, p. 174.

[70] Or 3299, ff.262a, 268; *Tutinama*, c.1565–70, Chester Beatty Library, MS No.21 f.29.

[71] *Patna–Gaya Report*, p. 651.

[72] Ibid., p. 657.

[73] Ibid., p. 651.

says that in Calicut washermen were both 'women as well as men': they were not only very competent but also cheap.[74] In Bihar too both men and women washed and bleached cloth for the English Company in c. 1810 and the earnings of husband and wife collectively were '1 anna short of 28 Rs' a year.[75] The women besides working with their husbands also washed the worn clothes of people, acting as domestic washerwomen.[76] Calico printing too was apparently carried out by both. Moti Chandra finds words for both male and female calico-printers, in the fourteenth–fifteenth century, namely, *chhimpaka* for female and *chhipa* for male printers.[77]

From the seventh century we have evidence of women putting patterns on cloth by the tie-and-dye process.[78] Women's role in this process has remained traditional, though often professional men and women worked together.

Another craft that the women pursued was embroidery. They stitched 'flowers' upon muslin, a profession said to be pursued by them at various places.[79]

Building Industry

In its detailed description of the staff of the building establishment of the Mughal government, Abū'l Faẓl's *Ā'īn-i Akbarī* does not indicate, directly or indirectly, any participation of women labourers in construction work. But Mughal paintings provide firm evidence of their participation. In a depiction (c. 1590) of the building of Akbar's capital city of Fatehpur Sikri, women are shown performing heavy tasks like breaking stones and old bricks by pounding to prepare rubble, preparing bitumen mortar-cement and staining and mixing lime used to surface walls.[80] In another painting of the same time depicting Akbar's construction of the Agra fort, women are seen preparing lime-mortar, and carrying it in pans, held in hand or over their heads,

[74] J. Fryer, *A New Account of East India & Persia being Nineteen Year's Travels*, Vol. II, pp. 121–2.

[75] *Patna–Gaya Report*, pp. 616–17.

[76] Ibid.

[77] Moti Chandra, *Journal of Indian Textile History*, Vol. V, pp. 51–2.

[78] Bānabhatta, *Harshacarita*, P.V. Kane ed., 2nd edn. Delhi, 1965, Ucchvāsa IV, p. 14. I owe this reference to my colleague Mr Ishrat Alam, who has also given me other help.

[79] *Purnea Report*, p. 544 and *Patna–Gaya Report*, Vol. II, p. 655.

[80] Binyon, *Court Painters*, Plate IX.

Fig.7.3: Women breaking stones and seiving material in lime-making, Fatehpur Sikri. Line drawing from miniature from *Akbarnama*, Victoria and Albert Museum, London

Fig.7.4: Women carrying bitumen, construction of Agra Fort. Line drawing from *Akbarnama* painting, Victoria and Albert Museum, London

to the masons at work. At least one of them walks up a slanted platform with the pan on her head.[81] It is worth noting that these jobs continue to be traditionally women's jobs in the Indian building industry even today.

Unfortunately, there is no information about women's wages. If the brick pounders (*surkhī kob*) in Abū'l Faẓl's account are women,

[81] Geeti Sen, *Paintings from the Akbarnama*, Calcutta, 1984, Plates 31 and 61.

we may take it that each woman worker earned 1.5 *dāms* (40 *dāms*=Re 1) for pounding 8 *mans* (200.88 kg) of bricks. If she then pounded 10.66 *mans* (267.83 kg), she would have earned the lowest daily wage specified for the same work for unskilled labourers.[82]

Petty Commerce

Women's participation in petty commerce seems to have been considerable. Milk and its products were usually hawked by them. Buchanan writing, c. 1810, about Bihar, describes the division of work among pastoral castes as follows: The young men were 'farmers', the old and the children tended cattle, and women sold milk and the cakes of dung that were used for fuel.[83] In fact, the collection of dung and the making of dung cakes for fuel was a task traditionally assigned to women and children. The author of the *Tashrīḥ-ul Aqwām*, 1825, a work on castes, describing the Gujjar and Ghosi castes, differentiates between the two castes according to the way their women sold milk, curd, butter, etc. According to him the women of the Gujjars hawked the products from door to door, while those of the Ghosis sold these at their own houses.[84]

Men and women of the Kunjra caste sold green vegetables[85] while only the women of gardeners hawked fruits and green vegetable in the markets and went from door to door.[86] The women of gardeners' caste also sold flowers, the *Tashrīḥ-ul Aqwām* mentions this and a miniature of the eighteenth century from Awadh depicts a female flowerseller.[87]

Bangle-makers sold bangles visiting the houses and hawking along streets and lanes: their women carried the basket of bangles while they emitted cries to attract customers' attention. The *Tashrīḥ-ul Aqwām* generally describes this as being the practice in Haryana around 1825.[88] Buchanan c.1810 gives a similar account of the glass and lac-bangle-makers in Bihar.[89]

At least in Bihar, about that time, all grain parchers and sellers of parched grains were women. They used to sit on the road sides with

[82] *Ā'īn*, Vol. I, p. 170. (1 *man-i Akbari* being equal to 25.11 kg, *ASMI, p.421&n*

[83] *Patna–Gaya Report*, Vol. II, p. 635.

[84] Br. Mus. Add. 27,255, f. 150a.

[85] Ibid., f. 235a.

[86] Ibid., f. 232b.

[87] T. Falk and M. Archer, *Indian Miniatures in the India Office*, Plate 26.

[88] Add. 27,255, ff. 326a–7a.

[89] *Patna–Gaya Report*, Vol. II, pp. 620–1.

small fire places while the customers brought their own grain to get it parched, the parchers keeping back small amounts of grain. In this way, according to Buchanan, women earned no more than 2 paisas a day (that is less than a rupee a month). But some had their own grain that they parched and sold sitting at their shops, their earnings then being a good deal more.[90]

Selling fish either door to door or in the market was also traditionally a women's profession among the fisher folk.[91]

Sundry Professions

There were various other professions where gender division of work was not well marked, and men and women both carried the same professions either separately or together. The potter's wife, for example, kneaded clay for the potter working at the kiln, as shown in an illustration, c. 1850–60.[92]

Men and women both worked as sweepers.[93] In making ornaments out of lac men and women worked together. Possibly, here women did not work full-time since, unlike men, they had also other chores to look after e.g., beating rice to supplement family earnings.[94]

The leaves widely used for serving meals in were gathered, dried, and stitched by men and women working together. A husband and wife making such platters earned approximately Rs 3 a month.[95] In the manufacture of nitre salt one man, one woman and two girls or boys were required to look after each furnace, though perhaps they performed different tasks.[96] In preparation of tobacco and charcoal balls, both the sexes were equally occupied.[97]

A profession where women had primacy, though it was not their sole preserve, was that of inn-keeping. The inn-keepers (*b͟hatyārīs*) were traditionally women. Rafi'uddīn Shīrāzī, a Persian merchant visiting India in the 1560s tells us:

[90] Ibid., Vol. II, p. 636.

[91] Ibid., p. 291.

[92] Reproduced in William Crooke, *A Glossary of North Indian Peasant Life*, Shahid Amin ed., New Delhi, 1989, Plate X.

[93] Add. 27,255, f. 178b.

[94] *Purnea Report*, p. 522.

[95] *Patna–Gaya Report*, Vol. II, pp. 617–18.

[96] Ibid., 667.

[97] Ibid., p. 629.

On roads used by people at every *farsakh* (2.5 miles) or half *farsakh*, notables of this country have founded or left behind in trust *sarāis* (inns), where persons of the caste of *bhatiyārās* (male) reside so that whenever the travellers arrive, they can on payment stay there and give provisions for food to the *bhatiyārī* (female) who then cooks the food according to their taste and takes her wage.

He calls such inns '*bhatiyārī's* houses'.[98]

Manucci records a tradition that Sher Shāh (1540–5) assigned the duty of looking after the travellers to married slaves and their wives.[99] Withington visiting India in 1612–6 mentions only women inn-keepers.[100] Peter Mundy in India, c. 1630, not only emphasizes that inn-keeping was the job of women but also informs us that their men were most commonly *Kahārs* (palanquin bearers), fowlers or fishermen.[101] G. Forster says more cautiously that 'many' of the inn-keepers were women.[102] In 1810s Buchanan still found inn-keeping as the job of old women.[103] The inn-keeping of course included the work of preparing and serving meals.

Women also served as wine-servers in taverns. There is an interesting pictorial representation in the *Miftāḥ-ul Fuẓala* of a tavern where women are serving wine and eatables and also entertaining the guests by singing with musical instruments. The fact that Emperor Akbar in 1582 appointed a woman belonging to the caste of wine-distillers to the official wine shop at the court[104] suggests that the *Miftāḥ-ul Fuẓala's* illustration was no fantasy, but depicted actual conditions.

Among the nomadic roadside entertainers called *nats* (male) and *natnīs* (female) forming a well-known caste of rope dancers and gymnasts, women performed various gymnastic feasts. Thevenot in 1660s describes a performance by a pair in Nander (Maharashtra) where the major role was played by the woman-performer. He provides an illustration as well.[105] The *Tashrīḥ-ul Aqwām* shows a woman

[98] *Tazkiratu'l Mulūk*, Add. 23883, ff. 172a–74b.

[99] N. Manucci, *Storia do Mogor, 1656–1712*, translated by W. Irvine, London, 1907–8, p. 115.

[100] W. Foster, ed., *Early Travels in India 1583–1619)*, London, 1927, p. 225.

[101] R.C. Temple, ed., *The Travels of Peter Mundy in Europe and Asia*, London, 1914, p. 121.

[102] G. Forster, *A Journey from Bengal to England*, London, pp. 86–7, 92.

[103] *Patna–Gaya Report*, p. 635.

[104] Badāūnī, Vol. II, pp. 301–2.

[105] *Travels of Thevenot and Careri*, pp. 107 and 109.

performing along with a man.[106] There was another class of female professional magicians (*Bhānmati*) who showed their tricks and magical articles. A description of them, with illustration, is provided in the *Tashrīḥ-ul Aqwām*.[107]

Women of a number of lower castes went to upper class houses on occasion of celebrations of births and marriages to sing and dance 'in order to earn their livelihood.'[108] Women of lime-makers did this, according to the *Tashrīḥ-ul Aqwām*,[109] and those of *doms* (*domīnīs*), according to a contemporary narrative from Lucknow.[110]

Singing and dancing at a higher professional level was also carried out by women who worked as free entertainers for higher classes. In most cases, their men acted as musicians playing instruments or in the case of less accomplished persons, took other sundry professions. These women singers and dancers usually acted as prostitutes,[111] a profession whose prevalence was acknowledged. Emperor Akbar allotted a special locality in his capital, Fatehpur Sikri, for the courtesans and tried to restrict their visits as dancers to the houses of nobles and gentry.[112]

A crucial role was played by women as primitive doctors and physicians. They served as midwives and as nurses to babies. The midwife and nurses invariably appear in Mughal paintings depicting scenes of births of princes, as for example that of Emperor Akbar himself[113] and those of his sons,[114] as well as of the birth of Lord Krishna, painted during the eighteenth century.[115]

A popular notion was that a number of diseases originated owing to excess or bad blood and it had, therefore, to be sucked out by leeches. Mrs Meer Hasan Ali (c. 1820) observed 'leech-women' at

[106] Add. 27,255, f. 304b (illustration) and f.306a.

[107] Ibid., f. 123b (illustration), f. 124a.

[108] Ibid., f.141a.

[109] Ibid.

[110] Mrs Meer Hasan Ali, *Observations on the Mussulmans of India*, Vol. II, London, 1832, p. 43.

[111] Add. 27,255, ff.138a–141b.

[112] Badāūnī, *Muntakhab-ut-Tawārīkh*, edited by Ahmad Ali, Vol. II, 1865, p. 186.

[113] Or. 12988, ff.20b and 22a, Plate 44;

[114] Chester Beaty Library Ms No.3 ff. 142b and 143b; Geeti Sen, *Paintings from the Akbarnama*, Calcutta, 1984, Plates 56 and 57.

[115] W.G. Archer, *Visions of Courtly India*, London, 1976, Plate 27.

Lucknow visiting homes with the insects and performing this operation, which required a certain amount of skill.[116]

It was common for women to work on wages as domestic servants. The practice of employing female domestic servants was certainly not confined to aristocratic establishments. A painting, c. 1740, depicts a rather modest home where a maidservant is seen killing a snake, the operation being observed by three other, one of whom is apparently the mistress of house.[117] Describing the practice in Bihar and eastern UP, Buchanan states that the wages given to women domestic servants were 'as high nearly as those given to men'.[118]

Elite Professions

Women's occupations do not seem to have been confined to manual labour and arts alone. There are at least a few references to women pursuing trade, and controlling agricultural land and urban property. In the seventeenth century, a Surat merchant left to his wife his merchandise and the conduct of his trade at Surat when he went to Mecca as the agent of another merchant. When he died there the widow went to the court of a *qāẓī* to claim her right to manage her deceased husband's affairs.[119]

In the territory of the present state of Uttar Pradesh, a Khatri woman, Sabhanu, is found selling her village land, c. 1680. There is evidence of other Brahman as well as Muslim women in the same region, who were proprietresses of village lands.[120] They also formed an important class of recipients of land grants from the imperial Mughal government.[121] Jahangir appointed a woman to process and recommend such grants.[122] Shāhjahān followed the practice and the head of department came to be designated as the *Ṣadru-n Nisa'*.[123]

[116] Mrs Meer Hasan Ali, *Observations on the Mussulmans of India*, pp. 143–4.

[117] T. Falk and M. Archer, *Indian Miniatures*, p.436, Plate 239.

[118] *Patna–Gaya Report*, Vol. I, p.287.

[119] Blochet, Supp. Pers. 482 ff. 185a–6b. For full translation of the document see my 'Travails of a Mercantile Community—Aspects of Social Life at the Port of Surat', *PIHC*, 52nd Session, Delhi, 1991–2, pp. 408–9.

[120] For full references see *ASMI*, pp.191–2, f.n. 95.

[121] Ibid., pp.352–3 and *n*.

[122] *Tuzuk-i Jahāngīrī*, S. Ahmad ed., Ghazipur, 1863, p. 21.

[123] Shāhnawāz Khān, *Ma'āṣir-ul Umarā'*, edited by Abdur Rahim and Ashraf Ali, Calcutta, 1881, p.241.

Sale deeds from such Gujarat towns as Surat, Cambay, and Broach show that during the seventeenth and eighteenth centuries women owned urban property which they themselves purchased, sold, or mortgaged.[124]

It was, perhaps, possible for women to fulfil responsibilities of such positions, whether by inherited ownership or grant or appointment, because among higher classes it was not uncommon for women to be lettered. The illustration depicting a school scene in the *Miftāḥ-ul Fuẓala* shows a young girl sitting with a boy learning to write the alphabet.[125]

Mughal court artists depict women reading letters and books.[126] From the Deccan School too comes similar pictorial evidence. Mughal royal ladies were learned enough to maintain their personal libraries and to compose poetry.[127] There are notices of accomplished Persian poetesses in the sixteenth and seventeenth centuries.[128] We know that

Fig.7.5: A girl at school. Line drawing from *Miftāḥ-ul Fuẓala* illustration, British Library, London

[124] National Archives of India, Acquired Documents.

[125] British Library Or. 3299, f. 278b.

[126] T. Falk and M. Archer, *Indian Miniatures*, p. 386; M.C. Beach, *Mughal and Rajput Paintings*, Cambridge, 1992, Plate 68, p.95.

[127] Gulbadan Bāno Begum (Emperor Bābur's daughter) wrote her memoirs, *A History of Humayun*, edited by A.S. Beveridge, London, 1902. A reference to her library is made in Bāyazīd Biyāt, *Tazkira-i Humāyūn-o-Bābur*, edited by M. Hidayat Hosain, Calcutta, 1941, p.

[128] Badāūnī (*Muntakhab-ut-Tawārīkh*, Vol. III, edited by Ahmad Ali, Calcutta,

some women worked as artists as well. Among Jahāngīr's (1605–27) court painters, there is mention of at least three women artists. The signed painting of one of them, Nādira Bānū, survives in the *Gulshan Album* (Imperial Library, Tehran). The ascription on the painting describes her as daughter of Mīr Taqī, a well-known calligrapher at Jahāngīr's court; she was herself a pupil of Aqā Raẓā, a master painter of Jahāngīr's atelier.[129] There are also pictorial depictions of women doing painting.[130]

Fig.7.6: A princess reading a poem. From Dārā Shukoh's Album, India Office Library

Women in Aristocratic Domestic Establishments

Not an inconsiderable source of employment for women during the sixteenth–eighteenth centuries, was service in aristocratic households. Women were appointed to perform a variety of tasks high and low, skilled and unskilled. Writing about Emperor Akbar's household, Abū'l

1869, pp. 360–1) mentions a poetess, Nihānī, of the sixteenth century. From the seventeenth century we have names of a number of poetesses, most of them royal princesses. See S.M. Jafar, *Education in Muslim India*, Delhi, 1972, pp. 194–8.

[129] I am grateful to Professor S.P. Verma for this information. See also A.K. Dass, *Paintings during Jahangir's Time*, Calcutta, 1978, p. 235.

[130] T. Falk and M. Archer, *Indian Miniatures*, p. 531 and Ivan Stchoukine, *La Peinture Indienne à L'Époque Des Grands Moghuls*, Paris, 1929, Plate LXXV (Rajput School).

Faẓl gives the number of harem inmates as 5,000.[131] The number of royal ladies, out of 5,000 total harem inmates, could then not have been more than 500; and there was, therefore, a female labour force of 4,500 in the imperial household establishment alone. The establishments of the nobles were replicas of the imperial establishment in nearly all respects except in size; the latter naturally varied in proportion to the rank and status of the noble. Pelsaert goes on to say that Mughal nobles usually had three to four wives, and each wife was allowed ten or twenty or hundred female attendants.[132] The contemporary paintings bear witness to this, by invariably showing large retinues of women attendants, waiting upon royal or noble ladies.[133] Eighteenth-century miniatures from different regional schools suggest that the same conditions prevailed among the regional aristocracies.[134]

In these pictorial depictions we can often clearly identify the kinds of work they performed. On ceremonial occasions such as celebrations of births[135] or weddings[136] they are shown looking after the entire domestic arrangements except for the cooking of food, which seems to have remained largely men's work in the great establishments.[137] Abū'l Faẓl says that the meals in Akbar's entire harem establishment were distributed from one main kitchen, though some very high ranking royal ladies had kitchens of their own.[138] Pelsaert describes a similar distribution of cooked meals among the ladies of a noble's household from a single kitchen.[139]

Women attendants are shown fanning their mistress, massaging her feet and legs at bedtime, doing her bed, helping her walk, serving meals, eatables, and wines. The attendants also entertained their mistress by singing and dancing or by narrating fables and stories.[140]

[131] *Ā'īn*, Vol. I, p. 40.

[132] Pelsaert, 'Remonstrantie', c. 1626, translated by W.H. Moreland and P. Geyl, *Jahangir's India*, Cambridge, 1925, p. 64.

[133] T. Falk and S. Digby, *Paintings from Mughal India*, Plates 31–40.

[134] M. Archer, *Visions of Courtly India—The Archer Collection of Pahari Miniatures*, London, 1976, Plates 12, 19, 29; M.C. Beach, *Mughal and Rajput Paintings*, Plate J.

[135] Geeti Sen, *Paintings from the Akbarnama*, Plates 17, 18.

[136] Amina Okada, *Imperial Mughal Painters*, Paris, 1992, Plate 102, p.98.

[137] M.S. Randhwa, *Paintings of the Babur Nama*, New Delhi, 1983, Plate XI.

[138] *Ā'īn*, p. 40.

[139] Pelsaert, 'Remonstrantie', p. 64.

[140] Ivan Stchoukine, *La Peinture Indienne*, Plates LXXXV, LXXXI, LXXXIV;

Another very popular theme with the artists was that of a lady at her toilet, where she is shown attended by a large number of servants, doing her hair, holding the mirror to her, pouring out water, etc.[141]

The attire of the women servants, particularly those employed in the imperial establishment, seems to indicate a distinct hierarchy. In illustrations showing the celebrations at the birth of Emperor Akbar's son, a woman in a highly dignified dress is shown standing before a group of religious men (a pandit and mullas) and appears to be a matron or housekeeper.[142] Even among singers and dancers there seems to be a very clear distinction of rank. These appear to belong to two classes. One may be classified as that of artistes. These are usually shown dancing alone in classical styles or singing with the accompaniment of musical instruments, or playing musical instruments themselves.[143] Others of the more ordinary class sang and danced in the popular fashion with drums and in rather ordinary dresses.[144]

Fig.7.7: Women dancers performing at a Royal wedding. Line drawing from *Akbarnāma* painting, Victoria and Albert Museum

M. Archer, *Visions of Courtly India*, Plates 20, 25, 29, 46, 52, 73, 74.

[141] Amina Okada, *Imperial Mughal Painters*, Plate V; S.C. Welch, *Imperial Mughal Painting*, Plate 16; W.G. Archer, *Visions of Courtly India*, Plates 46, 56, 61.

[142] S.C. Welch, *Imperial Mughal Painting*, Plate 16.

[143] Ivan Stchoukine, *La Peinture Indienne*, Plates IX, XXI, LVII; Geeti Sen, *Paintings from the Akbarnama*, Plate 19; M.C. Beach, *Mughal and Rajput Paintings*, p.132; T. Falk and M. Archer, *Indian Miniatures*, Plate 7.

[144] Geeti Sen, *Paintings from the Akbarnama*, Plate 3; M.C. Beach, *Mughal and Rajput Paintings*, Plate 86, p.116, Plate 98, p.132; T. Falk and M. Archer, *Indian Miniatures*, Plate 7.

In Akbar's household establishment women employees were divided into two grades. Those in grade I received a monthly stipend ranging from Rs 20 to 51 and those in grade II, from Rs 2 to Rs 40.[145] The lowest wage of unskilled women servant was Rs 1.5 a month (2 *dāms* a day); the women employed in the imperial harem appear to have been much better paid.

Pre-colonial India was not a uniform mass, though the caste system did further a uniformity amidst much social diversity. But we can recognize throughout a tendency to assign certain jobs or stages in the labour process to women. The general exclusive attribution of spinning to women can be attributed to the expectation that their smaller and nimbler fingers suited the operation better. Spinning seems to have been allotted to women in the same manner in practically all civilizations. Certain jobs fell to the women's lot because with childbearing and rearing, pure domestic duties, like cooking food, were undertaken by them, and not by men (a feature perhaps as universal as spinning). Women's restricted participation in certain other jobs seems to have been determined by the fact that they could only work part-time, or that the work required a momentary application of such heavy muscular power as they did not generally possess. Thus they do not appear to have worked on the plough, or as weavers or blacksmiths, but assumed only supplementary roles in these spheres. Finally, male dominance, sanctified by faith and culture, determined that women should work as harem attendants, and as singers and dancers, and often combine the latter profession with prostitution.

Women were an important component of the labour force, and among the labouring poor an asset rather than liability. The insistence on remarrying a widow to the husband's brother, or alternatively the parents-in-law's right to marry a widow off to someone else, found in many castes,[146] implied this perception, which also meant the currency of bride-price, as against the pervasive dowry system of today's India. Women, as labourers, were not, however, mere extensions of their husband's persons. We have seen that they received wages themselves for their work, and often sold or hawked wares and goods produced by themselves or in conjunction with their menfolk. This suggested a certain amount of independence for the women of the lower orders in traditional India. This independence often was

[145] *Āīn*, Vol. I, p. 40.

[146] See, e.g., *Tashrīḥu'l Aqwām*, Br. Mus. Add. 37,255, f. 138a–41b.

sharply curtailed and seclusion and the veil enforced among both Hindus and Muslims, in the case of higher-class women.

Even among higher classes, women were legal persons in both Hindu and Muslim law. As such, they could hold, and, therefore, manage property. In the Mughal royalty and nobility, they received education, and some of them even took to literary and artistic professions, while others were assigned semi-bureaucratic or supervisory functions.

The colonial subjugation of the Indian economy, especially 'de-industrialization' during the nineteenth century, brought about considerable change in the conditions we have summed up above. Certain professions of women, notably spinning, were practically eliminated; others like work in plantations, mines, and factories (few and small as these still were) were created. The same women could not, of course, shift from the old sectors to the other new ones, and the process had therefore a most wrenching effect on women. A recognition of this made the Indian National Movement adopt the women's spinning wheel for its symbol, both as token of protest and declaration of intent. The fulfilment of the intention is, however, still a distant goal.

TAXATION AND IMPERIAL FINANCE

8

Problems of Mughal Revenue Administration

Todarmal's Original Memorandum, March 1582

The original text of Todar Mal's oft-cited memorandum on revenue administration, that accidentally survives in one of the MSS of the *Akbarnāma*[1] is of considerable archival interest. It is also of crucial importance in providing a more profound understanding of the actual working of the Mughal land revenue system. This memorandum appears only in an abridged (and stylistically refined) form in the final draft of the *Akbarnāma.*[2]

The original text is in the unvarnished language of the revenue ministry. There are in all twelve recommendations: most of these are clearer and more detailed in their original form than their revised version in Abū'l Fazl's final draft.[3] The observations of the emperor are duly recorded at the end of each recommendation (except for the last). Abū'l Fazl, in preparing the revised draft, has not only polished Todar Mal's unliterary language and dispensed with many technical terms but has also heavily pruned it. He has entirely omitted the Emperor's orders that are quite simple and direct, but by no means brilliant. Abū'l Fazl simply adds at the end that 'the proposals were examined and approved'. Such editing was in line with Abū'l Fazl's expressed intention to write the work in so polished a form as to be 'a boon for

[1] Br. Lib. Add 27247, ff. 31b–32b. The credit for bringing this document to light goes to Irfan Habib *(ASMI)*, p. 482. He has used it to explain certain intricacies of the Mughal revenue system (Ibid., pp. 159, 209, 244n., 254n., 256 and n., 293n., 295, 321n., 317).

[2] *AN*, Vol.III, pp. 381–3.

[3] In the case of some clauses, Abū'l Fazl's summary is of help in our understanding the original document.

the enlightenment of posterity'.[4] The historians of Mughal agrarian history might, however, be less grateful.

While in essence all the twelve clauses are more or less the same in both the versions,[5] the actual difference is in details and emphasis, and in certain additions and omissions. Both Moreland and Irfan Habib assigned much importance to this Memorandum and have used it to understand the various aspects of revenue administration, though Moreland had access only to the abridged final draft.[6] As has been stated, the original text was discovered and used by Irfan Habib long ago, but it is yet to be printed or translated in full.

There is no doubt that the original text of the Memorandum is of signal importance for getting an insight into the agrarian conditions during Akbar's reign, the problems of land revenue extraction and the structure and actual functioning of the Mughal revenue administration. It is proposed to analyse its information on these aspects and also to notice the departures Abū'l Faẓl makes from Todar Mal's original text and to guess whether some of these differences were owing to a moderation, if not modification, of certain views and policies of the administration between the time Todar Mal presented his proposals to the Emperor in 1582–3 and the time that Abū'l Faẓl prepared his final revision (probably in 1598).

This memorandum was drafted a little after the years of the so-called '*karori* experiment'. As a result of that experiment the imperial administration had already gathered a first-hand knowledge and experience of prevailing agrarian conditions and problems of revenue extraction. It must also have collected extensive data required for framing a new set of detailed regulations for officials of the *k͟hāliṣa*

[4] *AN*, Vol. III, p. 381.

[5] In the original text the clauses (*faṣals*) are all duly numbered but during the revision Abū'l Faẓl dispensed with the numbering. Beveridge in his translation introduced the numbering again; but this is faulty. He has mistaken clause 7 of the original draft as a part of clause 8; and clause 9 is put together with clause 8, so that there is no clause numbered 7. In this way his translation gives a false impression that there are all in all only eleven clauses. Beveridge's translation suffers from a number of other defects partly owing to the problems of his text and partly to his insufficient grasp of technical terms (*Akbarnāma*, translated by Beveridge, Bib. Ind., Calcutta, 1897, pp. 560–66).

[6] W.H. Moreland, *Agrarian System of Moslem India*, Cambridge, 1929, pp. 106–9. He also gives a summary translation, independent of Beveridge, of eight recommendations. *ASMI*, p. 159, 209, 244n., 254n., 256 and n., 293n., 295, 321n., 282–3n., 317.

and *jāgīrdārs*.

Todar Mal was closely associated with Akbar's attempt at systematizing and centralizing the revenue administration, but he was intermittently sent away on other errands. In the twenty-seventh regnal year he came back from a long campaign in Bihar and Bengal and was entrusted again with the work of the revenue ministry as its head.[7] It was as part of his renewed effort to improve the revenue machinery now entrusted to him that these twelve recommendations were submitted to the emperor for approval on 28 Isfandamuz 7th Safar 990 A.H. (3 March 1582).[8]

Todar Mal's memorandum helps us in understanding the agrarian conditions as the Mughal administration comprehended them: The document quite naturally categorizes the agrarian society in the context of land revenue collection. We thus repeatedly come across two categories, the *ri'āyā*, a term generally used to signify revenue-paying peasantry, and the 'contumacious' (*mutamarrid*) classes. But the *ri'āyā* is not invariably submissive; and it is further classified as *ri'āyā-i-khaṣ* (loyal peasantry) or the *ri'āyā* of *mawaza-i 'itimādī* (trustworthy villages), and the *ri'āyā* that is 'contumacious', from which revenue can be extracted only through use of force (Art. VIII).

The non-rebellious or submissive peasantry appears further classified according to its material conditions. A class of peasantry is referred to as *reza ri'āyā* (small peasantry). We come across it in two articles. In Art. VI and Art. IX the seditious and rebellious are reported as causing distress and loss to the small peasantry. Article IX complains by implication that the 'contumacious and bastards' did not pay their share of land revenue and passed it on to the small peasantry.[9] Todar Mal seems very keen to avoid any intermediaries and recommends that the loyal *ri'āyā* should be made to deposit their share of revenue directly (Art. VIII). But in the case of small peasantry (*reza ri'āyā*) it seems to be recognized that not only the collection from it had to be through the intermediaries but even the distribution of revenue burden too was left in the headmen's hands (Art. IX).

[7] *AN*, Vol. III, p. 38.

[8] Add. 27427, f. 31b. It should be remembered that the change from pre-Gregorian to Gregorian calendar occurred in October 1582. The final text does not give the exact date and only ascribes it to the twenty-seventh regnal year *AN*, Vol. III, p. 381.

[9] These details are altogether missed in the revised text.

Village society thus was not comprehended as an undifferentiated one, and the existence of stratification among the peasantry is duly recognized. Interestingly enough when Todar Mal refers to the destitute peasants lacking seed and oxen and recommends *taqāvī* loans for them, (Art. II), or when these are seen as so oppressed, either by the *muqaddam* and *chaudhurī*, or by the *karorī* (revenue collector) as to be compelled to take to flight (Art. IV), they are simply mentioned as cultivators (*muzari'ān*), not even as *ri'āyā*.

The document is perhaps too early in date for us to expect the use of the term zamīndār which seems to have been brought into vogue by Abū'l Faẓl's use of it in the *Ā'īn-i Akbarī* and makes its appearance as a common term in revenue documents only in the seventeenth century. In other revenue documents of Akbar's reign too, we do not come across the term *zamīndār*.[10]

However, if the familiar name was not there, the class itself could not be wished away. Article XI enjoins the *chaudhurīs*, *qānūngos*, and *muqaddams* to send to the court a report of each one 'who are loyal and dedicated to the prosperity of the peasantry' (*ri'āyā*) and of the 'contumacious and bastards',[11] who are the cause of 'sedition and disturbance'. The former were to be rewarded with *in'ām* (revenue-free grant), the latter to be chastised. In spite of the anonymity, the content clearly suggests reference to the two categories of *zamīndārs*, those who helped the administration in the realization of land revenue and the recalcitrant ones. The mention of grant of *in'ām* to the loyal elements certainly suggests a status superior to that of the peasantry. Another allusion to this class of persons is found in Article IX which, as already noticed, suggests that the dominant persons in the village did not pay their share of the land revenue and instead passed it on to the small peasantry (*reza ri'āyā*). There is also a mention of the *kalāntarān*[12] ('big ones') who along with the *muqaddams*, *chaudhurīs*, and *qānūngos* colluded with the petty revenue officials to oppress the peasants (Art. II). Here there is a clear recognition of the role of

[10] Fatḥullah Shīrazī's recommendations of thirtieth regnal year, *AN*, Vol. III, pp. 457–8. See also Irfan Habib and T. Mukherjee, 'Akbar and the Temples of Mathura and its Environs', *PIHC*, *48th Session*, Goa, 1987, pp.234–50.

[11] Todar Mal's use of uncivilized words for this class shows his extreme annoyance with them.

[12] Fatḥullah Shīrazī calls them *buzurgān* (*AN*, Vol. III, p. 457), and Aurangzeb finds a more appropriate term '*mutaghalabān*' (the dominant ones), *farmān* to Rasikdās.

zamīndārs in the collection of revenue, but with an effort to undermine it. There is a recommendation that the '*āmils* should fix a time-limit by which the peasants would themselves deposit their share in the land revenue at the treasury so that there should be no need of a collector (*taḥṣīldār*) (Art. VIII).

The document has some bearing on the question of the village community as well. Here we find perhaps the first mention of the term *malba-o-ikhrājāt* (exactions of the officials and other superior elements) and the 'village expenses' apart from the land revenue[13] (Art. I). But these exactions are considered to be against the interests of the peasantry; and Todar Mal tries to find out ways for eliminating them (Art. IX). If this was the objective, it was not attained, since not only does Fatḥullah Shīrāzī mentions *malba* and *ikhrājāt*, and their misappropriation, but much later Aurangzeb again complains more severely against these exactions.[14]

The Mughal administration apparently perceived the village potentates, *muqaddam*, *chaudhurī*, and *qānūngo* as the oppressors of the peasantry.[15] They are said to collude with the clerks of the revenue collector for unauthorized extortions of *malba* and *ikhrājāt* (Art. II). According to Todar Mal the harassment by the *muqaddam* and *chaudhurī* was one of the only two possible reasons for the flight of the peasantry, the other being the oppression by the *karorī* (Art. III).[16] In spite of it they had to be tolerated since they were essential for the functioning of the revenue system as long as the village was to remain the basic unit of revenue assessment and collection. It was the *muqaddam* and *patwārī* who were to sign bonds and be held

[13] The term does not occur in the final draft. For actual significance of the term see *ASMI*, pp.153–4.

[14] *AN*, Vol. III, p. 457, particularly Art. IV; Aurangzeb's *Farmān*, *AN*, Vol. III, Art. X.

[15] Fatḥullah Shīrazī seems to share this opinion in Art. IV *AN*, Vol. III, p.457; their misdeeds and Mughal administrations' complaints against them seem to grow with time. Aurangzeb found them guilty of unjust distribution of revenue burden (Art. IV), and of reliefs granted owing to calamity (Art. IX), as well as misappropriation of *malba* and *ikhrājāt* (Arts. X and XI).

In view of this evidence it seems surprising that to Athar Ali they should appear as the representatives of the larger and permanent interests of the imperial administration constituting a restraint on the exploitative tendencies of the revenue assignees (*Mughal Nobility under Aurangzeb*, Bombay, 1966, pp. 87–8.

[16] Abū'l Faẓl leaves out the whole passage in his editing, *AN*, Vol. III, p. 382.

responsible for realization of the land revenue from the peasant (Art. IX). The *muqaddam* was to stand sureties (*tamassuk*) for *taqāvī* loans (Art. III).[17] This perception of the 'village community' is thus in consonance with the characterization of it as a 'framework for sub-exploitation'.[18]

The fact that emerges fairly clearly is that notwithstanding all the protestations of the Mughal administration about individual assessment and collection of land revenue, the village remained the real unit of assessment. It is borne out from Art. III and, particularly Art. IX, where it is clearly stated that after the assessment of the village the division of the revenue burden among the cultivators (*kārindas*) was left to the *patwārī*.[19] The village is so prominently the unit of revenue assessment and collection that one finds them classified as 'trustworthy' (*mawaẓa-i 'itimādī*) and contumacious (*mawaẓa-i mutamarrid*) (Art. VIII).

However, as far as realization of the land revenue is concerned there seems to have been some effort to make it on an individual basis. In Arts. VII and IX there is insistence on the issue of receipts to the peasantry (*ri'āyā*), so much so that the *foṭadār* and the *'āmil* are warned that if receipts are not given to the peasants they alone would be held responsible and the word of the peasant and accounts in the papers of *patwārī* would be accepted. But all this seem to have been of no avail since even by the thirtieth regnal year, when Fatḥullah Shīrāzī was drafting his recommendations, this system was in total disuse, and he considered it futile to try to reintroduce it. He simply urged that the *patwārī*'s papers should be used as evidence of revenue payment (Art. II).[20] Interestingly enough Abū'l Faẓl in his summary of Todar Mal's recommendations in the final version of the *Akbarnāma* only makes a cursory reference to the instructions about issuing receipts to the peasants.

Unlike Aurangzeb's *farmān* to Rasikdās, this document does not reflect any trepidation about the state of cultivation or flight of the peasants, though it mentions both the phenomena. However, it does show some concern for peasants: Todar Mal recommends advancing

[17] In his summary Abū'l Faẓl leaves out all these details from Art. IX and modifies Art. III to say that peasant (*ri'āyā*) should give sureties for each other.

[18] *CEHI*, Vol. I, pp. 248–9.

[19] The system continued to be the same under Aurangzeb (Art. VI).

[20] *AN*, Vol. III, p.457.

taqāvīs loans to peasant, for seed and oxen and its recovery in easy instalments (Art. III).[21] The recommendation seems to have been seriously implemented because Fatḥullah Shīrāzī, formulating his proposal in the thirtieth regnal year, says that since *dādnī* (or loan, apparently his term for *taqāvī*) to peasants had become general, more staff should be provided to assist the *foṭadar* (treasurer) (Art. 17).[22]

If there is full concern for submissive peasantry, no leniency is shown to the head-strong: it recommends seizure of their harvested grain by force (Art. VIII) and the ravaging of their cultivation (Art. VI). However, the recommendation to compensate the *jāgīrdārs* in lieu of the loss of revenue from such destruction, by assigning them additional pay-assignments does not indicate an unsatisfactory state of revenue collection.

The document reflects an attempt at thoroughness in every matter. There is not only a full understanding of affairs concerning agrarian conditions but also an attempt to lay down all regulations with quite minute details, not leaving much to the discretion of the officials on the spot. It fixes detailed rates for waste lands lying fallow for different durations, detailed rates of conversion for coins of different metal and new and old coins, according to their weights, distribution, and scale of remission in the case of calamities.[23] The allowances to be paid to the member of surveyor's party in cash and kind, and the amount of the work to be done by them in a day are also fixed in detail.[24]

The Mughal administration seems to have had a healthy distrust of the revenue officials and a concern for the small peasant. The original text of Todar Mal displays quite a harsh attitude towards village officials and revenue collectors. The revenue collectors were to get only three-fourths of their salary, the remaining quarter to be given only after they had completed the full realization of assessed revenue. The practice was followed so severely that by thirtieth regnal year they were

[21] It is interesting that in spite of much trepidation shown, Aurangzeb does not mention *taqāvī* loans and only orders repair and digging of well, contrary to it Todar Mal has nothing to say about irrigation.

[22] Ibid., Art. XVII, pp.458–9.

[23] Aurangzeb (*farmān* to Rasikdās) simply contents himself by saying that proper remission should be allowed.

[24] How stringently the amount was sanctioned and paid is evident from Fatḥullah's comment that in case of longer stay of the surveyors, *'āmil* was to pay for them out of his own pocket Art. VIII).

generally getting only three quarters of their salary, irrespective of the fact whether they failed or succeeded in making full realization, as Fatḥullah Shīrāzī observes. This seems to be in keeping with what we know of Todar Mal's measures, through the criticism levelled against him, particularly by Niẓāmuddīn and Badāūnī.[25] Summarizing the memorandum much later for his final version, Abū'l Faẓl is much more careful. He not only moderates the language and omits certain adverse observations and details, but introduces additional proposals not at all occurring in the original, namely, that the revenue-collector's report should be sent to the court so that the worthy among them should be promoted and rewarded (Art. IX). In Art. IV, he makes another apparent interpolation, reflecting a lenient attitude, to the effect that if the revenue collectors bring about an enhancement in the total *jama'*, they should not be taken to task for shortfals in a few *maḥals.*

Incidentally, the original text of the memorandum of Todar Mal by its references to the value deemed to be lost through shortage in weight, shows that in 1582 the copper *tanka* was the usual coin in use and the *dām* was its mere fractional piece, equal to half of it in value (see Art. X). Abū'l Faẓl in his revised version converts *tankas* into *dāms*, by multiplying the number of *tankas* by two, in his summary of both Arts. X and XII.[26]

The full use of Todar Mal's original text for reconstructing our view of the working of the Mughal system is thus of considerable value. Its very contents belie the notion that Persian documentation is of little use in our comprehension of how rural society was structured and how the village was related to the larger exploitative framework in pre-colonial India.

Translation

At the beginning of this auspicious year [27 Ilāhī], Raja Todar Mal, who in the perception of the affairs of the *Dīwānī* (revenue ministry) and in the art of finding out the means of extension of cultivation in the empire, was among the renowned disciples of the Emperor. He (the Emperor) making him inclined to settle the affairs of the *khāliṣa*, brought his border attending heart from the concerns of the border over to undertake this major task. Despite the detailed regulations that

[25] *Ṭabaqāt-i Akbarī*, Vol. II, p. 331; *Muntakhab-ut Tawārīkh*, Vol. II, edited by Ali Ahmad and W.N. Lees, Bib. Ind., Calcutta, 1864–9, p. 189.

[26] *AN*, Vol. III, p.383.

His Majesty had issued in regard to every matter, from the knowledge that he had gained in service of His Majesty, he for additional care and renovation of those orders, he submitted through those proximate to the Court, a petition to His Majesty consisting of twelve articles. A response was accorded by the Emperor on *Dabīrīn*, 23 of the Ilāhī month of *Isfandārmuz* corresponding to 7 Ṣafar, in order to regulate the affairs of the *khāliṣa* territories (*khāliṣat*), etc. These articles are as follows:-

Article (*Faṣl*) I

That all the *'amils* of the *khāliṣa* and *jāgīrdārs* should be strictly ordered to collect the land revenue according to the regulations/scheduled cash rates (*dastūr-ul 'amal*) and not to harass the peasantry a jot by claiming more. If at all any excess is taken in *malba* and *ikhrājāt*, they should examining the state of the peasantry, make proper enquiry: Being accurately informed about the land surveyors and revenue collectors, whoever of this group they find to be dishonest to have misappropriated anything, that should be deducted from their monthly salary, and the amounts be credited to the peasantry for the revenue due upon each harvest. They should punish (the misappropriator) in accordance with his offence. Whoever does not endeavour in this matter should be reported to the Emperor so that he be singled out for punishment.

Imperial order: 'To assign the work to the competent is the work of that most efficient one (Todar Mal). Him we have deemed to be the for truth, correct conduct and knowledge of affairs of the *Dīwānī* and have assigned to him the duty of keeping watch so that he may, first, acquaint all people with the royal regulations that have been made in respect of revenue collection, and other matters, and, then, look into their conduct. Whoever for the sake of crass greed and blind inclination (to evil) acts contrary to orders and oppresses the peasants, let him so punish him that it be a lesson to all men of petty mind.'

Article II.

That each *karorī* and *'āmil* of the *khāliṣa*, has two writers, one styled *kārkun* (clerk) and the other *khaṣ nawīs*. In collusion with the *chaudhurīs*, *qānūngos*, *muqaddams*, and the 'big ones' of each village, they become the cause of increase in *ikhrājāt*. If instead of these two greedy writers one trusted, upright writer is appointed, in every respect there would be a saving in expenditure (*ikhrāj*) and the peasantry would become prosperous.

Imperial order: It has been well thought of. Assigning one job to two persons or assigning two jobs to one person is to violate the just order. These two greedy ones should be removed and at each place one of the trusted and upright ones should be appointed.

Article III

That it has appeared that the *ārāẓī* is (reported to be) less every year. (Therefore) when the cultivated land of every *pargana* has been once entirely and fully measured, based on actual survey, they should increasing it year to year according to the condition of the peasantry, establish a *nasaq* and, taking bonds from the *muqaddams*, realize the land revenue. Whatever *ārāẓī* has been lying waste for the last three or four years should be assessed for the first year at half (of the standard), in second year at quarter less (than the standard), and in the third year according to (the rates of) *polaj*. The *ārāẓī* lying waste for two years (should be assessed) in the first year at quarter less (than the standard) and the second year according to the *dastūr-ul 'amal* (revenue rates) of *polaj*. From the *banjar* land (*ārāẓī-i banjar)* the fixed amount of grain per *bīgha*, according to the previous order, should be realized. If the cultivators are in a distressed condition and do not have seed and cattle, they (*'āmils*) should, if they find it suitable, give them *taqāvī* (loans), taking securities from the *muqaddams*, so that whenever the harvest comes, they should recover it to the partly in kharif and the rest in *rabi'*. Year after year they should proceed in the very same manner. When the assessed land is (gradually) increased, year by year, the peasantry does not suffer.

Article IV

That during the time crops are still standing, the officials should choose five or ten *tanābs* (of land), according to the (size of?) the *jama'* of the *pargana*, and alighting in its midst, examine the single or double-cropped land in the vicinity, and bringing it under measurement, determine whether the yield is high or low. Every village where there is decline in yield, they should go there and find out causes thereof. If the peasants have fled from their homes or are destitute, this cannot be owing to any other but two causes: Either oppression by the *karorī*, or harassment by the *chaudhurī* and *muqaddam*. He should fully pursue the matter and should act in such a way that that *ārāẓī* should be brought under cultivation and the lapses be rectified. The actual report thereof should be prepared there and then and sent to the imperial office, so that it may be submitted to the Emperor and the loyal efforts and faults of the collectors be recognized. In the good year when, there is proper rainfall, owing to the grace of God, and in *parganas*, where the land lies under water and is good, a deduction may be made of one-and-half to two *biswas* [per *bīgha*] from total measurement and in the forest and desert a deduction of two and half to three *biswas* be allowed for the relief of the peasantry. They should so do everything that day by day there should be an increase in cultivation and habitation. The *siyāha* (record) of measurement (*ẓabṭ*) should be sent every week and the register of daily account of revenue receipts every month to the imperial office.

Imperial order: 'In a good year, one and half *biswas* of land should be deducted as *nābud* in flooded land, and two and half to three *biswas* in the desert. The record of *ẓabṭ* should be sent to the imperial office every week and the daily account of receipts every month.'

Article V

That, God forbid, if in a village any natural calamity occurs, from every part of the *pargana*, of that place, the *karorī* should reach there, measure the land, field by field, and send the *siyāha* of measurement along with his report to the imperial court; if it is considered suitable, or not suitable, either an *amīn* be appointed (to check it) or trust be reposed in the work (*'āmal*) of the [assigned] officials. This article too was submitted to the Emperor and a confirmatory imperial order was issued.

Article VI

That the contumacious who take refuge in forests and forts, and (behind) ditches, do not pay land revenue properly, but, instead, cause damage and loss to the peasants of the surrounding villages. Let every *jāgīrdār* and *karorī* in each *ṣūba* and *pargana*, giving protection to the peasantry, chastise the contumacious and seditious who oppress the small peasants. If it is later found that [in so doing] [in this] any loss is caused to the peasantry, (the official) would be held responsible for making good the loss. At first he should warn the contumacious so that if they still do not restrain themselves, the *faujdār*, *jāgīrdār*, and *karorī* would thereupon cut down forests and destroy the forts and ditches, and lay waste and plunder the cultivation of the contumacious.

If a *jāgīrdār* [should have had to do this], the *dīwān* should allow him one harvest worth, as salary, according to the *jama'* of his *jāgīr*. If [the place] is in the *k͟hāliṣa* and under the *karorī*, the financial officers (*mustaufīs*) should make due allowance for it so that he should not become the target of demand [for making good the loss in revenue]. Everyone who is found to protect the robbers and contumacious persons will receive punishment.

Imperial order: 'For the villages belonging to the contumacious that have become desolate the financial officers (*mustaufīs*) should not demand (from the *karorīs*) the amount of revenue falling short, up to one harvest and one year; and the *dīwāns* should assign pay [of like amount] in compensation to the *jāgīrdārs*.'

Article VII

That whatever has been collected from the peasantry should immediately be deposited into the treasury in the presence of the *fo̤t̤adār* (treasurer), and what is deposited in the treasury, the *fo̤t̤adār* should give receipts for it to the peasants. If he will not give receipts to the peasants, the *karorīs* and *fo̤t̤adārs* would not be allowed to refute whatever amount the peasants claim they have given. The *karorī* and *fo̤t̤adār* should be paid three-fourth of their salary according to their *sanad*, [deed of appointment], and the remaining one-fourth should be released when in the *maḥal* where something [of tax due] still remains with the peasantry, he has recovered [that amount], whereupon he should obtain the receipt from the treasurer (*fo̤t̤adār*).

Article VIII

That in the case of the peasants of trustworthy villages who conform in word and deed, the revenue collectors should lay down time-limit for (payment of revenue to) the treasury, so that they might themselves, within the said time-limits, deposit their share (*rasad*) of the revenue in the treasury and obtain receipt, and there is no need for a collector (*taḥsīldār*). In the case the peasants are contumacious and recalcitrant, securities should be taken, and appointing a competent grain-broker (*ahattiya*) so that whatever grain has been collected in grain-heaps, should be sold to obtain the part that is due for payment of revenue and dues of the *dīwān*, while the remainder should be left to the peasants. They should prepare for each *pargana* a detailed list of the villages of the loyal (*k͟hāṣ*) and the contumacious peasants and send it to the Court so that whatever is ordered thereon is carried out. The just imperial order has been passed (accepting the above).

Imperial order: [Approved.]

Article IX

That at the place (time?) where they harvest grain, the revenue collectors should, setting the *taujīh* (tax-assessment), *pargana* by *pargana*, and village by village, in accordance with the cultivated land, part by part (*rasad*) the *patwarī* of every village assigning the share (*rasad*) of each cultivator by name, put their signature on this assessment. They should take bonds from the *patwarīs* and *muqaddams*, and deposit the revenue (*mal*) collected into the treasury. The *foṭadār* should give the receipt for this to the peasants. If the accountant (*kārkun*) or *foṭadār* fails to give the receipt or the peasants fail to take it, whosoever be at fault, the responsibility shall be that of the revenue collectors (*'āmils*). If the peasants complain (about the amount of tax taken), the *'āmils* will not be heard, and the *dīwāns* and financial officials would consider the 'raw papers' (*kāg̱haẕ-i ḵhām*) of the *patwārī* as authentic. Care should taken that no one should take anything from the peasant without *taujīh*,[27] etc. Whatever has been brought under the *taujīh*, the amount to be realized (*wuṣūl*) and not-to-be realized (*lam-yaṣl*) should be determined in such a way that no injustice be done to anyone, and the bastards and the contumacious (of the village) keeping [only] their own share, [are compelled to] transfer [the remainder] to the small peasants (*reza ri'āyā*). (The revenue) should be collected, keeping in view everyone equally. What is aimed by these proposals is the extinction of *malba* and *iḵhrājāt* because the welfare of the peasants lies there. The *karorī* should investigate and report about everyone who acts according to orders. Submitted for orders.

Imperial order: 'To be implemented as proposed.'

Article X

That the *ashrafī*, *rupiya*, and *murādī* (copper money) whatever is coined should be issued by the officials of the mint in the presence of the custodians of the Treasury in return for coins of mintage of past years, (whether) rupees and *jalālīs*, so that the *karorī*, treasurer (*foṭadār*), and *ṣarrāf* change new with old coins, at the rates as have been decreed, for *ashrafīs*, etc., as follows:

[27] Reading *be-taujīh* for *ba-taujīh*.

La'l Jalālī and gold coin, whose weight and fineness is per standard, each	200 *tankas*
Jalālī rupee *chahār-gosha*, each	20 *tankas* Akbarshāhī
Ashrafī and round rupee; When years have passed since mintage, the years (of mintage) should be seen (on the coin):	
Ashrafī of full weight, to a maximum shortage of two or three *birinj* (rice-grain), each	180 *tankas*
Ditto, whatever is of shorter weight by more than three *birinj* up to *surkh* (*ratti*), each	177 *tankas* and 1 *dām*
Ditto, whatever is of shorter weight by more than one *surkh* up to one and half *surkh*, each	175 *tankas* and 1 *dām*
Rupee, of full weight, or of shorter weight upto one *surkh*, each	19 *tankas* and 1 *dām*
Ditto, of shorter weight of one and a half *surkh* to two *surkh*, each	19 *tankas*

It is obligatory that the greedy ones, freeing themselves from this temptation (?), should take to the right path. The *jāgīrdārs*, *karorīs*, and *foṭadārs* should allow the same rates to the peasants when realizing the land revenue, and deposit them in the treasury accordingly. *La'l Jalālī* of full standard and weight and *Jalāla rupiya*, till one-and-a-half *surkh* (to) two *surkh* shortage, of the past years of Akbarshahī (reign), (but) less than three rice-grains to one *surkh* [one] rice-grain short,[28] should be deposited in the treasury. What varies from this, the treasurer (*taḥwīldār*) shall put these apart, and the *musharraf* should with a detailed list enter into the daily register of receipts and send it daily to the headquarters. The *ṣarrāfs* should also change money at these rates, without allowing any deviations. Hereafter if any one acts against this order and charges different rates, report of this should be sent to the court after enquiry. Submitted for orders.

Imperial orders: 'Let them fix the rates for rupee and *ashrafī* according to the schedule; and the rupee that is old, should be listed[29] and the full-weight (*pora*) rupee should be accepted. The *ṣarrāfs* should follow the same rates. Any violation of this would attract punishment.'

Article XI

That the *chaudhurīs*, *qānūngos*, and *muqaddams*, should prepare a list name by name of such are loyal and dedicated to the prosperity of

[28] Insertion on margin of the MS, 'to one *surkh* [one] rice-grain short.' In Art. III, 383, Abū'l Fazl has the shortage restricted to one *surkh* only.

the peasantry and of such as are contumacious and bastards, who are the cause of sedition and disturbance, and send it to the imperial office so that the *dīwāns* may submit it to the Emperor. Those who have shown loyalty by striving for the welfare of the peasants and increase in the revenues will be given reward (*in'ām*), and the contumacious be admonished after enquiry.

Imperial order: 'Good, so be it.'

Article XII

That the surveyors (*ẓabitān*) be allowed in terms of Bahlolī *tankas*, ten copper *tankas* (*murādī*)[30] [as follows]:

Flour	15 seers [worth]	one *tanka* [A: 7 *dāms*]
Grain fodder	12 seers [A: 12½ seers] [worth]	two *tanka* [A: 4 *dāms*]
Butter (Ghee)	1 ¾ seers [A: 2 seers or less] [worth]	two *tanka* [A: 5 *dāms*]
Cash		six *tanka* [A: 8 *dāms*]

[This total of grain and cash is broken down as follows:]

Amīn (assessor)

Flour	5 seers
Butter (Ghee)	1 ¼ seers [A: ½ seer]
Fodder grain	7 seers
Cash	2 *tankas* [A: 3 *dāms*]

Navīsanda (writer), agent of the *kārkun* (clerk)

Flour	4 seers
Butter (Ghee)	1¼ seers [A: ½ seer]
Fodder grain	5 seers [A: 5½ seers]
Cash	2 *tankas* [A: 2 *dāms*]

Tanāb kash (rope-measurer), three in number

Flour	6 seers
Butter (ghee)	¾ seer
Cash	2 *tankas* [A: 3 *dāms*]

[29] I read *daul* for *awwal* in the text.

[30] Here Abū'l Faẓl improves our understanding by stating (*AN*, Vol. III, p.383) that a levy of one *dām*, 'as of old' (if *pāsbānī* is read as *pāstānī*, on Beveridge's suggestion) was levied per *bīgha*, and it was out of the amount so collected that the payment was to be made to the surveyors. Further, in Abū'l Faẓl's summary the

The sum of ten *tankas* is essential for the subsistence of the party, for otherwise they would tend to extort it from the peasants. The day the measurement takes place,[31] from every *tanāb* of measured land that is assessed, out of the total of *bahlolis* collected, twelve *tankas* should be allowed for allowance (*in'ām*) of this party.

total payment is put at 24 *dāms*, equal to twelve *tankas* and not ten. Other variations from the text are put within square brackets, prefaced by the abbreviation 'A' in the table that follows.

[31] Abū'l Fazl's final version here adds: 'During the rabi season when the days are long, they should not measure less than 250 *bīghas*, and during the kharif season, when the days are short, they should not measure less than 200 *bīghas*.' This implies that measurement took place close to harvests.

9

Reforming Revenue Administration

Aurangzeb's *Farmān* to Rasikdās, 1665

The seventeenth century, as it advances, becomes rich in official as well as unofficial documents; yet there is a peculiar handicap. From Akbar's reign, in spite of the relative paucity of documents, we are nevertheless fortunate in having memoranda and reports on revenue administration from Todar Mal and Fatḥullah Shīrāzī, and a general set of imperial regulations (*dastūr-ul 'amal*).[1] Such documents have not survived from the two subsequent reigns. Aurangzeb's farmān on general matters of revenue administration, issued to a revenue official, Rasikdās, in the eighth regnal year (1665) of his therefore, assumes great importance, being the first document of its kind coming to us after a gap of some seventy years.

The credit for bringing the farmān to light goes to Sir Jadunath Sarkar who published its text,[2] as well as a translation into English.[3] W.H. Moreland[4] and then Irfan Habib,[5] explained some of its technical terms and brought out its importance for analysing the agrarian conditions during Aurangzeb's reign.

Unfortunately, the text that Sarkar published was not collated with other available MSS and was based on only one MS, by no means the best of the surviving copies of the document. Many transcriptional errors, some of them serious, remained undetected by Sarkar. In his

[1] *AN*, Vol. III, pp. 381–3, 457–9. For the original version of Todar Mal's memorandum see Br. Lib. MS Add. 27247, ff. 31b–32b.

[2] 'The Revenue Regulations of Aurangzeb', *Journal of the Asiatic Society of Bengal*, June 1906, pp. 249–55.

[3] J. Sarkar, *Mughal Administration*, Calcutta, 1924, pp. 213–29.

[4] W.H. Moreland, *The Agrarian System of Moslem India*, Cambridge, 1929, pp. 132–8.

[5] *ASMI*, pp. 222 and *n*., etc.

translation, he was let into many errors by the defects of his text; but there are other slips as well, especially in the rendering of technical terms. For instance, he renders *sāl-i kāmil-o muttaṣil*, not as 'year of full realization and the year previous (to the current)' but as the 'past year and the year preceding it'. The *'amal-i jarīb* and *kankūṭ* (two distinct methods of assessment of land revenue based on measurement)[6] simply become 'actual valuation of crop'. Again, *jins-i kāmil* is translated as 'full crop' and not as high grade or cash crop. The term *dastūr-ul 'amal* though very clearly used in Mughal administration for cash revenue-rates, is rendered as 'revenue guide'. In clause 8 he misread *ṣarf-i sikka* (discount on mintage)[7] as *ṣirf sikka*, *ṣirf* taken to mean 'only', and the whole sense of the clause is lost. This list of Sarkar's errors, which is not exhaustive, suggests that a fresh translation is necessary to enable one to understand the *farmān* properly.

The translation that follows is based on a text collated with nine available copies of the *farmān*:

A: I.O. 1146 (Ethé 2185)

B: IO. 1566 (Ethé 2186)

C: I.O. 4014, ff, 8a–11b.

D: Br. Lib. Add. 19503, ff. 62a–63b.

E: Br. Lib. Or. 1735, ff. 162–64b, 129–32b.

F: Bodleian Pers. E-1 (I, 1385)

G: Berline Royal Library, Pertsch's Cat. 15 (23), ff. 267a–72a.

H: *Nigārnāma-i Munshī* (Nawal Kishor ed.), pp. 123–4 and 99–102.

I: Text as printed by Sarkar in *Journal of the Asiatic Society of Bengal*, N.S. II, 1906, pp. 249–55.

Of these, seven MSS are apparently copies of the *farmān* as issued to Rasikdās; in D his name is replaced by that of Mīr Muḥammad Mu'izz, *dīwān-i khāliṣa*, *ṣūba* Bihar. This led Irfan Habib to suggest that it was not a farmān issued to an individual, but a circular meant for all the *dīwāns* of the *khāliṣa*.[8] In that case, being a general order for at least the areas under the *khāliṣa*, it acquires much greater importance than it would have had if it was merely issued to an individual. However,

[6] For the significance of these terms see ibid., pp. 193, 200.

[7] See Irfan Habib, 'Currency System of the Mughal Empire', *Medieval India Quarterly*, Vol. IV, 1961, p. 5n.

[8] *ASMI*, p. 222 and *n*.

clause 7, which deals with the specific case of an area that was in a particular prince's *jāgīr* earlier, suggests that it was first issued in response to certain problems raised by Rasikdās; then, perhaps, in view of its general significance, it was circulated to others. The fact that it is preserved in so many MS copies also indicates that the *farmān* was deemed to contain regulations of relevance in general administration.

In Sarkar's printed text, Rasikdās's name is followed by the designation *karorī* (revenue-collector); no other MS carries this designation. Moreover, it is evident from the internal evidence in the *farmān* itself that it was addressed to a higher official, of the status of *dīwān*.[9]

The date of the *farmān* appears from the reference to the eighth regnal year of Aurangzeb in the Preamble, the year being styled as that of the commencement of implementation of the regulations contained in the *farmān*. The year began on to 18 March 1665 and ended on March 1666. Since the *farmān* was to come into effect from the beginning of the kharif harvest within that year, and this (meaning August) fell within AD 1665.

The translation is based on the text provided in version A. Variations from other versions are noted only if they are of any substance. Obvious spelling mistakes are not noted.

The translation is followed by a glossary of the technical terms used in the *farmān*. The terms are given in the translation in their original form. For well-known technical terms the meaning is given in brackets in the translated text.

Translation

Copy of the *farmān* of the Emperor Aurangzeb[10]

Let the *kifāyat-sha'ār*[11] (skilled in financial prudence), *Mutī'-ul Islām* (obedient to Islam) Rasikdās,[12] be hopeful of imperial favour, and

[9] Moreland, *Agrarian System*, p. 133 and *n*.

[10] D reads 'Copy of the *farmān* of Emperor Aurangzeb 'Ālamgīr issued to Mir Muḥammad Mu'izz *dīwān-i khaliṣa ṣūba* Bihar by way of a *dastūr-ul 'amal*'; B adds 'Alamgīr Ghāzī' after 'Emperor Aurangzeb'.

[11] A title commonly used for officers of the revenue ministry by the Mughal administration.

[12] D reads '*Sa'ādat Ma'āb* (receptacle of bliss), *Wizārat Panāh* (officer of ministerial status), *Kifāyt Dastgāh* (master of financial prudence) Mīr Muḥammad Mu'izz'.

know that, whereas the entire elevated attention and desires of the emperor are devoted to the increase in the population and cultivation of the empire and the welfare of the whole *ri'āya* (peasantry) and the entire people, who are the wonderful creation of the Creator; and now, therefore, an explanation having been desired of the actualities of *'amal* (revenue collection) of parganas of the *khāliṣa* and *tuyūldārs*,[13] it has been submitted to His Majesty by the imperial functionaries, that during the current year, the *umana'* (pl. of amīn, assessment officers) of the parganas of the imperial dominions assess in money the *jama'* (revenue demand) of most of the villages of the parganas at the beginning of the year, keeping in view the *ḥāṣil* (revenue collection) of the year of maximum realization (*sāl-i kāmil*) and of the immediately preceding year and the cultivable area and the condition of the peasantry's capability and other peculiarities. And if the peasants of certain villages are not agreeable to this mode of collection, they assess the *jama'at* the harvest time by the method of *jarīb* or *kankūṭ*. And in some of the villages, where they know the peasants and cultivators to be in distressed circumstances and with inadequate resources, they practise *ghalla-bakhshī* (crop-sharing) at the rate of a half or one-third or two-fifths (of the produce) or more or less. At the close of the year the *ṭawāmīr* (registers) of *jama'-i naqdī* (*jama'* stated in cash), (drawn up) in conformity with the regulations and actual practice, with his (the *dīwān*'s) own *taṣdīq* (confirmatory endorsement) and the *qubul* (acceptance) of the karorīs and the signatures of the *chaudhurīs* and *qānūngos*, are sent to the imperial office. But the imperial office does not receive the record of the *ārāẓī* (measured area) of each pargana, specifying the cultivated land and details of the rabi and kharif crops, showing *(a)* how much (land) was (under) the *jins-i kāmil* (high-grade crops) and *jins-i nāqiṣ* (inferior crops) during the previous year, and whether there has been any change, i.e., an increase or a fall during the current year compared to the previous year, and *(b)* the number of *muzāri*'s (cultivators) classified as *mustājirs* (revenue-farmers), *ri'āyā* (peasants), etc. As a result the condition of each *maḥal* and the competence of the *mutaṣaddīs* (officials) of that place, who, upon the occurrence of a shortfall in the *ḥāṣil* (revenue collection) of that *maḥal*, after the assessment of the *jama'*, grant a reduction from the total *jama'*, invoking deficient rains, or the calamity of frost or the cheapness of grain or something

[13] E omits *tuyūldārs*.

else as the reason thereof, might become known [at the Court.] If they inform themselves, of the cultivators and cultivation in each village, they (the officials) proceed to (assess and) collect revenue (*'amal-numāyand*) on the basis of (such) detailed knowledge, and endeavour to get the cultivable land cultivated and to enlarge the cultivation of *jins-i kāmil* (high-grade crops), the (villages of) parganas will become inhabited and cultivated, the peasantry will be well-off and there will be an increase in the *maḥṣūl* (revenue, produce). In this situation if any (natural) calamity occurs, no great loss will take place in the *ḥāṣil* (revenue collection), owing to the abundance of cultivation.

(Accordingly) the World-subduing, Universe-governing order is (hereby) issued to the effect that he [the addressee] should inform himself of the actualities of each village of the parganas attached to his *dīwānī* and *amīnī* (office of *dīwān* and *amīn*), namely, how much is the (area of) cultivable *ārāẓī* (land) within it (his jurisdiction), how much out of it is cultivated, how much uncultivated, in what quantity was *jins-i kāmil* produced each year, and what is the cause of the said *ārāẓī* remaining uncultivated. He should further find out what were the *dastūrs* (rates) of the levy of *maḥṣūl* (revenue) in the blessed reign of *Ḥaẓarat 'Arsh Āshiyānī* [Āstānī] (Akbar) during the *dīwānī* of Rāja Todar Mal; and whether the *sā'ir* taxes are according to the old regulations, or have been fixed at a higher (rate) since the year of the beginning of this august reign; how many villages are inhabited and how many are desolate, and what is the cause of their desolation. After obtaining information on these matters, he should strive for progressively populating the desolate villages and getting the cultivable land cultivated, by granting an equitable *qaul* (pledged revenue-rate or tax-demand), appropriate *qarār* (agreement by assessees), and increasing (the cultivation of) the *jins-i kāmil*. Wherever there is a well that is out of repair, he should repair it and also endeavour that new ones are dug. He should make assessement of *jama'* in such a manner that the whole peasantry receives its due and the *māl-i wājib* (authorized land revenue) is realized in time, and not a single peasant is subjected to oppression. He should, every year, prepare records containing the number of cultivators of each village and the *ārāẓī* (area), cultivated and uncultivated, [as well as] irrigated by wells and dependent on rain only; and [under] *kāmil* (superior) and *nāqiṣ* (inferior) crops, and the extent of success in getting the cultivable land cultivated, and increasing the (area under) superior crops and populating the villages that have been desolate for years. He should then submit (to the imperial office), the details of enhancement between that which has (now) fixed and the previous *dastūr-ul 'amal*, together with the amount that has been collected in the whole year.[14]

This regulation and rule of procedure is to be deemed to be in effect from the beginning of the kharif of the Īlān Īl, the eighth year from the royal accession, and he should act in conformity thereto, and also instruct the *'āmils* of *maḥals* and *jāgīrdārs* to work in the manner here prescribed:

1. That he is not to allow the *chaudhurīs* and *'āmils* to see him in private and direct that they should attend at the *dīwānī* (office); he should (on the other hand) admit the *reza ri'āyā* (small peasants) and the poor, who come for making submissions as to their condition, into private as well as public audience, and make them familiar with himself so that they might not need any other person's mediation in representing their needs.

2. That he should direct the *'āmils* that they should at the beginning of the year find out the (number of) cultivators with the number of ploughs and extent of *ārāẓī* (area), village by village. If the peasants are well off, they should arrange that all of them, according to their condition, try to increase (the area under) sowing and so, in comparison with last year, bring about an enlargement in the cultivated area and, while shifting from the inferior crops (*jins-i adnā*) to high grade (*jins-i a'lā*), not leave waste any cultivable land, so far as they can. If any one from amongst the cultivators (*kārindas*) has fled, they should find out the reason thereof and try hard in the matter of his return to his native place. Similarly, they should use praiseworthy endeavour and much effort at soothing and conciliation, to gather cultivators from all sides and directions. [As for] *banjar* (cultivable waste) land, they should impose such *dastūrs* (revenue-rates) on it as to enable it to be brought under cultivation.

3. That he should direct the *amīns* of the parganas that they should every year discover the actual conditions (*maujūdāt*) of cultivation, village by village, peasant-wise (*āsāmīwār*), and, after minute scrutiny, assess the *jama'*, keeping in view the financial interest (*kifāyat*) of

[14] In three MSS this sentence reads as follows: 'He should send along with the previous *dastūr'ul 'amal* whatever he had proposed for the further increase [in production] and prosperity; and also report in detail whatever cesses (*abwābs*) have been enhanced from the beginning of the present reign over the previous rate (*dastūr*) together with the amount collected over the whole year.'

the government and the welfare of the peasantry, and submit the *daul* (register) of *jama'* to the imperial office without delay.

4. That, after the assessment of *jama'*, he should so settle that, in conformity with the settled procedure, the instalments (for payment) of *māl-i wājib* (land revenue) that[15] are established in each pargana. In this respect, he should direct that they (*'āmils*) should start the realization of *maḥṣūl* in time, they should demand (the payment) according to the fixed time; and taking himself weekly reports (of the collection), he should direct that nothing should be left (uncollected) out of the settled instalment, and in case some part of the first installment remains unpaid, it should be collected with the second instalment, and in the third instalment the full payment, without any arrears, be secured.

5. That, he should fix suitable instalments for the *bāqī* (arrears) of the (previous) years, according to the condition and capability of the peasants. He should instruct the *karorīs* that (these instalments) should be realized according to pledges given, and he should keep himself informed of the progress of collection thereof. There should not be any delay due to the fraudulent practices and negligence of the *'āmils*.

6. That, whenever he himself goes out to obtain information about the true condition of the parganas, in each village which he passes through, he should observe the state of cultivation, *rai'* (crop yields),[16] the capacity of the cultivators and the amount of the *jama'*. If (he finds that) in the distribution of the *jama'* fairness and proper calculation has been followed in respect of each individual payer, well and good; but if the *chaudhurī*, or *muqaddam* or *paṭwārī* is involved in oppression he should, comforting the cultivator, let him have his due; and take away the *gunjāyash* (gain) from the dominant ones (*mutaghallibān*). He should, devoting himself to a detailed, truthful inquiry into the assessment of the present year and the distribution of the produce (*maujūdāt*), report in detail (to the imperial office), so that the true state of efficiency of the *amīns* and the good management of that *Wizārat Panāh* (i.e., incumbent of office in revenue department; in this case, the addressee) may become known.

7. That, he should maintain the *nānkār* and *in'ām* (revenue-free grant) according to the revenue regulations of the *khāliṣa-sharīfa*

[15] So in the text; but the word *ki* (that) should be omitted.

[16] D, G. and H read '*rub*' (one-fourth) and the rest '*rafa*' (dismissal): these are obvious misreadings for '*rai*' (crop-yields).

administration. He should discover whatever the *'āmils* of the Prince have increased, so that, keeping in view such matters as how much is left in arrears and what deductions have been obtained, on account of scarcity (of rain) or calamity, by them (i.e., the *'āmils*) from the beginning of the assignment (*tankhwah*) of the *jāgīr*, he should recover [the unreasonable remissions from them]. And for the future he should settle that whenever they restore the parganas to their original state and the fact is reported to the imperial court, each would receive concessions in accordance with the amount of services rendered by him.

8. That he should arrange that in the *foṭakhāna* (treasury) the treasurers (*foṭadārs*) should (only) accept the auspicious *'ālamgīrī sikkas* (newly-coined money of Aurangzeb). In the event of the non-availability of this kind of rupee, they should accept the *Shāhjahānī chalnī* (current) coins[17] that are current in the market and collect the fee (*abwāb*) of *ṣarf-i sikka* (mintage). But they must never accept for the Treasury underweight rupees that are not current in the market. However, if he finds that by rejecting the defective coins, revenue collection (*taḥṣīl*) may be delayed, they should, taking right and fair discount from the peasantry, make the exchange in his presence.

9. That, if, God forbid!, any natural (lit. 'earth-raised' or 'sky-sent') calamity occurs in a locality (*maḥal*), he should strongly direct the *amīns* and *'āmils* that they should watch over the produce (*maūjudāt*) of cultivation with every care, and, finding out (the extent of loss) for each peasant, they should make an assessment of the *hast-o būd* (actual produce) by means of detailed scrutiny. They should not make a collective deduction on account of calamity (*āfat-i sarbasta*), whose distribution is left in the hands of the *chaudhurīs*, *qānūngos*, *muqaddams* or *paṭwārīs*, so that the small peasants (*reza ri'āyā*), receiving their due, remain safe from injury and loss, and the dominant ones are not able to oppress them.

10. That, he should stringently direct the *amīns*, *'āmils*, *chaudhurīs*, *qānūngos* and *muqaddams* in the matter of extinction of *malba*, elimination of *ikhrājāt* (expenses) that are in addition to the *māl* (land revenue) and the prohibited cesses, that are the cause of the distress of the peasantry. He should take bonds from them, that they would never make any increase in the *malba*[18] and (indulge in) extraction of

[17] H adds '*khazana*' (coins of the earlier reigns) after '*chalni*'.

[18] The correct reading '*malba*' is provided by D and H.

the cesses as are forbidden and remitted by the imperial court. He should always keep himself informed; if anyone still commits such acts and persists in them despite prohibition and censure, he (the addressee) should report the matter to the imperial court, so that he (the culprit) be dismissed from service and someone else be appointed in his place.

11. That, for translating the Hindwī papers into Persian for purposes of audit (*barāmad*),[19] he should discover the amounts of *bāchh*, *behrīmāl*, *ikhrājāt* (village expenses), and *rusūmāt* (perquisites), paid by each peasant (*āsāmī*). Having brought into the accounts of the Treasury, everything that comes out of the peasant's house, under all heads, he should record the balance appropriated by the *amīn*, the *'āmil*, the *zamīndārs*, etc., name by name. So far as possible, he should collect and translate the *kāghaz-i khām* (*paṭwārī*'s papers) of all the villages of the pargana. If, due to the absence of the *paṭwārī* or for some other reason, papers from a few villages are not obtained, he should, for that part, enter in the register the average, struck on the basis of the audit (*barāmad*) of all the villages. After the preparation of the register, the *Dīwān* should inspect it. If it has been drawn up in conformity with the rules (*dastūr*) he should accept it, and proceed to recover the amount misappropriated by the *'āmil*, in accordance with the regulations, as well as the amount the *chaudhurī*, the *qānūngo*, the *muqaddam* and the *paṭwārī* have appropriated in excess of the established perquisities (*rusūm*).

12. That he should write (the name of) everyone from amongst the *amīns*, *karorīs* and *fotadārs*,[20] who is serving with uprightness and devotion and, having acted in every matter in conformity with the rules that have been laid down, is rendering good service, so that he should get the reward for his economical management and honesty. If anyone has acted in a contrary fashion, he (the *Dīwān*) should report the fact to the imperial court, so that he may be dismissed from service and discharged from duty, and, being called to account and faced with recoveries, receive punishment for his improper conduct.

13. That, he should fully insist upon the receipt of the register in time. At the *maḥal* where he has himself taken residence, he should daily secure from the *'āmils*, along with the amounts collected, the

[19] In H some superfluous words are added that are not supported by any of the MSS.

[20] D reads '*jāgīrdārs*' in place of '*fotadārs*'.

roznāmcha (daily account) of the collection of the land revenue (*māl*) and the cesses (*sā'ir*) and the daily price list; and from other parganas, the *roznāmcha* of the collection of māl and *maujūdāt* (produce, balances?) every fortnight, and the *arhsatta*[21] of the account (*taḥwīl*, lit. money in custody) of the *foṭadārs*, the *jama' wāṣil-bāqī* (*jama'* collected and in arrears), every month, and the register of *jama'*, *mujmil*, and *jama' bandī* and the income and expenditure (*jama'-o-kharch*) from the custody of the *foṭadār*, every harvest. Having inspected these, he should call to account whomever has appropriated anything in excess of the due amount, and send the report to the imperial office. He should not delay (the collection of) the papers of the kharif till the rabi and of the rabi till the kharif.

14. That, he should strictly take papers from the *amīn*, the *'āmil*, and the *foṭadār*, whoever has been dismissd from service, and should settle his account. He should recover through audit the appropriations recoverable (*abwāb-i bāzyāftī*) in conformity with the rules of the *dīwānī*. He should send the paper with the record of the realization of the appropriations determined by aduit (*abwāb-i badarnawīsī*) to the imperial *kachehri* (office), so that he (the dismissed official) may obtain (the certificate of) 'accounts cleared' (*az muḥāsiba farāgh*) from (that) office.

15. That he should compile the papers of the *dīwānī* each harvest, in conformity with the established rules and send these to the imperial office, under his own seal and endorsement.

Glossary

Abwāb-i bāzyāftī: Abwāb (lit. gates), taxes, cesses; *bāzyāftī*, recovery resumption; hence cesses due to be collected or malappropriations that are due to be recovered.

Āfat-i sarbasta: Āfat, calamity; *sarbasta* (lit. closed at the head), aggregate; hence lumpsum deduction on account of calamity.

'Amal: (Lit. practice) collection of revenue, also term of office or assignment.

'Amal-i jarīb: For *'āmal* see prec.; *jarīb*, measuring rope; hence assessment of land revenue by measurement. *ASMI*, p. 240 & *n*.

Aṛhsaṭṭa: Abstracts of revenue accounts. Cf. S.P. Gupta, *The Agrarian System of Eastern Rajasthan*, Delhi, 1986, pp. 317–8. See also R.H. Thomas ed., *Memoirs on Sind*, 1855, p. 730 (*atsatha*).

Āsāmī-wār: Āsāmī (lit. named individual), individual peasant; *wār*, Persian suffix equivalent of English suffix '-wise'; hence (assessing revenue on) each peasant separately.

[21] H reads '*athata*'; I has '*tatma*' and G '*shubh*'

Behrī Māl: Behrī, levy on each share (*bahra*); *māl*, land revenue; hence amount demanded from each peasant, comprising, or over and above, the authorized revenue and other cesses (Wilson, *Glossary*, s.v.; cf. *ASMI*, 153 & *n*).

Bāqī: Balance, arrears.

Dastūr, dastūr-ul 'amal:Dastūr, regulation, rule; *'amal*, revenue collection. Hence revenue regulations; revenue-rates.

G͟halla bak͟hshī: G͟halla, produce; *bak͟hshī*, a portion; hence crop-sharing. Cf. *ASMI*, p. 237.

Gunjāyash: (Lit. profit) gains.

Hast-o-bud: Hast, is; *bud*, was. A method of assessment based on summary estimation of total produce (Wilson, *Glossary*, s.v., cf. *ASMI*, 238 & *n*.)

Ik͟hrājāt-i deh: Village expenses paid out of revenue collection. Cf. *ASMI*, p. 284 & *n*.

Jama'-o-k͟harch: Collection and expenditure. See also *aṛhasṭṭa.*

Jama' wāṣil bāqī: A statement of total assessment of revenue (*jama'*), amount realized (*wāṣil*), and the balance outstanding (*bāqī*) (Yāsīn's Glossary, Add. 6603, f. 58b, and Wilson, *Glossary*, s.v.).

Jins-i kāmil, Jins-i a'lā: High grade crops, cash crops (Yāsīn's Glossary, Patna, f. 66a).

Jins-i nāqiṣ, Jins-i adnā: Inferior crops, ibid.

Kankūṭ: Method of assessing revenue, based on measurement of land and estimation of yield. Cf. *ASMI*, p. 232.

Malba: Cesses above authorized revenue, collected ostensibly for village expenses. *ASMI*, pp.154*n*, 284*n*.

Nānkār: Allowance paid to zamīndār out of the revenue collection or by allotment of tax-exempt land for services rendered in collecting land-revenue. *ASMI*, p.182.

Reza ri'āyā: Small peasants.

Sāl-i Kāmil: Abbreviated form of *sāl-i ḥāṣil-i kāmil*, year when the revenue realized was the maximum.

Ṣarf-i Sikka: Discount on account of mintage.

Sarishta-i wuṣūlī abwāb-i badarnawīsī: Sarishta, register; *wuṣūl*, receipt; *Badarnawīsī*, audit. Hence audited register of collection of unauthorized appropriations.

Tiyūldār: Tiyūl, area whose revenues were assigned by the Emperor. Hence holder of *tiyūl* or *jāgīr*, which are synonymous.

10

A Programme of Reliefs for the People of Kashmir

An Imperial Edict of Shahjahan

The Mughal administration tended to assume great uniformity not only in aspects of administrative organization but also in regard to its fiscal and revenue systems. There was a general policy of extending systems of revenue assessment and realization, and uniform units of weights and measures from its core area to the outlying regions.

But in spite of the high level of systematization attained, the Mughal revenue administration was not unduly rigid and modifications were affected and allowance made to accord concessions to the geographical and traditional variations prevailing in regions away from the heartland of the empire.[1]

The working of the Mughal revenue administration in Kashmir, after its conquest by Akbar in 1586, offers an interesting example of this dual process of systematization and adjustment: imperial measures in Kashmir were further influenced by the fact that the province repeatedly came under the personal scrutiny of the Mughal emperors who made frequent visits to the Valley at least till the early years of Aurangzeb's reign.[2]

Abū'l Faẓl has provided us with important information on the introduction of Mughal revenue system in Kashmir under Akbar, mentioning some of its attendant adverse effects and the consequent measures that Akbar was obliged to take to ameliorate the situation.

According to Abū'l Faẓl, during his first visit to Kashmir in 1589, Akbar made some efforts to make a fresh estimation of revenues, but

[1] For details see *ASMI*, pp. 259–71.

[2] Akbar made three visits to Kashmir, in 1589, 1592, and 1597 — the first two were rather short. Jahāngīr as emperor visited the Valley six times while Shāhjahān paid four visits. Aurangzeb went to Kashmir only once in the early 1660s, and then discontinued the practice of his predecessors.

in spite of the fact that detailed information was collected about the yields of various crops, the emperor remained engaged in sightseeing, and the actual demand to be imposed could not be worked out. Only a summary enhancement being effected, the *jama'* was raised from twenty lakh ass-loads of rice to twenty-two lakh. He, however, justifies this summary way of dealing with the matters by suggesting that a close enquiry would have resulted in some oppression, and in a newly conquered region the peasants should be encouraged.[3]

But after some time, the emperor changed his mind. Har Tota, a former confidant of Mirza Yusuf Khān, the deposed ruler of Kashmir, advised that the latter used to receive fifty per cent more ass-loads of rice, and each ass-load was exchanged for twenty-eight *dāms* instead of sixteen at which it had been earlier reckoned.[4] Thereupon Akbar despatched trusted officials to make enquiries,[5] and thought of taking Kashmir into the imperial *khāliṣa*.[6] On his arrival in Kashmir in 1592, he in fact incorporated Kashmir into the *khāliṣa* for a short while.[7]

Whatever be the arrangements, Abū'l Faẓl himself was compelled to admit that the economic conditions of Kashmir worsened owing to the tyranny of *jāgīrdārs*. They demanded revenue in 'gold and silver in that country of crop sharing.'[8] During his third and last visit in 1598, Akbar found Kashmir under the grip of a severe famine that was further accentuated by the arrival of the emperor with a large retinue.[9]

Akbar took immediate relief measures by remitting the revenue and opening free kitchens. He also ordered a fresh assessment based on actual village papers (*kāghaẕ-i-khām*) and fixed the demand at a half of the produce.[10] He also remitted fifty-five cesses and made new

[3] *AN*, Vol. III, pp. 548–9.

[4] Ibid., Vol. III, pp. 595, 617. Qāẓī Nūrullah and Qāẓī 'Alī had been entrusted with this task.

[5] Qāẓī 'Alī seems to have prepared a detailed assessment (Ibid., p. 627).

[6] Ibid., p. 626.

[7] Ibid., p. 627. On the recommendation of Prince Salīm, Kashmir was given in *jāgīr* to Mirzā Yūsuf but saffron was retained on the *khāliṣa*.

[8] Ibid., pp. 726–7.

[9] Mu'tamād Khān, *Iqbālnāma-i Jahāngīrī*, edited by Nawal Kishor, Kanpur, 1870, pp. 453–4; *Akbarnāma*, Vol. III, p. 727.

[10] *AN*, Vol. III, p. 727. Mu'timad Khān says that Abū'l Faẓl was made responsible for providing relief work and around seventy thousand people were fed daily (*Iqbālnāma*, Vol. II, p. 454).

arrangements for the picking of saffron. To provide employment to people, a fort was ordered to be built at Nagar Nagar.[11] It is interesting to note that the inscription at the gate of the fort explicitly says that no unpaid labour was used and one crore and ten lakh *dāms* were given for the purpose from the imperial treasury.[12]

Abū'l Fazḷ's further statements show that the Mughal administration accepted for Kashmir a fixed system of revenue assessment and collection, namely, *nasq-i g͟halla bakhshī*, in which yearly revenue assessments were not made and the same numbers of ass-loads of rice were demanded every year from each village.[13]

We have little direct evidence from the subsequent reigns to find out how appropriate or efficient the arrangements turned out to be and whether any further adjustments were made. Jahāngīr, as emperor, made five rather long visits to Kashmir; and he has also left striking notices of the Valley in the *Tuzuk*, but his concern was largely the flora and fauna, and he appears to have found little of interest in the details of the revenue system.

Even the chroniclers of Shāhjahān's time provide little information of use to us on the taxation system of Kashmir. A *farmān* of Shāhjahān issued in the fifth regnal year (1633) thus becomes especially significant as a piece of evidence for the functioning of the Mughal administration in Kashmir during the first half of the seventeenth century. It has already received some attention from the historians[14] but still merits a thorough analysis.

There are three surviving versions of this imperial order. The most noticed is the one engraved on the gate of the Jāmi' Masjid at Srinagar.[15] The second version (apparently a summary) is given by Qazẉīnī in his *Bādshāhnāma*.[16] Ṣāliḥ Kamboh provides us with the text of a third

[11] *AN*, Vol. III, p. 727.

[12] The inscription is reproduced in G͟hulām Ḥasan, *Tārīk͟h-i Ḥasan*, Vol. II, p. 443.

[13] Irfan Habib, *Agrarian System of Mughal India*, p.258.

[14] P.N.K. Bamzai, *A History of Kashmir*, Delhi 1962, pp. 397–8; G.M.D. Sufi, *Kashmir*, London 1974, p. 268, has offered a summary translation of the inscription but without any annotation.

[15] Personal observation as well as reproduced in *Tārīk͟h-i Ḥasan*, pp. 500–2 and in Birbal Kachni's, *Majmu'at-ul Tawārīk͟h*, Abdus Salam Collection, Aligarh Muslim University (MS. 289/59).

[16] Amīn Qazẉīnī, *Bādshāhnama*, transcript of the Rampur MS in the Department of History Library, Aligarh Muslim University, pp. 509–10.

version which in form and language is different from that of Qaẓwīnī.[17] Lāhorī does not even mention the issue of this order. Broadly speaking, all the three versions are similar in essence, though there are certain very interesting variations. The versions given by Qaẓwīnī and Ṣāliḥ are closer to each other than to the actual inscription.

In the Appendix, I offer full translations of all the three texts. The three texts, namely, the inscription, that of Qaẓwīnī and Ṣāliḥ from now are cited respectively as (A), (B), and (C).

The inscription (A) gives the date of the *farmān* as 7 Isfandārmuẕ, i.e., c. 24 February (1633) and the date of it being inscribed in stone on the Jami' Masjid, Srinagar, as 26 Āẕar, or 17 December 1633; Qaẓwīnī (B) puts it under 15 Isfandārmuẕ, i.e., 5 March (1633); Ṣāliḥ, does not mention any specific date, but places the issue of the *farmān* during Isfandārmuẕ.

The version inscribed on the gateway of the Jāmi' Masjid contains some exceptional features. The mere fact of placing it on such a public place is at least unusual if not entirely novel.[18] But the more striking feature is the fact that a preceding *ṣūbadār* is repeatedly criticized by name, only in (A); Qazwīnī and Ṣāliḥ appear more discreet than the inscription and avoid mentioning the name of the allegedly erring *ṣūbadār* I'tiqād Khān.[19]

[17] Ṣāliḥ Kamboh, *'Amal-i* Ṣāliḥ, Vol. I, edited by G. Yazdani, Calcutta 1918, pp. 543–5.

[18] The text of an order of Aurangzeb's time issued in the 22nd regnal year, remitting the *sā'ir* in favour of bankers, Brahmans and merchants of Shahabad, has been found inscribed on a pillar that was fixed in front of the *Kotwali* of the town (*Epigraphia Indica*, Arabic and Persian Supplement, 1968, p. 70). Like the Srinagar Mosque Inscription this too has a *la'nat-nāma*, that is, it calls upon all concerned to respect the order in the name of God and Rama.

[19] In all probability, the repeated references to I'tiqād Khān by name as the erring governor occurred in the *farmān* itself, since the public mosque inscription is not likely to have contained any unauthorized insertions in the *farmān*. However, this rather an unusual practice might have been simply a result of the draftsman of the *farmān* too closely following the contents of the report sent by Ẓafar Khān; Qazwīnī in his own summary and the other official Ṣāliḥ in his text, probably exercised due discretion here since Mirza Shāhpur I'tiqād Khān was a high ranking noble (4,000 *ẕat* and *sawār* in 1632), and a member of one of the leading families (being son of I'timādud Daula and brother of Nūr Jahān), and exactly reproducing the censure might have seemed discourteous for a person of his status. Even soon after his removal from Kashmir he was appointed governor of Delhi (by November 1633) and subsequently, held the posts of *faujdār* of Jaunpur and *ṣūbadār* of

The *farmān* was apparently issued on the solicitation of Aḥsanullah Ẓafar Khān who was acting as *ṣūbadār* on behalf of his father Khāwaja Ab'ul Ḥasan. The latter was appointed the *ṣūbadār* of Kashmir in the fifth regnal year, succeeding I'tiqād Khān[20] who was transferred from there after being posted there for almost eleven years.[21] Ẓafar Khān was confirmed as full-fledged *ṣūbadār* of the province one year afterwards, upon the death of his father.[22]

The preamble in all the three copies asserts that certain innovations had been made by the former *ṣūbadārs* that caused hardship to the people and peasants of Kashmir; and Qazwīnī and Ṣāliḥ also mention that these yielded large sums. Interestingly enough the inscription attributes the entire credit of getting the order to Ẓafar Khān while Salih says that it was issued on the receipt of reports of intelligencers and the petition of Ẓafar Khān. Qazwīnī simply attributes it to the petition of officials of government (*Mutaṣaddiān-i Muhimmāt*), giving no personal credit to Ẓafar Khān.

The first clause deals with the practice of using unpaid labour in picking saffron flowers.[23] In all the three versions it is alleged that it was an innovation of the former Mughal *ṣūbadārs*. This does not appear to be correct in the face of the information given by Abū'l Faẓl in the *Akbarnāma* as well as in the *Ā'īn-i Akbarī* and the testimony of Jahangir. Abū'l Faẓl describes in some detail how in each saffron flower there were only three inner stigmas that yielded pure saffron. After the flowers were gathered these stigmas were picked by hand.[24]

Bihar, Bengal, and Awadh successively, and reached the rank of 5,000 *zat* and *sawār* (for tracing his career see M. Athar Ali, *Apparatus of the Mughal Empire*, Delhi, 1986).

The apparent hostility of Ẓafar Khān to I'tiqād Khān might reflect some factional rivalries and personal grudges, (Khawaja Abū'l Ḥasan lost his coveted post of the *Dīwān-i kul* to I'timādud Daula in 1611). An imperial order obtained to undo the 'innovations' of I'tiqad Khān, in Kashmir, was perhaps a means of discrediting a prominent member of I'timādud Daula's house.

[20] Lāhorī, *Bādshāhnāma*, Vol.I, No. 1, edited by K.D. Ahmad, Calcutta 1866–72, p. 432; Ṣāliḥ, Vol. I, p. 410.

[21] He was appointed governor in the eighteenth regnal year of Jahāngīr (*Tuzuk*, p. 356) and was confirmed in the post by Shāhjahān at his accession, Ṣāliḥ, Vol. I, p. 226.

[22] Lāhorī, Vol. I, No.1, p. 474; Ṣāliḥ, Vol. I, p. 485.

[23] In (A) it is mentioned that a small amount of salt was given in wages.

[24] W.R. Lawrence, *Valley of Kashmir*, London 1895, p. 344, describes the process in detail.

Earlier the practice was that people were forcibly made to separate the stigmas from the petals and for cleaning one *pal*[25] of saffron, two *pals* of salt was given. However, during the time of G͟hāzi K͟hān Chak (1555–63) a different practice was introduced. The saffron flower was given to the traders and cultivators for cleaning; for every eleven *turks* of saffron flowers they were asked to give two *sers* of dry saffron that was supposed to be the yield of ten *turks* only. In other words, for returning ten cleaned *turks* of saffron flowers, one *turk* of flowers was left to them. According to Abū'l Faẓl, the practice was very inefficient, and much loss was incurred especially during the rains. It is reported that during his third visit in the forty-second regnal year (1598) Akbar abolished this practice and the flowers were handed over to the *Umara'* (nobles) for being cleaned; they apparently got it picked by employing paid labour because Abū'l Faẓl explicitly says that the yields under the new arrangement largely increased from earlier days when forced labour had been used.[26]

However, this new arrangement did not last long since Jahāngīr in his fifteenth regnal year mentions the old practice of payment in salt for picking saffron; and he seems to find nothing inappropriate in this practice. He adds that salt is not available in Kashmir and is brought from Hindustan.[27]

It was this practice that was ordered to be discontinued by Shāhjahān's *farmān*. According to Qaẓwīnī, forced labour was exacted from the people of the city; Ṣāliḥ specifies them as hapless poor, old women, and orphan children. Qaẓwīnī simply records that the practice was ordered to be discontinued; Ṣāliḥ is more explicit and says that the order was issued to pay wages out of the imperial treasury. The text (A) is however far more detailed, and tells us that for (the portion of) saffron belonging to the *k͟hāliṣa*, wages were to be paid, and that belonging to the *jāgīrdārs* was to be handed over to them in the form of flowers (and not in picked form). It seems from this that the saffron crop was shared between the *k͟hāliṣa* and *jāgīrdārs*. Previously, the crop was taken over by the *k͟hāliṣa* officials, who set forced labour to the task and handed over the picked saffron to the *jāgīrdārs* in lieu of their share. Now, they were to receive flowers only.

The second clause mentions that there was an old practice of collecting two *dāms* so in (A), but two and a half *dāms* in (B) and

[25] One *pal* was equivalent to 2 *dāms* weight, *Ā'īn*, Vol. I, p. 570.

[26] *Ā'īn*, Vol. I, p. 96; *AN*, Vol. III, pp. 727, 734.

[27] *Tuzuk*, p. 315.

(C)—on each ass-load of rice being transported, for the purpose of meeting the officials' needs for firewood. But I'tiqād Khān—his name is mentioned in only (A)—increased the levy to four *dāms*. The charge was now ordered to be abolished altogether. The practice of taking wood from the peasants is also mentioned by Abū'l Fazl among those cesses that had been abolished by Akbar in 1598.[28] The practice perhaps either survived or reappeared, the demand for firewood being commuted into cash. In (B) and (C) it is mentioned that this charge belonged to the category of toll and transit dues which had been remitted in the imperial dominions; therefore, this too should be abolished. These particulars are not given in (A).

The third clause is about a perquisite under which previously two sheep were taken from every village having a *jama'* of more than four hundred ass-loads of rice. But according to the version (A), I'tiqād Khān commuted this charge into cash and started realizing sixty-six *dāms* in lieu of each sheep. The rendering of this clause is almost identical, in substance, in all the three versions except that (B) and (C) add that the amount of sixty-six *dāms* that was realized as the price of one sheep in fact amounted to the price of three sheep. (A) alone names I'tiqād Khān as the innovator of the enhancement in the levy.

The fourth clause in (A) and (B), which is the fifth one in (C), deals with the remittance granted in the uniform levy of seventy-five *dāms* per head imposed by I'tiqād Khān, on boatmen irrespective of their age. Under the old rule the tax on boatmen varied according to their age, the young paying sixty *dāms*, the children thirty-six, and the old only twelve. The old rates were now restored.

The enhancement in levy on boatmen whether made by I'tiqād Khān or anyone else must have had very severe effects since the entire movement of men and goods, especially that of grains, was through the river transport and totally depended on boats.[29] According to Jahāngīr, there were 5,700 boats in the city (Srinagar).[30] Mu'tamad Khān gives the same number for the city as well as the districts and adds that the number of boatmen was 7,400.[31] The boatmen also worked as fishermen, and Jahāngīr describes a special type of fishing

[28] *AN*, Vol. III, p. 727.

[29] *Iqbalnāma*, p. 569.

[30] *Tuzuk*, p. 298; Abu'l Fazl however gives the number as 30,000 (*AN*, Vol. III, p. 550).

[31] *Iqbalnāma*, p. 569.

in which he found old fishermen to be more efficient.[32]

This clause too has little variations of substance in the three versions except the usual one, namely, the mention of I'tiqād Khān's name occurs only in (A). In (B) and (C) this levy is designated *mīr baḥrī*.

The fifth clause in (A) abolishes the practice of the seizure of choice fruits from private orchards by the *ṣūbadārs*. The matter perhaps appeared so trivial to the two chroniclers that they omitted it, but for the people of Kashmir it was also quite important. On the other hand, the clause relating to the multiplicity of *qānūngos* in the villages of Kashmir, a phenomenon causing a loss to the *jāgīrdārs* as well as to the peasants, does not appear in (A). It was perhaps not considered of interest to those who were expected to read the order; or were the Kashmir officials not ready to enforce this part of the order?

Ẓafar Khān is also reported to have collected all the people of Kashmir and read out the *farmān* to them.[33]

Ẓafar Khān as *ṣūbadār* of Kashmir appears to have remained quite popular since, when a famine broke out in Kashmir in 1641–2 and hoards of destitute people started reaching Lahore, one of the main measures the emperor took was the reappointment of Ẓafar Khān as *ṣūbadār*. He immediately went there and started taking steps for relief. He was given Rs 1,50,000 from the imperial treasury to meet the expenses on relief measures,[34] but he demanded a further sum of Rs 30,000 for giving loans to the peasants, expressly for buying oxen and seed.[35] He is said to have thus earned the gratitude of the people of the Valley and they praised him to the Emperor. As a reward for his good work the Emperor made a remission of one lakh rupees in the state demand against him.[36]

The Srinagar Mosque Edict then may well be the evidence of the work of one of the more humane governors in the annals of the Mughal empire.

[32] *Tuzuk*, p. 315.

[33] Qazwīnī, p. 510.

[34] Khafi Khān, *Muntakhab-ul Lubāb*, ed. K.D. Ahmad, Calcutta 1860-74, pp.587-8.

[35] Ibid., p.595.

[36] Ibid., p.608.

APPENDIX

(A) The Srinagar Mosque Inscription

'God is Great'[37]: Shāhjahān Pādshāh, the Just, the Victorious

Copy of the august order of His Solomon-like Majesty, Ṣāhib Qirān Ṣānī,[38] issued on the seventh of Ilāhī month Isfandārmuẕ [24 February 1633] upon the solicitation of the humblest of old imperial servants (*khānazādān*) Aḥsānullāh, bearing the title of Ẓafar Khān, for setting aside the innovations which have been made during the terms of the former governors of the *ṣūba* (*ṣūbadārān*) in the town of the pleasant vale of Kashmir and have been the cause of ruin of the peasantry and the inhabitants of this region:

Whereas Our attention is entirely engaged in securing the welfare of the people, We, owing to certain practices which in the pleasant territory of Kashmir used to cause hardship to the inhabitants of the region, have decreed that they be discontinued.

The first of these items is that at the time of picking saffron the people used to be forcibly taken to pick saffron and a little amount of salt used to be given to them by way of wages. On this account hardship is caused to them. We have decreed that no one must ever be compelled to pick [saffron]. [For picking] such as belongs to the *khāliṣa* the labourers should be engaged voluntarily and paid actual (i.e., market) wages. Whatever belongs to the *jāgīrdārs* should be handed over to them in kind in saffron flowers, so that they may get [the stigmas] picked in any manner they desire.

Item: In the time of some governors of Kashmir, on each ass-load (*kharwār*) of paddy two *dāms* of firewood used to be collected. During the tenure of I'tiqād Khān four *dāms* began to be realized on each ass-load on that ground. Whereas on this account too much hardship has been caused to the peasants, we have therefore decreed that peasants be fully exempted from this demand, and nothing must be realized from them on grounds of the claim for firewood.

Item: From every village whose *jama'* is more than four hundred ass-loads of paddy, the men in authority (*ḥukkām*) have been collecting two sheep every year; and I'tiqād Khān during his governorship of the *ṣūba* took in lieu of the sheep sixty-six *dāms* for each sheep. Whereas from this cause again great hardship occurs we have decreed

[37] This is preceded by some words of invocation.

[38] Title of Shāhjahān.

that it be totally discontinued; neither should they take the sheep nor the money on this ground. They should exempt the peasants (*ri'āya*) from the levy of this tax (*wajh*).

Item: During the period of his governorship of the *ṣūba*, I'tiqād Khān, imposing a summary rate, levied seventy-five *dāms* per head on all boatmen, whether young or old or juvenile. The old established practice was that from young [boat-] men they used to take sixty *dāms* per head, from the old, twelve per head, and from children thirty-six *dāms* per head. We have decreed that, maintaining the previous regulation (*dastūr*), the innovation made by I'tiqād Khān be considered abolished, and none should act according to it.

Item: The governors of the fruits in every garden and orchard, the excellence of whose fruits they have fancied, have been setting their men to guard those fruits for them and not allow the owners of these gardens and orchards to get those fruits. On this account much hardship has been caused to those people, so much so that some of them have turned away from [raising] fruit trees. We have [therefore] decreed that no governor of the *ṣūba* should requisition the fruits of anyone's garden or orchard.

Let the dignified men of authority (*ḥukkām*), careful *dīwāns* and the present and future *'amils* (revenue officials) of the *ṣūba* of Kashmir consider these orders as permanent and everlasting and not allow any alteration and change [therein]. Anyone who allow alteration and change herein will earn condemnation (*la'nat*) from God and the wrath of the Emperor. Written [i.e., inscribed] on the twenty-sixth of the Ilāhī month of Āẕar.

(B) The Version in Qazwīnī's *Bādshāh Nāma*[39]

Whereas from the petitions of the government officials (*mutaṣaddiān-i muhimmāt*) of heaven-like Kashmir it had been represented to the imperial court that in that *ṣūba* certain innovations have been instituted and these have become the cause of hardship to the peasantry and the poor, His Majesty Ṣāhib-i Qirān-i Ṣānī, who is the mark of the mercy and grace of the creator, closing his right-seeing eye to the revenue (*ḥāṣil*) obtained from them (such practices), remitted all of them. The world-regulating order was issued, addressed to Ẓafar Khān, that henceforth, treating the inhabitants of that region as exempted

[39] Qaẕwīnī, *Bādshāhnāma*, transcript of the Rampur MS in the Department of History Library, Aligarh Muslim University, pp. 509–10.

from those burdens, on no account should he oppress any one of the peasants and people of that *ṣūba* with these exactions (*jihāt*). Any of the officials of the revenue department (*dīwānī*), who acts in violation of this august order, would incur the Emperor's wrath, which is the manifestation of divine terror.

The description of each of the innovations about which the order was issued is now recorded by the chronicler. First, the inhabitants of the city used to be ordered to perform unpaid labour (*bagār*) of picking saffron, and this inflicted hardship on the artisans and men whose subsistence comes from their daily work. It has been decreed that hereafter the inhabitants of the town must not be harassed on this account. Second, in former days on each ass-load of paddy (*shaltok*), that the people of Kashmir call *shālī*, two and half *dāms* used to be levied and now this had been raised to four *dāms*, and the difference (owing to the increase) amounted to a large sum. The emperor ordered that since toll and transit dues (*zakat wa rāhdārī*) are remitted in most of the imperial dominions, and [as] this (exaction) is of that category, it should be wholly remitted and hereafter no demand shall be made on this account.

Third, from every village having a *ḥāṣil* of four hundred ass-loads or more (of paddy), two sheep used formerly to be collected, and some of the *ṣūbadārs*, fixing the value of sheep at sixty-six *dāms*, which (actually) is the price of three sheep, realized the levy on that basis. From this practice great loss used to befall the peasants. The emperor decreed that the innovations must be discontinued, and in this regard the old regulation should be acted upon.

Fourth, in every village there were many co-sharing *qānūngos* and they used to collect large amount of money from the peasants on account of the *qānūngoī* (perquisites), which caused hardship to the peasantry and loss to the *jāgīrdārs*. The Emperor ordered that henceforth there shall be only one qānūngo in each village and the co-sharing *qānūngos* should be removed.

Fifth, from all boatmen whether juvenile or old or young, they used to collect seventy-five *dāms* per head by way of *mīr baḥrī*. Owing to this many boatmen, choosing exile, abandoned their profession. It has been decreed by the Emperor that henceforth they should act according to the old rule and take from each old (man) twelve *dāms*, from each young man sixty *dāms*, and from each child thirty-six *dāms*.

Upon the receipt of the obedience-exacting imperial order, Ẓafar Khān, *ṣūbadār* of Kashmir, having collected all the people of that territory, had the destiny-framing order read out, causing happiness to the hearts of the select as well as the mass of the people. He issued severe, strict instructions for the carrying out of these obedience-exacting decrees, and had them inscribed on a stone, along with a curse for any infringement (*la'nat-nāma*), this being inscribed on stone and placed by him over the door of the Jami' Masjid. The entire peasantry and people of that paradise-resembling region, obtaining relief and comfort, let loose their tongues to pray for this everlasting empire.

(C) The Version in *'Amal-i Ṣāliḥ*[40]

The present is witness to the removal, by the kind attention of His Majesty Ṣāhib-i Qirān-i Ṣānī, of the shameful, notorious innovations that had been introduced in the capital city of Kashmir and its dependencies by the tyranny of the successive governors (*ḥukkāms*) had with passage of time come to yield large sums. Whereas, now that the facts about them were conveyed to His Majesty through the reports of the intelligencers of the said *ṣūba* and the petition of Ẓafar Khān, *ṣūbadār* of that region, a decree was forthwith issued addressed to Ẓafar Khān, in this regard, to the effect that all of these cesses that have been imposed by the perpetrators of oppression should be removed from the face of the registers, indeed from the pages of the age, and hereafter let nothing be taken from the peasantry on this ground [of cesses], except what had been fixed in the olden past. The details of those items and cesses are as follows:

Item: The government officials (*mutaṣaddiān-i muhimmāt*) compel the inhabitants of the city in general and the hapless poor, old women consumed by years, and children brought up by widows, for picking saffron by *begār* (forced unpaid labour). It has been decreed that these people should not be harassed by this objectionable practice. The workers of this necessary task should be paid their wages from the imperial establishment (*sarkār khāṣa sharifa*).

Item: It was fixed from the olden times that per ass-load of paddy they took two and half *dāms*, a copper coin (*falūs*) of a special weight. During these days four *dāms* have been fixed. It has been decreed that whereas in this everlasting reign the collection of toll and transit dues amount to a large sum, have been abolished in the entire imperial dominions, they should not trouble anyone with these miscellaneous

[40] Ṣāliḥ Kamboh, *'Amal-i Ṣāliḥ*, Vol. I, pp. 542–4.

cesses (*faru'āt-i juzwī*) which have no sanction whatsoever, and not collect anything on account of this exaction.

Item: From every village bearing the *ḥāl-i ḥāṣil* (realization) of four hundred ass-loads of paddy, two sheep used to be taken in the past according to the settled practice. At present, owing to the tyranny of the former *ṣūbadārs*, in lieu of the price of each sheep, they take from the peasants, in cash, sixty-six *dāms* which (actually) amounts to the price of three sheep. It has been decreed that in this respect they must act according to the former regulations and restrain their grasping hands from all [unjust] exactions.

Item: In every village numerous *qānūngos* have appeared and they realize from peasants a large sum under the head of *qānūngoī*. In this way much loss is incurred by the peasants and the *jāgīrdārs*. The Emperor has ordered that one *qānūngo* shall suffice (for each village), and the others shall not be allowed to intrude therein.

Item: From the aged and young, the children and the old among the boatmen, they take seventy-five *dāms* per head, calling the levy *mīr baḥrī*. It has been decreed that, regarding the older practice as the prescribed regulation (*dastūr-ul 'amal*), they should in this matter too stop the realization of the fiscal innovations, and from old ones take no more than twelve *dāms*, young men sixty *dāms*, and juveniles thirty-six *dāms*. (Further to that) Ẓafar Khān, the *ṣūbadār*, should, relieving the weak and poor from the bonds of hardship and the heavy fiscal demands, get the text of the imperial order inscribed on a slab of stone and have it placed on the gate of the Jami' Masjid.

11

Expenditure on Buildings under Shahjahan

A Chapter of Imperial Financial History

A proper delineation of the Mughal imperial finances seems essential for any serious study of the Mughal economy. For Akbar's reign (1556–1605) the unique information in Abū'l Faẓl's *Ā'īn-i Akbarī* makes it possible to work out the main features of the financial organization even if in outline. But there is no comparable repository of such data available to us from the seventeenth century. Mughal sources of this period do not usually go beyond providing the revenue statistics (*jama'* and *ḥāṣil* figures) or the lists of *manṣabdārs* and pay-schedules. Though the primary documentation is incomparably more extensive than for the sixteenth century, but it does not let us have the aggregate figures.

To make any attempt at a study of imperial finances during the seventeenth century, one has to resort to indirect evidence or to build upon bits and pieces. Though the related data are admittedly scattered and scanty, certain information on imperial financial expenditure can still be studied.

'Abdu'l Ḥamīd Lāhorī, the official historian of Shāhjahān (1628–58), gives the expected net revenue income (*jama'*) of Shāhjahān's empire in 1648 as 880 crore *dāms*.[1] The greatest charge on the revenue income was the total salary-bill of the *manṣabdārs*.[2] A.J. Qaisar estimates that in 1648–9 the pay-claims of the *manṣabdārs* accounted for 82.9 per cent of the total *jama'* of the empire.[3] In other words

[1] 'Abdul Ḥamīd Lāhorī, *Bādshāhnāma*, edited by Kabiruddin Ahmad, Vol. I, Part 1, p. 710.

[2] Under Akbar, in 1595–6, 82.13 per cent of the net revenue income went to meet the pay claims of the *manṣabdārs*, see *IESHR*, Vol. XVII, No. 3, p. 338.

[3] 'Distribution of the revenue resources of the Mughal empire among the nobility', *PIHC, 27th session*, pp. 237–42.

about 17 per cent of the total assessed revenue was left for the emperor's establishment (*khāliṣa*), after the salary payments of the *manṣabdārs*. Even out of this a part might have been alienated in the form of land revenue grants to the devout and the needy.[4] Taking the *jama'* assigned to the imperial *khāliṣa*, we must remember that the actual realization always fell far short of the assessment. Amīn Qazwīnī, the official historian of Shāhjahān, very helpfully informs us that the emperor in the early years of his reign fixed the income of the *khāliṣa* at 60 crore *dāms* (=Rs 150 lakh), while *khāliṣa* expenditure varied from 100 to 120 lakhs of rupees.[5]

This amount went, in part, to maintain the imperial military establishment that included 7,000 *aḥadīs* and mounted musketeers; 40,000 foot soldiers, gunners, musketeers, and archers,[6] as well as the animal stables, arsenal, and armoury. Part of additional expenditure on military campaigns must also have formed part of the *khāliṣa* expenditure.[7] Then there were expenses incurred on the harem, wardrobe, kitchen, and numerous other departments (*kārkhānas*) and buildings, all comprised under household expenditure (*bayūtāt*).

With the limited amount of data available to us, it does not seem possible to work out the pattern of imperial expenditure in any detail. Nevertheless the surviving monuments of Shāhjahān give us the impression that the financial investment in them should have accounted for a very considerable proportion of the *khāliṣa* expenditure. Fortunately, the costs of construction of most of the major edifices and the periods during which those were under construction are recorded either by the contemporary chronicles or are mentioned in some of the inscriptions on the buildings themselves. It thus seems possible to compute the minimum expenditure on imperial buildings erected by Shāhjahān and its relative significance in the imperial budget. This may also provide archaeologists with the possibility of relating the recorded estimates of expenditure to the surviving buildings though the fact that portions of certain complexes have disappeared, as in

[4] Abū'l Faẓl expressedly includes the amount alienated in *Suyūrghal* in his *jama'* figures, *Ā'īn*, Vol.I, pp. 386–595.

[5] Qazwīnī, *Bādshāhnāma*, transcript of the Rampur MS in the Library of the Department of History, Aligarh Muslim University, p. 423.

[6] Lāhorī, Vol. II, Part 2, p. 715.

[7] Qazwīnī states that in years when major expeditions took place the *khalisa* expenditure rose to Rs 120 lakh (*Bādshāhnāma* transcript, p. 423).

Mumtazabad, must complicate the task.

Shāhjahān's interest in building construction is evident not only from his surviving edifices, but also from the statements made by his historians. Qazwīnī says that 'during the present reign the building activity has reached such a level as had neither been attained in any earlier time nor would be possible in the future'.[8] The importance attached to the building department as well as the continuous pace of construction is apparent from the fact that the consideration of building plans was a part of the emperor's daily routine. Every afternoon the *dārog͟has* of the imperial buildings and the architects presented the plans and designs of the buildings for his approval and suggestions. The emperor not only modified them but often made the sketches of the plans himself which were then drawn (or faired out) on paper by Yamīn-ud Daula Aṣaf K͟hān.[9]

In spite of such importance attached to the building establishment, none of the sources of Shāhjahān's reign provide us with data on the wages of the workers employed in the building department nor the cost of the building material. (In this as in so many other things, they fall far behind Abū'l Faẓl). They make up, however, by giving us so many details on the actual costs incurred.

Construction on a large scale was undertaken in the very first year of Shāhjahān's reign.[10] The new emperor did not find to his taste most of the buildings in the Agra fort built by Akbar with red sandstone at a cost of Rs 35 lakh.[11] Shāhjahān, therefore, ordered construction of a number of buildings within the fort using marble.[12] Even the marble structures added by Jahāngīr were demolished and rebuilt by 1636–7.[13] In his tenth regnal year, 1636–7 Shāhjahān planned to build

[8] Qazwīnī, p. 266.

[9] Qazwīnī, p. 266; Lāhorī, Vol. I, part 1, p. 149.

[10] Ibid., p. 221.

[11] *Tuzuk-i Jahāngīrī*, edited by Saiyid Ahmad, Ghazipur and Aligarh, 1863–4, p. 2. Badāūnī gives the expenditure on the Agra fort by Akbar as 3 crore (*tankas*), i.e., Rs 15 lakh (*Muntak͟habut Tawārīkh*, edited by Ali Ahmad and Less, Vol. II, Bib. Ind., Calcutta, 1864–9, p. 74). While Pelsaert gives an estimate of Rs 25 lakh, F. Pelsaert, *A Contemporary Dutch Chronicle of Mughal India*, translated by Brij Narain and S.R. Sharma, Calcutta, 1857, p. 21. The amount reported by Jahāngīr should be allowed precedence over the other two estimates.

[12] Lāhorī, Vol. I, Part 1, p. 221.

[13] Ibid., Vol. I, Part 2, pp. 237–41.

a suitable mosque at Agra; a site was selected and the land acquired. Lāhorī and, following him, Ṣāliḥ inform us that the land of the site which was outside the *khāliṣa* was bought at prices one and a half times the presumed actual, while some of the owners opted for taking buildings in compensations elsewhere.[14] Princess Jahānāra sought permission from the emperor to build the mosque from her own resources, and so the construction work was handed over to the officers of her establishment.[15] One of the inscription on the main arch mentions the cost of construction as five lakhs rupees and the date of completion 1058 A.H.(AD 1648).[16]

It seems that all the alterations in the Agra fort by Shāhjahān except the mosque in the fort that was built later on had been completed around 1637–8.[17] While we have no separate estimates for the cost of construction of various buildings, Lāhorī as well as Ṣāliḥ record the total imperial expenditure on the buildings of Agra (excluding the Taj Mahal and Mumtazabad complex) as Rs 60 lakh. This amount includes the expenditure of Rs 3 lakh incurred on the mosque inside the fort.[18] Perhaps we will not go far wrong in assuming that in the first decade of the reign Rs 50 lakh were spent on the erection of buildings at Agra. It was during the same decade that a tomb was erected on Jahāngīr's grave. According to Jahāngīr's will it should have been a simple structure of mostly red stone and only partly of marble. It actually cost Rs 10 lakh and was completed within ten years.[19]

While Jahāngīr's mausoleum was still in progress, Shāhjahān's favourite queen Mumtāz Maḥal died in 1630.[20] The emperor decided

[14] Ibid. Vol. I, Part 2, p. 253; Ṣāliḥ Kamboh, '*Amal-i Ṣāliḥ*, Vol.II, edited by Ghulam Yazdani, Calcutta, pp. 230–1.

[15] Wāriṣ, p. 203

[16] S.K. Banerji, 'Shahjahan's Monuments in Agra', *Journal of the United Provinces Historical Society*, Vol.XVII, Part 2, Lucknow, 1944, p.70.

[17] Lāhorī, Vol. II, p. 405.

[18] Lāhorī, Vol. II, p. 714; Ṣāliḥ, Vol. II, pp. 557–8. In the printed text of Lāhorī the expenditure on the Agra fort mosque alone is wrongly given as 60 lakhs of rupees. The figure is not only inconsistent with Lāhorī's own account but we have the correct figure of 3 lakh in Wāriṣ (p. 240) and Ṣāliḥ (Vol. III, p. 175), as well as the inscription on the facade of the mosque (personal reading).

[19] Qazwīnī, pp. 36–7; Ṣāliḥ, Vol. I, p. 11; Jahāngir, following Bābur, had willed that no building should be erected on his grave.

[20] Lāhorī, Vol. I, Part 1, p. 204.

to build a marble mausoleum for her at Agra. The engineers and architects estimated the cost at Rs 40 lakh.[21] The work began in a big way. Marble was brought from Rajputana, skilled stone cutters were collected in large numbers and within a period of about twelve years, 1631 to 1642–3, the entire complex including the markets, inns, and other imperial buildings in the township of Mumtazabad was completed under the supervision of Makarramat Khān and Mīr 'Abdul Karīm. The total expenditure came to Rs 50 lakh. It included Rs 10,000 spent on the railing-gate made of jasper (*sang-i yasham*) that was joined by gold plated iron bars and was built in the Ottoman style, as well as the railing around the false grave that was built of marble in ten years at a cost of Rs 50,000.[22] Private merchants too built inns and other buildings in Mumtazabad at much expense, but that was separate from the imperial expenditure.[23]

The buildings within the Lahore fort too did not appeal to the emperor and he ordered the rebuilding of the *ghusulkhāna*, bedchamber, and the palace. Wazīr Khān, the Governor of Lahore, was made responsible for supervision and the buildings were renovated within ten years' duration at the expense of Rs 20 lakh based on plans drawn by Āṣaf Khān.[24] Some structures were also erected on the banks of the river Ravi at an expense of Rs 1,40,000 in two years.[25]

In 1639–40 'Alī Mardān Khān promised that he could cut a canal from the place where river Ravi leaves the hills, to bring water to Lahore. The emperor immediately sanctioned Rs 1 lakh for the purpose.[26] In 1641–2 Khalīlullah Khān, the *Akhtabegī* was asked to select a site 'with the help of the architects', on the bank of the canal, for laying out a garden.[27] The buildings of the garden were erected in exactly one year, five months and four days (during 1642), a sum of

[21] Ibid., p. 403.

[22] Ibid., Vol. II, pp. 324–30; Ṣāliḥ, Vol. II, pp. 370–5. Lāhorī says that in the beginning (sixth regnal year) the railing around the grave was gold enameled that weighed 40 thousand *tolas* and was worth Rs 6 lakh; but Shāhjahān ordered that it should be replaced by a marble railing (p. 326).

[23] Ṣāliḥ, Vol. II, p. 374.

[24] Qazwīnī, p. 589; Ṣāliḥ, Vol. II, p. 8. Ṣāliḥ says that the buildings in fort were neglected for a long time.

[25] Wāriṣ, p. 109.

[26] Lāhorī, Vol. II, pp. 168–9; Ṣāliḥ, Vol. II, p. 312.

[27] Ibid., p. 341.

Rs 6 lakh being spent on them.[28] However the canal failed to bring water down to the garden and Rs 1 lakh more had to be sanctioned out of which Rs 50,000 were wasted owing to the bad alignment of the canal by the officers concerned. Finally, the task was assigned to Mulla Ala-ul-Mulk who retained 5 *kuroh* of the original channel and excavated a new line 32 *kurohs* in length, thereby providing requisite supply of water to the garden.[29] This was the famous Ravi Canal of Shāhjahān.

In 1638 began one of the most important building projects of Shāhjahān's reign, namely, the construction of the new capital Shahjahanabad at Delhi. The fort complex took almost ten years to be completed and involved an expenditure of Rs 60 lakh.[30] Wāriṣ̤ provides us the expenditure on each building as follows:[31]

The imperial palaces:

(i)	Shāh Maḥal	Rs 14,00,000
(ii)	Imtiyāz Maḥal with sleeping chambers and other surrounding structures	Rs 5,50,000
	Diwān-i k͟haṣ-o 'aām	Rs 2,50,000
	Ḥayāt Bakhsh with *ḥamām*	Rs 6,00,000
	Palaces of Jahānāra and other royal ladies:	Rs 7,00,000
	Bāzārs and *chowk* within the fort for imperial *kārk͟hānas*	Rs 4,00,000
	The fort along with the ditch	Rs 21,00,000
	Grand Total:	Rs 60,00,000

As is apparent from the above break-down, the amount of Rs 60,00,000 was spent on the fort and the buildings within it alone. The expenses on decorations of the buildings do not seem to have been included in the estimates given by Wāriṣ̤. Ṣāliḥ records that Rs 9 lakh were spent on the decoration in gold of the ceiling of the *G͟husulk͟hāna* done in European and Ottoman styles,[32] while Wāriṣ̤ gives the expenditure on

[28] Lāhorī, Vol. II, pp. 311–15; Ṣāliḥ, Vol. II, pp. 373–6. But an inscription mentions the date of foundation as 1637. S. Muhammad Latif, *Lahore, Its History, Archaeological Femans and Antiquities*, Lahore, 1892, p. 142 and n.

[29] Lāhorī, Vol. II, p. 315.

[30] Wāriṣ̤, p. 54; Ṣāliḥ, Vol. III, p. 32 however gives the figures of 50 lakh for the expenditure.

[31] Wāriṣ̤, p. 54.

[32] Ṣāliḥ, Vol. III, p. 35. It is recorded under the account of A.H. 1058/1647–8.

Hayāt Bakhsh including *ḥamām* as Rs 6 lakh only. Other major buildings were built outside the fort. The Jāma' Masjid was built during 1651–6. The imposing edifice required 50,000 stone cutters, masons, and other workers daily for six years and a huge sum of Rs 10 lakh was spent on it.[33] This excludes the amount spent on the *madrasa* and the *chauk*. The famous canal of Fīruz Tughluq between Khizrabad and Safaidun was repaired and extended 30 *kurohs* more to reach the fort. This was carried out at an expense of Rs 2 lakh in four years (1646–50).[34]

Besides the imperial buildings, Shāhjahān also granted money to the princes for building their houses (*ḥavelīs*) in the new capital. In 1650–1, a further sum of Rs 2 lakh in cash was given to Prince Dāra Shukōh for his *ḥavelī* in Shahjahanabad, while he had already received Rs 2 lakh for the purpose previously.[35]

In 1647–8, when, at the completion of the six main buildings of the fort, the emperor officially moved to his new capital, a tent, made especially at the imperial *kārkhānas* at Ahmadabad, was erected in the *Dīwān-i khās*. It was made of velvet and gold brocade and was woven after many years of work. Its cost excluding the forty silver pillars, weighing 4,09,000 *tolas* of silver, was Rs 1 lakh. It covered 3,200 square *gaz*; and 10,000 people could get shelter under it. Ten thousand workers erected it in one month.[36] In 1651 another tent made by the Ahmadabad artisans at the cost of Rs 86,000 was set up at the *Dīwān-i khās*.[37]

Shahjahanabad did not get its city-wall until the twenty-fourth regnal year of Shāhjahān (1650–1). Before his departure for Kashmir, the emperor gave an order for its immediate construction. Hurriedly a wall of mud and stone was erected within four months at an expense of Rs 1.5 lakh. But it gave way under heavy rains the very next year. Therefore another order was given in the twenty-sixth year to build the wall afresh with stone and lime mortar. This long wall (6,364 *dira'* or

[33] Wāriṣ, pp. 351–2; 355–6; Ṣāliḥ, Vol. III, p. 52. Wāriṣ compares it with Akbar's mosque at Fatehpur Sikri and says that the domes of both the mosques are equal in size while the area of Shāhjahān's mosque is bigger. Moreover, Akbar's mosque is of red sandstone while Shāhjahān's mosque has been built of marble.

[34] Wāriṣ, p. 39; Ṣāliḥ, Vol. III, pp. 115–6.

[35] Ṣāliḥ, Vol. III, p. 118.

[36] Wāriṣ, p. 55; Ṣāliḥ, Vol. III, pp.56–72 and 181.

[37] Wāriṣ, p. 250–1; Ṣāliḥ, Vol. III, p. 159.

yards) with six big and five small gates and seven towers was built at a further cost of Rs 4 lakh, but the material left of the previous wall worth Rs 50,000 was reused, and so the actual additional burden on the imperial treasury amounted to Rs 3,50,000 only.[38]

The emperor kept on adding new buildings to his capital at least until 1656, when he constructed an *'Idgāh* outside the city wall at a cost of Rs 50,000. This was built within one and a half years.[39]

In the same year Shāhjahān built a summer palace at Mukhlispur at a distance of 48 *kurohs* from Shahjahanabad. Wāriṣ records under A.H. 1065/1654–5 that Rs 5 lakh had already been spent on buildings there, and an amount of Rs 1 lakh more was required to complete the work. The palace was built in about two years and four months. He further informs us that Rs 2 lakh were granted to Prince Dārā Shukōh and Rs 50,000 to Prince Sulaimān Shukōh to construct buildings at a place which the emperor now named Faizabad.[40]

Even after building Shahjahanabad, the emperor did not lose his interest in buildings at the Agra fort. In 1647 he decided to add a mosque at the fort. The work on the mosque was completed within seven years, i.e., in A.H. 1063/1653.[41]

Another rather minor building of Shāhjahān was a structure on the hunting ground (*shikār-gāh*) at Samogar (usually miswritten Samugarh). Wāriṣ records (under A.H. 1064/1653–4) that there was a hunting place built by Jahāngīr, which was in depleted condition, and the emperor gave order to Āgāh Khān to build a hunting ground in a village called Imadpur that was half a *kuroh* from the town of Samogar. This hunting ground was built in two years and Rs 80,000 were spent on it.[42]

[38] Wāriṣ, p. 378; Ṣāliḥ, Vol. III, p. 243. *Bādshāhnāma's* text here seems a little corrupt; it says that the material of the old city wall was worth Rs 1,50,000, which seems an error for Rs 50,000. Ṣāliḥ, however, does not give this break-down.

[39] Wāriṣ, p. 308; Ṣāliḥ, Vol. III, pp.211–2.

[40] Wāriṣ, pp. 373–8; Ṣāliḥ, Vol. III, pp. 90, 237 and 241–3. All these buildings were of marble and a canal was built from the river Yamuna to these palaces. The river was at a distance of one *kuroh* from the imperial palace. See also A. Fuhrer, *The Monumental Antiquities & Inscriptions in the North Western Provinces & Oudh*, Allahabad, 1891, p. 17.

[41] Wāriṣ, pp. 240, 243; Ṣāliḥ, Vol. III, p. 175; The entire mosque is built of marble and the inscription on the gate of the mosque says: 'Built within a period of 7 years at the expense of Rs 3 lakh, and completed in 26th R.Y./A.H. 1063'.

[42] Wāriṣ, p. 243; Salih, Vol. III, p. 178.

Shāhjahān also erected buildings and laid out gardens in Kashmir. The constructions started on a large scale during his visit to Kashmir in 1633.[43] Qazwīnī, Lāhorī, and Ṣāliḥ all describe a number of buildings constructed by the emperor in Kashmir during 1633–40, at various places such as Lok Bhawan, Machhi Bhawan, Islamabad, and Wintipur.[44] They do not provide us with estimates of cost of construction of these buildings individually. But Lāhorī and Ṣāliḥ both say that the total expenditure on Shāhjahān's buildings in Kashmir amounted to Rs 8 lakh.[45]

In the twenty-first regnal year Ghazi Beg, the *Mīr 'imārat* of Kabul, was ordered to rebuild the fort at Kabul. He carried out the work in two years and the expenditure amounted to Rs 2.5 lakh.[46] A few years earlier in 1056/1646–7 Shāhjahān had completed the work on his own buildings at Kabul, started by him when a prince, by spending a further sum of Rs 5 lakh. Out of these Rs 2.5 lakh were spent on the palace and the balance went in laying out gardens particularly the Chahār bagh and in repairs of Bābur's mausoleum.[47] In all, Rs 12 lakh were spent on buildings at Kabul.[48]

Lāhorī and Ṣāliḥ also state that the buildings within *ṣūbas* Ajmer, Ahmadabad, and other places accounted for an expenditure of Rs 12 lakh. Shāhjahān is reported to have built a marble mosque at Ajmer in 1651–2,[49] but the cost is not stated. Shaista Khān in 1651–2 received Rs 29,000 for the repair of the fort at Ahmadabad.[50] We are told that Rs 8 lakh were spent on the forts at Qandahar and Zamindawar.[51] These were subsequently lost to Iran (1648).

At the close of his work under the twentieth regnal year (1647–8), Lāhorī records that the total expenditure on buildings under Shāhjahān

[43] Qazwīnī, pp. 674–6; Lāhorī, Vol. I, Part 2, pp. 160–1.

[44] Lāhorī, Vol. I, Part 2, pp. 24–31, 50–1; Ṣāliḥ, Vol. II, pp. 40, 42–4.

[45] Lāhorī, Vol. II, p. 714; Ṣāliḥ, Vol. II, pp. 557–8.

[46] Wāriṣ, p. 109.

[47] Wāriṣ, p. 109; Ṣāliḥ, Vol. II, pp. 505–6. Wāriṣ also mentions an expenditure of 40,000 rupees on the repair of fort at Ghaznin.

[48] Lāhorī, Vol. II, p. 714; Ṣāliḥ, Vol. II, pp. 557–8.

[49] Wāriṣ, pp. 210–11; Ṣāliḥ, Vol. III, p. 193. Wāriṣ also says that Shāhjahān ordered the rapid reconstruction of the buildings of Rana Udai Singh at Udaipur that were demolished by 'Abdullah Khān during Jahāngīr's reign (pp. 106–7).

[50] Ibid., p. 208.

[51] Lāhorī, Vol. II, p. 714 and Ṣāliḥ, Vol. II, pp. 557–8.

amounted to Rs 2.5 crore.[52] Ṣāliḥ, who gives an account of the entire reign of Shāhjahān, repeats the same figure at the end of the account of the twentieth regnal year.[53] This suggests that this expenditure was incurred by that year only. This impression is further strengthened by the fact that though Lāhorī mentions the construction of the Jama' mosque at Shahjahanabad (built between 1651–6), he does not give the expenses incurred on it. A glance at the statement of expenditure on individual buildings at Shahjahanabad offered by Wāriṣ[54] confirms beyond doubt that Lāhorī's estimate includes only the costs of buildings constructed down to the twenty-first regnal year.

However, there is one exception. Both these historians mention the cost of the mosque built inside the Agra fort, though it was actually completed in the twenty-eighth regnal year, which is explicitly mentioned as the date of its completion.

On the basis of the information discussed above we may now attempt to work out the minimum imperial expenditure on buildings, gardens, and canals during the successive years of Shāhjahān's reign. Our computation of imperial expenditure on buildings should also include the amount given by the emperor to princes for the purpose of constructing buildings as well as the expenses on tents installed within the fort complex.

Table 11.1 sums up the information available to us on the cost of various buildings and the period during which those were built. Table 11.2 gives the minimum expenditure during the successive years and its share of the total *khaliṣa* expenditure of Rs 1,00,00,00. In working out the annual expenditure I have made the following assumptions:

(a) The cost of construction of each building was evenly distributed over the period that it was under construction.

(b) The building expenditure given by Lāhorī that cannot be assigned to particular buildings or to particular years is to be divided uniformly over the first twenty-one years of the reign.

(c) In converting the regnal and Hijra years into the Christian calendar, the Hijra year may be assigned to that Christian year in which its larger portion falls.

The minimum expenditure on buildings as computed above amounts to Rs 2,89,21,445 for the entire reign. Distributing it uniformly over

[52] Lāhorī, Vol. II, p. 714.

[53] Ṣāliḥ, Vol. II, pp. 557–8.

[54] Wāriṣ, p. 39.

the years from the beginning of the reign (1628) to 1656 (twenty-nine solar years), the year until which building activity is reported in our

Table 11.1

Name of Buildings	Period of Construction	Cost in Rs.
Jahāngīr's mausoleum	1628–37	10,00,000
Buildings in Agra fort except mosque	1628–37	50,00,000
Tāj Maḥal, Mumtāzābād complex	1631–43	50,00,000
Lahore Fort	1632–41	20,00,000
Buildings on the bank of river Ravi	1636–37	1,40,000
Shāhjahānabad	1638–48	60,00,000
Tent for Dīwān-i khaṣ	1647–8	1,00,000
Decoration of ceiling of *Ghusulkhāna*	1647–8	9,00,000
Lahore, 'Alīmardān Canal 1	1639	1,00,000
Shalimar Garden	1641–2	6,00,000
Lahore, 'Alīmardān Canal 2	1642	1,00,000
Buildings in Kabul, etc.	1646–50	5,00,000
Agra fort mosque	1647–53	3,00,000
Delhi city wall I	1651	1,50,000
Ahmadabad fort	1651	20,000
Shāhjahānabad Jāma' mosque	1651–6	1,00,000
Grant to Dārā for buildings in Shāhjahānabad	1651–4	4,00,000
Faizabad complex	1653–6	6,00,000
Samogar Hunting-place	1653–4	80,000
Tent for Fort (Shāhjahānabad)	1651	86,000
Shāhjahānabad city wall	1655	3,50,000
Extention of canal to Shāhjahānabad	1646–50	50,000
'Idgāh in Shāhjahānabad	1655–6	50,000
Grant to Dārā and Sulaimān Shikoh for buildings at Faizabad	1656	2,50,000
Buildings at Kabul	1628–48	7,00,000
Buildings at Lahore	1628–48	19,60,000
Buildings at Agra	1628–48	3,00,000
Buildings at Ahmadabad and Ajmer, etc.	1628–48	11,80,000

Source: See text.

Table 11.2

Years	Annual expenditure In Rs	Years	Annual expenditure In Rs
1628	7,99,545	1643	11,61,666
1629	7,99,545	1644	7,44,999
1630	7,99,545	1645	7,44,999
1631	7,99,545	1646	8,45,999
1632	14,16,212	1647	9,45,999
1633	14,16,212	1648	18,45,999
1634	14,16,212	1649	1,51,000
1635	14,16,212	1650	1,51,000
1636	14,86,212	1651	5,72,667
1637	14,86,212	1652	3,16,667
1638	13,61,666	1653	4,56,667
1639	14,61,666	1654	4,56,667
1640	13,61,666	1655	6,91,667
1641	17,61,666	1656	5,91,667
1642	14,61,666		

Source: See text.

sources, the average annual expenditure works out at Rs 9,97,291. This amounts to 8.33 to 9.99 per cent of the annual *k͟hāliṣa* expenditure or 6.66 per cent of the annual *k͟hāliṣa* income.[55]

The minimum expenditure on buildings naturally varied considerably from year to year. It was lowest during 1649–50 but this was preceded by a very high expenditure amounting to Rs 18,45,999 in 1648 when Shāhjahān formally moved to his new capital. The lower figures for the years 1649–50 and even afterwards till 1654 can possibly be attributed to the diversion of the emperor's attention to attempts to recover the Qandahar which were made after much preparation in 1649, 1650, and 1653.

The amount spent on building construction by Shāhjahān was thus considerable. In absolute terms it was much higher than the average annual expenditure under Akbar that I have estimated at Rs 3,75,000

[55] Qazwīnī records the annual income of the *k͟hāliṣa* as Rs 1,60,000 and the expenditure in normal years as Rs 1,00,000 (p. 423).

per year.[56] The scale of expenditure on individual buildings too indicates the same trend. Akbar is reported to have spent Rs 15,00,000 to 20,00,000 on his capital city Fatehpur Sikri[57] and, as mentioned earlier, Rs 35,00,000 on the Agra fort. On the other hand, the known expenditure by Shāhjahān on his capital Shāhjahānābād exceeded Rs 80,00,000.

One rather obvious reason for the higher costs under Shāhjahān was the extensive use of marble instead of the red sandstone mainly used under Akbar. Wāriṣ explicitly mentions that marble for the buildings of Shāhjahānābād was brought from Makrana in Rajasthan, over a distance of 100 *kurohs* (over 250 miles).[58] The cost of transportation must have added to the expense.[59]

Another important factor for increase in expenditure on buildings under Shāhjahān was the much greater use of decoration. In Akbar's buildings the concentration was on structural design, and decoration was usually confined to incised and fresco work such as at Fatehpur Sikri. In Shāhjahān's buildings 'pietra dura' inlay work after the Persian style predominates. The inlay work with gold and semi-precious stones was naturally excessively expensive. As noticed earlier only the inlay work of the ceiling of the *G͟husulk͟hāna* in Delhi fort cost Rs 9,00,000. The emphasis on decorations and other details seems to have increased the cost in another way as well. The work being extremely specialized, the remuneration of the craftsmen and their supervisors was very high. R. Nath has discovered two nineteenth century MSS that give the wages of the builders of the Tāj Maḥal. The monthly salary of a *Tug͟hrānavīs* (writer of a decorative calligraphy inscribed on walls)

[56] *EME,* p.266.

[57] The amount given by Pelsaert is Rs. 15,00,000 but it is not clear whether the cost of the mosque is included in it or not. See Irfan Habib, 'Fatehpur Sikri — The Economic and Social setting', *Fatehpur-Sikri*, edited by Michael Brand and Glenn D. Lowry, Bombay, 1987, pp.73-82.

[58] Wāriṣ, p. 39.

[59] 'Imperial *farmāns* relating to the construction of the Tāj Maḥal', *Medieval India— a Miscellany*, pp. 158–9. Also reproduced in R Nath, *The Tajmahal and Its Incarnation*, Jaipur, 1985.

R. Nath has reproduced two *farmāns* of Shāhjahān dated January and September 1632 addressed to Mirza Rāja Jai Singh of Amber; it appears from these *farmāns* that an amount was sanctioned from the imperial treasury to meet the cost of transport of marble to Agra for the building of Tāj Maḥal.

was set at Rs 1000; that of a *khushnavīs* (calligraphist) at Rs. 500, and of a *gultarāsh* (sculptor), at Rs 400.[60] These were high salaries, since an ordinary unskilled workman's wage in 1637–9 was Rs 3 a month at Agra[61] and the salary of a *manṣabdār* of 20 *ẕāt* of class III was only Rs 750 a month.[62] However, the authority these late writers had for their statements is suspect.

The scale of building construction under Shāhjahān was certainly not smaller than under Akbar. Shahjahanabad was an immense enterprise; and Shāhjahān built extensively at other places as well. The use of marble and decoration was accordingly on a vast scale and the cost too therefore correspondingly enlarged.

Finally, the rise in prices during the seventeenth century were also responsible for a part of the higher costs of the buildings. The influx of silver began a process of depreciation of the value of the rupee, which led to a rise in the price-level between the first and sixth decades of the century. Seen in terms of copper, the increase by 1656 amounted to about 79 per cent to what it was in 1609.[63]

The costs of building construction represented a significant share of expenditure from the *khāliṣa* under Shāhjahān. It does not, however, seem to have been so excessive as to set a heavy drain on imperial finances, or to interfere with military expenditure.

The splendour of Mughal architecture did not, therefore, bring about a financial crisis for the imperial treasury. That the same funds could have been more gainfully employed in making other buildings of larger welfare is, of course, another question—one that involves the basis of the purpose and objectives of Mughal rule.

[60] R. Nath, 'Scrutiny of Persian Data Related to the Builders of Taj Mahal', *Indo-Iranica*, Vol. XXXI, Nos. 182, 1979, pp. 1–9, also reproduced in his *Taj Mahal and Its Incarnation*, pp. 36–40.

[61] W.H. Moreland, 'Some Sidelights on Life in Agra, 1637–9', *Journal of the United Provinces Historical Society*, Vol. III, Part I, 1923, pp. 148.

[62] *Selected Documents of Shahjahan's Reign*, edited by. Yusuf Husain, Hyderabad, 1950, p. 84.

[63] *CEHI*, Vol. I, p. 380.

12

The Mughal Empire and the Deccan
Economic Factors and Consequences

The Deccan has generally been treated by modern historians as a geographical entity so far separated from northern India that attempts by the Delhi Sultans or the Mughals to extend their frontiers beyond the Vindhyas have been looked upon as over-ambitious and potentially disastrous.[1] There is no denying that the barrier of the Satpura range, called the 'Bindha' (Vindhyas) in Mughal documents[2] was not easy to pierce, and the terrain beyond it was quite different from the alluvial plains of the North, being cut into regions and sub-regions by narrow river basins, hills, and plateaus. But the resistance offered by these physical features was certainly not insurmountable.

The fact that the fall of the Mughal empire came close at heels upon the complete annexation of the Deccan by Aurangzeb has lent further strength to criticisms of the Mughal Deccan policy. It has been held that by extending into the Deccan, the Mughal empire became unmanageable administratively as well as politically. Sarkar put the argument succinctly when he said, 'Aurangzeb like a boa constrictor, had swallowed more than he could digest.'[3] But little attention has

[1] See, for such a statement, Ishwari Prasad, *History of Medieval India*, Allahabad, 1952, p. 23. Lane Poole declares 'the Deccan was never intended by nature to have any conversion with Hindustan', and 'to conquer the Deccan was another phrase for risking the loss of Hindustan.' (*Aurangzeb*, Bombay, 1957, p.143). Athar Ali, (*The Mughal Nobility under Aurangzeb*, Bombay 1966, p. 102), also emphasizes the geographical difficulties. R.P. Tirpathi, however, considers the North and South as part of single 'well defined unit' (*Rise and Fall of the Mughal Empire*, 2nd ed. Allahabad, 1978, p. 312.

[2] That 'Bindhachal' was the Satpura and not the modern Vindhyas as shown by the *Ā'īn*, Vol.I, p. 476. (Cf. Atlas, pp. 24 and 37). The Satpura are much higher and have sharper slopes on either side than the Vindhyas, which form, in a larger section, merely the southern wall of the Malwa plateau.

[3] Jadunath Sarkar, *Studies in Aurangzeb's Reign*, Calcutta, 1933, pp. 17–18.

been paid to the specific factors which induced the Mughal emperors from Akbar to Aurangzeb to follow a policy of expansion into the Deccan ('a sleepless aim of the Mughal Emperors', to quote Sarkar again),[4] in spite of the obvious problems of distance and geography. It is sometimes said that this derived from Akbar's desire to be a 'Chakravartin' or from his self-imposed obligation to provide 'good government.'[5] In a recent article Satish Chandra has made a refreshing departure when he argues that there were, indeed, complex factors responsible for the Deccan policy pursued by the Mughals.[6] By and large, however, in the debate on the fall of the Mughal empire and the role of the 'Deccan factor' the economic significance of the Mughal expansion into the Deccan has largely escaped notice. As a result, as we will see, the admitted elements of weaknesses of the Mughals in the Deccan have over-shadowed some of their strengths and achievements.

In considering Mughal expansion, we may begin by asking whether for the Mughals, except for some geographical complications, the Deccan was any different, say, from Bengal or Gujarat. The Mughal ruling class naturally sought larger revenues; and the emperors had to have expanding resources to reward their particular confidants and favourites as against the established nobility. It was, therefore, the pressing need, in the short as well as the long run, for enlarging imperial resources that dictated to some degree the policy of the Mughal emperors towards the Deccan. Starting from Akbar down to Aurangzeb all attempts for conquests in the Deccan can be seen to have been not as simple matters of choice of the individual emperors, but practically matters of compulsion, given the structure of the Mughal ruling class.

By the 1590s Akbar's empire encompassed almost the whole of northern India barring some parts of Bengal; for the Mughal arms to turn now in the direction of the Deccan was only natural. Akbar annexed Berar by 1596 and Khandesh by 1601.[7] Ahmadnagar too was formally annexed, but its actual absorption had only progressed partially after Akbar's death.[8] Jahāngīr found it difficult to recover the annexed

[4] Jadunath Sarkar, *History of Aurengzeb*, Vol. IV, Calcutta, 1919, p. 5.

[5] B.P. Saxena, *History of Shāhjahān of Delhi*, 2nd ed., Allahabad, 1976, pp. 127–8. He also mentions the need to find resources.

[6] 'The Deccan Policy of the Mughals—A Reappraisal', *IHR*, Vol. IV, No. 2, and Vol. V, Nos. 1 and 2.

[7] *AN*, Vol. III, pp. 780–1.

[8] No *jama'* figures or any other details for Ahmadnagar are given in the *Ā'īn-i Akbarī*.

Table 12.1

S. No.	Year	Reference	'A' *Jama'* of the Empire	'B' *Jama'* of the Deccan	'C' 'B' as % of 'A'	'D' Area of the Empire	'E' Area of the Deccan	'F' 'E' as % of 'D'
1.	1601	*Āʼīn*, Vol.I, 386	5,03,82,56,318.5	(a) 94,61,32,760 (b) 1,00,91,85,579	(a) 18.8 (b) 20.0	9,79,644	(a) 60,336 (b) 73,011	(a) 6.2 (b) 7.5
2.	1605	*Iqbālnāma-i- Jahāngīrī*, Or. 1334 ff 231b–2b	5,83,46,90,344.5	1,10,08,17,069	18.7	9,85,592	64,627	6.6
3.	Pre.1627	*Majālis-Sālaṭīn* Or. 828 ff. 114a–115b.	6,30,00,00,000	1,15,67,00,000	18.4	9,85,592	64,627	6.6
4.	1628–33	*Bayāz-i-Khush bui*, I.O. 828, ff.180-1a.	6,57,73,57,625	1,25,08,05,955	19.0	9,86,577	67,268	6.8
5.	1646	Lāhorī, Vol. II, pp. 709–12	8,80,00,00,000	1,82,00,00,000	20.7	10,10,266	95,998	9.5
6.	G-1658	*Dastūr ul 'Amal-i 'Alamgīrī* Add. 6598, la–128b	9,12,24,45,846	1,85,64,48,000	20.4	10,10,266	95,998	9.5
7.	1667	*M'īrat-i 'Alam*, Add. 7657. ff. 445b-6a.	9,24,17,16,082	2,96,70,00,000	32.1	10,10,266	1,17,681	11.6
8.	1687–91	*Ẓawābit-i-'Alamgīrī*, Add. 6598 ff. 130b–29	13,80,23,56,000	6,50,14,52,140	47.1	10,28,535	1,17,681	11.4
9.	1687–95	Fraser 86, ff.57–61b	12,07,18,76,841	4,75,20,09,370	39.4	12,52,367	3,46,459	27.7

10.	1687	*Intikhab i-Dastūr- ul 'Amal-I Pādshāhī*, Edinburgh, 224, ff.1b–11b	13,21,98,53,981	5,91,72,36,140	41.2	12,52,367	3,46,459	27.7
11.	1702–7	*Dastūr-ul-'Amal-i Shāhjahānī*	13,26,00,56,263	6,09,61,92,104	46.0	12,52,367	3,46,459	27.7
12.	1709	Jagjīwandās, Add. 253, 51a–54a	13,33,99,91,841	6,03,73,74,000	45.3	12,52,367	3,46,459	27.7

Note: The *jama'* figure of the empire are taken from *ASMI,* pp.454-5 & 461-2, except for 1601 & 1702-7. The figure for the *jama'* in 1601 is based on the sum of the totals stated for the *sarkārs* (cf. *Atlas, p.8).* The *jama'* of 1702–7 is directly taken from the *Dastūr-ul 'Amal-i Shāhjahānī* (B.L. Add.6588, ff. 15a—47b). For the Deccan some of my totals are in disagreement with those set out in *ASMI.* I have generally accepted the dates to which Irfan Habib assigns these figures. Only in the case of the *Bayāẓ-i Khushbui*' it seems that the date can be further narrowed. Irfan Habib assign these figures to 1628–36, but the period can be limited further to 1628–33 on the basis of figures for Khandesh which being identical with those of the *Iqbālnāma*, show that the *ṣūba* had not till then been enlarged, by the transfer in 1634 of certain portions from Malwa.

The map-area is based on the *jama'* and map-area statistics set out in the *Atlas*, pp. vii and viii. For transfers to Khandesh, the area has been directly measured from sheets 9A, 14A, and 15A of the *Atlas*. The *Iqbālnāma* does not mention the *sarkārs* of Ramgir and Manikdurg under Berar. Manikdurg was perhaps included in *sarkār* Kalam; but Ramgir, though included in the *Ā'īn*, was not yet actually annexed, and so its area is excluded from the area of the Mughal Deccan shown for 1605.

The change in frontiers of the Deccan with the enlargement of the limits of *ṣūba* Khandesh in the early 1630s, and the annexation of Baglana in 1638 necessitated separate column 'B', with different corresponding figures in the *Ā'īn* for *jama'* and map-area.

areas within Ahmadnagar (Ahmadnagar and Bir), which had been lost during 1610–16[9]. Shāhjahān's reign saw two major spurts of expansion. Between 1632–6 almost the entire Ahmadnagar kingdom was annexed, though its southern parts were ceded to Bijapur. In 1656–7 came the second spurt with the district of Ramgir taken from Golkunda, and large portions (including Bidar and Parenda) seized or claimed from Bijapur. Under Aurangzeb the pressure on the Deccan sultanates continued unevenly during the first part of the reign; but in 1686 and 1687 both the remaining Deccan sultanates, Bijapur and Golkunda, were liquidated and their territories annexed.

These waves of territorial expansion in the Deccan are duly reflected in the fluctuations in the estimated revenue income (*jama'*) of the empire. Table 12.1 sets out the *jama'*, of the empire (column A) along with the *jama'*, of the Mughal territories in the Deccan (column B) drawn from various authorities. Column 'C' gives the *jama'*, of the Deccan as per cent of the total *jama'*. The total area of the empire is set out in column 'D' and that of the Mughal Deccan in column 'E'. The last column 'F' shows the area of territory held in the Deccan as per cent of the total area of the empire.

An important feature that emerges from the statistics is the large size of the *jama'* of the Deccan territories. The figures suggest that right from the beginning the revenue resources of the Deccan were quite significant. At the beginning of the seventeenth century when only Berar and Khandesh were annexed, the *jama'* of the Deccan was nearly 19 per cent of the *jama'* of the empire, though the area of the annexed territories was only about 7 per cent of the total area of the empire. After the annexations of 1636, the Mughal Deccan contributed over a fifth of the total *jama'* of the empire (1646–7), while its area was less than one-tenth of the total area. But proportionately, the increase was smaller than could be justified by the area gained. Whereas the area of the Mughal Deccan increased in comparison with 1601, from 7.45 to 9.50 per cent of the total area of the empire, i.e., a net increase of 2.05 per cent of the area of the empire, the *jama'* of the Deccan increased by 0.65 percent of the *jama'* of the empire. For this lag in the *jama'*, the great famine of 1630–2[10] might perhaps have

[9] *Tuzuk-i Jahāngīrī*, edited by S. Ahmad, Ghazipur and Aligarh, 1863–4, pp. 86–8, 148.

[10] Amīn Qazwīnī, *Badshāh Nāma*, Br. Mus. Add. 2073, pp. 442–4. Cf. *ASMI*, pp. 115–17.

been partly responsible. The *jama*‘ of the Deccan remained at about the same levels in 1650 as well. But after the subsequent annexations, the increase in *jama*‘ greatly outpaced the territorial additions. The *jama*‘ of the Mughal Deccan rose from less than 21 per cent in 1646 and 1656 to over 32 per cent of the empire in 1667, though the area of Mughal Deccan increased only from 9.5 per cent to nearly 11.5 per cent. Thus while the increase in the area amounted to 2 per cent of the whole empire, the increase in the *jama*‘ amounted to 11 per cent of that of the empire. The same trend continued till the end of our period. In 1709 the revenues of the Deccan accounted for over 45 per cent of the *jama*‘, though it comprised only over 27 per cent of the entire area. Compared to 1667, the Deccan was enlarged by an area equal to 16.2 per cent of the empire, and the *jama*‘ increased by an amount equal to over 13 per cent of the *jama*‘ of the empire.

The estimation of the *jama*‘ of the Deccan thus was from the beginning quite disproportionately large relative to its area. One must infer that it was artificially inflated. This process of inflating the *jama*‘ had begun under Akbar himself. Abū'l Fazl says that the *tanka* of Khandesh was first reckoned at 16 *dāms* but soon afterwards (before the *Ā'īn* was closed), Akbar decreed it equal to 24 *dāms*,[11] implying that the revenue of Khandesh was enhanced by 50 per cent at a stroke of the pen. The inflated nature of the *jama*‘ of the two Deccan *ṣūbas* (Berar and Khandesh) in the *Ā'īn-i Akbarī* becomes very obvious if we compare the *jama*‘ per square mile of map area of these *ṣūbas* with those of the various provinces of the empire. Table 12.2 below exhibits the *jama*‘ in thousand *dāms* per square mile.[12]

Even at the lower rate of conversion (16 *dāms* to the *tanka*) the *jama*‘ of Khandesh per square mile was not only the highest but was much more than double of that of even Agra, where the incidence of *jama*‘ was the highest in the whole of northern India. The ratio for Berar too exceeded that of every northern province including Agra and was more than double the *jama*‘ incidence in Malwa and Gujarat, the two provinces which adjoined it to the north and west. This artificial ‘inflation’ seems to have continued throughout the seventeenth century. As we have seen, the increase in relative size of the *jama*‘ of the Mughal Deccan in one phase radically outpaced the size of the territory

[11] *Ā'īn*, Vol. I, p. 474.

[12] The calculations are based on the *jama*‘ and map area figures given in the *Atlas*, pp. vii and viii.

Table-12.2

Provinces	*jama'* per sq. mile (in thousand *dāms*)
Lahore	10.3
Multan	2.3
Delhi	9.0
Agra	11.8
Awadh	7.6
Allahabad	6.1
Bihar	4.0
Bengal and Orissa	4.7
Ajmer	2.4
Thatta	2.5
Malwa	2.1
Malwa (excluding Garh)	4.6
Gujarat	5.6
Berar	12.9
Khandesh (at 16 *dāms/tanka*)	25.7
Khandesh (at 24 *dāms/tanka*)	38.6

gained within the Peninsula. The outcome was that in 1709 the *jama'* in thousand *dāms* per square mile was 7.6 in the northern Indian province and over twice of it, namely, 16.3 in the Deccan.

Such overestimation in the *jama'* of the Deccan was a fact well recognized by the Mughal administration. During his second viceroyalty, Aurangzeb made repeated complaints about the enormous difference between the estimated income (for salary assignment purposes) and actual income. He says that the realization (*ḥāṣil*) of the Mughal provinces of the Deccan was Rs 88 lakh which did not amount to even *sih-māha* (three monthly) or one-fourth of the *jama'*, which was put at 1,44,90,00,000 *dāms* (equal at 40 *dāms* a rupee to a nominal sum of Rs 362.26 lakh).[13] *Jāgīrs* in the Deccan were at best 'four-monthly' (*chahār māha*) and often of much lower yield,[14] so

[13] *Ruqa'āt-i 'Alamgīrī*, edited by Najib Ashraf, Azamgarh, 1930, pp. 121–2. For the significance of 'month-ratios' see *ASMI*, pp.306–8*n* and M. Athar Ali, *Mughal Nobility*, pp. 46–9.

[14] *Ruqa'āt*, p. 129.

that most *jāgīrdārs* held 'three-monthly' *jāgīrs* or those of still lower income.[15] This situation persisted despite a reduction (*takhfīf*) in the *jama'* that had been granted in the Deccan during the early years of Shāhjahān's reign, owing to the famine of 1630–2.[16]

The reasons for the overestimation of the *jama'* in the Deccan can be partly explained by reference to the military problems faced by the Mughals. The Mughal possessions south of the Satpura Range were in the nature of frontier territory, facing a group of hostile or potentially hostile powers. Thus the position was quite different from the North Indian provinces where maintenance of internal peace was practically all that was required of troops stationed in them.[17] As a result, the Mughals had to post a much larger number of *mansabdārs* (in terms of contingents they had to maintain) in the Deccan for comparable areas than in any other region of the empire. As Bernier put it, the Deccan was held to be the bread of the soldiers of Hindustan.[18] To maintain this army, *jāgīrs* had to be found in the Deccan, since assignment of *jāgīrs* outside Deccan to the *manṣabdārs* posted there raised other problems. If *jāgīrs* were assigned outside the Deccan, management of *jāgīrs* at a distance becoming more expensive, the size of the contingents had to be reduced from 'one-third' to 'one-fourth' of the *sawār* rank.[19] Thus there would then have to be a reduction in the size of the Mughal army posted in the Deccan. Moreover, there would be difficulty of providing supplies to troops serving in the Deccan if the *jāgīrs* of their *manṣabdārs* were situated at a distance from their camps. This would raise the expenses of troopers as well as make them vulnerable to the vagaries of caravan

[15] Ibid., p. 116.

[16] 'Abdul Ḥamīd Lāhorī, *Bādshāhnāma*, Vol. II edited by Kabiruddin, Calcutta, 1868, p. 712.

[17] Aurangzeb, when Viceroy of the Deccan, wrote to Shāhjahān to urge that 'the Deccan is a frontier province' and that 'for various reasons it cannot be compared with Bengal or Gujarat; thus a strong army is required to be always maintained here.' (*Ruqa'āt*, pp. 106 and 122).

[18] François Bernier, *Travels in the Mughal Empire, 1656–68*, tranlated by A. Constable, London, 1916.

[19] Lāhgorī gives the rule that *manṣabdārs* posted in the same province where their *jāgīrs* were situated were required to maintain troopers (*tābīnān*) equal in number to a third of their *sawār*-rank, but if their *jāgīrs* lay in other provinces, they were required to bring to the brand a contingent equal to one-fourth of their *sawār*-rank (Lāhorī, Vol. II, pp. 505–7). See M. Athar Ali, *Mughal Nobility*, pp. 54–9.

traffic. Finally, if to avoid this, the troops were garrisoned in *jāgīrs* outside the Deccan, it would be difficult to mobilize them rapidly in case of need in the Deccan. The last must have been a very important factor in the eyes of the Mughal court.

If *jāgīrs* were then to be found for the very large number of *manṣabdārs* posted in the Deccan, the temptation to raise the *jama'* so as to meet, on paper at least, the total salary demand (*talab*) of as many *manṣabdārs* as possible would have been irresistible. Thus as we have seen, even Akbar was compelled to raise the *jama'* of Khandesh by 50 percent, by a single stoke of the pen.

Conditions for the Mughal nobles and soldiery posted in the Deccan became even worse owing to the fact that 'Deccani'[20] nobles won over for the Mughal cause in the Deccan had also to be assigned *jāgīrs*. The Mughal administration tried to moderate the pressure of claims of the Deccani nobles by reducing their pay claims by a fourth when assigning them *jāgīrs*. This practice was well established by 1634[21] and continued under Aurangzeb, who clearly reiterated it in his eleventh regnal year.[22]

Thus there was multiple pressure on the revenues of the Deccan. This inevitably led to the intensification of tax-realization from the peasants. The assignees in their anxiety to collect whatever proportion of their sanctioned salary they could, necessarily neglected the long-term interests of agriculture. It was perhaps owing to this excessive exploitation that agriculture failed to recover even after a lapse of more than fifteen years following the famine of 1630–2. The shortfall in the revenues was not made good even by 1647.[23] The fall in cultivation seems to have continued, and Aurangzeb found it in a precarious position on his arrival in 1652–3.[24] The concern of the Mughal court over this declining agriculture is evident from the fact that Shāhjahān, while appointing Aurangzeb as the viceroy of the Deccan for the second time in 1652, gave him special instructions to

[20] The nobles who were previously in the service of Deccan Sultanates were designated 'Deccani'. See Yusuf Husain, ed., *Selected Documents of Aurangzeb's Reign*, edited by Yusuf Husain, Hyderabad, 1958, p. 64; cf. *Mughal Nobility*, pp. 26–7.

[21] Ibid., *Selected Documents of Shahjahan's Reign*, edited by Y. Husain, Hyderabad, 1950, pp. 1–23, 88.

[22] Ibid., *Selected Documents of Aurangzeb's Reign*, p. 64. For the actual deductions see Ibid., pp. 8, 120, 126, 144.

[23] Lāhorī, Vol. II, p. 712.

[24] *Ruqa'āt*, pp. 70, 84, 91.

strive for improving cultivation and resettling villages.[25]

For the agricultural decline in the Deccan, Aurangzeb himself held the mismanagement by previous governors to be chiefly responsible, besides the confusion caused by the prevalence of different forms of assessment and collection (*ẓawābiṭ-i gunāgūn*).[26] Accordingly, Murshid Qulī Khān was appointed *dīwān* with the task of improving conditions. He introduced a particular form of crop-sharing with a differential scale, depending upon crops and irrigation.[27] He carefully fixed a *rai'* (crop-rate) and brought land under measurement. The introduction of crop sharing, in the beginning, was naturally expensive[28] and was resorted to presumably as a temporary expedient, designed to help in evolving a reliable *rai'*.[29] *Taqāvī* advances (agricultural loans) were made to peasants to enable them to buy seeds and cattle.[30] The Mughal court was so anxious about the situation that Shāhjahān criticized Aurangzeb for not sanctioning forty to fifty thousand rupees on his own, as *taqāvī* for construction of irrigation bunds in the provinces of Khandesh and Berar.[31] Nevertheless, the desired results were not obtained at least in the short run. The revenues of the Deccan, not even on paper, could suffice to meet all the claims the Mughal administration imposed on it.[32] Aurangzeb, as viceroy, sought the grant of extra-Deccan *jāgīrs* to those serving in the Deccan provinces, as also cash payment from the treasuries of Malwa.[33] Shāhjahān would not accede to this. On the other hand, the size of troops that the *manṣabdārs* were required to maintain in the Deccan was increased by an order that reduced the allowed rate for the troopers from Rs 20 to Rs 15 and 17.[34] By this device the *manṣabdārs* were called upon to maintain 9,000 more horsemen.[35] Aurangzeb protested

[25] Ibid., pp. 69 and 84.

[26] Ibid., p. 97. See also Khāfī Khān, *Muntakhab-ul Lubāb*, Vol. I, edited by Kabiruddin Ahmad and Haig, Bib. Ind., Calcutta, 1860, p. 735.

[27] Ibid., p. 733.

[28] Ibid., p. 117.

[29] *ASMI*, pp.268–9.

[30] Khāfī Khān, Vol. I, p. 733n.

[31] *Ruqa'āt*, p. 131. The plan was that of Multafat Khān.

[32] Ibid., pp. 106 and 121. Aurangzeb complains that no *pāi-bāqī* (land to be assigned in *jāgīr*) was left in the Deccan.

[33] Ibid., p. 118.

[34] Ibid., p. 116.

[35] Incidentally, this would suggest that there were supposed to be 27,000 to 51,000 horsemen posted in the Deccan at this time.

that the new rate was too low to maintain a suitable horse, and complained that the increase in number of the troops would only be theoretical.[36] The order had finally to be reversed.[37]

The critical problem of difference between the paper *jama‘* and actual collection thus persisted. Neither the reforms of Murshid Qulī Khān, in spite of Aurangzeb's claims of doubling of revenues in certain *maḥals*, nor Shāhjahān's manipulation of salary rates for cavalry could be of much help. It was in this situation that any possible scheme of territorial aggrandizement in the Deccan could look so attractive. Peace had been established in 1636 by a settlement imposing tribute on Golkunda and portioning Ahmadnagar with Bijapur. Yet the Mughals could not honour it for more than twenty years. Since the Marathas were not yet an independent power or a real menace for the Mughals, it is not possible to see them as an excuse for the fresh wave of annexations which came in 1656–7.

By Aurangzeb's campaigns against Golkunda and Bijapur, dealt with successively, the territory of Mughal Deccan was enlarged by about 21 per cent. Yet the increase in the *jama‘* in 1667 over that of 1656 (before the annexations) was about 58 per cent (see Table 12.1). This disparity between the proportional increase in area and the *jama‘* shows that the solution was only partial, and the pressure on revenue resources continued. This was all the more so because the annexations involved the Mughals in expensive campaigns in the 1660s, largely to seize territories and forts of Bijapur that were theirs by the treaty of 1657, but which Bijapur was unwilling or unable to deliver. Shaista Khān's campaigns ended in a fiasco at Puna (1663); this was followed by sack of Surat by Shivaji (1664). The Deccan had thus to be filled with more troops, with the resultant expedient of inflating the *jama‘*, which our *jama‘* figures for 1667 so clearly brings out. Thus the Mughals were back to square one, with Mirza Raja Jai Singh trying to recoup the losses by an alliance with Shivājī against Bijapur.[38] These plans, however, did not meet with success; and Aurangzeb lost interest in the Maratha alliance. This was shown in the episode of Shivājī's arrival at and escape from Agra in 1666. Henceforth, the Marathas would act as an independent power; and the Mughal problems in the

[36] Ibid., p. 116.

[37] Ibid.

[38] Jai Singh's letters in *Haft Ajnuman*, analysed by J.N. Sarkar, *Military Despatches of a 17th century General*.

Deccan would be intensified even further.

In other words, while the Marathas increased their pressure upon the Mughal dominions in the Deccan, the same inducements to the Mughals to expand their frontiers, which had caused them to make a breach of the 1636 settlement in 1656–7, continued to operate.

With Aurangzeb reaching the Deccan with large armies in 1682, the compulsion towards aggrandizement increased, with still larger strain put on resources. This then was the essential factor behind the annexations of Bijapur (1686) and Golkunda (1687) and the subsequent campaigns to take effective possession of their territories. This was not only because these had become the refuge of the Marathas, or because the Sultans of Golkunda and Bijapur were unable to 'tame Shambhuji', as Sarkar believes.[39] The presence of the Marathas was undoubtedly a factor in the further Mughal expansion in the Deccan; but our argument is that this was secondary to the economic considerations.

The annexations of Bijapur and Golkunda on paper completed the conquest of the Deccan. But the advantage gained did not prove a sufficient counterweight to the drain of resources caused by the burden of continuous campaigns. The *jama'* of the Deccan continued accordingly to be highly inflated. The *jama'* and *ḥāṣil-i akhir* (the revenue of the previous year) statistics set out in the *Ẓawābiṭ-i 'Alamgīrī*[40] suggests a *ḥāṣil-jama'* ratio of 67:100 for the entire empire, as against 52:100 for the Deccan. Thus tax realization in the Deccan amounted to still only half the *jama'*, although there seems to be something nominal and inflated about these 'realization' (*ḥāṣil)* figures as well.

There was also the absolute decline in the internal revenues that have to be considered. Bhīmsen's well-known passage brings out the unending cycle of agrarian depredations, fall in revenues, increase in revenue pressure, internal disturbances, and further agrarian depredations of which the Maratha *sardārs* were the chief beneficiaries, with the peasant-*bargīs* as their instruments.[41]

There simultaneously occurred an influx of the Deccani nobles into Mughal service. According to Athar Ali the number of Deccani officials holding ranks of 100 *z̤āt* or above increased between 1658–

[39] Jadunath Sarkar, *History of Aurangzeb*, Vol. IV, p. 6.

[40] *Ẓawābiṭ-i 'Alamgīrī*, Br. Mus. Add. 6598 ff. 130b–132a. Cf. *ASMI*, p. 466.

[41] *Nuskha-i Dilkusha*, Br. Mus. Or. 23, ff. 138–140a. Cf. *ASMI*, pp.400–1.

78 and 1679–1707 from 58 to 170, i.e., by 290 per cent[42] while the *jama'* of the Deccan rose by 20.3 per cent (see Table 12.1).This increase in the size of the Deccani elements was thus even disproportionate to the rise in the *jama'* of the Deccan. It naturally exacerbated what has been called the *'jāgīr* crisis'[43] reflected in the scarcity of lands to be assigned in *jāgīr*. It seems difficult to agree with Richards' criticism[44] of the established view for which there is enough support in contemporary accounts. The large size of *pāi-bāqī* (land to be assigned in *jāgīrs*) in Hyderabad that Richards' discovers that a document cited by him[45] is by no means decisive. Substantial amounts of revenues were needed in the Deccan for the imperial treasury owing to the prolonged stay of Aurangzeb and the need to finance his own (*khāṣa*) troops and artillery. These had to be paid out of revenues collected for the imperial treasury, and for this purpose large areas of the Deccan needed to be kept unassigned, so that their revenues might be collected for the treasury. In this respect revenues from the *pāi-bāqī* were practically no different from those of the *khāliṣa* being collected by the imperial administration. The presence of *pāi-bāqī*, therefore, need not imply actual availability of *jāgīrs* that could in fact be assigned.

The crisis of *jāgīrs* created discontent among the Mughal nobility and weakened the very basis of the empire. The Mughals thus met with a political failure side by side with their military difficulties.

And yet the Mughal record in the Deccan was not one of unqualified failure. Indeed Mughal achievements in the Deccan were by no means negligible. The long survival of the Nizam's power in the Deccan and the rise of Mysore under Hyder Ali and Tipu bear testimony to the strength of Mughal institutions. It was no small contribution of the Mughal empire that most of its political administrative institutions got firmly transplanted in the Deccan. The two successor states right from their inception till their end thrived on the institutions that were simply survivals of, or borrowed bodily from those of the Mughals.[46]

[42] M. Athar Ali, *Mughal Nobility*, p. 28.

[43] Satish Chandra, *Parties and Politics in the Mughal Court, 1707–40*, 1959, pp. XLVII–XLIX; Athar Ali, *Mughal Nobility*, pp. 92–4.

[44] J.F. Richards, *Mughal Administration in Golkunda*, Oxford, 1975, p. 214. Athar Ali has persuasively contested Richards' view in his *Mughal Nobility under Aurangzeb*, revised ed., New Delhi, 1997, pp.xxi-xxii.

[45] Ibid., pp. 158, 199–204; see also J.F. Richards, 'Imperial Crisis in the Deccan', *Journal of Asian Studies*, Vol. XXXV, No. 2, 1976, pp. 239–40.

[46] For the Nizam, see Yusuf Husain, *The First Nizam The Life and Times of*

The Mughals had an important impact too on the economy of the Deccan. The Deccan had so far been a separate economic zone, symbolized by its gold money as against the silver money of northern India. The separateness is shown by distinctly higher interest rates that prevailed in the Deccan throughout the seventeenth century: even after the universal fall in the rates during the 1640s, these continued to be higher than at Agra or Surat.[47]

In all the territories annexed by the Mughals, they introduced their standard rupee coinage, and thus unified the monetary system. With Mughal conquests, gold coinage was progressively replaced by the silver in the Deccan. By the end of Akbar's reign there were three mints uttering silver rupees in the Deccan: their number rose to six during Jahangir's reign and to eight under Shāhjahān. By the end of Aurangzeb's reign silver mints in the Deccan had risen to twenty-four, spread all over the Deccan and southern India.

The process of replacement of gold by silver can be seen still better by the increased output of the Deccan mints as reflected in the surviving coins. The number of surviving rupee coins throughout faithfully reflected the expansion of the Mughal system into the Deccan. The data have been compiled from the catalogues of Museum Collections at Calcutta, Lucknow, Lahore, and Nagpur and in the British Museum, London (see Table 12.3).

From the last decade of Akbar's reign there are seventy-five coins uttered in the Deccan mints; under Jahangir the number of coins declined in correspondence to falling Mughal activity in the Deccan. His two decades yield only twenty-one and eighteen coins respectively. During the first spurt of conquest under Shāhjahān the surviving rupees rise to a spectacular eighty, though there is a trough immediately afterwards. The lower military activity after the 1636 settlement seems to be reflected in the small number (twelve and twenty-two coins) belonging to these decades. Thereafter military campaigns and annexations lead to a constant rise barring a small decline during 1676–85, until the apex is reached by the close of Aurangzeb's reign. In this

Nizam ul Mulk Asaf Jah I, Bombay, 1963. For Mysore see N.K. Sinha, *Haider Ali*, Calcutta, 1941; Mohibbul Hasan, *History of Tipu Sultan*, Calcutta, 1951.

[47] Irfan Habib, 'Usuary in Medieval India', *Comparative Studies in Society and History*, Vol. VI, No. 4, 1965, pp. 402–4. The general worldwide fall of the 1640s is evident from the data collected in Sidney Homer, *A History of Interest Rates*, New Brunswik, 1963, pp. 128–39. (See also Chapter 1, Table 1.11)

Table-12.3

Decaded	No. of coins from 'Deccani' mints	No. of coins from North Indian mints	Active mints in the Deccan
1596–1605	75	683	3
1606–15	21	629	5
1616–25	18	757	6
1626–35	80	824	5
1636–45	12	486	4
1646–55	22	350	5
1656–65	83	703	6
1666–75	95	304	6
1676–85	93	264	10
1686–95	179	604	15
1696–1705	238	686	18
1706–07*	54	138	15

* Only two years not a full decade.

Source: Nelson Wright, *Catalogue of Coins in Indian Museum*, Calcutta, Oxford, 1907. Shamsuddin Ahmad, *Supplement to Volume III of the Catalogue of Coints in Indian Museum*, Calcutta, Delhi, 1939. C.J. Brown, *Catalogue of Coins in the Provincial Museum*, Lucknow, Oxford, 1920. C.R. Singha, *Supplementary Catalogue of the Mughal Coins* in the State Museum, Lucknow, 1965. C.J. Rodgers, *Catalogue of Coins in Government Museum, Lahore*, Lahore. V.P. Rode, *Catalogue of Coins in the Central Museum, Nagpur*, Bombay, 1969. Lanepoole, ed. Stuart Poole, *The Coins of the Mughal Emperors of Hindustan in British Museum*, London, 1892.

last decade the Deccan mints account for a third of the silver coin output of northern India.

The introduction of silver currency in the Deccan did not only result in the achievement of uniformity in the monetary system, but also had economic consequences for northern India. A substantial part of the silver influx into India must have been absorbed by the process of replacement of gold in the Deccan, and this could have acted as a break upon inflation in northern India.[48]

[48] Irfan Habib finds a 'Price Revolution in India' (*ASMI*, pp.445–9). The rise in prices during the seventeenth century is further elaborated by Aziza Hasan, 'Silver Currency Output of the Mughal Empire and Prices in India during the 16th and 17th Centuries', *IESHR*, Vol. VI, No. 1, March 1967, pp. 85–116.

On the effects of interest rates in the Deccan we have unluckily no information after 1675. It remains to be investigated whether a unified currency also helped to lower interest rates in the Deccan.

Side by side with the monetary unification, the reforms of Murshid Qulī Khān initiated a process of extending Mughal method of revenue assessment and collection in the Deccan. The survivals of the Mughal land revenue system were visibly present at the opening of the nineteenth century when Buchanan made a survey of the lands of southern Mysore spread between Kaveri Pura Ghat and Coimbatore, and then towards Malabar. The measurement of land was in vogue, the cash nexus was established, and the conventional claim was a third of the produce. Even the differential rates based on the extent of irrigation were fully established. In the traditional Mughal way 'lands were divided into three qualities according to the goodness of their soil.' The *taqāvī* were advanced and recovered in instalments.[49]

Munro too in his Ryotwari system was influenced by the survivals of the Mughal–Mysore system of cash revenue-rates fixed on individual surveyed fields of peasants that he found in Baramahal.[50] He also classified the land on almost the same basis as the Mughal administration; and even his fixation of a third share of the produce had respectable Mughal antecedents.[51]

[49] Francis Buchanan, *A Journey From Madras Through the Countries of Mysore, Canara, and Malabar*, London, 1807, pp. 187, 188, 212–13.

[50] A report of the 'Board of Revenue at Madras' declares 'the Ryotwari system had its origin in the Baramahal and Salem districts', cited in R.C. Dutt, *The Economic History of India under Early British Rule*, London, 1908, p. 147.

[51] *Fifth Report from the Select Committee on the Affairs of the East India Company*, 1812, facsimile reprint in Irish University Press series of *British Parliamentary Papers*, Colonies, East India, Vol. III, p.947.

13

Scarcities, Prices, and Exploitation

The Agrarian Crisis, 1658–70

Modern studies of the Mughal economy generally deal with its long-term performance. One tends to ask whether there were factors inhibiting the expansion of production and commerce;[1] whether, on the other hand, there were potentialities of capitalistic development;[2] whether the agrarian sector was overwhelmed with excessive tax realization;[3] and whether there was or was not a price revolution over the entire period.[4] There seems to have been in these discussions a neglect of the short-term fluctuations in the cycle of production and consumption which individually, or in the aggregate, could have also greatly influenced the performance of the economy in secular terms. There is an obvious analogy here with the effects that business cycles, which individually are short-term phenomena, have upon the course of capitalistic development in the long term.

It has of course been recognized that famines and natural calamities had an excessively disturbing effect on the Mughal Indian economy.[5] With the development of the market and the cash-nexus, an abundant harvest and the resulting fall in prices could equally appear as a

[1] As W.H. Moreland mainly did in his *India at the Death of Akbar*, London, 1920.

[2] Irfan Habib, 'The Potentialities of Capitalistic Development in the Economy of Mughal India', in *Enquiry*, n.s., Vol. III, No. 3, 1971; V.I. Pavlov, *Historical Premises for India's Transition to Capitalism*, Moscow, 1979.

[3] W.H. Moreland, *Agrarian System of Moslem India*, 1929; *ASMI*; T. Raychaudhuri, *Enquiry*, n.s., Vol. II, No. 1.

[4] Aziza Hasan, 'The Silver Currency Output of the Mughal Empire and Prices in India during the 16th and 17th Centuries', *IESHR*, Vol. VI, No. 1, 1969, pp. 314–33.

[5] W.H. Moreland, *From Akbar to Aurangzeb*, London, 1923, pp. 205–20; *ASMI*, pp. 112–22.

'calamity'.[6] In other words, not only climate but also monetary phenomena had begun to have a hand in causing economic dislocation. Yet except for catalogues of famines, there has not been any attempt so far to analyse any of the great scarcities and depressions of the seventeenth century.[7] Admittedly, the evidence is usually not of the kind and size one would like to have. But some of it is still there, and invites consideration.

I propose to take up here the evidence for the vast economic disturbance in northern India that occurred late in the fifties and continued practically throughout the sixties of the seventeenth century. It has almost entirely escaped recognition in modern studies, being seen at best as a chance cluster of some regional scarcities.[8] I hope to show that it was much more than this, and also that it may well have a significant place in the agrarian, and perhaps, the general history of Mughal India.

I

Bihishtī Shīrazī, a court poet of Prince Murad Bakhsh, gives a moving depiction of the widespread famine, plague, desolation of towns, and disruption of trade and commerce that occurred after that prince's fall in the summer of 1658.[9] According to Aurangzeb's own official historian, Muḥammad Kāẕim, the author of the *'Ālamgīrnāma*, the scarcity that now began continued throughout the years 1658–62. It led to an exodus of destitute peasants (*ri'āya maḥnatzada*) from the countryside to the towns. Conditions became so serious that the emperor was obliged to order the opening of ten free kitchens (*langar*) in the capital (Delhi) and twelve more in the surrounding *parganas*, as well as in Agra and Lahore. Besides these imperial *langars*, all the *manṣabdārs* down to those of the ranks of 1,000 were asked to run free kitchens of their own. People living in the city, unable to pay the high prices prevailing in the town, went in large numbers to villages to buy grain. Here 'the strong' oppressed the 'weak'; and officials were

[6] Aurangzeb's *farmān* to Rasikdas puts the fall in prices among calamities (*āfāt-i arzānī*). Text in the *Journal of Asiatic Society of Bengal*, (*JASB*), n.s., Vol. II, 1906, pp. 223–35). See also Chapter 9.

[7] The only notable exception is Moreland's analysis of the causes and effects of the great Gujarat famine of 1630–1 (*India at the Death of Akbar,*, pp. 210–18).

[8] Moreland, *India at the Death of Akbar,* p. 209; *ASMI,* pp. 112–22.

[9] Durga Prasad, *Gulistān-i Hind*, Vol. II (Supp.), Sandila, 1897, p. 105, for extracts from Bihishtī's *Āshob-i Hindustān*.

appointed to maintain order there with the aid of soldiers. To reduce the pressure on grain supplies in Delhi, the *manṣabdārs* were asked to send away half of their retainers to their respective *jāgīrs*. Muhammad Kazim ascribed the scarcity to a breakdown of administration during the War of Succession, an added factor being the insufficiency of the rains.[10] Khāfī Khān too gives an account of the severe famine in the eastern and northern provinces and offers a narrative similar to that of the *'Ālamgīrnāma*. The causes, according to Khāfī Khān, were the ravages of the War of Succession and, at certain places, the failure of the monsoons.[11] The *Ma'āṣir-i 'Ālamgīrī* implies that the high prices continued until 1670, when relief was obtained owing to better harvests.[12]

These general statements are corroborated by information relating to specific areas. The English records show that Gujarat suffered from an acute scarcity in 1659 that lasted until 1663–4. The prices of foodgrains as well as of indigo rose so much that they touched the price-level of 1630–2, the years of the great Gujarat famine.[13] The scarcity and high prices in 1663–4 led to apprehensions of large-scale depopulation, but this was happily averted by timely rains in 1664.[14] The famine in Gujarat was thus attributed largely to the failure of rains. Famine, plague, and very high prices were reported from Sind during 1658–60.[15] The distress further increased in 1658–9 due to the arrival of Prince Dārā Shukoh with his army.[16] Malwa witnessed a year of scarcity since the kharif crop was destroyed owing to the

[10] Muhammad Kāẓim, *'Alamgīrnāma*, edited by Khadim Husain Abdul Hai, Bib. Ind., Calcutta, 1865–73, pp. 436–7, 609–12. He actually ascribes the breakdown of administration to the illness of Shāhjahān; but it was this illness which precipitated the War of Succession.

[11] Muhammad Hāshim Khāfī Khān, *Muntakhab-ul Lubāb*, Vol. II, edited by K.A. Ahmad and Haig, Bib. Ind., Calcutta, 1860–74, pp. 87, 124.

[12] Sāqī Musta'idd Khān, *Ma'āṣir-i 'Alamgīrī*, edited by Bib. Ind., Calcutta, 1870–3, p. 98.

[13] W. Foster, ed., *English Factories in India, 1655–60*, Oxford, 1906–27, pp. 306–7, 320. In the allusion to prices prevalent forty years earlier, 'forty' is an obvious mistake for 'thirty'.

[14] *EFI, 1661–4*, pp. 25, 200, 255, 329, 320–1, 333. Cf. 'Alī Muḥammad Khān, *Mi'rāt-i Aḥmadī*, edited by Nawab Ali, Baroda, 1927–8, p. 257.

[15] *EFI, 1655–60*, p. 210 & n. 307.

[16] 'Alī Sher Qānī', *Tuḥfatu-l Kirām*, completed 1767–8, Litho., Vol. III, n.d., p. 96.

War of Succession.[17] Rajasthan suffered from famines and drought in 1660–3 and 1665. The famine of 1665 was particularly acute and widespread, and the peasants fled towards Malwa and Mathura.[18] In the eastern region a famine occurred in Dhaka in 1662–3. It was alleged that it obtained particular severity owing to the exaction of high tolls and official interference with transport.[19]

The continuous scarcity (or succession of scarcities) that this evidence suggests for the late fifties and early sixties of the seventeenth century is reinforced by two well-known *farmāns* issued by the emperor in the 1660s. The *farmān* to Rasikdās was issued in 1665–6,[20] and the one to Muḥammad Hāshim in 1669–70.[21] The issuing of two *farmāns* of general import for the agrarian administration of the whole empire would in itself seem to be an indication of the concern that the situation was causing at the imperial court. But the *farmāns* are actually explicit on the matter.

Both the *farmāns* express anxiety about the decline in cultivation, and the abandonment of land by the peasants; their provisions aim at

[17] *'Arẕdāsht* of Ja'far Khān in Munshi Bagchand, *Jami'-al Insha'*, B.L. Or. 1702, f. 10b; *Faiyaẕ al Qawānīn*, Br. Mus. Or. 9617, Vol. I, f. 130b.

[18] *Chitthi* of Sri Ram *'Āmil* of *pargana* Naraina to *Dīwān* Kalyandas, V.S. 1722/1662 AD. In the same letter he refers to the years V.S. 1717/1660 AD and V.S. 1720/1663 AD as famine years. See also S.P. Gupta and Dilbagh Singh, 'Famines in the Territories of Amber (c. 1660–70)', *Proceedings of the Rajasthan History Congress*, Vol. VII, Ajmer Session 1975, Jodhpur, 1976, pp. 52–6.

[19] Shihāb-ud Dīn Tālish, *Fatḥiya-i 'Ibriya*, supplement, Bodleian Or. 589, ff. 79b–80a, 110b–11a. This supplement has not been printed in the published text of the work.

[20] Text published by Jadunath Sarkar in the *Journal of Asiatic Society of Bengal*, n.s., Vol. II, 1906, pp. 223–35. In a copy of the *farmān* (Br. Mus. Add. 19,503, ff. 62a–63b) the name of the addressee is given as Mir Muhammad Mu1izz, the *Dīwån-i Khaliṣa* of Bihar (*ASMI*, p. 222n). In the preamble the addressee is asked to instruct also 'the *'āmils* of the *parganas* of the *jāgīrdārs*'. This suggests that the *farmān* was a general order meant for the *dīwāns* of the *khāliṣa* as well as *jāgīrdārs*. This makes it all the more important. Clause 7 appears to refer to some particular locality that had been transferred to the *khaliṣa* from a prince's *jāgīr*. But all other provisions are of a general applicability.

[21] Text published by Jadunath Sarkar in *JASB*, n.s., Vol. II, 1906, pp. 238–49; it is also given in *Mi'rāt-i Aḥmadī*, Vol. I, pp. 268–72. Though the *farmān* is addressed to Muhammad Hasim, the *Dīwān-i Khaliṣa* of Gujarat, it announces that all the officials of the empire are to enforce it. All of its clauses, without any exception, are of general applicability.

checking this process. This is in sharp contrast to the contents of Todar Mal's memorandum (1582–3)[22] as well as Fatḥullah Shīrāzī's recommendations (1585)[23] which became general decrees upon approval by Akbar. Unlike the two *farmāns* of Aurangzeb, there is no mention there of any general falling off of revenues or of decline in cultivation. The two documents from Akbar's reign generally lack the urgency and trepidation so noticeable in the two *farmāns* of Aurangzeb. Even when Todar Mal refers to a fall in the reported *ārāẓī* (measured area) from the *kh̲āliṣa* lands, he does not seem to consider it as a fall in actual cultivation but assumes it to be a paper reduction due to either concealment by the cultivators or corruption and inefficiency of the revenue officials. The remedy he suggests is a stringent measure, namely, taking the measured area as previously fixed and simply increasing it without further measurement by way of *nasaq* (clause 3).[24] He assumes that the increase of revenue demand so enforced would compel the peasants to cultivate more land.

In the *farmān* to Rasikdās the situation described is quite the opposite. The officials, it says, simply report large areas as 'cultivable' without indicating what area is being actually cultivated. The suspicion is voiced that this is done to conceal a real decline in the area of land under the plough. The officials are instructed to find out the reason for the cultivable land being left uncultivated and discover the causes of the flight of the peasants (clause 2). They are particularly warned to prevent exactions and oppressive practices by the village and local officials, the *muqaddam*, the *chaudhurī*, and the *qānūngo* (clauses 6, 9, 10, and 11). The officials are further asked to strive to bring the peasants back by giving assurances and concessions.

One should normally expect that the agrarian crisis should have found its reflection in a decline of the *jama'-dāmī* or the officially recognized revenue income. The *jama'-dāmī* of the *jāgīr* of an officer was supposed to equal his pay. Granting a reduction (*takh̲fīf*) in *jama'-dāmī*,[25] however, was a very rare step for the administration, because

[22] *AN*, Vol. III, pp. 381–3. See also the original text that is preserved in a unique copy of an earlier draft of the *AN*, B.L. Add. 27247 ff. 331-b. It is interesting that Aurangzeb's *farmān* to Raskidas itself should have enjoined the *dīwān* to find out the conditions that had prevailed in Akbar's reign during Todar Mal's *dīwānī*.

[23] *AN*, Vol. III, pp. 457–8.

[24] For the significance of the *nasaq* see *ASMI*, pp. 255–9.

[25] Cf. M. Athar Ali, *The Mughal Nobility under Aurangzeb*, Bombay, 1966, p. 77.

it required the provision of a fresh *jāgīr* to meet the balance of pay-claims of the *jāgīrdārs*. Thus normally, the *jama'* should not have exhibited a decline unless the decline in actual revenue collection was fairly substantial. Moreover, since prices must have risen during scarcities, the revenue rate in money terms should have also been raised, as is indicated by a specific statement in the *Mi'rāt-i Aḥmadī* from this period.[26] Thus the *jama'-dāmī* could have still been sustained, despite a contraction in actual cultivation, so long as the fall in production was not greater than the proportionate rise in prices. Table 13.1 gives figures at roughly twenty-year intervals (1646, 1667, and 1687) for the North Indian provinces.

Table 13.1

Suba		*Jama'-dami*	
	1646	*1667*	*1687*
Bengal	50,00,00,000	52,37,39,110	52,46,36,310
Orissa	20,00,00,000	19,71,00,000	14,28,21,000
Bihar	40,00,00,000	72,17,97,019	40,71,81,000
Allahabad	40,00,00,000	43,66,88,072	45,65,43,278
Awadh	30,00,00,000	32,00,72,193	32,13,17,119
Agra	90,00,00,000	1,05,17,09,283	1,14,17,00,157
Delhi	1,00,00,00,000	1,16,83,98,269	1,22,29,50,177
Lahore	90,00,00,000	90,70,16,125	89,89,32,170
Multan	28,00,00,000	24,53,18,505	21,43,49,896
Thatta	8,00,00,000	7,49,86,900	6,88,16,610
Ajmer	60,00,00,000	63,68,94,883	65,26,45,602
Kashmir	15,00,00,000	21,30,74,826	22,49,11,687
Malwa	40,00,00,000	42,54,76,670	40,39,80,658
Gujarat	53,00,00,000	44,88,83,096	45,47,49,135
Total	6,64,00,00,000	7,37,11,54,951	7,13,55,34,829

Source: The *jama'* figures for 1646 are from 'Abdu'l Ḥamīd Lāhorī, *Bādshāhnāma*, Vol. II, Bib. Ind. Calcutta, 1866–72, pp. 709–12; those of 1667 from Shaikh Muhammad Baqa, 'Baqa', *Mi'rāt-i 'Ālam*, Br. Lib. Add. 7657, ff. 445b–46a, and of 1687 from *Ẓawāḇit-i 'Ālamgīrī*, Br. Lib. Add. 6598, ff.130b–132a/ Or. 1642, ff.4a–6a.

[26] *Mi'rāt-i Aḥmadī*, p. 263.

If we take the *jama'dāmī* figures for 1667 as those which should have shown the effects of the crisis to at least some degree, it comes as a surprise to us that except in Gujarat, where the fall is perceptible[27] (from 53.0 crore *dāms* to 44.9 crore *dāms*), in all provinces either the 1667 figures exceed those of 1646 or are very close to them. In the case of Bihar, the increase seems more to be due to a misreading in the original of 72,17,97,019 for 42,17,97,019 (possible in *raqam* notation). Even if we then allow the total to be reduced by 30 crore *dāms* the total for all the north Indian provinces in 1667 would stand at 7,07.11 crore, as against 6,64.00 crore in 1646, an increase of 6.1 per cent over some twenty years. It may, however, be argued that the increase took place because prices rose in the meantime quite considerably offsetting the fall in production, a phenomenon in which both scarcity prices and the silver influx played their part, as we have just seen. But clearly owing to high prices prevailing now, the *jama'dāmī* of 1667 carried much less real value than the slightly lower *jama'dāmī* of 1646.

We do not unfortunately have the actual tax realization (*ḥāṣil*) figures for these *ṣūbas*; but that the *ḥāṣil* could have fallen considerably as a result of scarcity despite high prices, is suggested by figures from a locality in Rajasthan. We are fortunate in possessing revenue-realization figures of *pargana* Merta (Rajasthan) for twenty years, 1644–63.[28] Though the *ḥāṣil* fluctuated from year to year, a sharp decline occurred after 1661; the realization fell from Rs 5,71,301 in 1661 to Rs 3,28,576 in 1662; it fell further to Rs 1,60,550 in 1663, giving the lowest figure in the entire period of twenty years.

The late 1650s and early 1660s were thus marked by a definite contraction of cultivated area, the flight of the peasantry, and a likely fall in real revenues (i.e., revenues adjusted to prices). François Bernier who came to India during the War of Succession and remained in Delhi till 1666, obtained an impression of agrarian conditions that must have been strikingly heightened by the distress of that period. He tells us that:

Even a considerable portion of the good land remains untilled from want of *laboureurs* (peasants) ... many of the peasantry, driven to despair by so execrable a tyranny,

[27] The noticeable decline in the *jama'* of Gujarat (around 15%) was most probably the result of the successive famines of 1659, 1660 and 1663 (*ASMI*, p. 119).

[28] Muhnta Nainsī, *Marwār ra pargana ri Vigat*, edited by N.S. Bhati, Vol.II, Jodhpur, 1969, pp. 78–9.

abandon the country ... [29]

II

While there is thus indisputable evidence that the opening decade of Aurangzeb's reign witnessed an agrarian crisis, its causes remain rather obscure. It appears from our authorities that in northern India, the monsoons failed or were unsatisfactory for about three or four years.[30] Nevertheless, even contemporaries do not seem to have thought the failure of the rains occurring in certain regions in some years to have been the major cause of the scarcity. The official account at any rate ascribed the distress to a failure of administration and the ravages of the War of Succession. According to the author of the *'Ālamgīrnāma* the closing phase of Shāhjahān's reign was marked by disturbances of refractory elements, who gravely injured the peasants (presumably by destroying their crops and cattle). Indeed, part of the scarcity was supposed to have been due to a breakdown in commerce, especially grain transport. In order to expressly overcome this, Aurangzeb issued a *farmān* in 1660, abolishing all road tolls.[31] Its futility is commented upon by Khāfī Khān, who says that the *jāgīrdārs* refused to desist from collecting the tolls.[32] In any case these political or administrative disturbances should have caused only short-term dislocations.

Besides these factors which are described by contemporaries, there is perhaps one which has uniformly escaped identification by them. This was the inflationary effect of the influx of silver into the country. The prices of silver in terms of both gold and copper fell sharply between 1661 and 1666.[33] Indeed silver became so depressed in value that gold began to replace it in Indian imports of treasure during the

[29] François Bernier, *Travels in the Mughal Empire 1656–8*, translated by A. Constable, edited by V.A. Smith, London, 1916, p. 205. I have replaced the word 'labourers' in the translation by the original French word, which, of course, means peasants.

[30] In addition to the authorities quoted above, Bernier too says that two entire years passed without scarcely a drop of rain, *Travels in the Mughal Empire 1656–8*, p. 432.

[31] *'Alamgīrnāma*, pp. 435–9.

[32] Khāfī Khān, Vol. II, pp. 87–91.

[33] *CEHI*, Vol. I, pp. 361–71. Table 9 gives the rupee values of the *muhr* and Table 10 the indices of the rupee-price of *dām*, 1595–6=100. The table has been revised by Irfan Habib with additions and corrections in 'A System of Trimetallism in the Age of Price Revolution', J.F. Richards, ed., *The Imperial Monetary System of Mughal India*, Delhi, 1987, Tables 2 and 3, pp.148-9.

1660s.[34] Obviously, all prices quoted in silver would have greatly risen in such a situation. If they kept pace with copper, the increase in the general price-level should have been of the order of 60 per cent between 1659 and 1661, though thereafter there should have been a slide bringing it by 1666 to a level only 40 per cent above that of 1659.[35] If the price-movement kept pace with gold, the increase would have been substantially less.[36] By this time, copper had by and large ceased to be the ordinary medium for non-fractional payments.[37] The cheapening of silver should, therefore, have affected the entire commodity sector of the agrarian economy.

To some extent, the high prices in Gujarat (see section I) tend to confirm the role of the monetary phenomena, since Gujarat was the major entry-point of silver from Europe.

The silver influx would explain a price-rise, and distress among consumers. But why should there have been distress among the producers? If prices increased, and the revenue demand lagged behind, the peasants might make a gain, and then make an effort to increase cultivation. If this happened, the revenue should have gradually risen for two reasons; first, in 'pursuit' of prices; and, second, owing to extension of cultivation.

But our evidence indicates, as shown earlier, a fall in the revenue as well as a fall in the area under cultivation.[38] It, therefore, does not seem possible to attribute the crisis of the 1660s purely to monetary factors either, though like climate and political disruption these too might have had a contribution to make.

Finally it was during the very period of the crisis of the 1660s that Bernier offered his exposition of the process of agrarian decline of the

[34] K.N. Chaudhuri, *The Trading World of Asia 1660–1760*, Cambridge, 1978, p. 175.

[35] The indexed value of copper *dām* in terms of silver increased from 167 in 1659 to 267 in 1661; in 1666 the index was 242.4 (price in 1595=100).

[36] In 1661 a *muhr* was worth Rs 14.63, thereafter it appreciated and in 1666 fetched Rs 16.

[37] Irfan Habib, 'Aspects of Agrarian Relations and Economy in a Region of U.P. during the 16th Century', in *IESHR*, Vol. IV, No. 3, 1967. The point has now been firmly established. See Irfan Habib, 'A System of Trimetallism' and J.S. Deyell's note thereon, Richards, ed. *Imperial Monetary System of Mughal India*, pp.137-70.

[38] Table 1 indicates that the *jama'-dāmī* declined in ten out of fourteen provinces of northern India between 1656 and 1667.

Mughal empire. According to him the system of transfer of *jāgīrs* induced the *jāgīrdār* and his agents to extort the maximum from the peasants, since no benefit would accrue to them from any concessions granted in the interests of long-term improvement. On this view, a steady tendency towards agrarian devastation was a built-in feature of Mughal polity.[39]

Bernier was not the first to offer this reason for the decline in agriculture, though he sets out by far the most cogently argued theory. Much before him Xavier,[40] Hawkins[41] and Manrique[42] too had commented on the ill-effects of the *jāgīr* system. Xavier remarked as early as 1609,

> during the time that someone holds certain lands he squeezes out of them whatever he can and the poor laboureurs (peasants) desert them and run away.

It was not the European travellers alone who noticed this inherent defect; the Mughal administration too was apparently aware of it. It was perhaps to restrain the over-exactions by the *jāgīrdārs* that Fathullaḥ Shīrāzī in 1585 had recommended promotions in the ranks of *jāgīrdārs*, if they improved the land assigned to them.[43]

It has been argued that while the *jāgīrdārs*' individual interests might have been served by oppression, the Mughal government was effective enough to impose positive checks upon the avarice of the *jāgīrdārs*. Athar Ali suggests that the local potentates, the *qānūngo* and *chaudhurī* whose positions were almost hereditary, represented the permanent interest of the localities and could put a stop to the excessive exactions of the *jāgīrdār* or his agents.[44]

While it may be recognized that unlike the individual *jāgīrdārs*, imperial policy might have looked to improvement in agriculture and placed some restraint over revenue realization (*ḥāṣil*) in the interest of

[39] Bernier, *Travels in the Mughal Empire*, p. 227.

[40] Xavier, Tr. Hosten, *JASB*, translated by Hosten, n.s., Vol. XXIII, 1927, p. 121.

[41] Hawkins, *Early Travels in India, 1583–1619*, edited by W. Foster, London, 1927, p. 114.

[42] Fray Sebastian Manrique, *Travels, 1629–43*, Vol. II, translated by C.E. Luard and Hosten, Hakluyt Society, 1927, p. 372.

[43] *AN*, Vol. III, p. 459. It is interesting to note that Prince Aurangzeb also recommended promotion to Rāo Karan on this very count (*Ruqa'āt-i 'Alamgīrī*, edited by S.N.A. Nadvi, Azamgarh, 1930, pp. 112–13).

[44] M. Athar Ali, *The Mughal Nobility under Aurangzeb*, pp. 89–92.

future increase in *jama'-dāmī*, it is difficult to agree with the view that it possessed an effective instrument in the hereditary local officials by which such a policy might be put into effect. The *qānūngos* and *chaudhurīs* were themselves the beneficiaries from a larger realization of surplus (they gained a fixed percentage of the realization), and it is therefore difficult to suppose that they were interested in reducing the amount of revenue collection. Indeed, the Mughal administration was itself aroused on many occasions to denounce these officials' own oppressive practices. Todar Mal in his memorandum warns the *'āmils* against the oppression by the *chaudhurīs* and *muqaddams* as well as the attempts of the 'dominant ones' to pass on the revenue burden on to the shoulders of the small peasantry.[45] The conditions seem to have only worsened by Aurangzeb's time. In his *farmān* to Rasikdās a number of clauses are exclusively devoted to prescribing measures by which to limit extortions and oppression by the village officials. The *dīwāns* are repeatedly warned against their illegal appropriations and the oppression caused thereby to the small peasantry (clauses 6, 8, and 10). The *farmān* expressly orders that the distribution of remissions (on account of 'calamities') should not be left in the hands of the *chaudhurīs*, the *muqaddams*, and the *qānūngos*, since the benefit would not then reach the small peasants (*reza-ri'āyā*). It also orders that the *dīwān* should not let these officials meet him in private, a prohibition which implies awareness of collusion between them and the revenue officials.

It is, therefore, difficult to contest Bernier's thesis that the maximization of exploitation was inherent in the Mughal revenue system. It was only other factors such as perhaps a lag between rising prices and cash revenue rates in the earlier part of the seventeenth century,[46] a factor that gained in importance because of the extension of the cash-nexus, which tended to set limits to agrarian devastation inherent in *jāgīr* transfers. By the mid-seventeenth century, the process of monetization had largely been completed. It was perhaps now that the Mughal system became especially vulnerable to effects of weather

[45] *AN*, Vol. III, p. 382. The words are much stronger, almost abusive in the original version preserved in Add. 27247. See Appendix to Chapter 8.

[46] The gold and copper prices of silver show that the bulk of increase in prices during the seventeenth century took place in the first fifty years. By 1653 the silver price of gold had increased by 35.3 per cent; the price of copper by 1656 had gone up by 79 per cent. *CEHI*, Vol. I, pp. 367, 370.

fluctuations and monetary disturbances. With no further 'cushion' offered by inflation the inherent destructive tendency in *jāgīr* transfers could become particularly virulent. Yet quite possibly, the exceptional virulence too was a passing phenomenon, as the pressures for higher revenue fuelled by steady inflation continued in the initial phase of a slow deflation. As the effects became too destructive even for revenue collection in the short-run, the *jāgīrdārs*' pressure on the peasants may have moderated somewhat. An opening would, then, be created for recovery.

III

The crisis apparently receded in the 1670s since no further complaints of a general nature were reported about agrarian distress. The *rabi* crop of 1670 was a bumper one and the prices declined—a fact recorded with great satisfaction by the author of the *Ma'āṣir-i 'Ālamgīrī*.[47]

The recovery, however, seems to have been superficial and could partly be attributed to monetary factors. The silver price of gold showed a downward trend after 1666 and a major crash in the gold price occurred in 1676. Thereafter, a slow recovery began, marked by fluctuations. The silver price of copper began to decline after 1671, though it was not a very sharp one. The rise in the value of silver was therefore real and not simply due to the heavy gold imports. This appreciation of silver in terms of gold and copper must have checked inflation to a certain extent, relieving the pressure on consumers.

The 'deflation' of the 1670s and 1680s was, however, at a low rate. The silver price of copper fell by about 21 per cent in eastern Rajasthan between 1666 and 1686, giving a price movement of 1 per cent per annum. The silver price of gold fell between 1666 and 1688 by 33 per cent, a rate of 1.4 per cent. This suggests that if agricultural production had remained static, the revenue collection should have fallen by about 20 per cent between 1667 and 1687 (going by copper prices). We are able to compare the *jama'-dāmī* figures of 1667 with those of 1687, but these exhibit an almost stationary level as may be seen in Table 13. 2 (abstracted for convenience from Table 13.1).

As Table 13.1 shows there is probably a serious error in the 1667 figure for Bihar, which should be 42,17,97,019. The small decline in the *jama'-dāmī* of Bihar which would still be present between 1667

[47] Sāqī Musta'idd Khān, *Ma'āṣir-i 'Alamgīrī*, p. 98.

Table 13. 2*

Ṣūba	*Jama'-dāmī*	
	1667	*1687*
Bengal	52,37,39,110	52,46,36,340
Orissa	19,71,00,000	14,28,21,000
Bihar	72,17,97,019	40,71,81,000
Allahabad	43,66,88,072	45,65,43,278
Awadh	32,00,72,193	32,13,17,119
Agra	1,05,17,09,283	1,14,17,00,157
Delhi	1,16,83,98,269	1,22,29,50,177
Lahore	90,70,16,125	89,89,32,170
Multan	24,53,18,505	21,43,49,896
Thatta	7,49,86,900	6,88,16,610
Ajmer	63,68,94,883	65,26,45,602
Kashmir	21,30,74,826	22,49,11,687
Malwa	42,54,76,670	40,39,80,658
Gujarat	44,88,83,096	45,47,49,135
Total	7,37,11,54,951	7,13,55,34,829

* For sources see Note to Table 13.1.

and 1687 may be explained by the great Bihar famine of 1671–2.[48] The *jama'* of the northern provinces in fact declined in absolute terms, though only marginally. In view of our present information about the monetary phenomena of this period, these figures would suggest a possible recovery in agricultural production (though at a rather slow rate) during the 1670s and 1680s.

But it should be remembered that the Mughal administration was extremely reluctant to grant reductions in *jama'-dāmī*. Thus even the slow rate of recovery that we are inferring here from a stability in *jama'-dāmī* might be largely illusory.

If, therefore, there was a recovery from the crisis of the 1660s it must have been on a very limited scale. What was achieved was some increase in agricultural production through possibly an extension of cultivation. But it is difficult to say how far the loss of the 1660s was

[48] John Marshall, *Notes and Observation on East India*, edited by S.A. Khan, *John Marshall in India— Notes and Observation in Bengal, 1668–72*, London, 1927, pp. 125–7, 138, 149–53.

really made up. In monetary terms, the Mughal revenues do not seem to show an increase, and it is also not clear how far the postulated recovery in agricultural production was due to an absence of drought, except for Bihar. This fortunate exemption from natural calamities disappeared from the beginning of the 1690s, when a new cycle o scarcities and epidemic began in Northern India.[49]

The excessively exploitative element within the *jāgīr* system presumably continued to operate in the 1670s and 1680s, and may be the best explanation for the constricted nature of the recovery. On our present information then, the long crisis of 1658–70 may well have formed a watershed between the earlier and more vigorous phase of Mughal Indian economy and its later phase of decline.

This is no more than a hypothesis; but it is one which may partly help to explain some of the acute problems of Aurangzeb's reign and his efforts to resolve them. The agrarian revolts beginning in northern India in the 1660s; the discriminatory religious policy designed to reinforce the political base of the empire among Muslims at a time of financial difficulties; and the annexations in the Deccan with a view to augmenting imperial resources, beginning in the 1680s. If so, the agrarian crisis of the 1660s seems to have initiated a cycle of political developments which led ultimately to the ruin of the empire.

[49] *ASMI*, pp.120–1.

SHIPPING AND PORTS

14

Shipping and Navigation under Akbar

It has long been an axiom in Indian historiography that the Mughal empire being a 'continental' power was only marginally interested in sea-borne commerce. Indian states, noted Moreland, 'appreciated the benefits of foreign commerce, and the revenue which it brought to their seaports, (but) they did nothing to protect it on the way'. Speaking specifically of Akbar, he admits that he 'sent ships from Gujarat to the Red Sea', but was content to let them sail 'under license from the Portuguese'.[1] Moreland, as always, spoke with a certain amount of caution. Pearson is convinced of the fact that 'the revenue resources of the Mughal empire were overwhelmingly from the land ... interlocked with ... a North Indian Muslim elite ethos which was again oriented to land'.[2]

This paper does not necessarily take issue with this perception in the broad sphere of land *versus* sea. What it sets out to do is, first, to establish what really was the attitude of the Mughal court, especially Akbar and his nobility towards shipping and navigation, and then to see how far the established hypothesis fits in with this information.

Akbar's empire touched the sea only when he conquered Gujarat in 1572. On 12 December he arrived at Cambay and went out on a vessel (presumably a *taori*) to enjoy the sea.[3] Significantly, Akbar did not leave to a subordinate the task of reducing Surat, soon to be the major port of the Gulf of Cambay, but proceeded there himself. The fort of Surat surrendered to him on 26 February 1573.[4] Akbar had,

[1] W.H. Moreland, *India at the Death of Akbar, an Economic Study*, London, 1920, p. 202.

[2] M.N. Pearson, 'The Sixteenth Century' in *India and the Indian Ocean, 1500–1800*, Calcutta, 1987.

[3] *AN*, Vol. III, p. 9.

[4] Ibid., Vol. III, p. 29.

therefore, a personal view of both Cambay and Surat; and though he had no further occasion to view the sea again, he had considerable opportunity to obtain much information of both the ports and the trade.

What is noteworthy is that within three years of the taking of Cambay and Surat, Akbar had built or acquired two ships, the *Salīmī*, obviously named after his eldest son, and *Ilāhī*, a favourite word with Akbar to recall God's particular benevolence to him. It was on these two ships that a party of very high ladies of Akbar's family, headed by his aunt, famous as a writer of memoirs, Gulbadan Begam, was to go on the *ḥajj* pilgrimage in 1576.

The decision of the imperial ladies to go for their pilgrimage is of much interest. Akbar's step-mother Ḥājjī Begam, the senior wife of Humāyūn, had gone for pilgrimage in 1563–4, but she might have gone by land, or by sea taking ship through Sind, and not Gujarat. At least she did not return through Gujarat, because she had remained in Delhi after her pilgrimage (indicating a return journey through Multan) and only came to see Akbar at Agra after his triumphal return from Gujarat in 1573.[5]

The party that now was to go to Mecca included besides only Gulbadan Begam, the recognized head of the party, Akbar's cousin and wife Salīma Ṣultān Begam, two daughters of Akbar's uncle Kāmrān, the widow of his uncle 'Askarī, and other ladies of the harem.[6] Very high officers accompanied the party, but doubts persisted as to whether the Portuguese would not interfere or try to capture the women, which would have been a personal disaster for Akbar.

Such worries are attributed by Abū'l Faẓl to inexperienced persons accompanying the party and who spread rumours among the pilgrims. The fears did not abate despite Gulbadan Begam's counsel to the contrary and the encouragement of the escorting nobles. Akbar, therefore, had to summon Qulich Khān from Idar in Gujarat to receive instructions from him (he was then camping near Udaipur) and to set off to Surat to arrange for the ladies' departure. The narrative up to this point is identical in both the final (printed) text of *Akbarnāma*,[7] and the earlier version, preserved in MS in the British Library.[8] The

[5] Ibid., Vol. III, p. 77. For her departure in 1563–4, see Ibid., Vol. II, p. 243.

[6] Ibid., Vol. III, pp. 145–6. Mu'tamād Khān, *Iqbalnama-i Jahangiri*, Lucknow, 1870, Vol. II, p. 298, offers a clearly written summary.

[7] *AN*, Vol. III, p. 195.

[8] Add. 27, 247, f. 285b.

latter version not only adds a few details, but goes on to tell us what happened in a way different from the brief reference in the final version. A translation of it is given in Appendix A.

From the passage as given in the MS version, it is obvious that Qulich Khān, who belonged to a family long in Timurid's service, was called upon to help because he had been Akbar's first governor of Surat[9] and was, therefore, thought to be well informed about the situation with regard to the Portuguese.

What Abū'l Faẓl omits to say is that on reaching Surat the initial reports from Qulich Khān were not encouraging, and Akbar's own fears were the same as those attributed by Abū'l Faẓl to inexperienced persons. This we come to know only from the chance survival of an undated *farmān* of Akbar to Qulich Khān, in a mid-seventeenth-century collection of documents.[10]

A translation of this is given in Appendix B. The Portuguese, Qulich Khān reported had not violated any passes they had issued, nor obstructed anyone's passage in recent years; but no one had yet gone for *ḥajj* by sea trusting to their word. Akbar, as will be seen was unnerved, and wrote to his 'Esteemed Mother', which must mean his aunt Gulbadan Begam, to consider her journey to Surat as equivalent to *ḥajj* and defer the voyage at least for a year. He openly expressed his fear of a blow to the honour of the imperial family, and his own great pain, if something happened to the imperial ladies at the hands of the Portuguese.[11]

Quite possibly, Gulbadan Begam, intent on her *ḥajj* pilgrimage,[12] was adamant and Akbar gave way. The earlier version of the *Akbarnāma* says that Qulich Khān first tried to put the ships on their voyage without a pass (*qaul*) from the Portuguese; but, then, Rāi Kalyān used tact with the Portuguese and obtained passes for both the 'junks', *Salīmī* and *Ilāhī*. I use the word 'junk', not only because these large ships, carrying one main sail, and therefore very fast when winds were favourable, were known by this name both to Europeans and in Persian (*jank*), but also because in the MS *Akbarnāma* the ships carrying the ḥajj pilgrims is explicitly called *qāfila-i jank*, 'or convoy of junks'.[13] Incidentally, we learn from Badāūnī that Kalyān,

[9] *AN*, Vol. III, p. 31.

[10] Bib. Nat., Paris, Blochet Sup. Pers. 482.

[11] Ibid., f. 30b–31a.

[12] Cf. *AN*, Vol. III, p. 145, on the project having come about at her insistence.

[13] Add. 27, 247, f. 285b.

an imperial officer, was a *baqqāl* (i.e., *Banya*; or, in this case, Vora?) of Cambay.[14]

The ladies boarded the *Salīmī* and their main escort Ṣulṭān Khwāja and all (male) pilgrims set sail on the *Ilāhī*. What happened on this voyage which must have taken place during the winter monsoons of 1576–7, was reported to Akbar by Ṣulṭan Khwāja in December 1578. The details do not appear in the final version,[15] and, therefore, the passage in the earlier version is given in translation in Appendix C. The first incident was the recovery of a child who had fallen overboard at night, a boat being sent out for him from the fast-moving ship, and a lamp was set alight on the ship to guide the boat back. Lighting lamps aboard ships is stated to have been against navigational custom, possibly because lamps might cause fire, though a purely superstitious reason—the fear of large sea beasts was advanced by Ṣulṭan Khwāja. The other strange thing was that both the ships which left together, were able to keep close company and reached the Red Sea together.[16]

While the imperial ladies were performing their *ḥajj* pilgrimage, an official of Akbar, Bāyāzid Bayāt, who too has left his memoirs wished also to undertake the same pilgrimage. His account of his voyage is most valuable.[17] He took permission of the Emperor to go on *ḥajj* with his three sons in March–April 1578, and departed for Surat. Here the permission for him to sail was not given, for Akbar did not wish that in the name of going to *ḥajj* wealth should be taken away from India. This, one may consider to be an Indian version of the mercantilist approach to treasure exports! Ultimately, Bāyazīd was allowed to board ship only when the effects he had put on boats (for being taken to the ship) had been inspected and found in cash and purchased goods, to be worth Rs one lakh. This was reported to the emperor, who ordered that he be allowed to leave. All this took time, and it was not until 11 March 1580 that he could board ship.[18]

This ship was the *Muḥammadī*, and had been built jointly by Quṭbuddīn Khān and Qulīch Khān. The former belonged to Akbar's

[14] 'Abdul Qādir Badāūnī, *Muntakhabu-t Tawārīkh*, edited by Ali, Ahmad and Lees, Vol. II, Bib. Ind., Calcutta, 1864–9, p. 242. Kalyan after finishing this business was to join his posting with the army in Malwa.

[15] *AN*, Vol. III, p. 263.

[16] Add. 27, 247, f. 297a–b.

[17] Bāyazīd Bayāt, *Tazkira-i Ḥumāyūn wa Akbar*, edited by M. Hidaya Hosain, Bib. Ind., Calcutta, 1941, pp. 353–61.

[18] Ibid., pp. 353–4.

foster mother's family (the *Atka Khail*) and was posted to Gujarat (as commandant of Baroch), after its conquest; and we have already seen who Qulīch Khān was. Their 'land ethos' did not prevent them from immediately entering into a shipping and commercial enterprise and going into partnership like any merchants.[19]

Muḥammadī on sailing from Surat proceeded to the Daman estuary, where it had to pay for the Portuguese *cartas* or pass. The procedure is here described from the Indian point of view. The price of the pass, which was taken on behalf of Diu by the 'tax-farmers of Daman', was assessed after the inspection of the ship's hold. As the Portuguese arrived to board the ship, they took a son of Bāyazīd as hostage: clearly neither party trusted the other. The elder son of Bāyazīd, Sā'dat Yār, it transpires, had learnt Portuguese and negotiated with the inspectors. The Portuguese demanded 10,000 *maḥmūdīs* in cash, to be paid by the passengers. Since the passengers had only goods, Bāyazīd paid the sum on their behalf, they promising to reimburse him at Jedda, after they had sold their goods. The agreement was registered with the 'captain of the Surat ships', Ḥasan Chunnu, and the '*chaudhuri* of the port', Tajpāl, left the ship. Bāyazīd's own son was returned from the 'Portuguese galliot' (*ghurāb-i Farang*) in the evening.[20] Clearly, the financial burden of the Portuguese cartas system upon Indian shipping was not inconsiderable, and amounted to little more than regularized blackmail.

The ship left Daman Estuary on 18 March morning, and, though it was near the end of the season, the winds proved favourable, and the sight of Aden was obtained after fourteen days. Here the ship was espied by the ship on which Gulbadan and Salīma Sulṭan Begam and their party were returning, accompanied by Khwāja Yaḥaya. Anxious to find out news from home, they sent out a boat, and Bāyazīd had the ship's sail pulled down, to stop his own ship. He immediately wrote out a full report to the ladies, to which he received their reply by land at Mecca.[21]

When Bāyazīd wished to return to India in 1582, he took a ship which as it came out of the Red Sea, found it was too late in the season, and so anchored for four months at the port of Zufar (Zofar) in southern Oman. Here the news was received of the rebellion of

[19] Ibid., p. 354.
[20] Ibid., pp. 354–5.
[21] Ibid., pp. 355–6.

Muẓaffar, the former ruler of Gujarat, in which Qutbuddīn K͟hān, the part owner of *Muḥammadī*, was to lose his life.[22] Bāyazīd notes that the *tandil*, the head sailor,[23] and the *k͟hallāṣis*, the sailors, were Gujaratis, and were so sympathetic to Muẓaffar's cause that they had gathered all sorts of weapons in order to mutiny. Bāyazīd had to retire with another Mughal officer to a special cabin (*dabosa*).[24] Ultimately the mutiny was averted, a happy eventuality in which a convenient omen drawn from Ḥāfiz also helped. The ship at last set sail, but took two months to reach Gogha in Gujarat, the port having just been retaken from Muẓaffar. Like any modern passenger, Bāyazīd does not forget to record that he had trouble clearing his goods from the customs (*furẓa*). He had been on the vessel for full eight months.[25] Gogha was the outer port (on the Saurashtra coast) for Cambay.

Almost any important noble posted in Gujarat, it would seem, had a ship or two built for himself to engage in traffic. The Governor of Gujarat, Mirza 'Azīz Koka, Akbar's foster brother, built a ship of his own, *Ilāhī* (presumably different from the one on which Gulbadan Begam's escort had sailed). In 1593 he had it furtively brought to Velaval, from which he set sail in March to the Red Sea for the *ḥajj* pilgrimage, out of professed resentment against Akbar's religious policy.[26] But dissatisfied with Mecca as well, he returned, setting anchor at Velaval: the news reached the court on about 20 September 1594).[27] Apparently, he had made use of his own ship, and a reference to it occurs in an undated document. When K͟hān-i 'Āẓam ('Azīz Koka) wanted to set sail from Jedda on his own ships, all the merchants cried out against his taking out his ship empty, though he had a Portuguese pass. 'Azīz Koka apparently did so, because he wished to keep his voyage secret. But merchants saw it as a wasted voyage:

[22] On this rebellion see the account in Ali Muhammad Khan, *Mi'rāt-i Aḥmadī*, edited by Nawab Ali, Vol. I, Baroda, 1928, pp. 142–57.

[23] See the definition in Abū'l Faẓl, *Ā'īn*, Vol. I, p. 203.

[24] 'Cabin in ship or boat, which is below the elevated part of the deck, where the captain's wife and women of the passengers sit'. Tex Chand Bahar, 1739–40, *Bahār-i 'Ajam*, S.V. *dabusa*.

[25] Bāyazīd Bayāt, *Taẕkira*, etc., pp. 358–61. Gowa (Goa) on p. 361 is an obvious misprint or misreading of Gogha.

[26] A well-known incident. For the flight see *AN*, Vol. III, p. 638; *Mi'rāt-i Aḥmadī*, Vol. I, pp. 181–2. Abū'l Faẓl says the vessel normally used to ply from Diu.

[27] *AN*, Vol. III, p. 654–5.

why, they asked, did he not simply board a Portuguese ship?.[28] (Document translated in Appendix D).

Another officer who had ships at Surat was 'Abdur Raḥīm Khān-i Khānān. He was Governor of Gujarat under Akbar (1584–5, 1586–8),[29] and apparently held Surat in *jāgīr* as well, since he had a garden there.[30] He had three ships built, the *Raḥīmī*, *Karīmī*, and *Sālārī*, with 'captains, navigators, and staff' employed and paid by him, mainly to cater to *ḥajj* traffic.[31] None of these ships is mentioned in documents of Akbar's reign, but the great ship *Raḥīmī* 'at least' 1200 'Tonnes' was described as 'the Queen Mother's ship' in 1612 in an English report.[32] Apparently, the Queen Mother was Salðma Sulṭān Begam, who was first married to Bairam Khān, had borne him 'Abdur Raḥīm; after being widowed early, she was taken to wife by Akbar. She had gone with Gulbadan's party, as we have seen; and it is possible that the ship *Raḥīmī* (with 'Abdu'r Raḥīm's name clearly in mind) had been built for her by his son.

Some unpublished documents shed light on the shipping activities of another officer of Akbar, Ṣādiq Muḥammad Khān, Khān-i Jahān. Ṣādiq Khān held Surat and Broach in *jāgīr*, having been assigned to him in 1593. He died on 29 March 1597.[33] One ship that he had built was *Ṣādiqī*. This ship ran aground near Daman. The document which is translated (in Appendix E), dated 24 September 1594, is addressed to the captain of Daman, warning him that if anything belonging to the ship or its cargo was touched, his son Dost Muhammad would march on Daman with the troops of Broach and Surat, and Ṣādiq Khān himself would to join him (from Ahmadabad?).[34] Another document, dated 17 February 1595, (translated in Appendix F) gives

[28] Bib. Nat. Blochet: Sup. Pers. 482, f. 182.

[29] M. Athar Ali, *Apparatus of Empire*, Delhi, 1985, p. xxxxiv.

[30] 'Abdu'r Raḥīm Khān Khānān's influence in Surat is shown by a *parwāna* issued by Khān-i Jaḥān (miswritten Khān-i Khānān) to his officer Khwāja Muḥammad Ma'ṣūm, at Surat 18 June 1595, to send fifty or sixty pineapples for the Khān-i Khānān's table (Blochet Sup. Pers. 482, f. 132a).

[31] 'Abdul Ḥaqq Nihawardī, *Ma'āṣir-i Raḥīmī*, edited by M. Hidayat Hosain, Bib. Ind., Calcutta, 1910–31, p. 611.

[32] John Saris' journal in Samuel Purchas, *Purchas His Pilgrimes*, edited by Mac Lehose, Vol. III, Glasgow, 1905, p. 399.

[33] For these details, see Irfan Habib, *PIHC*, 55th session, 1993, Mysore, p. 247.

[34] Blochet, Sup. Pers. 482, f. 170a–b.

us the sequel. The viceroy (at Goa) had also been written to, and he had directed the captain at Daman to return everything aboard the ship to Ṣādiq Khān's men. The letter gives details of how this was to be done.[35] Unluckily, it does not transpire whether the *Ṣādiqī* itself could be salvaged.

There is, finally, an undated document of Akbar's reign, which is a *parwāna*, possibly issued by an officer or Ṣādiq Khān himself (see Appendix G for translation).[36] A very high noble (titles given, but name lost), possibly Ṣādiq Khān himself, was having a ship built at Surat and was sending Maḥram Khān to oversee the matter. The addressee is to help in seeing whether it could be ready in time to sail for Jedda during the season. If it did so, the ship *Akbarshāhī*, which apparently belonging to the same master, should be loaded with cargo to sail for Acheh (in Sumatra, Indonesia). If the new ship was not likely to be ready, the *Akbarshāhī* was to be prepared for Jedda. The calculations were thus purely commercial, and we can see that the nobles' ships were not only involved in the *ḥajj* traffic or Red Sea trade, but also with South-east Asia.

Let us now turn to Akbar himself. Unluckily, the general belief that the *Ā'īn-i Akbarī* consists merely of hyperbole and the statement of the ideal ('normative') has often led to the ignoring of its evidence. It should surely modify one's ideas of the 'land ethos' of Akbar's court, when we find that Abū'l Faẓl has a regular chapter on the command over sea ('*Ā'īn-i Mīr Baḥri*', characteristically rendered by Blochmann in his translation as 'Admiralty'). In this chapter Abū'l Faẓl begins by noting that on the sea-coast, in the east, west, and south, large ships have been built, which 'have become a source of comfort to the seafarers, the ports have obtained prosperity, and knowledge has grown'.[37] He is not necessarily referring here to imperial ships alone, but perhaps to the general progress of ship-building. He then proceeds to give a detailed statement of the twelve categories of staff manning the ship, headed by the captain, with a short description of the functions of each. Indian terms such as *tandil*, for head of sailors, *bhandārī*, for store keeper, *panjrī*, for look-out, and *gunamtī*, for bailing out water, show actual familiarity with navigational terminology of the time. That many men, sometimes, more than twenty persons,

[35] Ibid., f. 167b–8a.
[36] Ibid., f. 132b.
[37] *Ā'īn*, Vol. I, p. 202.

designated *sukangars* had to be ready to set the course of the ship at the direction of the navigator (*mu'allim*) shows how difficult it was to alter the junk's direction. Abū'l Faẓl tells us that on the sea, sailors (*mallāḥs*) are known as *khāllṣīs* and *kharwas*, and that good sailors came mostly from Malabar. The same realism is visible when he states the salaries and wages for each voyage, which 'in the terminology of these people is called *kosh*'. These vary for different ports, and Abū'l Faẓl quotes those of Satgāon (Bengal) for each class, (the captain having ten times the pay of the ordinary sailor). The right to four *malikh*, or passengers' places (?) was an extra privilege of the captain, along with the right to carry much cargo. The pay for captain at Cambay was much higher and in Lahari Bandar lower. In other ports, in South-east Asia and Portugal, we are told, the pay was much higher.[38]

The collection of such detailed data attest the Mughal court's interest in shipping. But there is evidence of such interest in practice as well. Two imperial sea-going ships were constructed at Lahore in 1594 and 1596, whose technological importance has been studied by Irfan Habib.[39] The large use of iron in the ships should set to rest the speculation that Indian ships did not have nails, and the planks were bound only by ropes. The use of a barge on which the second ship was built, for carriage down to Lahari Bandar, gives Akbar precedence in the invention of the 'ships, camel' (a barge on which a ship is built and then carried over shallows into open sea). But of equal significance is the strategic nature of the effort.

As is well known, the Portuguese were able to control the Gujarat shipping from their two strong points at Diu and Daman on each side of Gujarat. However, it was not possible to come out of the Gulf of Cambay, without being caught by their vigilant eye. But they had no means to control shipping at Lāharī Bandar, the port of Sind, since from their position at Hormuz they could control only ships entering the Persian Gulf. Musqat, which might have helped them to control Lāharī Bandar, they were unable to seize. Akbar was able to annex Sind in 1591 after a successful expedition under 'Abdu'r Raḥīm Khān-i Khānān. The ruler Jānī Beg was allowed to hold his dominions, as a

[38] Ibid., Vol. I, pp. 202–3.

[39] Irfan Habib, 'Akbar and Technology', in Irfan Habib, ed., *Akbar and His India*, Delhi, 1997, pp. 144–6. For the translations of the two passages in *AN*, Vol. III, pp. 651–2, 715–6, see S. Moosvi, *Episodes in the Life of Akbar, Contemporary Records and Reminiscences*, National Book Trust, New Delhi, 1994, pp. 98–9.

noble of the empire, but Lāharī Bandar, was kept within the *khāliṣa*, i.e., under direct imperial control.[40] The difficulty was that since Sind had no close access to forests, ships could not be built there, and the port had to be dependent on ships built and repaired in south Gujarat. Akbar, therefore, hit upon the idea of building ships at Lahore, which could get supplies of Himalayan timber and send them down to Lāharī Bandar through the Indus river system. Two of these were built, as we have seen, and were used for the Red Sea trade.[41] Unluckily, the names of the ships are not vouchsafed to us, and so we cannot trace their later history.

Perhaps because of the distance from Lahore to Thatta, and the fact that Akbar himself left Lahore in 1598 for campaigning in the Deccan, the experiment was not continued. But surely the project cannot be just treated as a curious episode. It could equally well be held to be the design of genius. That geography was, perhaps against it is another matter; but, surely, even if they were bound by 'land ethos', it did not prevent Akbar and his court from thinking big on affairs of the sea.

Appendices

A

Akbarnāma, BL, MS. Add. 27, 247, f. 285b.
Under Ilāhī Year 21/A.H. 984=AD 1576
During the journey of the sky-high imperial Camp in the vicinity of Udaipur, reports (*'āra'iẓ*) reached the Court from the intelligencers of *ṣūba* Gujarat that some of the inexperienced ones in the train of the *ḥajj* pilgrims abroad the convoy of junks (*qāfila-i junk*) have spread [among them] fear of the authorities of the Portuguese ports. However, much the imperial ladies counsel them with words of wisdom and the high officials give them encouragement, the general body of persons do not seem to be satisfied. Since His Majesty has summoned Qulīch Khān from Idar, he may be sent to that destination (Surat). Accordingly, a gracious *farmān* to summon Qulīch Khān was sent with 'Alī-Murād, and some brave troopers were sent with him so that

[40] Cf. Fatima Zehra Bilgrami, 'The Mughal Annexation of Sind' in *Akbar and His India*, p. 53 & n., citing the *AN*, Vol. III, p. 642.

[41] This is explicitly said of the first ship, Ṭāhir Muḥammad Sabzevārī, *Rauẓatu't Ṭāhirīn*, Br. Mus. MS, Or. 168, f. 556a–a.

he may not come to harm in the arduous way through the mountains …'Alī Murād brought Qulīch Khān to the imperial camp, and His Majesty sent him to set the ships on their voyage. He (Qulich Khān) first wanted that he should set the ships on voyage without a pass or assurance (from the Portuguese). This was not possible. Rai Kalyān by proceeding tactfully brought the pass (?word illegible) from the Portuguese for the ships *Salīmi* and *Ilāhī*. And the chaste ladies went aboard the ship *Salīmī*, while Sulṭān Khwāja and the entire party of *ḥajj* pilgrims took their place aboard the ship *Ilāhī*, and sailed for their destination.

B

Blochet Sup. Pers. 482 f. 30b–31a

Akbar's farmān to Qulich Khān,

The learned, the noble of the realm, the perfect of faith and sincerity, deserving of favour and consideration, Muahammad Qulīch Khān, comforted by our kindness, should know that the report (*'arẓdāsht*) that he had sent to the court was received on the seventeenth of the current month, and its contents have been comprehended. He had written that although the Portuguese (*Farnagīān*) have not within this period violated their promise (*be-qauli na-kardaand*) and not obstructed any ship's passage, yet during this same period, no one has put his trust in the pass (*qaul*) of the Portuguese, to set sail to Mecca. He is right in what he has written, and it has appeared reasonable to us. We have therefore written, to Our Esteemed Mother that as she has herself reached Surat with sincere intention, her *ḥajj* has been approved (by God). There is a likelihood that a party of the Portuguese, thinking of the money and assemblage (accompanying her) might obstruct the passage, and so vexation and trouble might be caused to her. That would really be vexation for us. It is (a matter of) protecting one's honour, a matter regarding one's good repute (*sharīfī*). Let it not happen that an indecorous incident occurs, and that news spreads through the world. Her/Their[1] going this time is not at all proper; the voyage can be undertaken next year, at some other time.

When he (Qulīch Khān) learns of the contents of this *farmān*, he should so endeavour keep (the journey) in suspense, which this time is better. Let him put into effect what has been written above (date omitted).

[1] *Īshān* here can refer to the Queen Mother as well as the entire party of the imperial ladies who were going with her.

C

Akbarnāma, BL, MS Add. 27, 247, f. 297a–b

23 *Ilāhī*/A.H. 986=AD 1578

Since His Majesty approved of the sincerity, good faith, and obedient demeanour of Sultan Khwāja , it was reported to His Majesty that out of a yearning (to see His Majesty) he is coming to the court. His Majesty on the Day Khūr, Eleventh Dī Month Ilāhi, corresponding to Monday 22 Shawwal (22 December 1578), went out for a hunt, so that pleasure may be obtained from hunting, while his (Sulṭān Khwāja) good faith and sincerity may receive greater credit, that [to receive him] His Majesty went out into the country. Sulṭān Khwāja ... first of all tendered to His Majesty the ladies' (*Begamān*) joy-increasing greetings and then conveyed the prayers of the great men and saints of that land (Arabia), conveying their words of greetings to the ruler of the realm of spirit (the Emperor), and gave with proper details a statement of the distribution of charities and the fulfilment of wishes thereby of various groups of people. He also presented the precious commodities of that land, such as Arabian horses, etc. Of the strange incidents that transpired the Khwāja related that during the time the ship was going on its voyage, one night a child fell from the *satbās* (?) of the ship into the sea, and the sound of his cries came for quite some time. With the wind blowing into the sails, the ship was set on a speedy sail. Out of kindness, the Khwāja sent out a boat (*sunbak*), with attendants, since despite the speed of the ship the sound of the cries came still. Assuredly [they felt], there is some reason for it. Though no one believed [rescue] possible, they took out the boat. The people on the ship lost hope (even for the boat). Out of care (for it), a lamp was lighted—though this is not the custom on board ship, in order to avoid a large beast pursuing it—in order to guide the sailors (*khallāṣis*) of the boat back to the ship. After some time the sailors (*mallāḥs*) returned, with the child safe and sound. Another event he reported was from which from the port of Surat that we sailed from up to Jedda we accompanied the Begams' ship, and our ship never got separated from it. Such a thing seldom occurs. The Khwāja was further elevated by imperial favours on this occasion.

D

Blochet Sup. Pers. 482, f. 168b

Another (*parwancha*): if it happens that the Portuguese raise the question that the pass (*qaul,* 'cartas') had been given for the ship that had been laden at the port of Ghoga, where has the pass for this ship come from? He is to answer that when Nawwāb Khān-i 'Ā'ẓam ('Azīz Koka) had wanted that he should set on (return) voyage from Jeddah on his own ship, all the merchants cried out, 'you are taking your ship with a pass (*qauli*) empty, when you do not need a pass, since you can go on Portuguese ships' (no date).

E

Blochet Sup. Pers. 482, f. 170a–b

Parwāna of Nawwāb Ṣādiq Muḥammad Khān to the Captain of Daman

The chief of notables, select of the age, the renovator of the customs of the Divine Spirit, Captain of Daman, is informed that the ship known as *Ṣādiqī*, which is owned by my *sarkār* (i.e., by me) had gone to Tarapur and there ran aground. It is proper that good care and great effort are taken to protect her and the goods that are aboard her. Let him so act that the bond of friendship is not snapped, and no harm comes from your men, and so endeavour that the ship returns safely to the port of Surat. Please understand with full assurance that if the bond of friendship is snapped over that ship, I will write to my son of good fortune, Muḥammad Dost, that he should march to Daman taking with him the troops of Surat and *sarkār* Baroch, and I will myself march from here (Ahmadabad?). Do not please do anything which may end in remorse, and for a small thing you lose your whole territory. In this matter no more need be said. Dated: 9 Muharram 1003 (24 September 1594).

F

Blochet Sup. Pers 428, ff. 167b–168a

Parwāncha

Written: The high one among the select, of good faith and sincerity, Mahābat Khān, assured of favour of attention (from us) should know that the report ('arẓdāsht) he had sent has been received, and the contents have been comprehended. He had written, 'The letter of the (Portuguese) viceroy (*Bazri*) that he has written to Nawwāb Qudsī Alqāb and Nawwāb Nāmdārī is to the effect that he has written to the Captain of Daman to return all the goods and cargo of the ship. Do send that letter so that, by giving it to the Captain of Daman, the goods of the ship can be recovered. One store-keeper (*taḥwīldār*) should be sent from amongst the staff, so that whatever belongs to the goods and cargo of the ship should be handed over to him'. The

Viceroy's letter has been sent, and Farīd Phaluri, the Keeper (*taḥwīldār*) of the cargo, has also been sent. He should hand over whatever belongs to the goods and cargo of the ship to Farīd Phalaurī. Rāgho has also been posted, so that he writes in detail whatever goods and cargo is handed over to the [designated] keeper. It is necessary that he should, persuading the Captain (of Daman), make all efforts that the cargo and goods are recovered soon. Now there remains nothing more to be said, except that he must make efforts to recover the goods ...[Promises to look into the flight into Mughal territories of a slave and *sarnāī* (a hautbois player?)]. Dated 7 Jumada 11, 1003 (17 January 1595).

G

Blochet Sup. Pers. 132 (Order)

His Highness, of High Titles, Good Fortune, Elevated Position (name omitted) has sent Maḥram Khān to Sūrat, in order that in regard to the ship of the sarkar of His Highness that is being prepared for a voyage to a suitable port, he and the honoured brother Khwājagi Jīū,[2] after inspecting the ship, should decide whether this year that ship can go on a voyage to Jedda or not. If they think that it can be ready by the arrival of the (sailing) season and it can go on its voyage to Jedda, that would be good. In that case, he (the addressee) should, for the ship *Akbarshāhī*, buy cargo for Achhi (Acheh). But if it is not possible for that ship to go to the port of Jeddah this coming season, he should buy cargo for the ship *Akbarshāhī* accordingly (i.e., for a voyage to Jeddah/Red Sea). End of our Message. Post-script: A storekeeper (*taḥwīldār* will be arriving soon (Date and Year missing).[3]

[2] Out of politeness the reference to the Khwaja is preceded by *khuddām* (servants) of *nawwab* prefacing name of noble or *bandagan* that of king.

[3] So stated in text.

15

Mughal Shipping at Surat in the First Half of Seventeenth Century

There is considerable interest in Indian shipping during the sixteenth and seventeenth centuries. The researches of Tapan Raychaudhuri, Ashin Das Gupta, M.N. Pearson, and Arsaratnam, have contributed richly to our understanding of the extent and nature of Indian participation in the overseas trade.[1] The Mughal emperor himself, princes and princesses, as well as nobles felt little hesitation in participating in overseas trade. This naturally meant their building and owning ships to carry their cargo as well as the cargo of other merchants and passengers. Such state and aristocratically owned shipping formed a distinct part of Indian shipping, which was of a considerable size.[2]

Till now our knowledge of seventeenth-century Indian shipping has come mainly from European sources especially the records of English East India Company.[3] The information in Persian works so far studied has been sparse and in aggregate small.[4] It is, therefore, in the nature of a rarity when very interesting information on Indian shipping is found in a collection of Mughal documents, the unique

[1] Ashin Das Gupta, *Indian Merchants and the Decline of Surat*, Wiesbaden, 1979; M.N. Pearson, *Merchants and Rulers in Gujarat*, Berkely, 1976; *Coastal Western India*, Delhi, 1981; Ashin Das Gupta and M.N. Pearson eds., *India and the Indian Ocean 1500–1800*, Calcutta, 1987; Satish Chandra, ed., *Indian Ocean*, Delhi, 1987.

[2] Cf. A.J. Qaisar, 'Merchant Shipping in India during the 17th Century', *Medieval India—A Miscellany*, Vol. II, 1972

[3] *Letters Received by the East India Company from its Servants in the East 1607–17*, 16 vols., Vol. I Danvers; Vols. II–VI, edited by W. Foster, London, 1896–1912; W. Foster, ed., *English Factories in India*, 13 vols., Oxford, 1906–27.

[4] The *Anīsul Ḥajāj*, transcript in Library of Department of History, AMU, a work of Aurangzeb's time may be considered an exception.

manuscript of which is preserved in Bibliotheque Nationale Paris, (Blochet, supp. Pers. 482). An unknown official at Surat in 1647 (to judge from the last date found in the collection) brought together numerous documents of all kinds, principally relating to Surat, and of the reigns mainly of Jahāngīr and Shāhjahān (although it also contains a few documents of Akbar's time as well). From this collection, first introduced to Indian scholars by B.R. Grover at the Delhi session of the Indian History Congress, 1961, I have selected some documents relating to shipping at Surat, not hitherto examined, and have translated them in the 'Appendix'. These deal with three Mughal ships, the *Shāhī*, the *Ganjāwar*, and the *Sāḥibī*.

These documents are not the only ones concerned with Indian ships in this collection. One comes across a number of ships that are not mentioned in other sources, such as the *Ṣādiqī* of Akbar's noble, Ṣādiq K͟hān, wrecked off Daman (f. 17a–b), the *Samandar Nāyak*, being repaired at Ghogha in 1624 (f.125a) and the *Shukōhī* and the *K͟hozrī* that were abandoned at Surat Bar and from which twelve guns were taken in 1646 (Doc. No. 7).

Bāyazīd Bayāt who took ship for *ḥajj* pilgrimage from Surat in the 1570s gives an account of the ships crew, which corroborates the information given in the *Ā'īn-i Akbarī*[5] since he mentions the *nāk͟huda* (captain) the, *mu'allim* (navigator), the *ṭandīl* (head-sailor), and the *k͟hallāṣīs* (sailors) aboard the two ships on which he travelled.[6] The documents here translated for the first time mention some other officers serving on the ship, namely, *dārog͟ha* (supervisor), *mushrif* (accountant), *taḥwīldār* (treasurer or store-keeper), *qābiẓ-i māl* (cargo master), and clerks (Doc. No. 2).

Of the terms used in the documents is *naul*. This meant the freight charged on the cargo; and besides this the passengers were to pay fare (*kirāya*) and charges for carrying provisions on journey (*āẕūqa*), (Doc. No. 13). On the imperial ships the rates for *naul* (freight) were sanctioned under certain regulations. Usually the captain and crew of the ship as well as other officials such as the *dārog͟ha* and the *mushrif* were appointed by Prince Shāhjahān himself when he owned the ship (Doc. Nos 2 and 3). On her ship *Ṣāhibī*, Princess Jahān Ārā once left the selection of the captain and crew to her officials (Doc. No. 13),

[5] *Ā'īn*, Vol. I, pp. 202–3.

[6] *Taẕkira-i Ḥumāyūn-wa-Akbar*, edited by H. Hosain, Calcutta, 1941, pp. 353–6.

though the next year she made the appointment of the *dārogha* of the ship herself (Doc. No. 14).

The Mughal emperor seems to have kept himself well informed about the affairs of his ships, received not only the dispatches and reports sent by the officials responsible for the ship but also from the regular official news reports sent from various places. Thus Shāhjahān learnt from the news report of Surat the real cause of the loss of the *Shāhī* (Doc. No. 5). He similarly learnt about the arrival of the *Ganjāwar* at Surat from Jedda with some horses aboard from the newswriter's report (Doc. No. 10).

The emperor also gave detailed instructions about the loading of the cargo, spaces allotted to the various merchants such as reserving *dabosa* (a cabin below the highest deck)[7] exclusive chamber on the ship under the deck) and sanctioning the rates for *naul* (freight). But the emperor was practical enough to insist that decisions about the time of dispatch of the ships and cargo should be made by local officials on the advice of experienced merchants (f. 83b). The advice of the merchants was so much respected that the emperor rescinded Jahān Ārā's order to send her own ship *Ṣāhibī* to Jedda, and ordered that, since going by merchant's advice, Jedda could not provide a sufficient market for two such large vessels as *Ṣāhibī* and *Ganjāwar*, the former should set sail for Mocha.

We learn that the imperial ships also made voyages to South-east Asia (f. 182b). English records confirm this, for Methwold wrote in June 1636 that a 'lesser ship belonging to the king' was nominated to make the voyage to Achin.[8]

The documents that I have translated in the Appendix provide us with interesting details of three ships, the *Shāhī*, originally owned by Shāh Jahān when prince and becoming an imperial ship with his accession; the imperial ship *Ganjāwar*; and Jahān Ārā's own ship *Ṣāhibī*. We are lucky to have references to these ships in English records as well. As a result, we are now able to reconstruct rudimentary 'life-histories' of all the three vessels: in the case of *Shāhī*, we have the narrative of her complete life from construction to loss.

[7] *Bahar-i 'Ajam*, s.v. *dabosa*, describes it as 'the chamber in a ship or vessel below the *'arsha*, occupied by the captain's wife or women of the ship's passengers'. As for *'arsha* it is defined (s.v.) as 'the elevated place provided in a ship for accommodating rich persons.' Bāyazīd's account (p.356) shows that *dabosa* was a cabin where men could meet in safety.

[8] *EFI, 1634–6*, p. 255.

I offer below a summary of our information on all the three vessels.

The Shāhī

The *Shāhī* owned by Prince Khurram was constructed before 1617.[9] When the construction began at Surat the *desāis*, *muqaddams*, and peasants were instructed by an official (most probably Jamāl Khān, the *mutaṣaddī* of Surat)[10] to supply timber for the ship, being promised good prices. Those holding state funds were asked to go to the forest and cut and send timber either overland or by water (Doc. No. 1). Soon after the ship being built, it was named the *Shāhī* by Prince Khurram, now holding the title of Shāhjahān, who at that time was the governor of Gujarat. 'Shahi' was perhaps chosen as an allusion to the title 'Shah Jahan', this being a unique privilege not accorded to any of the other princes who only bore the title of Sulṭān. The *dārogha*, mushrif, and *taḥwīldār* (treasurer of the ship) were appointed according to the *ḥasbu-l ḥukm*, and the two officials on the spot took the opportunity to appoint one each of their own clerks for watch and ward and keeping of records, and requested the prince to confirm these appointments. The prince duly confirmed them but also gave permission to the officials to appoint others whom they considered suitable (Doc. No. 2). Later on Muhammad Parkār was appointed captain of the ship (Doc. No. 3).

In 1619, the *Shāhī* 'the greate shippe' was on its way back to Surat from Jedda, and the merchants were hopeful that she would soon make another voyage to the same port. The English planned to detain the ship in order to compel Shāhjahān to lift the embargo he had imposed on their Red Sea trade.[11] They apparently did not succeed in this and she not only reached Surat safely in August, 1623, but Captain Hall was obliged to 'give attendance' at the ship. She seems to have been the only ship that made profitable voyages to Jedda.[12] On a subsequent voyage to the Red Sea, in September–October 1623, the English factors again sought permission to seize here in order to obtain release of their compatriots, though they were not sure if she was to

[9] On its voyage in 1617 the English claimed to have rescued the *Shāhī* from pirates, *EFI, 1618–21*, p. 127, and *Letter Received*, Vol. II, p. 173 and c.

[10] Jamāl Khān who is mentioned (ff. 181a–1833b) is reported to be the Governor of Surat in 1618–19 in *EFI, 1618–21*, p. 100.

[11] *EFI, 1618–21*, p. 113; and Br. Mus. Add. 405 (Hari Vol. 43, A, 4); see also *EFI, 1618–21*, pp. 176–7.

[12] The Shahee 'shee onlie reforms from Judda rich', Ibid., pp. 253, 265.

return that year.[13] She did return and was captured along with the *Ganjāwar* in December 1623.[14] Soon after a compromise between the Mughal officials and the English was affected, and the ship was released and accounts settled.[15]

The *Shāhī* attained the status of an imperial ship when its owner became the emperor in 1628. The ship not only made voyages to the Red Sea ports but also went to the 'Ādil Shāhī port Danda Rajauri where the English reported it in March 1628. It is then said to be 'drawing 25 feet'.[16]

At Surat, in 1629, the *Shāhī* required repairs and in April 1629 an imperial agent, Malik Muḥammad, was deputed to purchase the material needed for the purpose. The prices paid for the material were to be certified by the qāẓī wherever available, or otherwise by Saiyid Muhammad, the customer (*mutaṣaddī*) (Doc. No. 4).

In March 1629, Nicholas Sharp while on sea reported that he had seen 'the *Shāhī* of Surat' and six frigates, which brought letters warning that a Portuguese squadron was looking for the Indian ships.[17] Subsequently, the Mughals asked the Dutch and the English to seek her and protect her against the Portuguese, and escort her to Surat.[18] The English, keen to appease the Mughal officials and Surat merchants, made some endeavour, but could not trace the ship for quite some time. The merchants and the Mughal authorities were worried since the *Shāhī* was 'most richly fraught' and the 'greater' ship was bringing from Mocha 'wealth far surpassing the others'. She was sighted in December 1630, and she was followed by the Portuguese frigates off Daman.[19] The *Shāhī*, does not seem to have reached Surat that year because the English search for her continued in 1631.[20] In November 1632, it safely arrived at the Surat Bar and Captain Bangham went aboard the ship.[21]

[13] 'Of which there is some doubt', Ibid., p. 267.

[14] Ibid., p. 340.

[15] Ibid., *1634–6*, p. 252.

[16] Ibid., *1624–9*, p. 253.

[17] Ibid., p. 362.

[18] Ibid., *1630–3*, p. 49.

[19] Ibid., pp. 46, 52, 56, 58, 64, 72. The Portuguese threat was 'menacing' and the English were reluctant to trace and protect the ship, but they deceived the officials and merchants at Surat who were 'under the impression that the English intend to sail in search of the *Shāhī*'.

[20] Ibid., p. 1631.

[21] Ibid., p. 245.

The *Shāhī* was a 'vessel of immense bigness' and was held to be one of the prime ships of Surat. In June 1636, it was first nominated to go on voyage to Jedda at a formal function attended by the English, but in September, it was still being prepared for the voyage.[22]

We come to know from an undated *farmān* of Shāhjahān to Ḥakīm Masīḥ-uz Zamān, the governor of Surat (appointed to that post in 1637), that the *Shāhī* sank off port of Danda Rajapuri. The emperor came to know of it not only from the Ḥakīm's letter but also through the news report sent by the news reporter of Surat. The latter reported that the ship was sent on voyage after seventy days had passed after the beginning of the shipping year (*Nauroz-i Daryāi*). The emperor censured Masīḥ-uz Zamān for the loss of the vessel, remarking that sending this kind of a vessel so late in effect meant sinking it (Doc. No. 5). The sinking of the *Shāhī* is reported also in the English records.[23]

The emperor issued a separate *farmān* to Adil Shah, enjoining him to make his governor return whatever cargo he had taken from the ship or the merchants back to the merchants and also to try to salvage the ship, promising to meet the expenses incurred (it is not absolutely clear if these latter injunctions are addressed to 'Ādil Shāh or to Ḥakīm Masīḥ-uz Zamān). But there was no possibility of salvaging the ship. The emperor, therefore, simultaneously ordered the construction of two vessels one with a capacity of 10,000 *korīcha* and the other of 8,000 *korīcha* (Doc. No. 5). Unfortunately, there is no means of knowing what a *korīcha* is represented in terms of modern measures of weight or capacity.

The Ganjāwar

It is not possible to say when the imperial ship, *Ganjāwar* was constructed. The first reference to her comes from August 1619 when the English factors mention it as an important Surat ship preparing for the voyage to Mokha.[24] The ship generally plied between Surat and

[22] Ibid., *EFI, 1634–6*, pp. 255, 295.

[23] The English factors at Gambroon in his dispatch dated 13 June 1638 corroborates this report. He says the vessel was dispatched for Mocha from Surat too late in the season. She was trying with haste to reach her destination but encountered a 'violent storme' which drove it to Danda Rajapuri, where it ran aground. There was no loss of life but cargo estimated worth Rs 1,100,000 was lost (*EFI, 1637–41*, pp. 38–9).

[24] Ibid., *1618–21*, p. 113.

Mokha, because in September 1623 she was again ready at Surat to sail for Mokha when the English planned to seize her. They finally succeeded in capturing the vessel in October 1623, and it was still detained by them till December 1623.[25] But soon thereafter, the hostilities with the Mughals ended and the *Ganjāwar* with her cargo and money was handed over to the governor of Surat and a receipt obtained.[26]

In March 1626 the same vessel was being loaded under the scrutiny of an official Āqā Jamāl, whose certificate that the ship was duly loaded and properly prepared was required by the Mughal authorities (Doc. No. 6). In April 1629 it was given to the Queen (Mumtāz Mahal) along with the instruments, valuables, drugs, and material. It was actually handed over to the representative of Āqā Jamāl, and a receipt taken (Doc. Nos.4 and 7).[27] The ship was also ordered to go on voyage soon though the destination is not mentioned (Doc. No. 7). The official *Mutaṣaddī* of Surat?) was asked in December 1629 to guard the ship against fire or any other harm and not to let strangers come near it (Doc. No. 8).

Presumably, after the death of Mumtāz Maḥal, it returned to the emperor's formal possession. Sometime before 1642 it is found to be directly under imperial management. Two *dustaks* addressed to *ūparī* (apparently, from context, the control of loading) of the ship reveal that cargo of some merchants being sent upon *horīs* (small boats) was to be loaded aboard it (Doc. Nos. 9 and 10). In 1643 it came back from Jedda, some horses being brought on it. It was soon to go to Jedda again and the emperor sanctioned two lakhs of rupees to the *mutaṣaddīs* of Cambay and Ahmedabad, to buy merchandise to be sent aboard the *Ganjāwar* to Jedda. On the return journey the ship was to bring pearls, horses, and other rarities for the emperor, to be procured out of the sale proceeds of the imperial cargo (Doc. No. 11).

In 1644, the vessel seems to have been mainly reserved for carrying the imperial cargo and the cargo of some principal merchants who were to be given concessions and special treatment, such as the use

[25] Ibid., *1622–3*, pp. 264, 267, 341 and 344.

[26] Ibid., *1634–6*, p. 252. However, even ten years after the Mughal officials were not fully satisfied with the settlement of claims.

[27] In Doc. No. 4 the titles are *Nawwāb Qudsī-alqāb Jahānbanī*, and in Doc. No.7, *Nawwāb Qamar Rikāb 'Āliya ul 'Āliya*, which cold only apply to Mumtāz Maḥal.

of the *dabosa* and were to be exempted from paying the freight on their own goods. Other merchants recommended by them were to be allowed to put their cargo on board but at full rates. She was then sailing to Jedda (Doc. No. 12).

In January 1646, the ship needed repairs as her *ṭonk* (prow)[28] became unstable and the elevation was found to be insufficient. She was duly repaired and 5,000 *maḥmūdīs* spent on the work (Doc. No. 13).

The vessel was a very sturdy one and received commendation from Shāhjahān that she always came back safe whenever she went on voyage, (Doc. No. 11). We last hear of her in October 1650 when she was intercepted by the frigates of the King of Persia on her way to Basra.[29] There were hostilities, then, between the Mughal empire and Persia over Qandahar at the time, and there is a likelihood that *Ganjāwar* was not restored to the Mughal government.

The Ṣāhibī

The *Ṣāhibī* was constructed by Princess Jahān Ārā at Surat, and was clearly named after herself, since she was known as Begam Ṣāhib. Shāhjahān in a *farmān* in October–November 1643, noting that the construction of the ship was now complete, orders the officials at Surat to send the ship on voyage in the same shipping season (Doc. No. 11).

Princess Jahān Ārā left the selection of captain, navigator, and cargo-master to the officials (Doc. No.15). The princess seems to have decided to use the ship with an eye to profit as well as to assist *ḥajj* traffic. When the *Ṣāhibī* was preparing for her first voyage, the Princess by her order, on 29 October 1643, reserved the ship for pilgrims to Mecca and Medina, and ordered that every year fifty *koni* of rice should be sent by the ship for distribution among the destitute and needy of Mecca. The pilgrims were exempted from paying the fare, as well as the charges on provisions on journey and freight on their own goods. However, the princess warned that the pilgrims should not be allowed to carry the goods of merchants in their names.

The ship was ordered not to set sail without taking merchants and their cargo, though the *naul* (freight) collected from them was to be

[28] The Hindi word *ṭonk* literally means 'a beak, a bill' (J.T. Platts, *Dictionary of Urdu, Classical Hindi and English*, p.30). In relation to a ship it must, therefore, mean the prow.

[29] *EFI, 1646–50*, p. 324.

given away in alms. The vessel was also to carry the cargo of the princess worth ten to fifteen thousands of rupees; the cargo was to consist of goods in demand at Jedda and these goods were to be procured during the rainy season. The treasurer of the ship was to keep in his custody the amount received from freight as well as the principal and profit received from sale of the princess's cargo at Jedda. The ship was also to carry 50 *gonis* (or 1674 kg) of rice for free distribution at Mecca on behalf of the princess.[30] The captain of the ship was also under instructions to bring as many horses as he was able to procure at Jedda (Doc. No. 15).

The next year (August 1644) Jahān Ārā appointed Muhammad Rafi' the *darogha* of the ship in place of the previous incumbent Mīr Ghiyās. Some other officials of the ship were also changed by her. She ordered that the older officials hand over charge and accounts to the new *darogha* and *mushrif*; and only when the charge was given over to their satisfaction were the previous officers to be relieved and sent to the court (Doc. No. 14).

The *Ṣāhibī* remained in service till 1663, the year in which we last hear of her. In July 1663, the English at Mokha were advised to board her for Surat after closing down their trade there.[31]

The lifespans of these three leading Mughal ships were thus as follows:-

Shāhī	1617	21 years
Ganjāwar	1619–50	31 years
Ṣāhibī	1643–63	20 years

Given the dates of construction (or in the case of *Ganjāwar* the first notice), the first two ships were almost certainly 'junks', and so of considerable size. This may be the reason for the complaint (Doc. No.13) that the *Ganjāwar* was of low elevation, its *tonk* or prow being so low as to be struck by waves. The *Ṣāhibī* built in 1643 might, perhaps, have been affected by European models, for 'an unchronicled revolution in the Indian ship-building industry' took place after the 1630s, with a shift from junks to European-style ships.[32]

[30] A *gonī* is a said in the document itself to weigh 20 *man-i Shahjahānī*, and the latter was equal to 33.48 kg in weight, *ASMI* , pp.421–2).

[31] *EFI, 1661–4*, p. 191.

[32] Cf. Irfan Habib, 'The Technology and Economy of Mughal India', *IESHR*, Vol. XVII, No. 1, pp.14–5.

Appendix

Doc. No. 1 ff. 159 a–b
(*Parwāna*) To the desāīs, *muqaddams* and peasantry (*ri'aya*) of the *pargana* Telari [*sarkār* Surat] (from Jamāl Khān, 'Customer' of Surat) (1618–19).

The construction of an auspicious (*mubārak*, an epithet for ships used for *ḥajj* pilgrimage), new ship has auspiciously begun. Now [therefore] timber is required. Whatever amount of timber is available, should be sent to Surat by all possible means, of which information shall be sent in writing. In case the source of supply is near the inlets of sea, they should inform in writing so that I may send a *horī* (rect. *taurī*), (*khārī-hā)*, for there is great need of timber. Whoever will provide timber at the earliest would receive appropriate price and be allowed due credit. Whoever has money of the (Customer's) *sarkār* in his hands should be sent to the forest to cut timber and send it immediately. When, God willing, the road for carts are open; they will load carts (with timber) and sent them to Surat. Much attention must be paid in the matter of timber.

Doc. No. 2, ff. 181a–183b.
[Memorandum of the *dīwān* of *sarkār* Surat to Prince Shāhjahān and his replies thereto, c 1618–19.]
Memorandum: the humble of disciples, X, submits to His Highness' court as follows: This humblest of disciples has been appointed to the post of *dīwān* of the *sarkār* of Surat and his entire attention is devoted to the performance of his duties, in such manner, God willing, that his sincerity, honesty, and loyalty can come to the notice of His Highness....

Item: Submitted: On the auspicious ship, that is being newly constructed, *darogha* (superintendent) X, and *mushrif* (accountant) X, (the new one, that has been appointed by Khwāja X according to the *ḥasbu-l ḥukm*), the *taḥwīldār* (store-keeper) X are all at work. For watch and guard, so that (there is no) loss or destruction, one clerk of this servant along with a clerk of [Jamāl] Khān and X should be appointed so that they should maintain the records. Orders solicited. Also solicited: The name of the new ship may please be given by His Highness. Order: If Jamāl Khān and he considers the person X as proper for this service let him continue as heretofore; otherwise let him be reverted to the *sarkār*, and whomever they think suitable they should appoint. [Further] ordered: The ship has been named *Shāhī*. Also ordered that one *muḥarrir* (writer) of Jamāl K͟hān and one of the petitioner should supervise this undertaking. If they consider it advisable they should ask the *mushrif* of the customs for [advice on] how to fill the post of *mushrif* of that [undertaking].

Item: Submitted: For managing the affairs of the port and the voyages of the ships there are no firm regulations, and divergences occur in respect of *naul* and expenses of ships such as on *sarail* (?) *aryad* (?) *qual* (European pass), etc., and later the imperial auditors (*mustaufiān-i 'uẓẓām*) raise objections. It is requested that the order be issued that in this regard whatever is certified under the seals of Jamāl K͟hān, and this servant and officials be accepted by the auditors who should not object, so that the officers may, with due honesty and integrity, carry out their duties. Order: Whatever in the regard is certified by Jamāl K͟hān and him, should be accepted by the auditors, who should not claim recovery on account of differences between expenses of different years.

Item: Submitted: Since the basis of prosperity and profit of the port is from the coming and going of the ships and in respect of such commerce there is no regulation and permanence, especially in matters of the sea and the calamities, that God forbid, occur. The officials of *sarkār* Surat and the port have on the advice of the merchants sent His Highness' ships and cargo to Arabia, South-east Asia, etc. If it is so ordered, hereafter [too] relying on the protection of His Highness, the officials may send ships and cargo to Arabia, etc. Order: Relying on royal protection, ships should be sent on voyage and similarly cargo in whatever way and to whatever amount that they deem suitable. God willing, they would reach [their destinations] safely.

Doc. No. 3, ff. 163a–b
Parwāna (of appointment) of captain (*Nā-k͟hudā*) of the ship (*Shāhī*) c. 1618–37.
On the recommendation of loyal servants, the noble captain ('Umdat-un Nawak͟hīd), Captain Muḥammad Parkār, has been appointed the captain of the auspicious *Shāhī*. The merchants, passengers, and crew of the said ship should consider him their permanent captain and not deviate from his instructions and guidance which shall be always

conducive to rectitude, economy, and administration. The conduct and manner of the noble captain should be to so endeavour sincerely and honestly as to contribute to the advantage and prosperity of the imperial establishment (*Sarkār-i Khāṣa Sharīfa*) and keep contended and satisfied the crews and persons on the ship. That would be put to his credit.

Doc. No. 4, ff. 122b–123a
Parwāncha:
Sayid Muḥammad at Surat is to know that some material is required for the repairs of the auspicious ship *Shāhī*, which has been attached to the *sarkār* of Her Highness, the Queen. Whatever material is needed and has been purchased by Her Highness' agent the honourable Malik Muḥammad, the price thereof should be ascertained and the record of purchase be certified by the *qāẓī* under his seal, wherever he be. He should not spare himself in giving him [Malik Muḥammad] assistance, deeming service to the prince a compulsory obligation. Dated 27 Farwardīn 2 Ilāhī = 16 April 1629.

Doc. No. 5, ff. 59a–61a
Farmān of Shāhjahān regarding the sinking of the *Shāhī* to Ḥākim Masīḥ-uz-Zamān, governor of Surat (1635–8).

......

With regard to the sinking of the ship that was on voyage to the port of (Danda Rajauri) in the estuary of..., what has been reported by the addressee, has been noted. It makes one wonder how with the efficiency and competence of the loyal officer in these matters, it happened that at a time that seventy days had passed after the *nauroz-i dariyāī* (beginning of shipping year), he yet sent on voyage that kind of a ship, as has come to be known from the news report of the town of (Surat). We have given the news report to the *Sipāh Sālār* [Asaf Khān] so that he may sent it to the addressee. Really, to send on voyage this kind of vessel at such a time amounts to sinking that vessel. Anyhow, a *farmān* has been issued to 'Adil Khān that whatever from the cargo of the merchants, the governor of Danda Rajauri has taken from the ship or from those merchants, the addressee should take it from him and give to the merchants. If possible, he should attempt to bring out the ship from the sea and whatever expenses are incurred on this should be paid out of the funds of the imperial treasury. If the ship is salvaged safely, he should carry out whatever repairs are needed and prepare it for voyage in the coming season. If this cannot be achieved, let it be deemed a sacrifice for imperial good fortune.

That loyal officer should now construct a vessel with a capacity of 10,000 *korīcha* at port X for the imperial establishment. Further according to terms of a *ḥasbu-l ḥukm* (separately issued), officers will construct a vessel of a capacity of 8,000 *korīcha*.

Doc. No. 6, f. 129b
Parwāncha
The honourable Sayyid Muhammad is informed that the petition that he sent has been received, along with the log, which has been seen. He had written concerning *Ganjāwar* that 4,000 *korīcha* have been loaded aboard the ship and that he is striving day and night that the ship be sent on voyage as desired. It is certain that he has not spared himself in performing the duties of his office, nor would he do so in future. He would receive credit however, only when the ship is loaded as desired and set sail. The honourable Āqā Jamāl would report w̱hen the loaded ship starts on its voyage. He should so endeavour that Āqā Jamāl writes to the writer (at an early date) that the loaded ship has set sail. Dated 2 Farwardīn R.Y. 21=22 March 1626.

Doc. No. 7, ff. 125b–126a
Parwāncha
The honourable Saiyid Muḥammad [at Surat] should know. The ship *Ganjāwar* has been attached to the establishment of Her Highness [the Queen]. The said ship along with whatever is on it, instruments, drugs, and materials, should be handed over to the representative of the honourable Āqā Jamāl and receipt be taken. He should not spare himself in assisting him. It has also been decided that till the time that this ship starts on its voyage, cargo should not be loaded on any other ship. The rates (*dastūr*) (of charges for carrying cargo) should be such as have been approved. Dated 24 Āẕar R.Y.2=16 December 1629.

Doc. No. 8, f. 123a
Parwāncha
The honourable Saiyid Muḥammad may know that he had written previous to this, recommending (assistance to) the ship *Ganjāwar*. In assisting the agents of Āqā Jamāl he should not spare himself. He should so endeavour that the ship should set out on its voyage soon. He should be careful in providing watch and ward and be vigilant

against fire and not let anyone light a fire close to the ship, or for any reason harm the ship. The intention is that he should be aware of friend and foe, and not let any stranger go near the ship. He should not make any mistake in guarding the ship. What more need be written. Dated 2 Dī R.Y. 2=23 December 1629.

Doc. No. 9, f. 130a
Dustak: Ūparī (official in charge of loading ship?) of the *Gunjāwar* should know that one *jhalla* (?) of 'Abdul Wahāb and Mānikji according to the regulation of *malīkh*,[33] has been dispatched for being loaded aboard the auspicious ship. Let it be received. Dated 24 Ẕīqad, R.Y. 16, 1052 = 13 February 1643.

Doc. No. 10, f. 129b
Dustak: Ūparī of the ship *Gunjāwar* should know that one *horī*[34] with cargo belonging to Hari Dar, Donki, Hāniyā, Dabash, 'Azīz Beg, and Mullā Jalāl has been loaded and dispatched. It should be checked with record and [the cargo] loaded aboard the ship. Dated ẓīlhij, 1052 A.H., R.Y. 16 (= March 1643).

Doc. No. 11, ff. 37a–38a
[*Farmān*] The Sayyids, deserving of Our favour Mir Sharfuddīn Husain and Mīr Ḥāshim, honoured by royal grace, should know that it came to be known recently from the news report of the port of Surat that the ship *Gunjāwar* that had sailed to Jedda has safely returned... Information about Mirza Ibrāhīm has been received from them [those aboard *Ganjāwar*] and from the ships that had voyaged (to Jedda) from Surat.... The news reporter wrote that five horses have also come aboard the said ship. He should see the horses and whichever is worth buying he should buy and dispatch (to the court).

Two lakh of rupees were sanctioned to the *mutaṣaddis* (officials) of Ahmadabad, Cambay, etc., for the purchase of goods (to be sold in Arabia). They must have made the purchases by now. The said amount (in form of goods for sale) should be taken by Shaikh 'Abd-ur Raḥīm and out of it one lakh of rupees have been set apart for distribution

[33] The *A'īn*, Vol. I, p.203, describes *malīkh* as the compartments into which a ship was divided for accommodating passengers and cargo.

[34] Hindustanī *horī* 'a small flat-bottomed boat' (J.T. Platts, *Dictionary of Urdu, Classical Hindi and English*, Delhi, 1977, p.241).

among the indigent and needy ones of Mecca and Medina, and out of the remaining one lakh of rupees pearls, horses, and other rarities should be purchased.

By the time, Shaikh 'Abdur Raḥīm and Shaikh 'Abd-us Ṣamad arrive, the honourable Sayyid (addressees) should repair the *Ganjāwar* which is the best of ships and whenever it has set on a voyage has returned safely, and make it ready [to sail] so that when the above-named persons, along with the goods and cargo should reach there and board it and the season arrives, the ship sets sails at the very beginning of the season.

It has also been ordered that they should also strive hard that the ship *Ṣāḥibī* of Our beloved daughter Princess Jahān Ārā that has been constructed should go on voyage this year. Their credit lies in this; let them not be negligent. Dated Sh'ābān, 1053, R.Y. 17=Oct–Nov. 1643. Submission by Disciple and Son [of the Emperor] Muhammad Dārā Shukoh through the humblest disciple Islām Khān.

Doc. No. 12, ff. 28–b

[*Farmān*] During the preparation of this *farmān*, another petition of that loyal servant arrived, and was seen by the Emperor. He had written that the ships that went on voyage from Surat have all returned safely. He has repaired the *Ganjāwar* and made it ready. The moment Shaikh 'Abdur Raḥīm and Shaikh 'Abdus Ṣamad arrive and the cargo of the royal establishment is brought to Surat, he should set the ship on voyage at the very beginning of the shipping season.

(He has further reported that) in the meantime an order from Her Highness Princess Jahān Ārā has been received that the ship *Ṣāhibī* be sent on voyage to the port of Jedda. The merchants are required to constantly loading the ships and setting them sail. Persons who are familiar with the Jedda market say that the cargo of the two ships [*Ganjāwar* and *Ṣāḥibī* cannot be sold in Jedda. It is advisable that one ship should go to Jedda and the other to Mocha. This having been submitted, it is ordered that in case conditions are what the merchants state them to be, the *Gunjāwar*, as ordered earlier by *farmān*, should be sent to the port of Jedda. Shaikh 'Abdur Raḥīm and Shaikh 'Abdus Ṣamad Maḥmūdī should go aboard that ship, the *dabosa* (deck cabin) of the ship should be given to Shaikh 'Abdur Raḥīm and as much of the cargo belonging to the imperial establishment as it can be held should be loaded on the *Ganjāwar*, the rest should be put in another appropriate place (ship?). *Labbas* (?) should be given to Shaikh 'Abdus

Ṣamad, and the *naul* (freight) thereon should be remitted. As for his ('Abdus Ṣamad's) cargo whatever the honourable Sayyids (addresees) may recognize to be his own, should be loaded on the ship, its freight remitted. From amongst the companions and friends of the Shaikh, whomsover wishes to come on board the ship should be allowed to do so, but the freight and *'ushr* (customs) should be realized from them. Freight should also not be similarly demanded on the cargo owned by Shaikh 'Abdur Raḥīm himself. If the auspicious ship *Ganjāwar* gets filled up with the cargo of the imperial establishment and that of Shaikh 'Abdur Raḥīm and Shaikh 'Abdus Ṣamad and their companions, they should consider it sufficient. Otherwise as much of the cargo of the merchants as can be accommodated on board the auspicious ship should be loaded. Let them send it on its voyage, early in the shipping season, to the port of Jedda....

The *Ṣāhibī* should be loaded and sent to the port of Mukha so that the merchants and passengers should reach their destination and gain profit. Dated 27 Shawwāl, 1052, R.Y. 17 = 1052 [miswriting for 1053] = 8 January 1644,

Doc. No. 13, f. 93b
Farmān in response to the petition of 'Abul Qāsim, *diwān* of *sarkār*, containing orders of transfer from his post.

He had reported that the height of the auspicious ship *Ganjāwar* was insufficient and its *tonk* (prow) was low and unstable when hit by the waves. Three 'planks' (*takhta*) were added to the elevation [deck] and the *tonk* was raised higher. Five thousand *maḥmūdīs* were spent on this. This has been commended.

The action in moving twelve guns from the ships *Shukohī* and *Khiẓrī*, which were laying in disuse outside the fort (of Surat) were approved.... Dated 2 Zīlḥijj, 1055 = 19 January 1646.

Doc. No. 14, ff. 20b–21a
[*Nishān* of Princess Jahān Ārā]
The valiant and favour-deserving Sharfuddīn Ḥusain and Mir Hāshim, expecting favours, should know that Muḥammad Rafī' (?) has been appointed the *darogha* of the auspicious ship *Sāhibī*, on the transfer of Mir Ghiyās. They should, as in the past, assist him in all matters concerning the ship and so endeavour that the duly loaded ship may set sail early in the shipping season, and merchants and passengers and the indigent/pilgrims who go aboard this ship should travel safely

and at ease. From the derveshes they should not charge the fare. As for the previous officials as soon as they have cleared their transactions and accounts to the satisfaction of the present *darogha* and *mushrif*, and have that trusty addressee's seal affixed on the report of their period of work, they should be relieved and sent forthwith to the Court. Dated 7 Jumāda 18 R.Y. =11 August 1644.

Doc. No. 15, ff. 35b–36a
[*Nishān* of Jahān Ārā]
The valiant Sayyid Sharfuddīn Ḥusain and the general officials of the auspicious *Ṣāhibī* should know that we have reserved the said ship (*Ṣāhibī*) for the pilgrims to the holy city of Mecca and Medina. They should put aboard the ship as many scholars, Mughal and Hindustani, etc., desirous of going on pilgrimage, as can be accommodated, to send them on voyage from the port of Surat to Jedda, which is the port serving Mecca. The fare from them on their persons, journey provisions, and their own goods should be remitted in accordance with the regulations; but if they enter cargo of merchants under their own names this should not be allowed. Most (of these passengers) will bring *ḥasbu'l ḥukm* certificates from the *dīwān* of Our *sarkār*. Since the ship cannot go without the cargo of the merchants, the Princess orders that they should load the cargo and merchandise of the merchants. We order that the cargo and merchandise of the merchants be also loaded on this ship and the merchants be given accommodation taking *naul* (shipping freight) from them. That amount we wish to be distributed among the destitute and needy. The merchants should be looked after so that they should travel on this auspicious ship safely and at ease, and all people gain advantage from this ship and pray for His Majesty and Us. In loading the cargo, provisions, and passengers, all prudence should be shown so that the ship is sent on voyage quickly. Care should be taken in this matter, and competent men should be appointed as captain (*nākhuda*), navigator (*mu'allim*), cargo-master (*qābiẓ-i māl*), etc. It has been ordered that every year fifty *goni* of rice, each *goni*, being twenty *man-i Shāhjahānī*, should be sent to Mecca aboard the said ship, so that the captain of the ship may distribute it among the derveshes and destitute of that place. Every year ten to fifteen (thousand) rupees should be invested in buying such cargo as they know to be in demand (at Jedda), to be purchased in the rainy season and then put (aboard the ship) for its voyage. This year according to the *ḥasbu'l ḥukm*, the

honourable Mu'izul Mulk was given Rs 20,000 for purchase of goods for Arabia. These goods should be taken from him and (goods worth) fifteen thousand of rupees should be put as cargo on the ship and the remainder be sold, at the port of Surat. The principal and profit along with the proceeds of the freight of the ship, (charged) from the merchants, should be placed in custody of the treasurer (*taḥwīldār*) of the ship, as ordered earlier to be kept in the treasury under the addressee's seal. The captain of the ship should be asked to buy and bring from Mecca as many horses as he can get. He should be careful in managing the ship in all aspects, so that nothing is lost or damaged. He (the addressee) should consider this as a means of getting credit for his service and loyalty so as to be hopeful favours. Dated 15 Sha'bān, 1052, R.Y. 17 (1052 is a misreading for 1053) = 29 October 1643.

16

Travails of a Mercantile Community

Aspects of Social Life at the Port of Surat (Earlier Half of the Seventeenth Century)

Surat was the main port of the Mughal empire during the seventeenth century. It was not only the focal point of the overseas trade of Mughal India to the Red Sea and the Persian Gulf and Europe via the Cape of Good Hope, it also maintained a brisk trade with Southeast Asia, and conducted considerable commerce down the western coast. Oceanic commerce thus naturally dominated the town, and both administration and law had to respond to the needs and problems generated by such dominance. The Mughal imperial government recognizing the special status of the port, permitted modifications in the local administration by appointing particular officials or by assigning special duties to certain officials such as the *mutaṣaddī* ('customer' in English records) of Surat and the *Shāhbandar* (port-master).[1]

Contemporary sources, particularly the records of the European companies, are fairly rich in information on life in seventeenth-century Surat. The material has been explored by Ashin Das Gupta, B.G. Gokhale, Surendra Gopal, and M.J. Mehta.[2] A very vivid picture of the 'Blessed port of the Mughals' has been especially reconstructed by Ashin Das Gupta who had command over the large Dutch material in addition to the English records.[3]

[1] 'Alī Muhammad Khan, *Mi'rāt-i Aḥmadī*, supp. edited by Nawab Ali, Baroda, 1930, pp. 194, 222; also Ibid., Vol. I, pp.260–2. See also Ashin Das Gupta, *Indian Merchants and the Decline of Surat c. 1700–50*, Wiesbaden, 1978, pp. 24–8.

[2] Ibid.; B.G Gokhale, *Surat in the Seventeenth Century*, Bombay, 1978; Surendra Gopal, *Commerce and Crafts in Gujarat, 16th and 17th Centuries,* New Delhi, 1975; M.J. Mehta, 'Some Aspects of Surat as a Trading Centre in the 17th Century', in *IHR*, Vol. I, No. 2, 1974, pp. 247–61.

[3] Ashin Das Gupta, *Indian Merchants and the Decline of Surat, c. 1700–50*, pp. 20–93.

The European material has not however, been supplemented in much of this work by the Persian, which, if not so extensive as the European, is not altogether insignificant. There is, for example, an important collection of Persian documents, mainly relating to Surat, collected by an anonymous Mughal official about the middle of the seventeenth century, now preserved at Bibilotheque Nationale, Paris.[4] This has much that is of interest for any historian of the port.

Besides a number of documents relating to the administration and commerce at Surat, this collection contains documents that shed light on the social life of the town, including marriages, master–servant relations, and disposal of property. For the present study, I have selected here three marriage contracts, one claim for marriage-dower, one divorce settlement and two claims of inheritance by women. Translations of all these documents are given in the Appendix. These documents assume some importance because besides providing information on Surat they shed light on a rather obscure aspect of Mughal-Indian society, namely, the position of urban middle and lower-middle class women and their rights (and plight) as wives.[5]

I

Since marriage is based on contract in Islamic law and as such is customarily evidenced by a written agreement duly signed and witnessed, *nikāhnāma* (marriage contract) may contain certain conditions specific to the particular marriage. In general, the *nikāhnāma* contains the name and parentage of the bride and the groom and specifies the amount of dower (*mihr*) payable to the wife, and whether this payment is to be immediate or deferred.[6] But these marriage agreements coming from Surat go further and specifically lay down certain other conditions in detail that the wives imposed on

[4] MS. Blochet, Supp. Pres. 482. Some of these documents relating to the administration of Surat have been translated and analysed by Farhat Hasan in *PIHC*, Golden Jubilee Session, 1989, pp.284–93; those relating to the Dutch by Jawed Akhtar, ibid., 48th Session, 1987, pp.251-60; and relating to Mughal imperial shipping by me in, ibid., 51st Session, 1990, pp. 308–20 (for the last see Chapter 14).

[5] Rekha Mishra, *Women in Mughal India, 1526–1748*, Delhi, 1867 devotes a chapter to position of middle and lower class women, pp. 129–48, but the information given is sketchy.

[6] For a specimen *nikāhnāma* of this kind, see *Inshā-i Fāi'q*, edited by Mirza Mahdi Ali, Lucknow, 1268 AH, p. 31.

their husbands. Three of these four agreements besides spelling out the amount of marriage-dower (*mihr*), that incidentally appear to be quite substantial in all the three cases, set out four conditions the husbands were to follow. These four conditions were most probably quite commonplace among middle class Muslims in Surat. Doc. No. 1 (dated 1639) indeed characterizes them as 'commonly prevalent among the Muslims' and Doc. No. 3 (of 1639) without spelling them out simply says 'the four conditions that are well known among theologians'. In fact, two illustrative *nikāhnāmas*, one in a collection of documents of Akbar's time and the other in an accountancy manual (*Siyāqnāma*) of Aurangzeb's time also contains precisely these four conditions, which we discuss below.[7]

The first of these conditions imposes monogamy on the husband by denying him the right of a second marriage while married to the present wife. This is an important restriction and shows that there was a general sense that polygamy gravely affected the wife's position. By the second condition the wife was spared from severe beating, at least to the extent that no marks should be left on her body by the stick used! Wife-bashing thus appears to be not an uncommon practice and was not objected to even in the case of women of some status.[8] However, Doc. No. 1 prohibits severe beating unless the wife commits a transgression under the law.

The third condition seeks to provide redress to the wife if deserted for a long duration by the husband without making provision for her maintenance. This problem seems to be typical for a place where quite a few persons were obliged to leave their homes on long and distant voyages. Taking the wife or family along was not always practical (see Kāmrān Beg's advice to his servant Muḥammad Beg, Doc. No.8), though his was not totally rare. Fāṭima's father took his wife and daughter along to Acheh (Doc. No.7) and Muḥammed Beg did send his wife from Hyderabad to Surat with a caravan of merchants

[7] Abu'l Qasim Khan 'Namakin', *Munshāt-i Namakīn*, Aligarh: Lytton Farsiya, 3-26 and 3-27, ff 195b-196a (=selections from this work, ed. Ishtiyaq Ahmad Zilli, pp. 333-4, which drawn from the India Office MS, seems to have more errors than in Aligarh MS); and Munshī Nand Rām, *Siyāqnāma*, litho. Nawal Kishor, Lucknow, 1875, pp.88–9.

[8] Wife-bashing was also common in medieval France where according to Ladurie, even the women of the aristocracy formed no exception (Emmanuel Le Roy Ladurie, *Montaillou*, translated by B. Bray. New York, 1979, pp. 92–3).

(Doc. No.8). All the four agreements impose the obligation on the husband to neither leave the wife nor fail to provide her maintenance for more than a particular period, varying from six solar months (Doc. No.2, probably pre-1637) to one lunar year (Doc. Nos. 3 and 4, the latter dated 1619). In the *Siyāqnāma* contract mentioned above, the maximum period is put at three years.

All the three conditions were to be followed so stringently that a violation of anyone of these entitled the wife to automatic divorce or annulment of marriage. It is, however, not mentioned whether in such circumstances she would be entitled to her dower.

These marriage agreements suggest that the practice of maintaining a slave-girl as a concubine was quite common. The fourth condition imposed was that the husband, could not keep a slave-girl as a concubine. But if he committed a breach of contract in this respect, it was not considered serious enough to entitle the wife to seek automatic annulment of marriage. She was, on the other hand, entitled, upon discovery of her husband's maintenance of a concubine, to take the slave-girl away from her husband and sell her and keep the proceeds in part payment of her *mihr*; she could also deny the slave girl to her husband by gifting her to someone or manumitting her[9] or marrying her off (Doc. No. 1).

Out of these four conditions, three were palpably applicable in the case of women belonging to the middle-class only. These appear in the marriage agreements of 'Lady' Ḥabība whose *mihr* was fixed at three thousand silver rupees of Surat mintage and one gold *dinār* of Mecca (Doc. No.1), of a 'lady' whose *mihr* has been stated as five thousand silver rupees and one gold *dīnār* of Mecca (Doc. No. 2), Bī'Āyisha, fetching a *mihr* of 1,000 gold *Ibrāhīmīs*[10] (Doc. No. 5), and another 'lady', the actual amount of whose *mihr* is not stated, but the currency is in which to be paid is the gold *asharfī* and the titles used for the husband suggest some status (Doc. No. 3). In the case of Mariyam, wife of Muḥammed Jiu, whose daily subsistence allowance was fixed at one *tanka-i murādī* only[11] and two *sārīs* and

[9] Interestingly enough, in the same collection of documents there is a copy of letter of manumission where one lady Mariyam Ji daughter of Aḥmad and wife of Ḥasan Muḥammad manumits a slave-girl of wheatish complexion (ff. 194a–b).

[10] *Ibrāhīmī* was a Turkish gold coin. In 1661 an official price list from Aurangzeb gives its value as Rs15±½ anna (Y.H. Khan, *Selected Waqai' of the Deccan, 1660–1671*, Hyderabad, 1953, p.35).

[11] We may remind ourselves that the lowest wage in the imperial establishment,

two bodices a year, suggesting quite poor circumstances, the only condition in the marriage agreement was that her husband would not leave her for more than a year and also not fail to provide her the maintenance allowance specified above. She was not provided any protection against the possible second wife or the acquisition of a concubine by her husband (these were probably not likely events among poorer people) or against severe beating. The privileges of women thus seem to vary according to their class. One may argue that in the case of Mariyam whose husband Muhammed failed to provide even such a small amount of maintenance to her, the two conditions relating to second marriage and concubine were superfluous. However, the women of Mariyam's class were apparently expected to submit to some level of violence by their husband, for this is not expressly prohibited in her marriage contract.

The poorer class of women had apparently little sense of relief even if the divorce was granted from an impecunious husband. In the case of Mariyam, the *qāẓī* after satisfying himself about the failure of Muḥammad Jīū to keep the terms of contract and give maintenance to his wife, gave his verdict in her favour. Yet she seems still to have agreed to remain his wife because we find two years after the above verdict that a person called Ibrāhīm is now taking surety before the *qāẓī* on behalf of Muḥammad Jīū for his payment to her of maintenance (one *tanka-i murādī* daily and the provision of two *sārīs* and two *kānchulī* or bodices a year) (Doc. no. 4 A of 1621). Perhaps to find a suitable and dependable husband was not so easy for Mariyam and women of her class, and thus the theoretical safeguards provided in the marriage agreements could be of little use. It is also significant that if a husband violated the conditions of contract and divorce ensued, there seems to be no obligation imposed on him to pay the *mihr* upon the break-up of the marriage. On the other hand, if a woman sought divorce from her husband, she could receive it by paying him money—seventy silver *mahmūdīs* for *khula'*(release) being paid and accepted in one case, in front of the *qāẓī* (Doc. No. 6 of 1628).

In the case of people of substance the terms of marriage had value. When Bi 'Āiysha daughter of Āqā Aḥmad and widow of Ḥajji 'Ābdi

under Akbar, was 2–3 *dāms* a day and according to Pelsaert 5 or 6 'tackas' a day at Agra during the 1620s: Moreland and Geyl, *Jahāngiri's India*, Cambridge, 1925, p.60. A *tanka-i murādī* was a copper coin equivalent to a *dām* or at best a double *dām*.

Qirāmānī, proved before the *qāẓī* the claim of her *mihr* of one thousand *Ibrāhīmīs*, he granted her the full right to realize her claim from the property left behind by her husband, wherever that might be found (Doc. No. 5 dated 1613). It appears that the claim of *mihr* had primacy over other claims. The practice of giving *mihr* among Gujarat merchants was so prevalent that even Hindu merchants gave marriage-dower (*mihr*) to their wives.[12]

However, all the widows even of substance were not as fortunate as Bi 'Āiysha. Some faced grave problems after the death of their husbands. How the widow of a merchant suffered at the hand of her husband's senior slave when her husband died at Acheh is narrated in Doc. No. 8. Since Gujarat's commerce with Acheh seems to have ceased about 1615, with a brief revival in 1618 only,[13] the merchant must have died in the early years of Jahāngīr's reign or still earlier. His slave (who was apparently his main business servant) fraudulently took the widow in marriage to himself, against her knowledge or will, so much so that she even tried to commit suicide by taking opium. Even though the king of Acheh wished to punish the slave, the community of Gujarati merchants at Acheh sided with him and coerced the widow to yield. However, back at Surat, her daughter Fāṭima, on reaching majority, persistently asserted her claim to the property of her father seeking to recover it from the slave and his two sons. The decision on the claim is unfortunately not known but the vigour with which she fought her case and the support she enjoyed from the number of people who testified on her behalf is noteworthy.

Another interesting case involving a widow's claim to property is set out in Doc. No. 8 (undated), addressed to Princess Jahānārā to judge from the titles used for the addressee. The complainant was the widow of Muḥammad Beg, a trusted servant of the merchant Kāmrān Beg. The woman originally belonged to Hyderabad. She protests against the action of a slave of Kāmrān Beg who forcibly took into his possession not only the male slaves and slave-girls, and other property of Kāmrān Beg which had been left with her husband at Surat by Kāmrān Beg on his departure for Arabia, but also her husband's own

[12] Sundar Dās Baqqāl (Banyā) son of Mathurā Dās purchased a house in Cambay at a price of 701 'Alamgīrī rupees in 1686 to give it in payment of mihr to his wife Sundar Bai, daughter of Gokul Baqqāl (Cambay Documents, National Archives, Item No. III-5, Doc. No. 8).

[13] Ashin Dasgupta, in *CEHI*, Vol. I, p. 431.

effects left to her against her claim of *mihr*. He had evicted her out of Muḥammad Beg's house as well. In this document, thus, the problem of custody of an absent merchant's property, and the private effects of his factors, is presented to us alongside the claim of a widow for *mihr* and succession to her husband's rights and obligations.

What these documents disclose to us is a little of the social history of merchants and a little of 'women's history'. Altogether they add interesting touches to the reconstruction of the personality of seventeenth-century Surat. They bring to us the instability and inscrutability of overseas commerce for the humbler individuals, of that great port, whom, like so much flotsam and jetsam, it held closely in its thrall.

Appendix

Document No. 1, ff. 201b–202a
Agreement of Marriage

Statement: Whereas the honourable 'Abdullah, son of Ḥajjī Mubārak, sought and took in marriage as wife the chaste, virtuous lady Ḥabība, daughter of X, in lieu of the marriage-dower (*mihr*) of three thousand rupees of Surat mintage, and one *dīnār* of gold, by the weight of Mecca, one-third to be paid forthwith and two-thirds deferred, with four conditions that are commonly prevalent among Muslims. The first condition: that beside the said wife he shall not marry another. The second condition: that the husband shall not beat the wife, without her committing any perfidious transgression of law, in rage and fury, so as to leave marks of the stick visible on any part of her body. The third condition: that the husband shall not leave the wife without her consent, continuously for a lunar year during which period he does not provide maintenance and clothing and his own company. In the event of any one of the three things contemplated coming to pass from her husband's side, she shall make herself by a single act of divorce forbidden (*ḥarām*) to the said husband. The fourth condition: that (if) the said husband keeps a slave-girl as a concubine, according to the custom of concubinage, whatever be the manner in which the aforesaid fact occurs, the aforesaid wife shall be the agent (*wakīla*) on behalf of the said husband (entitled) to sell that slave-girl and take the proceeds in lieu of her marriage-dower (*mihr*), and if she so desires make that slave-girl forbidden (*ḥarām*) to the said husband by manumitting her or by marrying her off or by giving her in gift. The said husband accepts all the conditions in the presence of witnesses. The agent (on behalf of the wife) being Y, son of Z. The witnesses of the authorization of the agent A, son of B, and C, son of D. Witnesses as present in the assembly E, son of F (etc.), written dated 18 Rajab 1039 (=3 March 1630) (or 18 Rajab 1049, =14 November 1639).

Document No. 2, ff. 217a–b
Agreement of Marriage
Sought and took in marriage the honourable (titles indicating some status), X, son of Y, the chaste lady A, daughter of B, in lieu of marriage-dower (*mihr*) worth so many current *asharfīs*, ... the conditions of the aforesaid (marriage-contract) being as follows: The first condition: that the husband shall not take in fresh marriage another women in addition to the said wife. Second: that he shall not keep a slave girl as concubine. Third: that without a reason valid in law he shall not hit his wife in such a manner that the traces of the stick-blow appear on her body. Fourth: that he shall not let pass six solar (*ilāhī*) months without providing food and maintenance to her. In case of anything contemplated in these conditions coming to pass, except for the condition relating to concubinage, the right to divorce shall vest with the lady aforesaid.... As for the slave-girl who is maintained as a concubine, the wife shall have the right to sell her and keep the proceeds as part of her *mihr*, the husband having no right or authority to prohibit her ... Dated — and — month.

(Since the year mentioned in the text is solar (*ilāhī*), the documents should be pre-1637).

Document No. 3, ff. 198a–b
Agreement of Marriage
... Whereas on 29 Safar 1049 (1 July 1639) X, son of Y according to the Quranic verse ... sought in marriage lady A, daughter of B and the amount in lieu of marriage dower to be five thousand rupees newly minted coins of Surat and one *dīnār* of gold by the weight of Mecca, whereas a third shall be paid forthwith and two-thirds shall be deferred on the four legal conditions that are well known among the theologians, he entered into marriage with her, with her consent and acceptance ... Dated 29 Safar 1049–1 July 1639.

Document No. 4, ff. 206b–207a
Agreement in the Presence of People Assembled
Whereas Muhammad Jīū, son of Miyān Jīū, came to the [*qāzī*'s] court

of the blessed town of the port of Surat and brought with him his wife, the lady Mariyam, daughter of Mūsā Jīū, son of Ibrāhīm, and alleged: 'My wife, for a long time abhors me and does not come to my house. Let the Court order that she should come to my house'. When Muḥammad Jīū's allegation was put to his wife in the presence of the people assembled, she showed a written statement of a group of Muslims containing the agreement of Muḥammad Jīū to the following effect. 'I will give to my wife Mariyam, daily one *ṭanka-i Murādī* for food and every year two *sārīs* for her clothing. If I fail to provide this and I leave her for a period of one year during which she does not receive her maintenance and clothing, she shall become a divorcee (automatically) by this act of divorce and the aforesaid Muḥammad Jīū will have no access to her.' (She then said): 'About four, five years have passed and I did not receive maintenance and clothing from him. I have thus become divorced from him.' Thereafter Mariyam was asked to submit a written statement in accordance with her oral assertion. She brought it and submitted it. Ya'qūb, son of Walī Bohra and Ḥasan Jīū, son of Mām Jīū Nassāj (carpenter) and others came and in conformity with that written statement gave evidence in the presence of the said Muḥammad Jīū. After the evidence of the said witnesses, it is established, in conformity with the words and sense of the evidence, that there has been separation (*tafrīq*) of the said wife (from the husband). Written in the presence of the people assembled so that it may be used on occasion of need. Dated, close to the month of Rabi' I 1028–17 March 1619.

Document No. 4 A, ff. 207a–b

Agreement of Surety

Whereas Ibrāhīm, son of Muḥammad Jīū, son of Pīr Muḥammad, presented himself at the court of [the qāẓī of] the blessed town of the port of Surat, gave a surety on behalf of Muḥammad Jīū, son of Miyān Jīū, that 'if he does not deliver to his wife the lady Mariyam, daughter of Mūsā, one *ṭanka-i murādī* daily for diet and two *sārīs* and two *kānchulīs* (bodices) for clothing every year, I will, as surety give the allowance for daily food and yearly clothing. (If) after this statement, aforesaid Muḥammad Jīū is unable to provide maintenance and clothing and two months pass, he shall make his wife his authorized representative (*wakīla*) to state the facts before the court of law and having given evidence of the absence or receipt of maintenance and clothing, make herself released (from her marriage).

Written dated 2 *Ẕilhij* 1030 (=18 October 1621)

Document No. 5, ff. 207b

Legal Agreement

Whereas 'Abdu'l Laṭīf, son of Malik Pīr Muḥammad, Chānd Jīū, son of Malik Jīū, and 'Abdu'l Ghanī, son of Shaikh Chānd, came to the *qāẓī*'s court of the port of Surat, and stated that we are witness of and solemnly testify to the fact that it was in our presence that Bī 'Āiysha, daughter of Āqā Aḥmad was married to the late Ḥājjī 'Ābdī Qarāmānī, in lieu of one thousand *Ibrāhīmīs* of gold, half of which in actual is five hundred *Ibrāhīmīs*. After hearing the testimony of the above-mentioned independent persons, the *qāẓī* ordered that whatever be the property of Ḥājjī 'Ābdī deceased, the said wife should take and realize her claim from it. Such is the record of proceedings. Written, dated 9 Zilhij 1021 (=31 January 1613).

Document No. 6, f. 194a

Agreement of whereby a wife is released from her contract by paying some amount to the husband:

Whereas X, son of Y, alias Z, came to the [*qāẓī*'s] court of the town of the blessed port of Surat and by the custom of his community and tribe, gave up his turban after tearing it up after obtaining the sum of seventy silver *maḥmūdīs Akbarī*, the half of which is thirty-five *maḥmūdīs*, as release money (*khula'*) from his wife the lady A, daughter of B, and by this act of divorce made her a divorcee and made access to her person forbidden to himself. It is thus settled that after this date the aforesaid X has no conjugal relationship with the aforesaid lady A. If any claim of conjugal relationship is now made by him, it shall not be entertained and shall be invalid. These few sentences have been written by way of attestation that may be used on occasion of need. Dated 12 Muḥarram 1038 (=9 September 1628).

Document No. 7, ff. 226a–b

Agreement of Assistance

What is the opinion of the scholars of the Muḥammadan religion and theologians of the blessed Law of the Prophet in the matter that Lady Fāṭima lays before them: When I was a child, my father died in the port of Acheh and from amongst his slaves the senior slave by fraud and falsehood, did not inform my mother of this, and took her in marriage himself. When my mother came to know that such and such slave has taken her in marriage, she wailed and wept and even took opium (to kill herself). When this matter reached the ears of the king of Acheh, the above-mentioned slave was given harsh punishment and put into prison. Afterwards the merchants persuaded my mother (to relent) by threats and temptations, and the slave was also released from prison by the king at the request of the merchants. Thereafter, the aforesaid slave brought me and my mother along with all the effects and goods (of my father) from Acheh to the port of Surat. Time and again that slave, while in full possession of his senses, repeatedly admitted before the assembly of Muslims that 'the entire effects in cash and kind that are in my possession and control belong to Fāṭima and I too am her slave'. After some time my mother died. When I grew up and reached majority, I took the slave to the *qāẓī* and *ḥākim* (commandant) of the town and claimed that this slave had against the law taken my mother in marriage and at present he is in possession and control of the property of my deceased father and mother. Whatever cash my mother had given us that too he has seized by force from me and is withholding it from me. The *qāẓī* and the *ḥākim* placing that slave under the rigour of the law told him, 'Whatever effects of the deceased you have are the property of Fāṭima. You must give these to her.' The said slave agreed to hand property over to me. Soon after I fell seriously ill, and the matter remained in abeyance for some time. Fate willed that that slave also died. Since the said slave left two sons, I brought those two before the *qāẓī*, and claimed that this much is the original property and whatever effects are left behind by that slave belong to my father, and asked that they be made to give these to me. The *qāẓī* demanded a written statement. I took a number of Muslims before the *qāẓī* and all of them unanimously, in letter and meaning testified that whatever effects the said slave left behind, belong to Fāṭima's father, that slave had not been manumitted. Now whether these effects are those of Fāṭima or not, may be inscribed by them here, so that they may be rewarded by God and thanked by people. Undated.

Document No. 8, ff. 185a–186b
Representation:
I, destitute old widow, X (by name), submit to Her Highness the Ṣāhiba (Princess Jahān Ara) that Muḥammad Beg, my lawful husband, was a trusted servant of the honourable Kāmrān Beg. As willed by fate, they came in pursuit of their mercantile activities to Hyderabad, and at that place by the will of God, my marriage with Muḥammad Beg took place. When this news reached the ears of the honourable

Kāmrān Beg, he said to Muḥammad Beg that 'my relationship with you is not that of servant (and master), but of brother, I have heard that you have established a relationship and got married. We are merchants: today we are in this town, tomorrow we will go to some other city. How can we carry with us a family?' He (Muḥammad Beg) did not listen to him and married me. Since a caravan in the meanwhile was leaving for Surat, he entrusted me to one of his acquaintances and sent me here. After some time he came to this port, along with Kāmrān Beg. Since Kāmrān Beg was preparing to leave for the *Khair-ul Balād* (Mecca?), he insisted that Muḥammad beg should accompany him. The latter did not agree and wished to leave his service. Kāmrān Beg realized that he would leave his service. He therefore told him: 'Some goods(?), slave-girls and male slaves whom I cannot take in this voyage, I am leaving here and entrust them to you.' He (Muḥammad Beg) declined even to do so, but I persuaded him and he agreed. At this place (this house), he kept custody of the belongings of Kāmrān Beg. During this season, Mushtāq, a slave of Kāmrān Beg, came from Arabia and for five–six months he kept paying visits to Aḥmad (Muḥammad?) Beg. When the call for Aḥmad (Muḥammad) Beg arrived, and he lay ill, and he realized that he would not survive this illness, he invited the representatives of the *qāẓī*, the *kotwāl*, and the *dīwān*. Whatever were the effects and belongings of Kāmrān Beg, he prepared an inventory thereof and stored the goods at one place and affixed his own seal thereon. Whatever were his own effects, he gave those to me and said, 'These are yours. Although these do not fully cover claim of marriage- dower (*mihr*), you should stay in this house after me and as I have guarded and taken care of the belongings of my master and of those whom he left behind, you do likewise. I am hopeful that when my master Kāmrān Beg comes back, he will make further provision for you.' I acted according to the will of my deceased husband and took custody of the effects. After a few days the same slave Mushtāq imposed his presence upon me and took away the *mihr-nāma* and (my husband's) will from me, and whatever were the effects of my husband that belong to me he seized and threw into the store and told me, 'You have no right to them'. This was the kind of cruelty the slave inflicted upon me after the death of my husband. I have no one in this town except Your Highness (*bandagān-i Ṣāḥib*) to whom I can go for redress. For the sake of God, for that of salvation, please have mercy upon my distress and deprivation, and give me redress, for there will be great reward for it from God and from the Prophet. At the time of the making of the will and recording of effects (by my husband), the representative of the *qāẓī* was present. You may please call him to your presence and enquire what settlement the deceased made in the presence of the representatives of the *ḥākim* and the *dīwān*. If you consider that I am right, please have my share that he has seized restored to me, and let me be in that house so that till the arrival of Mirzā Kāmrān Beg I should perform the same service that my husband was engaged in. If you do not trust me, please employ someone from the men of the town and place him at the house and the persons (left behind by Kāmrān Beg) so that he should keep watch day and night till the arrival of Mirza Kāmrān Beg. After the aforesaid Mirzā arrives, and deems my share to the worthy of restoration, let him give it to me; otherwise it is a matter for him to decide. At present when this slave exercises mastery over the effects, what authority and legitimacy does he have? You may please give this much attention so as to ensure that the right of none is usurped or destroyed. Since this was obligatory for me, I have made this representation ….

17

The Gujarat Ports and Their Hinterland
The Economic Relationship

The Gujarat ports and their relations with hinterland form a fascinating subject of study. In the third millennium BC, there was a small port of Lothal near Cambay, an emporium for collecting agate and cornelian found in the Rajput territory, beyond the Narbada river, and sending them overland or by coastal shipping to the major towns of the Indus basin. In subsequent centuries, as the centres of economic activity shifted, trade lines multiplied and realigned, and the terrain and nature of Gujarat hinterland also changed. Barygaza or Broach on the Narbada river was the major port in the first century of the Christian era, with Ozene (Ujjain) an important emporium of its hinterland.[1] The presence of Indo-Greek coins at Barygaza also suggests strong trade links with the upper Indus basin. The silk it re-exported probably came from as far as China over the Great Silk Road.[2]

I

In the medieval period Broach continued to be an important port attracting silver coinage from all over the world as shown by the Broach coin-hoard;[3] but Cambay too developed and established direct

[1] 'Periplus Maris Erytheraei', in R.C. Majumdar, ed., *The Classical Accounts of India*, Calcutta, 1960, pp. 302–3. The commodities supplied from Ujjain, according to the *Periplus*, were mainly onyx stones, various kinds of muslins, and considerable quantities of ordinary cottons.

[2] Among the goods exported from Barygaza, the *Periplus* mentions not only ivory, muslins, and cottons of all sorts but also silk, silk-thread, and long pepper. Ibid., p. 304.

[3] O. Codrington, 'On a Hoard of Coins found at Broach', *The Journal of Bombay Branch of the Royal Asiatic Society*, Vol. XV, No. 1881–2, pp. 339–70. The hoard contains gold and silver coins from Egypt, Syria, Yemen, Persia, Geneva, Venice, and Armenia. Gold coins number 448 and silver coins over 1,200.

trade links with the Persian Gulf and the Red Sea.[4] The Khalji annexation of Gujarat must have enlarged trade relations between Gujarat and upper Gangetic region; but on this there is little explicit evidence.

In the sixteenth century, Gujarat retained its importance owing obviously to its proximity to Ahmedabad, a city that became an important commercial centre in the preceding century. But geography also imposed a certain disadvantage on Cambay. Situated at the extreme end of the Gulf, the presence of large sand banks deterred sea-going ships from coming to it directly;[5] and there was also the dread of tidal bore owing to the narrowing of the Gulf at that point.[6] Cambay could only hold its ground by developing Gandhar and later Gogha as its outer ports, where the large ships could anchor, and receive, and deliver cargoes from and to Cambay by flat-bottomed light boats (*tauris*). It appears from the testimony of Ibn Batuta and from the Portuguese sources that during the fourteenth, fifteenth, and early sixteenth centuries, Gandhar, situated to the north of Narbada river, served as the main outer port of Cambay.[7] But during the first half of the sixteenth century Gandhar seems to have silted so much that it became unsuitable for anchoring ships. By the seventeenth-century it seems to have lost all importance. Gogha on the opposite (Saurashtra) shore had replaced it well before 1595, for Abū'l Faẓl duly records that large ships were anchored at Gogha, goods being trans-shipped to and from Cambay on smaller boats 'known as *tauris*'.[8]

Diu, at the southernmost point of the curve of the Saurashtra coast was a natural port, well suited for the anchoring of large ships. An

[4] We have Minhaj's testimony that Ulugh Khan (Balban) was brought from Baghdad to Gujarat to be sold as a slave: *Ṭabaqāt-i Nāsirī*, Vol. II, edited A.H. Habib, Kabul, 1964, p. 48. The Ilkhanid court historian Waṣaf reports that 10,000 horses were annually exported to Ma'bar (Tamil Nadu) and Cambay from Persia: *CEHI*, p. 148.

[5] *Atlas*, Sheet 7B and notes.

[6] According to Thevenot, 'The tides are so swift to the north of the Gulf of Cambay, that a man on horse-back at full speed, cannot keep pace with the first wave. And this violence of the sea is one reason also why great ships go but seldom thither.' S.N. Sen, ed., *Indian Travels of Thevenot and Careri*, Delhi, 1949, p. 18.

[7] Mehdi Hasan, *Rihla*, tr. Baroda 1953, p. 190. Ibn Batuta himself set sail from Gandhar in a flotilla of four vessels, three of them merchantmen and the one, with Ibn Batuta on board, a sufficiently large man of war. Cf. *CEHI*, Vol. I, p. 152.

[8] *Ā'īn*, Vol. I, p. 486. Jahāngīr gives the same information for early seventeenth century in S. Ahmad, ed., *Tuzuk-i Jahangiri*, Ghazipur, 1863, p. 206.

island protected its harbour. But it had no immediate hinterland of any consequence, since Ahmedabad was quite some distance away, and the route passed through various chieftains' territories. As Pearson points out, the port flourished despite these disadvantages during the opening decades of the sixteenth century under the efficient administration of Malik Ayāz (1500–22) and seems to have surpassed Gogha despite the continual disturbances created by the Portuguese.[9] Diu, owing to its suitable anchorage, received goods from overseas by ships, while Cambay had to depend upon trans-shipment at Gandhar or Gogha. Diu thus flourished as an important entrepot in the same fashion as Hormuz, Aden, Malacca, and other ports with limited immediate hinterlands. But with the Portuguese seizure of the port in 1536, it tended to be more a Portuguese base for extorting tribute from Indian shipping than a true entrepot, though for some time, Indian and Asian ships continued to use the port.[10]

Cambay (with Gogha as its outer port) was thus the main port of Gujarat at the time of the final conquest of Gujarat by Akbar in 1572. The conquest brought not only political and administrative integration of Gujarat with the Mughal empire, but had considerable economic consequences, notably, in terms of the enlargement of the hinterland of the Gujarat ports. From now onwards, the Gujarat overseas trade had to respond to the needs of the Mughal empire or, at least, of its inland core (Agra–Delhi area where the court mainly resided along with the great nobility). The Gujarat ports became increasingly the emporia for exports from the inner zone of the empire, and, perhaps still more, of imports like treasure and horses intended for that zone.[11] The exports too now included goods from the inner zone such as

[9] M.N. Pearson, *Merhants and Rulers in Gujarat*, Berkeley, 1976, pp. 67–73.

[10] Diu was still an important port in 1609. 'Many great ships' of Moores and Christians being laden here for Ormuz and Red Sea. Joseph Salbancks in Samual Purchas, *Purchas his Pilgrims*, published by MacLehose, Vol. III, London, 1925, p. 89.

[11] Arab and Persian horses brought by sea were still a prized commodity in the seventeenth century. A *fārman* of Shāhjahān of the seventeenth regnal year specifically orders that the horses brought from Jeddah to Surat should be purchased and dispatched to the court. Bib. Nationale, Blochet, Suppl. Pers. 482 f. 37b. In another *fārman* of the fourteenth regnal year, Shajahan orders that the merchants bringing horses and other commodities from Iran should not be obstructed. Ibid., ff. 44a–b. See also, 'Alī Muḥammad Khān, *Mi'rāt-i Aḥmadī*, edited by Nawab Alī, Vol. II, Baroda, 1927–8, p. 221.

Bayana indigo, raised near Agra, textiles (Daryabadis and Khayrabadis) from Awadh, and even Bengal silk. The inventories of cargoes of English ships sailing form Gujarat ports bear testimony to how important these exports had become.[12]

The new importance of the interior zone in its turn effected a major shift in the Gujarat ports. At the time Akbar conquered Gujarat, the major route connecting the inner core with the Gulf of Cambay was the one running through Ahmedbad to Agra via Ajmer.[13] On the map the distance was fairly short and it proved better in the rainy season. But the intervening desert and the interference of chiefs through whose territories it had to pass imposed difficulties.[14] An alternative route offering greater advantage became possible when Khandesh was annexed to the Mughal empire in 1601. The route ran south from Agra through Gwalior and Malwa to Burhanpur and then turned west crossing the Khandesh plains into southern Gujarat. Since it ran through fertile and directly administered regions, it was well-traversed and much safer from violent disturbance.[15] The route could also be used by *banjāras* carrying large supplies on oxen, owing to the presence of grazing lands all along the route. Once it became available, the rapid growth of Surat at the cost of Cambay in the seventeenth century can be seen to be inevitable. Surat was already a port of some importance for pilgrim traffic, since the Tapti river offered a harbour, while with its small discharge silting was not too great a threat.[16] Its advantage as a port was improved by the discovery of a hole, or a natural undersea though, opposite the village of Swally, offering excellent anchorage for large ships.[17]

[12] *EFI, 1618-21*, p. 61. The Bayana indigo alone accounted for 45.37 per cent of the total value of the cargo sent on board the *Royal Anne*.

[13] Tavernier, *Travels in India*, Vol. I, translated by V. Ball, edited by W. Crooke, London, 1925, pp. 80–4; 'Alī Muḥammad K͟hān, *Mi'rāt-i Aḥmadī*, Supplement, edited by Nawab Alī, Baroda, 1930, 1976.

[14] *EFI, 1648-50*, pp.192–3, complains that 'customs and extortion are intolerable'. See also, Tavernier, *Travels in India*, p. 31.

[15] This route has been described as, 'safer, speedier and cheaper'. W. Foster, *Supplementary Calendar of Documents in the India Office Relating to India or to Home Affairs of the East India Company, 1600-1640*, London, 1928, p. 89. See also, *Atlas*, Sheet 7B and notes.

[16] Ashin Das Gupta, *Indian Merchants and the Decline of Surat, c.1700-1750*, Wiesbaden, 1979, p. 3.

[17] The hole, situated just at the mouth of the river, was said to have been discovered by Henry Middleton: William Hawkins in W. Foster, ed., *Early Travels*

The rise of Surat as the major Gujarat port at the expense of Cambay is reflected in a dramatic shift of silver-minting from Ahmedabad (supplied with silver via Cambay) to Surat, to which the silver streams from Europe (via the Red sea and the Cape of Good Hope) were now diverted. Moreland had already noted this shift from catalogues of museum holdings.[18] I offer below the quantitatively larger data from the UP coin-hoards:[19]

Table 17.1

Decades	Ahmedabad	Surat
1566–75	30	-
1576 –85	97.5	-
1586–95	294.5	-
1596–1605	592	-
1606–15	24	67
1616–25	9	28
1626–35	7	111.5
1636–45	13	92
1646–55	6	121
1656–65	5	98.5
1666–75	12	127
1676–85	10	143
1686–95	3	101.5
1696–1705	3	89

Clearly, by the early 1610s, Surat had attained the pre-eminence which remained with it for the rest of the century.

in India, London, 1927, p. 96. For safer anchorage for Indian ships deep hollows were excavated in the channel of the Tapti river at Surat to receive ships: Godinho, translated in *Journal of Bombay Branch of the Asiatic Society*, N.S. XXVII, No. II, 1953, p. 124. There is an interesting *parwana* of Sa‘ādullah Khān of 1645 describing how the Dutch and the English tried to control Swally by attempting to build a fortress thereby recruiting over three hundred local Saiyyads, Shaikhzadas, Afghans, and Rajputs at Surat; their attempts were thwarted on the complaints of Gujarati merchants to the Mughal administration: Blochet, Suppl. Pers., 482 ff.133a–b.

[18] W.H. Moreland, *From Akbar to Aurangzeb*, London, 1923, p. 177.

[19] Unpublished official reports (signed by Secretary, Coin Committee, UP/ Curator, Lucknow Museum) of the treasure troves found in UP during the period 1884–1979 and presently with the State Museum, Lucknow. See also, A.K.

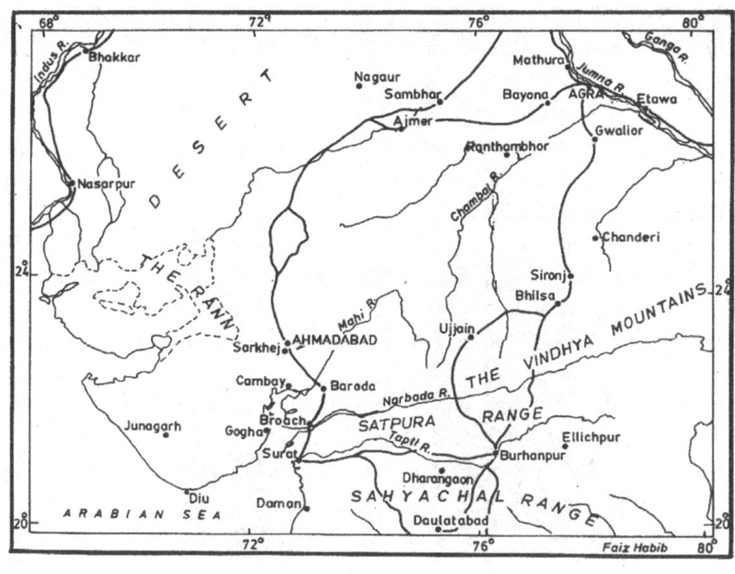

Map 17.1: Routes into the Hinterland

II

Having considered the shifts in routes and ports (see Map), as initial consequences of the Mughal imperial expansion, we may consider going beyond these, and touch on the sphere of composition and flow of commerce.

We may begin by considering the obvious fact that after the conquest of Gujarat the imperial exchequer must have received a steady flow of tax-revenues from Gujarat. The *jama'* statistics for Gujarat given by Abū'l Fazl exhibit two notable features. First, the central Gujarat region was fairly highly taxed, and, second, the level of urban taxation was exceptionally high in comparison with other parts of the empire.[20]

The gross revenue demand per *bīgha-i Ilāhī* of cultivated land in various *sarkārs* of Gujarat (c.1595), varied from 14.96 *dāms* (Godhra)

Srivastav, *Coin Hoards of Uttar Pradesh, 1884–1979*, Vol. I, Lucknow, 1981. Unfortunately, the number of coins for different years is not specified in this publication: I have used the original reports directly.

[20] *EME*, pp. 309–16.

to 82.88 *dāms* (Baroda), the average for all *sarkārs* being 46.51 while the corresponding figure for the territory comprising UP was 34.98 *dāms* and for the Punjab and Haryana 23.23 *dāms*.[21] This higher incidence of revenue demand in Gujarat is supported by the testimony of Geleynsen (followed by De Laet) (c.1630) that in Gujarat the demand was closer to three-fourths instead of one-half of the produce, the norm in northern India.[22]

In urban taxation the difference is even more remarkable. Ahmedabad was only a little behind Agra in the size of urban taxation (98.36 per cent of Agra); Cambay yielded 54.45 per cent of Agra in taxation; and Baroda and Nadaut each yielded almost 32 per cent.[23]

The figures suggest a higher tax collection on manufactures and trade in Gujarat than even at the capital of the empire. In turn one may expect that considerable net tax revenue flowed to the inner core of the empire, and this had to be in the form of manufactures, besides treasure (silver, bullion).

If Gujarat paid revenue in the form of its manufactures, more particularly Ahmedabad manufactures, the connection would have remained a purely inland one. But if the tax-flow was in part in money, or in imported commodities like horses, copper, broadcloth or even slaves,[24] the Gujarat ports would become involved in the exchanges; and a triangular relationship could develop between Ahmedabad, Surat, and Agra. For instance, bullion or other imports received at Surat might be transported directly to Agra, while Ahmedabad and inland Gujarat might supply indigo, cotton textiles, and other manufactures to Surat for export. The resulting claims of Ahmedabad on Agra would then be cancelled by the latter's tax claims on the former.

This relationship would explain why Surat becomes the principal Gujarat mint in the seventeenth century, and began to account for a surprisingly large share in the total mintage of the empire, if UP coin-hoards are any guide:

The enormous amount of rupees minted in Surat indicated that *a)* their diffusion inland was directly from Surat after the 1620s and not through Ahmedabad, whose mintage had lost its previous supremacy, as we have seen; and *b)* enormous coined money must have

[21] Ibid., pp. 136–41.

[22] *ASMI*, p. 194.

[23] *EME*, p. 313.

[24] Bib. Nat: Blochet., Suppl. Pers. 432 ff. 162–163a.

accumulated at Surat for transfer inland. This explains why all bills drawn at Surat on Agra carried a heavy discount but the reverse ones, that is, from Agra on Surat would carry a premium.[25]

Table 17.2

Decade	A Total No. of Coins	B Surat Coins	B % of A
1606–15	516.5	67	12.98
1616–25	432.5	28	6.48
1626–35	758	111.5	14.71
1636–45	499	92	18.43
1646–55	398	121	30.40
1656–65	365	98.5	26.99
1666–75	256	127	49.61
1676–85	294.5	143	48.60
1686–95	453	101.5	22.41
1696–1705	670	89	13.28

In return for bullion transferred inland, Surat might in part receive manufactures and goods from its immediate hinterland (Gujarat); but, additionally, exports of inland regions might develop. In this case, of course, Ahmedabad would have no more significance than a station on one of the two routes connecting Surat and Agra. The connection between the major Gujarat port and the capital city of the empire would be direct. Undoubtedly, Bayana indigo played a major part in sustaining this relationship till the 1650s; so also textiles from production centres in the upper Ganga basin and Bengal silk transported overland.

However, partly because Bengal silk rose to be such an important commodity of world trade after the 1650s, European companies

[25] The *hundi* drawn at Agra on Surat carried a premium of 4¼ to 5 per cent: Tavernier, Vol. I, p. 30. In 1636, a *hundi* at Surat on Agra was, however, discounted at ½ per cent only: *EFI*, 1634–6, p. 169. For a fuller discussion see Irfan Habib, 'The System of bills of exchange (Hundis) in the Mughal Empire', *PIHC*, 33rd Session, pp. 290–301.

developed direct sea-borne commerce with Bengal thereafter. At the same time, Bayana indigo began losing out to the West Indian competition. In the latter half of the seventeenth century, Agra and the imperial heartland would, therefore, have little for export through European companies via Gujarat. And yet Surat continued to inject large amount of bullion into the empire. The only explanation for this would seem to be that exports of inland textiles and other commodities to West Asia followed a different pattern, and that therefore much of the Surat mintage was of bullion received through the Red Sea and the Gulf. Unfortunately, owing to absence of data on the composition of trade on these two sea routes, this suggestion must for the moment remain just a hypothesis.

By and large, the role of the Mughal empire in sustaining the briskness of commerce through Gujarat seems to have been significant. Conversely, its decline beginning in Aurangzeb's later years, initiated a process of constriction of the hinterland of Surat which Ashin Das Gupta has so well depicted,[26] and which in the first half of the eighteenth century was so decisively to stifle the port.

[26] Ashin Das Gupta, *Indian Merchants and the Decline of Surat, c.1700-1750*, Wiesbaden, 1979.

Index